Reflections from the Heart of Educational Inquiry

SUNY series, Curriculum Issues and Inquiries

Edmund C. Short, EDITOR

REFLECTIONS FROM THE HEART OF EDUCATIONAL INQUIRY

Understanding Curriculum and Teaching through the Arts

Edited by

George Willis and William H. Schubert

State University of New York Press

Published by
State University of New York Press, Albany

©1991 State University of New York

All rights reserved

Printed in the United States of America

No part of this book may be used or reproduced in any manner whatsoever without written permission except in the case of brief quotations embodied in critical articles and reviews.

For information, address the State University of New York Press, State University Plaza, Albany, NY 12246

Production by Christine M. Lynch
Marketing by Bernadette LaManna

Library of Congress Cataloging-in-Publication Data

Reflections from the heart of educational inquiry: understanding curriculum and teaching through the arts/edited by George Willis and William H. Schubert.
p. cm. — (SUNY series in curriculum issues and inquiries)
Includes bibliographical references and index.
ISBN 0-7914-0556-7 (alk. paper). \ISBN 0-7914-0557-5 (pbk. : alk. paper)
1. Arts\Study and teaching\United States. I. Willis, George. 1941- . II. Schubert, William Henry. III. Series.
NX303.R44 1991
700'.7'073\dc20 90-9906
CIP

10 9 8 7 6 5 4 3 2 1

CONTENTS

PREFACE

This book has grown larger than we originally anticipated, but, we hope, its growth has been a fulfilling of some central convictions that both of us have held for many years. Because it consists largely of statements by individual educational scholars writing personally about how they have come to understand curriculum and teaching through the influence of the arts in their own lives, it has taken on a collective life of its own. As with all living things, it has become uniquely what it is; and as with any living person, it has thus become something which never can be known quite fully in only a cognitive sense. Fullest understanding requires something more: a prolonged, constant, sympathetic identification with, a reverent living through that engages the senses and changes the sensibilities. This kind of experience, in which one becomes open to new possibilities, is what we mean by reflective inquiry. In thus taking on a life of its own, the book has not only eluded the many constraints which our own limited visions, ideas, and plans would have imposed upon it; it has engaged us in reflective inquiry and so has taught us more than we alone could have imagined. The energy of its life has overcome whatever of our timidities or inabilities would have kept it smaller both literally and figuratively than what it has grown to be. Although it has grown mostly from the contributions of others, it has still become a book which does not simply talk about, but which concretely embodies, what we believe in. We intend the word *understanding* in its title not to be taken in any one particular sense, but in the fullest possible variety of senses. It is a book, therefore, which is composed of reflections and which invites reflection.

We began with the belief that making decisions about curricula is the heart of education, but that making such decisions is no mere technical matter. Education at its best is the same as how to lead a life, and, therefore, decisions about curricula are microcosms of everything that goes into wise living, as scholars such as John Dewey and James B. Macdonald have many times reminded us. Wise living, we believe, is not a matter of simple prudential calculation; it requires constantly extending ourselves through many acts of faith, and courage, and imagination. Hence, there are no simple answers about how or what to live, only opportunities continually to inquire reflectively into ourselves and the world around us as we continue to make decisions about how to act on what we believe. Furthermore, we have also come to believe through numerous experiences in our own lives and through our reflective inquiry on them, that this kind of inquiry, which is the heart of living and education, is the same kind of imaginative inquiry which is the heart of creative art. Therefore, it was natural for us to want to create a book that would embody these intrinsic connections among curriculum, education, reflective inquiry, and the arts. All people involved in living artistically or educationally feel the same essential pulse, we believe. We wanted a book that through its examples powerfully embodied that pulse, helping readers feel their own pulses more intensely within them and so encouraging them to further reflective inquiry of their own.

We started small. Our original intent was to focus directly and rather exclusively on curriculum inquiry, that part of educational inquiry with which we were most familiar. We asked a few scholars from the field of curriculum studies who had backgrounds in the arts or who we knew had been influenced by the arts to write short autobiographical essays. As these essays started to come in we began to understand how the book could honor something else we believed in: that curriculum and teaching are essentially the same process and so organically connected that both are at the heart of education. We therefore decided that *teaching* was another word that could be added to the title of the book. At the same time we kept finding more scholars in curriculum who had been personally and professionally influenced by the arts and who also saw curriculum and teaching as essentially the same. And so the book continued to grow in many ways.

While we were not surprised, we were gratified to see evidence for our convictions in the essays. The authors helped validate our beliefs in the centrality of curriculum and teaching to education and in the intrinsic connection between education and the arts through their mutual use of reflective inquiry. In each essay we can see quite easily how reflection on the arts engaged the author in inquiry on fundamental meanings of education. As authors considered the ways in which experience with the arts affected their views of curriculum and teaching, they found themselves addressing the essence of education and exemplifying the ways in which they have come to inquire about the process of education because of the arts. The more essays we requested and received, not only the larger the book grew, but the stronger the validation of these beliefs became. The book, we think, comes very close through the examples it provides to validating the belief that reflective inquiry in the arts is the central basis for reflective inquiry in education. That is not a point we argue directly, however, and readers can make up their own minds about the strength of the examples.

Readers will find the word *curriculum* but not the word *teaching* in the titles of chapters of the book. That is largely an accident of our first asking scholars in curriculum to contribute essays on the arts and curriculum inquiry before we were fully aware of how large the book would become. Words such as *teaching* and its synonyms are used frequently in the bodies of the chapters. Since most contributors assume that making decisions about curriculum and making decisions about teaching are essentially the same, few chapters actually maintain any distinction between curriculum and teaching. Readers will therefore find discussions and examples as germane to reflective inquiry on teaching as to curriculum inquiry. Clearly, a very similar book could be created from the contributions of scholars on teaching who have been moved by the impulse of the arts.

We have not begun the book with a conventional chapter outlining thesis, organization, or content. Instead, we have begun with some personal reflections written deliberately as an extended prologue. Following this prologue, the body of the book is divided into two parts. For reasons that we attempt to make clear in the prologue and in the short introductions to these two parts, this division is not highly significant, especially since all chapters are autobiographical to one degree or another. Chapters in the first part of the book do provide more general explanations of principles than do chapters in the second part. All chapters in both parts, however, provide personal examples of the influences of the arts on the lives of the authors, although chapters in the second part emphasize personal examples more than general explanations. The book ends with a brief epilogue.

The basic purpose of the book is to provide artistic examples, not discursive argumentation. For that reason we have written prologue, introductions, and epilogue in the form of a continuing dialogue, and readers will find that the individual chapters which comprise the body of the book even more directly invite participation in the immediacy of shared inquiry with their authors. We believe the nonlinear form our dialogue takes is consonant with the notion of the arts exemplified in the chapters throughout the book, and we hope most readers will find the dialogue an integral part of an aesthetic whole. Some readers, however, may find it a distraction or wish we had provided a shorter, easier, and more conventional way into the book. But we think the examples provided throughout the entire book invite reflective inquiry both by themselves and in conjunction with all other examples, and it is not necessary to read the book in its entirety to experience what it invites. Therefore, an individual reader may prefer to omit our dialogue altogether or to begin inquiry directly in any particularly appealing chapter. We have arranged the chapters of the book in one possible order, but they can be read and reflected upon in any order. Readers should have no difficulty in finding their own ways in.

To the extent that we have succeeded in creating an artistic book on reflective inquiry in the arts and education, we are indebted to the artistic and educational power of those scholars who have written for the book. We acknowledge them and their chapters here, but all of them are people who have provided us with helpful examples over and above the chapters they have contributed, examples helpful to us in a multitude of ways impossible to explain or acknowledge fully. Many of them have provided us with such personal and professional examples over many years.

We wish also to acknowledge some people who have contributed in other ways to the creation of this book. For help with word processing we are indebted to Marcia Chaimovitz, Sharon Coleman, Mary Ann Koch, and Bernadette Strykowski. For suggestions and advice invaluable in moving this project through its various stages of development we are indebted to Alex Molnar, Edmund C. Short, Lois Patton, Craig Kridel, William Ayers, Elliot W. Eisner, Priscilla C. Ross, Geneva Haertel, Janet L. Miller, Louis

Rubin, Thomas E. Barone, Michael Costigan, and anonymous reviewers selected by SUNY Press. Michael Costigan deserves special thanks for his work on the indexes. And for continuing examples and support both throughout this project and, especially, long before it had begun we are indebted to Nancy Willis, Ann Lynn Lopez-Schubert, and Pat Rolleum.

We dedicate this book to our children (Elizabeth, Kathryn, Elaine, Karen, Heidi, and Henry), and to the hope that the arts will continue to bring meaning to their lives and to the lives of all children, their parents, and their teachers.

G.W.
W.H.S.

GEORGE WILLIS AND WILLIAM H. SCHUBERT

PROLOGUE:
Reflections on the Origins of This Book

"George, now that most of the essays for our book are in I have been reflecting on how and why the book came to be. From our phone conversations I surmise that you have been thinking along these lines, too. Because of the autobiographical character of the book, I propose that we engage in an autobiographical dialogue (although I am not quite sure what that means) about its nature and intent."

"An autobiographical dialogue on how and why the book came to be? Well, Bill, that sounds both intriguing and challenging, and I admit agreeing earlier that we should try to do an opening chapter that is consistent with the spirit of the book. Certainly, we both have a lot we feel we would like to say about its being. So there is a part of me that resonates to what you say and immediately replies, 'Okay. Let's see what we can create here. Let's try a dialogue that opens to readers as much as possible about the book and ourselves.' That is the part of me talking which is intrigued.

"The part of me which is challenged is not so ready to just plunge in, however. It says, 'Don't be hasty. Opening up the book to readers is one thing; opening up yourself is something else. There are a lot of problems in writing personally for an academic audience. Likely any dialogue that Bill and you write will seem forced or stilted anyway, especially since you are going to have to do it gradually, by mail, over a period of weeks. Besides, neither of you is sure about what an autobiographical dialogue entails.' So this part of me—perhaps actually more intimidated than challenged—wants us to write a nice, safe, discursive, traditionally academic opening chapter, which describes the book in a straightforward, linear, impersonal way. Both you and I think the book itself is going to say a lot directly to anyone concerned with education, not just to anyone in curriculum or teaching, so why run the risk of losing readers before they have had the chance to fairly begin?"

"All well and good, George, but why delay the inevitable? You know you are going to accept what I have proposed."

"What persuades me to accept your suggestion is that deep down inside I simply don't think there is a safe way to introduce the book that is consistent with its spirit. The very notions of art, and education, and inquiry which are exemplified in virtually every chapter of the book embody risk. In fact, intrigue (in the sense of interest or fascination), challenge, risk, and change may be the essence of both art and education, what they have most in common, what one needs to feel in order to understand them. Inquiry may be the making explicit or bringing to consciousness of this essence; asking 'What about art is educative?' and 'What about education is artful?' is really asking the same question. Inquiry itself—simply asking the most fundamental questions—is really the basic form of teaching or curriculum development. Both the artist and the educator run enormous and similar risks when they begin to inquire, when they begin to bring forward some personal perceptions or interpretations of the world, which inevitably suggest to others how to live their own lives. The risks involved in perceiving and changing and inevitably perceiving and changing again and again are ultimately both personal and moral. Neither art nor curriculum exists out there someplace in the world independent of the people who do the making of them. You are always going to be intrigued and challenged by something beyond yourself, of course, but in making a creative response to it—whether that response be as purely personal as some form of self-expression or as broadly public as a curriculum intended for thousands of people—you are always going to risk your being. So art-making and 'curriculum-making' (as it was frequently called in the 1920s) are essentially the same thing. It does not matter what the scope of the making is. It does not even matter how private or public your response. What ultimately matters is whether you are responding to the intrigue and the challenge by changing for the better and whether your example might suggest to others how they, too, might so change. There is no getting around such personal and moral risks for either artists or educators about how to respond to the challenges of life and what the examples of these responses say both to the responders themselves and to others. Perceptive, self-conscious inquiry may reduce some of the risks, but it cannot do so entirely, since inquiry is also an artistic process."

"Well, George, the idea of art and curriculum as one, both being the same creative process which begins in inquiry and through which each person responds to the challenges of living a moral life, is one which appeals to me. I have often thought about both art and education in such a way, though not in quite the same words you have just used. But the idea itself will not appeal to everyone for a multitude of reasons, some of which you have hinted at. There are bound to be skeptics. The words you have used will be confusing to many people. You have already mentioned such risks. If you could be a bit more concrete . . . Perhaps provide an example or two . . ."

"Providing examples is the basic purpose of this book. I hope that much is clear from the start. So, consistent with the spirit of the book, I am willing to try here.

"Take, for example, the reality that neither of us knows what an autobiographical dialogue entails. In some ways that seems strange, since we have suggested that contributors to the book not write traditionally academic essays. We have encouraged them to speak in personal, autobiographical terms about the influences of the arts on their lives in general and on their professional lives in particular. We have wanted them to say what it is about the arts—or any specific piece of art—that has most moved them, that has caused them to question their ordinary, taken-for-granted assumptions about education and set them on new paths of inquiry. And all of them have opened up themselves to one degree or other. Much to our delight, the book we have now received from them is filled with such personal and artistic examples, examples which both of us think can speak directly to readers' lives and through that kind of autobiographical dialogue between writers and readers perhaps even move readers in ways which art itself can and which ordinary conversation and ordinary discursive analysis cannot. That is curriculum-making! But it is not strange that each example is different and that each writer and each reader brings something different and deeply personal to that kind of dialogue. So the same examples will still move different people in different ways, and the best examples will move the same people in many different ways many times over. Thus it is neither surprising nor particularly important that neither of us understands exactly what an autobiographical dialogue is. The important thing is to have one! All this means that the process of creative responding I have been describing is never complete, that we always have more inquiry to do about how we can best change our lives. Understanding is not solely cognitive; it arises through living. Certainly you do not think that we have both read the various contributions to this book in precisely the same ways?"

"Of course not. If I did think that, I would not have been certain that you were going to accept my suggestion to try a dialogue. But despite this query of me, you seem to be drifting into abstraction again."

"Then let me come back to the point I started with. I still have some specific things to say about it. Most simply, I am in complete agreement with you that it is only appropriate here that we try to emulate those good examples of the many contributors to the book instead of writing a traditionally academic opening chapter. In terms of the inherent risks involved, examples speak louder than words, even if in a book the examples are in words. Since I presume that is the kind of dialogue you mean—and since there are no other options consistent with the spirit of the book—I am willing to try.

"I think, however, despite our optimistic expectations about what the book can do, we still need to be circumspect about what we suggest to readers, particularly about what we suggest we can accomplish here talking to each other, even though we invite readers to participate as fully as possible. We should be specific about some of the risks. We ourselves may have nothing worthwhile to say, and nobody may care about hearing from us personally. Not every example is moving, and both abstractness and discursive analysis have their place. Readers should be aware that the book as a whole is limited, that all chapters in it are essays and the personal examples within, therefore, couched largely in ordinary language (especially in Part I, where we have asked contributors to include analysis of underlying theoretical issues), that there is—alas—no pure poetry. In this light, what is most unsettling to me in both a negative and a positive sense about our own effort here, is that there is an artificiality in our attempt at dialogue that is clearly transcended throughout virtually all the rest of the book. Here we are addressing the readers, but through an essay in which we are addressing ourselves. The essays elsewhere in the book (including our own individual ones) are written by single authors and addressed directly to the readers, and these essays speak powerfully for themselves, some of them, I think, remarkably functioning paradoxically in their simultaneous craftedness and ingenuousness as superior pieces of art, and all of them at least pushing in that direction. Certainly, all the essays throughout the rest of the book have something worthwhile to say which we here may not, and readers are going to be moved far more by the best of their examples than by our attempt at dialogue. Those essays are the art, the real dialogue, the real education. Speaking for myself, I know I have been moved by them in unexpected ways to inquire anew about directions in my own life, and that has made putting this book together the most stimulating professional project I have ever worked on. I am in the contributors' debt for that alone."

"So you warn readers that there is no pure poetry in the book, but you think—as I do—that there is poetry nonetheless?"

"That is true, I admit. I think different readers will find their own kinds of poetry in it.

"In any case, Bill, I think I know you well enough to sense that in suggesting we attempt a dialogue you have an additional motive, and I am in agreement with it, as well. In my own essay later in the book, I have suggested, as you know, that good education is much like good storytelling. Good stories are about people embodied in the context of their histories. I have no doubt you have such a story—likely a personal and professional story—you want to tell. I encourage you in that. Even though we have talked many times before about the origins of this book, I want to hear what you have to say, since some of it will surely be new. Besides, Bill, I have found you a good storyteller. Your major curriculum book (Schubert 1986), although conventionally discursive on its surface, is highly personal and self-consciously written as a conversation with its readers. I think at its best it attains the characteristics of the kind of dialogue we are striving for here and moves its readers to risk inquiry. So you are at heart a storyteller, and there is much yet to tell about how this book came into being. Perhaps we can create at least a partially artful example of how we have developed our own personal and professional consciousness as educators. Despite our limitations, putting within the contexts of our own histories how we further perceive the essential relationships between inquiry, curriculum, and teaching (really how in good education that functions as art all these are one) may help readers, who must be at least somewhat like us, find the connections between this book and their personal and professional lives. That seems to be a risk worth taking.

"You remain silent. Sorry. In replying too long to your proposal I have mostly monopolized our conversation-would-be-dialogue, and your patience has been admirable. I am sure you have a lot to say which you have contained up till now. Suppose, then, you begin your story, letting me and the readers know exactly what is on your mind."

"You're right—at last. And not exactly everything now on my mind is new!

"If memory serves correctly we first met at the Annual Meeting of the American Educational Research Association (AERA) in Washington, D.C., in 1975. As we talked after a Special Interest Group meeting on curriculum knowledge, I recall that we hit it off rather well. Part of the reason, surely, was our mutual interests in philosophy and history as necessary and neglected bases for curriculum inquiry. More unique for that time period in curriculum (a time when curriculum and objectives were almost always said in the same breath) was our conviction that literary and artistic perspectives of all kinds had contributed 'immeasurably' to our understanding of curriculum (and I use the term 'immeasurably' intentionally). Moreover, unlike many curriculum writers who dominated the field in those days, we saw curriculum as the heart and soul of education. It was the experience, the sources of meaning and direction that altered and improved the outlooks of those who participate in it. Therefore, it embraces the essence of the teaching–learning process. Other dimensions of education are necessary parts of the orchestration, but curriculum, we were convinced, is the music. Without the music, what good is the orchestration (the administration, the finances, the psychology, the methodology, the policy)?"

"Right. What you now call music is the same thing I called poetry. One form of art is as good as another for representing the underlying process."

"Exactly. In this position we thought ourselves in harmony with John Dewey and other progressive educators who were largely consistent with Dewey's perspective. Dewey's notion of experience, as developed in *Experience and Education* (1938a), is in harmony with his aesthetic theory. In fact, an aesthetic appreciation of patterns of experience is necessary to the ability to imagine and perceive consequences of different possible courses of action. This attention to the consequences of action, this artistic viewing of curriculum as embedded in the context of lived experience, was reemphasized for me in the late 1960s and early 1970s by Joseph Schwab's work on practical inquiry (1960, 1970, 1971, 1973, and later 1983). Both Dewey and Schwab seem to view understanding in a full way.

"I vividly remember that 1975 AERA meeting on a Tuesday afternoon when Schwab informally reflected at a graduate student seminar sponsored by the Student Committee of AERA. His discussion, titled simply 'Curriculum Theory: The Practical and the Educational,' lingers as memorable to me. I especially recall a brief history of inquiry that he recounted. He began by noting that natural science of the nineteenth century was preoccupied with statistics, but with the revolutions brought by relativity and quantum theory, natural science saw clearly that theory (not statistics alone) had to be the intellectual context of research. The burgeoning social sciences, however, in their attempt to move from social philosophy to something more credible in the modern technological world, turned to statistics and an array of quantitative modes of research to support their claims. Meanwhile, however, the natural sciences that they emulated had ironically turned to theory-based investigation. Similarly, at midcentury, when the social sciences began to tout the importance of theory, modern physics and chemistry had moved natural science investigation into a realm best referred to as situational analysis. More ironically, it was also at about midcentury that educational researchers scrambled for credibility in the scholarly community, but they did so too often by hanging on to statistical analysis, which had long left dry the mouths of natural scientists and which had recently been deemed inadequate by social scientists.

Thus, in the late 1960s Schwab began to promote a Deweyan epistemology of situational analysis for education. In one of the most well-known passages in the curriculum literature, Schwab began his article 'The Practical: A Language for Curriculum' by asserting:

> I shall have three points. The first is this: that the curriculum field is moribund, unable by its present methods and principles to continue its work and desperately in search of new and more effective principles and methods.
>
> The second point: the curriculum field has reached this unhappy state by inveterate and unexamined reliance on theory in an area where theory is partly inappropriate in the first place and where the theories extant, even where appropriate, are inadequate to the tasks which the curriculum field sets them. . . .
>
> The third point, which constitutes my thesis: there will be a renaissance of the field of curriculum, a renewed capacity to contribute to the quality of American education, only if the bulk of curriculum energies are diverted from the theoretic to the practical, to the quasi-practical, and to the eclectic. (Schwab 1969, 1)

"Schwab, of course, went on (over the course of almost two decades) to argue for inquiry in education that took problems from a state of affairs, not from a mere abstract conceptualization or state of mind. He wrote of the importance of focus on situational understanding through interaction with those situations and their complex contexts. And he admonished educational researchers to value the kind of knowledge that facilitated morally defensible decision and action, not just detached induction that brings law-like generalizations.

"It seemed to me that Schwab and Dewey were speaking the 'language' of art even more than 'instrumentalism' (as Dewey called his philosophy) or 'the practical' (as Schwab referred to his). And it was especially interesting that both Schwab and Dewey were scientists at heart. Throughout his long career, Dewey referred to inquiry and the thinking process as 'scientific' (Dewey 1910, 1929, 1938b). Similarly, Schwab was a geneticist by training, and he often wrote about the scientific process (Schwab 1960); in fact, a selection of his most important essays is entitled *Science, Curriculum, and Liberal Education* (Westbury and Wilkof, 1978). So when Schwab writes of science, I give his perspective greater credibility than that of educational researchers who proclaim themselves 'scientists'. In fact, when I hear the self-proclamations of such educational researchers, I think of Schwab's historical sketch portraying them as followers of 'science' long discarded by those very persons whose work they purport to emulate at the forefront of natural sciences.

"I see Schwab and Dewey as advocating a vision of science more compatible with that portrayed by Jacob Bronowski in *Science and Human Values* (1956). Bronowski (longtime resident poet and physicist at The Salk Institute and commentator on the history of human growth through the arts and sciences) demonstrates convincingly that excellence in science is strikingly similar to excellence in the arts. Both require the essence of analytic clarity, synthetic integration, and imaginative exploration. In a follow-up article (1971) on his 1969 piece that called for practical inquiry in education, Schwab presented the ideas of 'eclectic arts' or 'arts of eclectic' as a necessary basis for practical inquiry. He pointed out that practical inquiry is not devoid of theoretical perspectives provided by liberal education; it is not a mere muddling through. Fundamentally, persons grow in their capacity to carry out practical inquiry as their background in liberal education is expanded and deepened. Acquaintance with history, philosophy, the arts, literatures, the natural sciences, mathematics, and the social sciences provides a seedbed from which imaginative responses to practical situations can grow and flourish. This is a basis for Schwab's first eclectic art, that of matching theory and research to the needs of practical situations. Since such knowledge rarely matches exactly, the second eclectic art is needed to tailor or adapt existing theories to situations more fully. Finally, since extant theories account for only a partial view of experience, a third art, that of invention or the anticipatory generation of alternatives is needed. This is the kind of wherewithal required, I believe, by Dewey to engage in an everyday science of problem-solving that continuously searches to understand better the consequences of action."

"Well, Bill, your reflectiveness during the long wait I put you through while I considered the prospect of a dialogue seems to have encouraged you to speak your mind, and you still seem a long way from concluding your remarks. Right now you remind me of Marlow, the storyteller in Joseph Conrad's *Heart of Dark-*

ness; not because the story you are telling of how educational researchers generally misinterpreted Dewey and Schwab is quite as dark as Marlow's story of how modern, civilized people now seldom give themselves up to what he calls 'the devil of violence, the devil of greed, and the devil of hot desire; . . . strong, lusty, red-eyed devils . . . that swayed and drove [people formerly],' but instead now usually succumb to 'a flabby, pretending, weak-eyed devil of a rapacious and pitiless folly' (though, come to think of it, there are a lot of parallels between the two stories!); not because in your own reflections you at all resemble Conrad's physical description of the meditating, Buddha-like Marlow 'sitting cross-legged right aft, leaning against the mizzenmast . . . [with] sunken cheeks, a yellow complexion, a straight back, an ascetic aspect'; but because your meaning, like Marlow's, is basically moral and, thus, you are running the same risk that your meaning may not seem to some people to be found at the story's center, like a kernel, but remain indistinctly enveloping the outside—'brought . . . out only as a glow brings out a haze, in the likeness of one of these misty halos that sometimes are made visible by the spectral illumination of moonshine,' as Conrad has one of Marlow's listeners complain. That has a lot to do with losing our readers! The same listener also says about Marlow's beginning, 'we knew we were fated, before the ebb began to run, to hear about one of Marlow's inconclusive experiences.' "

"Is that your way of telling me I am being too abstract?"

"Only partly. Despite my teasing, I admit, Bill, I am in essential agreement with the story you have told thus far and have nothing I wish to add to it. The background is an important part of the whole story. You have said what this academic background means to you, and it means very much the same to me. My own epistemology and general approach to education are consistent with Dewey and Schwab. Still, I do suggest you now focus the story more directly on your own experience—conclusive or inconclusive as it may be! As you go along I can add some of my own. Let's see if making our examples more personal makes our meanings less hazy."

"That is quite suitable to me, George. Virtually all of your own lengthy, inconclusive, opening remarks about how art, education, and inquiry are essentially one were focused on the nature of experience, you know—only much to my surprise you did not use the word *experience* itself, an admirable restraint for you!"

"You seem to know my mind as well as I claimed to know yours."

"That is not at all difficult."

"Good, though knowing another's mind is only part of what one needs to know. By the end of Marlow's story the same listener seemed to know Marlow in a larger sense and—I don't think incidentally—to have lost much of his skepticism. In this larger sense he seemed to understand Marlow's meaning, though I doubt that he could have said exactly what that meaning was. Whether he was also a better person is the question."

"And what, exactly, does that have to do with our attempt at dialogue?"

"It has as much to do with you as Marlow. It also is my way of urging you to get on with our story."

"As you wish.

"The writings of Dewey influenced my teaching in elementary school more than those of any other. After six years of elementary school teaching, in 1973 I distanced myself from that situation to contemplate and build upon it more fully through doctoral studies at the University of Illinois at Urbana-Champaign. As I reflected and studied, it increasingly occurred to me that the imagination was the essence of good teaching. As I read educational classics, as I interacted with faculty members, as I taught students who wanted to become teachers, and as I observed these teachers and their experienced cooperating teachers in classroom activities, I became convinced of the necessary and neglected place of imagination in curriculum and teaching. Therefore, this topic became my dissertation, *Imaginative Projection: A Method of Curriculum Invention*. Through a variety of traditional and emergent research modes, I investigated imagination as a basis for understanding curriculum and teaching. With Schwab and Dewey, I saw imaginative literatures (classic and modern, philosophic and popular) as a foundation for the imaginative practice of teaching and reflection on curriculum. I incorporated ideas from philosophical classics and literary criticism into my understanding of imagination with the help of philosophers Hugh

Chandler and Harry S. Broudy. I considered further the nature of imagination in curriculum with J. Harlan Shores (my dissertation chairperson) and implications for teaching and contexts of learning with Louis Rubin, Bernard Spodek, Frederick Raubinger, Peter Shoresman, William F. Connell, and J. Myron Atkin, among others. I found that good teachers imagined in many directions simultaneously. In the course of action, their considerations rapidly traversed the following kinds of questions: What possible courses of action (practical hypotheses) might be helpful in this situation? What does it mean to be helpful? How does each possibility fit with or even alter my assumptions about human nature, knowledge and knowing, values, goodness or rightness, beauty, reason, and the ideals and realities of social life? What are likely to be the subtle side effects of a course of action within the social context of the school and in terms of the hidden curriculum? Who benefits and who suffers from each possible course of action? Similar questions are asked as action proceeds.

"As I considered these and related questions, I found educational theorists to be insightful who were then on the periphery of mainstream curriculum writing of the time. Maxine Greene, Dwayne Huebner, Elliot W. Eisner, and James B. Macdonald were especially helpful. I am sure that the main reason for this was that they drew upon literary, artistic, and philosophical sources that were not in the main stream of technical and outdated scientific modes of inquiry and understanding in education. They probed literary and artistic criticism, phenomenology, existentialism, hermeneutics, and theology, psychoanalysis, and critical theory, as well as literature and the arts directly."

"I must break in to say here these same sources were also a great influence on me. Perhaps I came to them a bit earlier than you, Bill, for as an undergraduate I attended a liberal arts college which encouraged me to pursue such interests, and pursue them I did. Officially my major was philosophy, but most of the faculty seemed engaged in the kind of inquiry I have been advocating, and crossing ordinary academic boundaries was no problem. I wound up thinking then, during my years as a secondary English teacher, and to this day that Shakespeare was not only a great poet, but a great phenomenologist.

"I did not know originally that these interests were crystallizing around the problem of how to comprehend the nature of educative experience, but I did so by the time I reached doctoral studies at Johns Hopkins University in the late 1960s. The Department of Education there was small and intellectually exciting; unfortunately, it was also beset by political problems which led to its termination a few years later, really a victim of the Vietnam War as much as anything else, through the social, moral, and financial crises the war brought on in academia. But I thoroughly enjoyed my time at Hopkins and was able to create my own course of studies, encouraged by faculty whose interests were at least as diverse and certainly more deeply directed than my own then were, particularly John Walton, the most insightful educational thinker I have known, and John S. Mann, my dissertation advisor, whose work still influences the curriculum field, though, regrettably, he left academia more than fifteen years ago. Mann introduced me to the writings of the selfsame Greene, Huebner, Eisner, and Macdonald who have so influenced you and many others now in curriculum, and he encouraged me to write an historical dissertation, which I did on how educative experience has been conceived by the curriculum field during much of this century.

"I joined the faculty of the University of Rhode Island in 1971, and really all the serious work I have undertaken since then has in some way or other been along lines of inquiry into the nature of educative experience—as you know so well.

"But getting back to your story, Bill . . . Thus far you have mostly described the origins of your interests but have not said much about how you have used them in your academic work. What about the differences these interests have made in your professional experience?"

"Since I joined the faculty of The University of Illinois at Chicago fifteen years ago I have continued several of the above interests. In preparing for articles and parts of books devoted to discussions of the nature of curriculum inquiry and educational research, Ann Lynn Lopez-Schubert and I vividly recall your influence, George, when in the introduction to your *Qualitative Evaluation* you admonished educators to think of personal, social, and educational significance, not merely statistical significance, which is often confused with 'importance' in a broad sense. Matters of personal, social, and even educational significance, for me, have derived from literary and artistic sources (especially from theatre, film, stories, novels, and abstract expressionist art) more than from social science discourse or educational research that is billed as scientific. Therefore, I found it a major contribution when William F. Pinar began to draw together experienced and emergent scholars who brought a broader array of perspectives to bear on curriculum issues. I especially think of his 1975 book, *Curriculum Theorizing: The Reconceptualists*, and conferences he started that have continued since 1973. We feel part of that tradition and part of the gradual entrance of it into the American Educational Research Association through the AERA Special Interest Group on Creation and Utilization of Curriculum Knowledge (see Short, Willis, and Schubert 1985), which is now called the Special Interest Group on Critical Issues in Curriculum. The point is that this concern for educational, personal, and social significance has over two decades emerged as the dominant thrust in curriculum theory today. It clearly develops and extends the spirit and vision of a Deweyan tradition and is represented by the authors of this book, who are indeed part of the pluralistic and emergent character of curriculum studies today that takes seriously the arts as a basis of inquiry."

"I could not agree more. But, Bill, the differences in *your* life? It is hard to know whether you think your experiences are conclusive or inconclusive if all you do is keep talking around the edges of them. You are certainly resisting my suggestions that you plunge into them directly. That is what I—and surely the readers—are waiting for you to do."

"It is your turn to be patient. I *am* talking about my experience. You know better than to imply that experience is the stereotypical stuff of soap operas. Even Conrad gave Marlow more restraint than that! You, after all, are the one who called me a storyteller and talked about the potential value of including in our story the context of our histories. Now I am the one who would like to get on with the whole story."

"By all means. I knew you had read *A Christmas Carol*, but I didn't know you had also read *Heart of Darkness*. Perhaps you have other surprises in store for me."

"You would be rather disappointed if I did not, I am sure, but that is a possibility I will let pass for the moment.

"I vividly recall being influenced by evaluation literature, as well. Perhaps more than anywhere else in the mid-1970s, the evaluation literature began to take on an artistic countenance. Along with your book, George, David Hamilton and others put together an anthology of artistic or qualitative orientations to evaluation referred to as having the intent to illuminate. Among the contributors to this book (Hamilton, et al., 1977) was Elliot W. Eisner, who also wrote the Foreword to your *Qualitative Evaluation*. In any event, Eisner's position that evaluation in education should seek to interpretively render educative experience for readers in ways that enable them to perceive that experience differently is well known today. Since readers of such rendition would often be educators, part of the hope is that new perspectives will bring new possibilities, and that imagining the latter will eventually provide improved practices. Eisner's work was, of course, based on connoisseurship and criticism in the arts. Thus, those who engage in educational criticism must be connoisseurs of educational phenomena. The notion of portrayal and interpretation in educational evaluation was pushed forward by Robert Stake's responsive evaluation, Malcolm Parlett's novelettes about his students, Egon Guba's naturalistic inquiry (later with Yvonna Lincoln), Michael W. Apple's ideological critiques, Maxine Greene's literary mosaics, William F. Pinar's and Madeleine R. Grumet's autobiographical explorations, Philip Jackson's rendition of classroom life, Louis Smith's portrayals of the complexities of schools, Max van Manen's and Ted T. Aoki's phenomenological interpretations of pedagogy; these scholars (along with Eisner) and others ushered in an expanded notion of educational scholarship itself. Expanding far beyond the parameters of conventional educational research, these authors, their contemporaries, and those influenced by them have pushed far afield the boundaries of educational inquiry in the past two decades. Many of these authors are found in the pages of this book."

"And this book?"

"That is, very simply, what our professional lives have come down to, at least for the moment, George, influenced by all the people I have just mentioned and many more. Surely, both you and I have lots of interests and have done lots of professional things, but this book is where we now stand. Do you find our experience embodied in it conclusive or inconclusive?"

"Inconclusive—without a doubt! Even though you have not finished telling the story of our experience with the book, I can still answer that question. (I was tempted to reply, 'Conclusively inconclusive,' but did not want you again to bring up my lack of restraint.) And not just our experience: everybody else's, too. You have just said as much. Come now, Bill, I was the one who began by being too solemn; now you seem to be the one. What else can experience be but inconclusive? This book is where we stand today, but if and when tomorrow comes, you, and I, and everybody else who put themselves into the book will be journeying on to someplace else. It won't be a case of any of us necessarily rejecting where he or she now stands, for we will all take our histories of today with us, just as we have brought yesterday's with us to today. It will simply be a case of encountering a series of new examples, the best of which will artfully portray experience and invite us to encounter them in artful ways. So there are always more examples worth seeking out, more lessons to be learned within them, more stories to tell. The what about experience that we sometimes think conclusive is when tomorrow's examples make us better than we are today. That is the what about a story that is moral. The arts necessarily aid in this, for all the arts speak to experience from experience. I, for one, am glad there is always more worthwhile to learn. Teaching and curriculum are always inconclusive in this same moral, artful way.

"Again I take your silence as agreement.

"I think all I have said thus far is borne out in what many of the contributors have told us about their own experience in writing for the book, an example I here add to our story. As we hoped, some of the contributors found writing short, non-academic essays about their own lives to be an easy task. They became open to new possibilities both for themselves and for their readers, and their writing flowed from within. Some even thought they had transcended anywhere they had previously been. Yet, as we had not sufficiently anticipated, still others found their task a highly daunting one. They, too, saw new possibilities, but possibilities that moved them to struggle within before they could begin to move outwardly at all. Some reported that their essays were the hardest pieces of writing they had ever done. The more autobiographical the essays, in fact, the more contributors seemed to find themselves at one extreme or the other; few remained near the middle. We did not know originally what we were asking of them. So whatever came out of them—solemn or humorous, about their personal lives or their professional practices—came at least in part as a surprise to us and to them.

"Don't you think so, too? . . . Still silent. Perhaps in your reflections you are more like a meditating Buddha than I originally anticipated."

"The question of how one's educational scholarship influences one's practice can be a haunting one. In 1983 Elliot W. Eisner reported on a study in which he surveyed faculty members at prominent research-oriented universities and asked them to relate the research that influenced their practice. Surprisingly few even acknowledged that they used research to guide their practice. Why, then, one wonders, were they such advocates of research as a guide for practitioners in schools? Are university professors beyond the need for guidance by research? Or is research simply being sold because it is what research universities have to sell? Or were these researchers merely delinquent in following their own prescriptions for success? None of the alternatives seem very flattering to university professors who promote research! Or, maybe, just maybe, educational researchers, like other educators (and human beings generally, for that matter) are influenced by something other than research findings. Perhaps that something is the integration of their lives with powerful messages from the arts.

"This possibility came home clearly to me in a meeting with J.P., a friend and former elementary teaching colleague. Since our days as teachers when we frequently got together to engage in ideas based on our teaching, we occasionally continue to meet and have these 'symposia' or 'seminars,' as we call them. Despite the fact that J.P. is now an award-winning filmmaker, and I have moved into the cloistered halls of academe, we gain insights from our talks on education. On one of these occasions, J.P. inquired about my recent work in curriculum. Of course, at a research-oriented university, the term *work* means research and publication, so I related my latest forays into curriculum theory and curriculum history. Then, as an aside, we began to talk about how I teach at the university. After a while, and showing more interest, he suggested that I consider deriving curriculum theory from my own teaching experience. I began to reflect on this, and was struck by the influence of the arts on teaching that I have found most successful. One of my favorite ways to deal with conflicting positions on curriculum is to role play as proponents of those views and encourage students to challenge each of the 'guest speakers.' Students seem less likely to be inhibited in challenging a fictional guest speaker than the professor of the course, the one who must eventually grade them. Vitality and enthusiasm for ideas is somehow heightened through role-playing. Sometimes after each student has read selections by authors that they have found illuminating, we set up an authors convention. We establish panels and I introduce the curriculum 'authors,' who then tell about the essence of a book or articles that they have written. This often emerges into dialogue with other 'authors' with conflicting views, or it results in the creative integration of positions among authors who have compatible views.

"While this certainly engages the artistic imagination in a theatrical way, I found the influence of other arts as well. I have asked students to create an advertisement, as a small poster, for a curriculum book or article that they would like to share with others. In some cases copies of the posters have been sent to actual authors of the books or articles, and students have received responses. Similarly, the art of writing has become enhanced when I have asked students to write a critique of a book to send to the author, not merely turn in for me to read. Finally, from colleague William Ayers, I became aware of a strategy whereby students are asked to make a collage of their pathway to teaching and share it with other members of the class (actually putting something on the walls of a university classroom!). Another approach sponsored by my acquaintance with the arts is derived from the prominent role of metaphor and analogy in all forms of art. I ask students to think of a topic that they know exceedingly well (not a topic within the realm of education) and to delineate several categories within it. Then I ask them to classify the curriculum theorists they have been reading into one of the categories by analogy and to provide reasons for their classification. In another activity, I ask students to reflectively consider the authors who have provided greatest enlightenment for them throughout the term. To do so, they enter eight of the authors who enlightened them the most in a 'curriculum enlightenment tournament.' The purpose of the activity, it is made clear, is not to finally determine who is wisest, Plato or Dewey or Sartre; rather, it is to facilitate reflection on ideas most influential for them at this particular point in their lives. Often this activity is extended to ask students to pose questions that they would like to ask some of these authors—and on occasion to try to anticipate the answers that they would provide.

"All of these activities enable me as a teacher to gain insight into how the course content integrates with the view of the world that students have. Surely these approaches get at that more fully than do multiple choice exams. If we want to know the impact of course experience on student outlooks, we need to seek it in more creative ways than the traditional requests to repeat knowledge disseminated. I think that is why many of us have used journals in recent years. Journals, too, are a kind of art form; certainly, when they involve the hermeneutic exchange of interpretations—student and teacher write and rewrite interpretations on each others' texts—it is a laudable kind of art. I think there was something quite right about J.P.'s suggestion that we should examine our own teaching for the theory embedded in it. Exposing that theory, we should then try to identify its sources. While I have found personal experience to be a powerful source of the 'theory' that guides my teaching, I have been surprised by the paramount influence of the arts on my teaching outlook. I think that I am not alone in this when I look at fellow authors in this book. We all seem to have come to understand in this same full but ever-changing way."

"Thank you, Bill, for following my suggestion to focus some remarks on your own professional experiences. You are a good storyteller, and the story you tell speaks for many people's experience and to virtually everyone's experience. It really is our story in the broadest possible sense. Personally, I don't think any reader should now have cause for complaint."

"Thank you for your kind words, George. I don't mind being compared to Marlow. However, I am still not as much like Marlow as you think, for I have not yet reached the conclusion of the story.

"A question that remains, and an important one, indeed, is about the import all of this has for the curriculum and teaching experienced by students. If our theories of experience are influenced in pronounced ways by the arts, if the arts have penetrated our conceptions of the world in ways that are difficult to decipher, what about the world views of our students? How do they live all this? This pulls the arts a long way down the road of significance (the personal, social, and educational kind) from the cut-and-paste art of the usual school setting. Our exposure to the arts gives us all (students included) a great deal of our sense of meaning and direction. As Sir Herbert Read (1943) observed, art evokes 'that instinct of relationship which . . . enables [a person] to distinguish the beautiful from the ugly, the good from the evil, the right pattern of behavior from the wrong pattern, the noble person from the ignoble' (p.70). Similarly, Malcolm Ross (1984), in *The Aesthetic Impulse*, points out that the central concern of arts education is 'the qualification of sensibility.' The essays in this book are intended to show that the arts have indeed educated us; they have helped us see (with Read) more of the beautiful, the good, the right, and the noble; and (with Ross) they have helped us perceive the kind and quality of educational patterns that move us toward greater qualification of sensibilities. The ultimate end of this journey, however, is not to enhance curriculum scholars alone through the arts, but through that enhancement to enable students of all ages to understand what it means to lead more artistic lives. We hope to contribute to educational settings in such a way that students experience alternative ways of knowing and being, a sense of playfulness of utmost seriousness, and a sensitive appreciation of possible worlds and possible lives through the arts. Such exposure, we trust, will inspire new and better answers to the basic curriculum question, What is worth knowing and experiencing?

"George? . . . That is the conclusion of the story. I feel nothing more I have to say now. . . . So you, too, in your reflectiveness have now fallen silent?"

"You are still more like Marlow than you think, Bill. Silence is the only appropriate conclusion to the story itself.

"As for our conversation-would-be-dialogue, there is a lot more about the coming into being of the book we both could say here, but, perhaps, not much more we need to say. The book began to come into being, of course, when we first asked ourselves how the arts have spoken to our lives. It has been a long time coming into being, but it is now here, and it now exists because of the contributions of others who have asked themselves the same question. I hope we all gradually have learned how to ask that question more broadly and more deeply, to thus be better inquirers, to thus be better hearers of and responders to what the arts say of living, to thus create our own examples, and to thus be better educators. In all that is the real understanding and the dialogue. Both you and I believe such dialogue is embodied in subsequent chapters of the book, artful chapters which say to readers, 'Please enter in.'"

I

GEORGE WILLIS AND WILLIAM H. SCHUBERT

PERSPECTIVES:
Reflections on the Arts and Educational Inquiry

"It seems only fitting, George, as we move from the prologue to the first part of the book that we continue a dialogue. When we decided to develop this book, I recall that we had two parts in mind at the very beginning. The first was to provide perspectives on the arts and what they offer to inquiry in education, and the second was to offer examples or illustrations of ways in which exposure to the arts has actually shaped the points of view of the author-educators of these essays."

"Your recollection of what we had in mind is correct. To reiterate what you said a bit differently, the first part of the book was to be relatively short, made up of a few essays intended to develop some general theoretical perspectives on how educators are indebted to the arts for their world views, for the very basis of how they live their personal and professional lives. The second part was to be longer, made up of a greater number of essays intended to provide sufficient specific examples of this living to illustrate the intimacy and the depth of the connections between the arts and the reflective, personal inquiry which is at heart educative and which education in a more public sense depends upon.

"The idea was not a bad one, I'm sure we both still agree, Bill. Many books contain a conventional distinction between a section on general theory and a section on specific examples. Our only trouble was that when we asked all contributors to the book to write autobiographically on the connections among these topics, those writing for the first part found they must necessarily include some specific examples from their own lives and those writing for the second part found themselves strongly compelled to include some general explanations for their own examples. That in itself illustrates how artistic, educative inquiry connects personal and professional living and why the two parts of this book inevitably reflect only different degrees of emphasis within the same overall process of how people come to understand. Thus all contributors to the book are fully reflective educational inquirers. The title we have given to the first part of the book, 'Perspectives: Reflections on the Arts and Educational Inquiry,' implies only that a primary focus within these autobiographical reflections is on providing some general explanations of the relationship between the arts and educational inquiry."

"Yes, and we also asked them to write longer essays than those in the second part of the book. Even so, the distinction between the general perspectives of the first part of the book and the illustrative examples of the second part is inevitably blurred, and the blurring is very sensible, I might add. We have learned—or at least were vividly reminded—that in touching individual lives there are generalizations in the Deweyan and Schwabian sense we reflected on earlier, but not in the sense of universal theory. To reiterate all this in still another way, the reflective inquiry and the artistry of the contributors have taught us that statements of perspective provide illustration and illustrations give perspective."

"Again we are in essential agreement, Bill, even though we have reiterated that agreement in different words. Perhaps the same could be said about the essays that now are the chapters in this part of the book. Readers will find that their authors have had different experiences, hold different ideas, and use different words, but that despite these differences, essential agreement perhaps prevails about the meanings of the arts, reflective inquiry, curriculum, and teaching for each other. Or is that too big a 'perhaps'?"

"Perhaps it is, George. Perhaps it is not. You will agree, of course, that readers must do their own inquiry on this matter. Since all the chapters are autobiographical to one degree or another, what readers will find are different perspectives on the topic, explanations that draw upon the different backgrounds of the authors.

"This part of the book begins with a chapter by Elliot W. Eisner, an artist and art critic as well as an educational theorist, researcher, and critic. He explains the basic lessons which his experience with the arts has taught him about education. The next chapter is by Louis Rubin, who was educated as a musicologist and has considerable experience as a musical performer, composer, and director. His chapter describes analogies between these activities and the kinds of composing, directing, and performing done in creating curricula and in teaching. Next, Harry S. Broudy calls upon his extensive background in philosophy of educ-•ation and aesthetic theory. In this chapter his perspective on the relationship between the arts and education focuses on a specific program of art education. Madeleine R. Grumet then opens up a much different approach to the general topic. Her depth of background in theatre, literature, other arts, and feminist studies is apparent in a chapter which suggests how the activities of daily living may be inherently artistic and educative. Next, Robert Donmoyer draws from literature, visual art, and especially theatre and his experience as an actor in a chapter which points out how the arts can engage people in fundamentally educative inquiry. And finally, Maxine Greene, who has developed a long line of books and essays that illustrate the literary artist and critic at work as a philosopher of education, contributes a chapter on how experience with the arts can inspire images of possibility and stimulate people to live education in new ways."

1

ELLIOT W. EISNER

What the Arts Taught Me about Education

What follows is a personal, autobiographical statement. To write about how the arts have influenced my thinking about education demands, at least for me, an examination of the role they have played in my life. I can see no other way to do it.

I must confess that I have thought about this matter many times, but it was not until I was invited to *write* this chapter that I confronted the task of thinking systematically about it. As almost all academics know, writing forces you to reflect in an organized and focused way on what it is you want to say. Words written confront you and give you the opportunity to think again. Thinking on its own, without the commitment that writing exacts, makes tolerable—even pleasurable—the flashing thought, the elusive image. When one writes, the public character of the form demands organization, and when autobiographical, the problems of appearing egoistic or saying too much or seeming self-promoting are constant threats.

I share these concerns with you because I want you to know that for me this is not the usual academic paper; the topic of the paper is me.

Let me begin with a confession that art—the visual arts—was a source of salvation for me in the two elementary schools I attended between five and thirteen years of age. I did not do well in elementary school: arithmetic was problematic and frustrating, my handwriting was and is at present not particularly good, spelling was a relentless bore, and English grammar—the diagramming of sentences whose features remain before me as vividly now as they were then—was largely meaningless, even when I was able to correctly indicate the difference between a direct and an indirect object. But art—ah, that was another story. I was good at art; indeed, I was the "class artist," and appreciation for this achievement motivated my third grade teacher, Mrs. Eva Smith (at that time a nearly ancient fifty year old), to suggest to my mother that I should be enrolled in art classes at the School of the Chicago Art Institute.

My mother was both an intellectual woman and someone who prized the arts, particularly music. She wasted no time enrolling me in Saturday morning art classes which I continued to attend throughout elementary school and into the beginning of high school. Art was then, as it is today, a deep source of pleasure.

High school was even more frustrating for me than elementary school. Aside from art, sports, and girls, my high school classes were dull at best. I did not do well. Out of a class of about 430 graduates, I managed to graduate in the thirty-second percentile of my class. The prospects for my future would be lackluster if I graduated today in the same position as I did then.

After graduating from high school, I enrolled in the School of the Art Institute of Chicago to study painting, and then attended Roosevelt College in Chicago to complete a B.A. in art and in education. It was during those four years—between seventeen and twenty-one—that the marriage of art and education occurred. Let me tell you how.

I grew up in a Jewish community on Chicago's west side. Although there was an exodus of Jews in the 1950s from this part of Chicago to the northern suburbs, our family was among the last to leave. The neighborhood that was once populated with delicatessens and synagogues—virtually one on every corner—became a haven for blacks not only from Chicago, but from other parts of the country. 'My' neighborhood had as one of its community resources a boys club, the American Boys Commonwealth, where as a child I spent countless happy hours working with clay, plaster, and paint, and learning to weave and draw. I returned to the ABC during my college years to teach arts and crafts to the black children and adolescents who had moved into the neighborhood. In fact, I taught my art and craft classes in the very same art room in which I had spent such happy days during my own childhood.

The children I encountered, and particularly the adolescents with whom I worked, were poor, and, as they were described at that time, were either "pre-delinquents" or "juvenile delinquents"—not all, to be sure, but enough of them to help me understand what those terms meant. Establishing rapport was tough but achievable, and such victories were very satisfying. My work with these children and adolescents, motivated initially by a desire to learn more about art by examining its sources, soon was converted into an interest in how art could be used to help children grow. My master's thesis at the Illinois Institute of Technology was titled "The Therapeutic Contributions of Art in Group Work Settings." I became as much interested in the children with whom I worked as in their art; no, even more so.

The opportunities to work with "children at risk," as we say today, and to teach art in the Chicago Public Schools after finishing a master's degree in art education provided a part of the foundation for my commitment both to art and to education. The other part of that foundation was built from the kind of social conscience that growing up in the home of a socialist father and an artistically interested and intellectual mother generated. Discussions about 'society,' 'the working man,' and 'equality,' as well as the importance of education, were almost daily fare.

As important as these two particular sources were, they do not tell the whole story. For example, while at Roosevelt College I had the good fortune of having some superb neoprogressive professors of education who were interested in "deep" learning and who cared about children. What they were concerned about I had become interested in years earlier, and so the congruence between their ideas and my interests were very close. My work as a student in the School of the Art Institute of Chicago taught me invaluable lessons about the importance of both intellectual and emotional commitment to one's own work. Painting was difficult, complex, challenging, and demanded time and the ability, even if one was only nineteen, to commit oneself to its seriousness. In its own special way, the School of the Art Institute of Chicago was a deeply intellectual place, as I think the really well-run high school auto mechanics program can be for today's adolescent. I, learned at the Art Institute of Chicago to take work seriously. The fact that some of my fellow students were a decade older than I, veterans of the Second World War going to school on the G.I. Bill, helped in this regard.

Also contributing to my views about education was my experience as a neophyte art teacher working on the fourth floor (where few administrators ventured) in Chicago's Carl Schurz High School. A school for thirty-six hundred students and middle class throughout, this setting gave me the opportunity to discover the deep satisfactions I could receive not only from seeing or making paintings and sculpture, but from helping fourteen and fifteen year olds immerse themselves in the process of creating their own art. I discovered at a level different from what I learned in the American Boys Commonwealth that initiating the young into the pleasures of art and the visual world was for me a very important source of satisfaction. These satisfactions and interests continued and provided a major theme during my doctoral studies in the Department of Education at the University of Chicago. No one on the faculty had a specialized or even a special interest in art education, but my professors provided the space and the support that made it possible for me to continue my interests in this field. I was very lucky.

Chicago also provided the theoretical tools and the intellectual climate that I needed; much of it was like my life as a child at home; ideas were prized almost for their own sake. Analysis, debate, and speculation were common. Much of my experience there was familiar and comfortable. More moments than one has a right to expect were like peak experiences. At Chicago, art and intellect had a happy marriage.

So much for foundations. What difference have these experiences made in the way in which I think about education?

Perhaps the most important contribution that my immersion in the visual arts has made to my views of education is the realization that neither cognition nor epistemology can be adequately conceptualized if the contributions of the arts to these domains are neglected. Those of us professionally socialized in education, not to say the culture at large, have lived in a sea of assumptions about mind and knowledge that have marginalized the arts by putting them on the back burners of mind and understanding. To engage in cognitive activities, we have been told, is to mediate thought linguistically, to use logic in order to monitor thinking, and to escape the limiting concreteness of the particular in order to experience the loftiness of the general. Plato's conception of knowledge as thought liberated from the senses and Piaget's ideal of formal operations as the apotheosis of cognition represent for most in education what it means to engage the mind (Gardner 1989).

As for knowledge, the legacies of Compte and positivism in its various forms put the arts beyond the margins of knowledge (Ayer n.d.). To know, the positivists tell us, is to make meaningful assertions—that is, to state propositions or make claims about the empirical world whose truth (or falsity, at least) can be tested.

What one cannot say one cannot know. Given this view, how can a nonpropositional form—and these forms include not only the visual arts, music, and dance, but also literature and poetry—be regarded as having any epistemic functions at all (Phillips 1987)? The answer is clear: they cannot.

The result of such beliefs—often unexamined, at that—is to promote a hierarchy of knowledge that enthrones scientific knowledge and expels the arts from cognition entirely. The arts, as everyone knows (given these beliefs), are affective, not cognitive, and in our educational institutions we are hell-bent on cognition. Given the prevailing view, the arts are nice, but not really necessary (Broudy 1979).

My own experience in the arts as a painter contradicted these narrow views of what the thinking mind did or how it was we come to know. It was clear to me, as a doctoral student at the University of Chicago, that the creation of a successful painting or an expressive sculpture could in no way be dismissed as a consequence of emotion finding its release in a material. The job of making a painting, or even its competent perception, requires the exercise of mind: the eye is a part of the mind and the process of perceiving the subtleties of a work of art is as much of an inquiry as the design of an experiment in chemistry. As a painter I grappled with the problem of trying to make a picture 'work'—often unsuccessfully. Painting was no easy task. Matters of visualization, technique, composition, sensibility, and inventiveness were required. And all of these skills and abilities were employed on a dynamic configuration; things were always changing, and the most subtle alteration of a passage in one section of an image required attention to a variety of others as well. To conceive of the arts as the discharge of affect was to miss the point of what they were about and, more important, to neglect a resource that could have a major contribution to make to the developing mind. Such ill-conceived notions, I thought, must surely be apparent. Yet all around, the arts were a nonissue. Even the educational scholars I respected the most paid little attention to their potential role in our schools.[1]

My work in the arts as a painter made it perfectly clear that cognition, by which I mean thinking and knowing, is not limited to linguistically mediated thought, that the business of making a picture 'that works' is an awesome cognitive challenge, and that those who limit knowing to science are naive about the arts and, in the long run, injurious to the children whose educational programs were shaped by their ideals.

I must confess that the foregoing beliefs were, early in my academic career, convictions that were derived intuitively from my experiences as a painter. It was not until I read the work of Rudolf Arnheim (1990), Susanne Langer (1942), and John Dewey (1934) that I encountered respected scholars whose work supported my intuitions. And when I read Michael Polanyi's *Personal Knowledge* (1958)—a book I encountered years after it was first published—my sense of being vindicated grew.

My appreciation for the kinds of thinking that qualitative mediation and qualitative problem-solving elicited led quite quickly to the view that if education was to do more than develop a small part of human cognition, it had to give the young opportunities to work in the arts. The arts were mind-altering devices and the curriculum the major means through which such alteration could be fostered. To underestimate their importance in the array of cultural resources that the school could make available was to do a significant disservice to the young. Making a place for the arts in our schools became for me a kind of cause, a cause in the name of a balanced and equitable education.

It is both interesting and gratifying to find that both developmental and differential psychologists have discovered the arts. Gardner (1983), for example, argues the case for a multiple theory of intelligence and makes place for the arts within the seven modes of intelligence he describes. Snow (1986), likewise, recognizes aptitude differences in learning and the importance of formulating curricula that allow children to play to their strengths. The new-found cognitive pluralism and the greater willingness of psychologists to recognize "practical knowledge"[2] harkens back to an Aristotelian distinction between the ways in which knowledge is secured and displayed. The upshot of these interests is the liberalization of views about the nature of intellect and the provision of a wider and more generous conception of what it means to be smart. I confess that I sometimes feel like someone standing on the sandy beach of a fog-swept sea watching a rowboat filled with cognitive psychologists searching for the shore. I sometimes see myself waving to those aboard and shouting to them, "Over here! Come over here! What's taken you so long?"

I know that such personal revelations make me appear smug;

I do not intend for that impression to be conveyed, but those of us who have devoted so much of our professional lives to trying to make a place for the arts in education have been waiting for a very long time. To be perfectly candid, although the rowboat is closer now to the shore than it once was, it has not yet docked.

You will recall that I said that cognition referred not only to skills, but also to knowledge. The creation of a picture, or a poem, or a musical composition requires, at minimum, knowledge of the unfolding qualities with which one works. These cognitively mediated qualities must be seen, modulated, transformed, and organized in the course of one's work. It is clear to anyone who has struggled with the task of doing so that there are no linguistic equivalents to the qualities experienced in this process. To reduce knowledge to warranted assertions, true propositions, or falsifiable claims that have withstood falsification is to be oblivious to the fact that, insofar as such claims refer to empirical qualities, they are never their equivalent. The map is not the territory. In order to draw the map, the territory first has to be known in other ways.

I was not willing to reduce knowledge to the kinds of truth tests that positivists or neopositivist philosophers required. Furthermore, knowledge of the qualities of works of art is not limited to the qualities found in works of art alone. It was clear that the qualitative subtleties of the world outside of art—the comportment of people, the look of a city street, the tone of voice as it speaks, and an infinite array of others—were objects of knowledge by a seeing eye and a hearing ear. Language is, in a way, our heroic effort to transform what we have come to know directly into that public surrogate we call *text*. When text is itself artistically rendered, we can begin to approximate the virgin experience it is intended to convey.[3]

Appreciation of qualitative sources of knowledge led me to reject conventional wisdom: why restrict knowledge to what verificationists *or* falliblists demand? To do so would be like limiting the content and aims of education to what psychometricians are able to measure. It made no sense to me to try to consign knowledge to a piece of paper the size of a bubblegum wrapper, all in the service of verification. Thus, it becomes increasingly important to me not only to broaden our view of what it means to think, but also to enlarge our view of what it means to know. In this effort cognitive pluralists such as Nelson Goodman (1978) became important allies.

To illustrate the ways in which the arts enlarge our knowledge of the world, consider two complementary processes that they engender: individuation and generalization (Arnheim 1990). The refinement of the perception of idiosyncratic features of objects or events is one of the two major lessons that learning to draw, sculpt, compose, or write artistically focused language develops. To draw a tree or the particular comportment of a seated figure, the artist must not only notice that the object to be drawn is a tree or a figure, but a *particular* tree or figure. To do this, the artist must avoid the premature classification that is typically fostered by schooling and instead remain open to the particular features and overall conformations of individual forms. No tree, no oak tree, no young oak tree is the same as any other young oak tree. The task the artist faces is to experience individual features of *this* tree, of *this* person, and to create a form that succeeds in revealing the essential and unique features of the object seen. In the process of revealing what is individual, the work also—ironically—becomes what Arnheim (1990) calls a canonical image through which the features portrayed through the visual rendering of a distilled particular can be used as a generalizable image to locate similar features found elsewhere. In this process the image becomes a concrete universal, a means through which perception is sensitized so that it can locate like qualities. Such functions are performed through literature, poetry, dance, as well as the visual arts. *Othello* is about more than Othello.

It is ironic, to say the least, that schools should pay so much attention to the process that Dewey (1934) called *recognition*, and so little attention to the processes of perception. All so-called abstract knowledge depends upon the ability to relate language to images: infinity, kindness, masculinity, envy are imagistic in character; the sources of these images are in the extrapolation of qualities seen: infinity—time and space; kindness—subtle degrees of care experienced; masculinity—the features we learn in our culture to stand for maleness; envy—the way in which individuals respond to each other. In fact, we have no words that can adequately reveal the meanings to which these terms refer. To the extent to which our imagination is impoverished, the meanings of these terms also will be. Imagination is fed by perception and perception by sensibility and sensibility by artistic cultivation. With refined sensibility, the scope of perception is enlarged. With enlarged perception, the resources that feed our imaginative life are increased. Thus, one of the lessons I have learned from art that has influenced my views of education is that it is through the refinement of sensibility that language secures its semantic character; another is that the eye is a part of the mind; a third, that not all that we can know, we can say. Polanyi (1967) was right: we know more than we can tell.

The practical and normative implications for curriculum of these ideas I believe to be more than substantial. Like the arts, the school curriculum is a mind-altering device; it is a vehicle that is designed to change the ways in which the young think. If the arts develop particular mental skills—the ability to experience qualitative nuance, for example—and if they inform about the world in ways unique to their form, then their presence in our programs for the young are likely to foster such outcomes; their absence, the opposite. Thus, when we think about the arts not simply as objects that afford pleasure, but as forms that develop thinking skills and enlarge understanding, their significance as a part of our educational programs become clear. Curricula in which the arts are absent or inadequately taught rob children of what they might otherwise become.

Thus far I have spoken of the contributions of the arts within the curriculum in fairly general terms. While it is true that all art forms share some common features, there are significant differences as well. The cadences of poetic language are not those of symphonic form; the rhythms of visual form are different from those found in literature or dance. At the most obvious level, differences among the arts are (usually) differences in the sensory modalities appealed to. They are images experienced through the funded perception of the form or genre in which any particular work participates. What this means is that the development of sensibility and judgment profits—indeed, often requires—a memory of forms related to the one being encountered (Eisner 1991). The curricular implications of this observation are that the educational benefits of the arts are secured not simply by their short-term presence, but by sustained experience with like forms. It takes time, effort, and experience to learn how to read a complex and subtle array of qualities. Each of the different art forms participates in a different history, has its own features, and utilizes different sensory modalities. By learning to create or perceive such forms, the arts contribute to the achievement of mind.

The differences among the various arts are not only differences that count in calculating their educational value. There are important differences *within* a specific art form. Different forms of visual art, for example, may be said to appeal to different parts of our body. Surrealist art, in both its perception and creation, calls upon the individual to take leave of reality and to enter into a *sur-real* world. Fantasy, dreams, reverie are the stuff that the surreal depends upon. Children introduced to such work or to activities that invite them to create it experience a different kind of 'ride' than those working with the French impressionists. My point here is that styles of art—cubism, de stijl, constructivism, minimalism, realism, pop and op art, expressionism—call upon different aspects of ourselves. Which art forms are selected and what tasks are set in the curriculum have consequences for that aspect of our being to which the form speaks. The same case can be made for music, dance, and literature.

Thus, another of the lessons I've learned from the arts is that while they share commonalities, different forms of art put me in the world in different ways. They speak to different aspects of my nature and help me discover the variety of experiences I am capable of having. I believe that such lessons have implications for educational policy and for deciding about what knowledge is of most worth.

As fundamental as curriculum is, no curriculum teaches itself. The curriculum is always mediated. It is in the description and improvement of teaching that the arts have a special contribution to make.

It has been relatively recent that it has become legitimate to think about teaching as an art form. The dominant image and ideal has been, and in most quarters still is, a technical one. The general model is for educational researchers to do the basic social science, to pass on to teacher trainers what they have discovered, who in turn inform would-be and practicing teachers of 'what works.' This model has increasingly been regarded as over-simplified and, by some, downright wrong (Broudy 1976). New and, I believe, more adequate views talk about the epistemology of practice (Atkin 1989) and about the differences between theoretical knowledge and practical deliberation (Schwab 1969). The importance of the context is recognized even by cognitive scientists when they talk about "situated knowledge" (Greeno 1989). Yet, for all of these developments, it is telling to note that the *Third Handbook of Research on Teaching* (Wittrock 1986), a tome weighing over four and a half pounds and containing over eight hundred entries in its index, has no listing under the heading "Art" with respect to teaching. To be sure, there is a heading referring to art, but it is to the teaching of art, not to the art of teaching.

My work in the arts has influenced my view that teaching is an artistically pervaded activity—at least at its best. Teaching is artistic in character in many of the ways in which all art is artistic: it provides a deep sense of aesthetic experience to both perceiver and actor when it is well done (Eisner 1982). It requires the teacher to pay attention to qualitative nuance—tone of voice, the comportment of students, the pervasive quality of the teaching episode. It requires the teacher to attend to matters of composition in order to give the day or lesson coherence. It often requires flexibility in aims and the ability to exploit unforeseen opportunities in order to achieve aims that could not have been conceptualized beforehand. Teaching is a constructive activity whose efforts result in forms that can provide what the fine arts are intended to provide: a heightened consciousness and aesthetic experience.

Because theoretical models are idealized structures, and research results, abstractions referring to absent populations, no teacher can rely upon them exclusively for dealing with particular students in particular classrooms in particular schools. Like all artistic activities, the features of the specific material or situation must be addressed without relying upon algorithms for decision-making.

These features of teaching seem perfectly plain to me. They are less clear to many others, although, as I have indicated, the field of education is moving toward a more artistically conscious view of the nature of teaching than it has in the past (Kagan 1989). When there is a willingness to recognize the artistic nature of excellent teaching and to acknowledge the inherent limitations of the social sciences in guiding teachers, possibilities emerge for treating the improvement of teaching in ways that are not unlike those used to improve individual performance in any art (Atkin 1989). When such ways are examined, attention to nuance in performance becomes crucial, and the use of a language through which it can be revealed, essential. These processes are examples of connoisseurship and criticism (Eisner 1985).

What the arts have taught me is that nuance counts in teaching no less than in painting. It has taught me that not everything can be reduced to quantity and that the attempt to do so creates a destructive form of reductionism and a misleading sense of precision. I have learned from the arts that poetic language is often needed to *render* a performance vivid, and that suggestion and innuendo are often more telling than stark statement of fact.

The logical categories and operational definitions that appear so attractive in the social sciences are, in my view, often misplaced in so fragile and delicate an enterprise as teaching. Although the traditional ambition of nailing down the facts and measuring the outcomes have long been sources of cognitive security for some, they are beginning to give way to a more elastic but relevant form of disclosure. That is one of the reasons why ethnography is now seen as a useful way to understand classrooms and schools. When Clifford Geertz (1988) says that anthropological authority often emanates from the ways in which some anthropologists write, he recognizes the artistic contributions to anthropological scholarship. Geertz is by no means alone. The previously sacrosanct methods and criteria for social science inquiry, methods that once aspired to those of physics, are being reconceptualized and widened in the process. The direction is toward the arts.

The conceptualization of teaching as an artistic activity and the acceptance of epistemological pluralism have opened the door to a form of evaluation that is rooted in the arts and humanities. Educational connoisseurship and educational criticism (Eisner 1985) are efforts to use and extend aims and methods employed to heighten awareness of works of art to educational practice. Connoisseurship is the art of appreciation; criticism, the art of disclosure. They are means with which to see and to articulate the qualities and values of particular works of art by using a language that helps others see those works more completely. The genre of educational criticism is literary. While an educational critic might use some of the techniques of the cultural anthropologist—interviewing students, for example—the aims of the critic's work are not anthropological, but educational. It is intended to heighten awareness of the classroom or of teaching or of the materials students and teachers use. It is critical, interpretive, and often poetic in flavor. From the arts I have learned that such efforts can amplify perception and expand consciousness of what otherwise might go unseen. Much of my own work over the last two decades has been aimed at elucidating that model and fostering its legitimation in the field of education. I believe much progress has been made.

Another lesson I learned from the arts deals with how we think about the outcomes of educational practice. In the standard model of rational educational planning, the task confronting the planner is, first, to be clear about his or her objectives, to specify them in detail and, if possible, to define them in measurable terms.[4] By using this model, curriculum development is believed to be made easier because clarity of aims is thought to facilitate the invention of means for their achievement. In addition, aims, by and large, are to be common among students of the same age levels, as are the tests they are to take to demonstrate competency. The education summit talk of September 1989 about national goals for America's schools, defined in measurable terms, is nothing less than the rationale I have described directing educational policy at the highest levels of our government. Clarity of expectation subjected to a common form of examination using standardized criteria meet the accepted canons of rationality and objectivity.

My experience in the arts has taught me a different lesson. From the arts I have learned that not only cannot all outcomes be measured, they frequently cannot be predicted. When humans work on tasks, they almost always learn more *and* less than what was intended. Furthermore, teaching that is not hog-tied to rigid specifications often moves in directions and explores ideas that neither the students nor the teacher could envision at the outset. In addition, virtue in education is much more than achieving uniformity in outcomes among students. Such an aim might be defensible in a training program, but when one values individual vision and personal creativity, the specter of all fourth graders marching at the same pace to the same drummer toward the same destination is a vision that better fits the current People's Republic of China than a nation aspiring to become a genuine democracy. In short, educational practice does not display its highest virtues in uniformity, but in nurturing productive diversity. The evocation of such diversity is what all genuine art activities have in common. Even art forms as apparently restrictive as the music of the baroque or the brush painting of the Meiji

Period in Japan made it possible for artists to improvise in order to reveal their own personalities in their work. Educational programs, I learned from the arts, should not be modeled after the standardized procedures of the factory; the studio is a better image.

When one seeks not uniformity of outcome, but productive diversity, the need to create forms of evaluation that can handle uniqueness of outcome becomes increasingly apparent: the multiple-choice test will no longer do. Any approach that prizes such outcomes forgoes commensurability, a source of deep security for many. When we cease putting all children on the same statistically derived distribution, we have to think and judge, we have to interpret what it is that they have done. We move more and more towards connoisseurship. And when we talk to others about what we have learned, we move more and more towards criticism, that age-old process of interpretation and appraisal. An artistic perspective, once taken, colors the way we see all facets of the educational enterprise; it is not restricted to a bit here and a piece there.

What, then, have I learned from the arts that has influenced the way I think about education? I have learned that knowledge cannot be reduced to what can be said. I have learned that the process of working on a problem yields its own intrinsically valuable rewards and that these rewards are as important as the outcomes. I have learned that goals are not stable targets at which you aim, but directions towards which you travel. I have learned that no part of a composition, whether in a painting or in a school, is independent of the whole in which it participates. I have learned that scientific modes of knowledge are not the only ones that inform and develop human cognition. I have learned that, as constructive activity, science as well as the fine arts are artistically created structures. I have learned these lessons and more. Not a bad intellectual legacy, I think. And not a bad foundation on which to build better schools for both children and teachers.

NOTES

1. Two exceptions were Jacob Getzels, whose background in literature permeated his observations about education, and John Goodlad, who intuitively knew that the arts were an important aspect of programs for children and adolescents. Both Getzels and Goodlad supported my

interest in the arts, although neither taught courses on the arts in education.

2. The concept "practical knowledge" reverberates in current discussions of "situated knowledge," a phrase being used increasingly among cognitive psychologists to underscore the differences between learning within an academic setting and the kind of knowledge that students can act upon in situations outside of the classroom. The family resemblance, it seems to me, between Aristotle's distinction between practical and theoretical knowledge is quite apparent, even when psychologists do not harken back to its roots.

3. Susanne Langer's point that both literature and poetry are nondiscursive is directly related to her argument that the artistic formation of language presents a form of feeling that can be known only through the way in which a form—language—has been shaped. Artistic form, for Langer, has an important epistemic function.

4. The salience of hyperationalized views of educational planning as represented in the work of Robert Mager and James Popham has diminished in recent years. However, it is well to recall how oversimplified conceptions of "intelligent" professional planning undermined genuine professionalism among teachers by its failure to appreciate the need for what Dewey referred to as "flexible purposing." As teachers have a larger say in schools, the acknowledgement of artistry and the need for flexibility is likely to increase.

2

LOUIS RUBIN

The Arts and an Artistic Curriculum

Since the walls of the first school were erected we have engaged in a seemingly endless—and unresolvable—debate over the school curriculum. Today's schools teach largely the same content and subject matter as those a half-century ago. Yet the debates—driven by changing societal norms, expectations, fears, and aspirations—are strikingly different. Virtually everyone has an opinion, inspired perhaps by some personal experience, private bias, media-fueled anxiety, or wishful thinking. Many are convinced that competitive sports teach teamwork and that the study of mathematics promotes logic. Some believe that AIDS education is simply a matter of instilling sound values, quibbling with those who think that contemporary youth must completely understand the physiology involved. In this maze of old and new ideas, the arts may provide partial direction.

Art education theorists frequently use terms such as *productive*, *expressive*, and *aesthetic* to describe the various dimensions of art. The instructional theory notwithstanding, schools place a predominant emphasis upon the productive: art education is expected to result primarily in poems, paintings, or choral presentations. As a consequence, whatever valuable learning is peripheral to the productive process falls by the wayside. Long ago, for example, I was the band instructor in San Francisco's largest high school. As a young teacher, I found it difficult to simultaneously conduct the band and react critically; I could detect obvious things like faulty intonation and rhythmic inconsistency, but I could not get a sense of the overall performance. Consequently, I taped the rehearsals and later listened, alone, with a critical ear. One afternoon, replaying a tape of a new piece the band had sight-read, I suddenly realized that it was not the primary exposure to a work of art, but rather the secondary contemplation, which evokes genuine understanding.

The true impact of a film is not immediately apparent during the viewing; it is the rumination that follows, the mental rehashing, which crystallizes one's reaction. We look at a sculpture, listen to a poem, and feel the texture of a clay pot, but it is in the subsequent cognitive processing—when we use our mind's eye, ear, or hand to relive the experience, free from the emotion attached to the initial encounter—that our imagination takes hold and we grasp the impact. One wonders, therefore— -to extrapolate curriculum implications—whether in schooling we too often stop short of the mark, judging the teaching successful when the learner has acquired preliminary knowledge instead of requiring that it be mentally recapitulated, interpreted, and resurrected in some realistic context.

The typical curriculum has both fixed and unfixed elements. The fixed embody what we take to be the knowledge of highest worth: a reasonable comprehension of the natural world, a conversance with history, a familiarity with literary classics, the ability to understand our own culture and others. The unfixed—those which lend themselves to continuous change—involve, first, substitutions and additions to the basic corpus and, second, alterations in ways of communicating information. For example, we may decide to replace *Silas Marner* with *Death of a Salesman* and add the music of Leonard Bernstein to the humanities program, or to incorporate ongoing societal concerns—such as international confrontations in the Middle East, the growing problems associated with various forms of addiction, and the potential dangers of genetic manipulation—into the social studies program. When we replace the old film strips with laser discs and equip new schools with fiber technology, however, we retain the substance but alter the medium.

It is curious that, in our approaches to curriculum design, we give so little attention to degrees of emphasis. We dissect the disciplines, extracting significant concepts and generalizations; we probe the societal fabric, searching out the weak threads and making provisions for at-risk youth, AIDS education, and drug abuse prevention; we periodically reexamine the ongoing youth culture and decide that it is once again time to stress moral values, citizenship, and idealism; and, alarmed at declining writing skills, we shore up our treatment of rhetoric, grammar, and clear prose. However, preoccupied with the concerns of the moment, we often fail to discriminate between matters of greater and lesser importance. Our courses of study dutifully list aims, objectives, and goals; we specify desirable outcomes and cobble together impressive-looking teaching guides that are model examples of comprehensive education. But in our concern about the overall instructional spectrum, we sometimes forget to hammer home intellectual ideas and values of overarching importance. Thus, the student may come away from the classroom assuming that the dates of the Civil War are as important as the guarantees in the Bill of Rights, that the correct spelling of Homer's name is as significant as his imagery, or that democracy is a governmental process rather than a way of life. Our only gesture toward paramountcy is repetition: we teach United States history in the fourth, eighth, and eleventh grades in the hope that reiteration implies consequence.

The arts, in this regard, provide an interesting contrast. Although artists seek to achieve works that have obvious appeal and demonstrate artistic merit, they are rarely satisfied with something that is merely pleasing or aesthetically satisfying. Their intent is to go beyond the art itself—to prod the intellect, stir the emotions, or excite the imagination. In the fine arts, particularly, the artist seeks declaration—a commentary on human travail, a warning about the societal plight, a plea for ethical values, or perhaps a protest against the decline of humanitarian impulse. Their art, in sum, produces both an object of beauty and a vehicle for expressing some deeper insight which goes beyond the aesthetic itself.

In all of the arts, vitality is critical. The artist's creative energy and the liveliness of the product are the primary sources of attraction. We find a vivacious departure from convention intriguing, just as we find clichés and time-worn modes boring. In TV commercials, for example—if an inspired advertisement can be conceived of as an artistic achievement, as, in a sense, it is—the artistic challenge lies in capturing viewer attention. One claim about the virtues of a particular soap is about the same as another. The lure lies, not in the assertion itself, but rather in the magnetism of the presentation: we respond to the creative flair of a commercial that seduces our interest through an imaginative notion, arrestingly presented.

In a curriculum, three particular aspects are likely to suffer when vitality is lacking: the instructional format, teacher performance, and learner incitement. The instructional format of a healthy curriculum must be more than a litany of topics, units, and tests. The relevance of the subject matter to the learner, the vividness of the learning materials, and the conceptual ploys used to reinforce powerful constructs heavily influence learner attentiveness and absorption.

Vitality in curriculum interpretation—teaching—is especially critical. A Bach fugue is no more than black spots on white paper until a great performer brings it alive. So it is with curriculum: the facts, concepts, principles, and generalizations specified in a lesson are subject to the beliefs, whims, preferences—and artistry—of the individual teacher.

Teaching artistry stems from a variety of factors. All artists have a lasting love affair with their art, and gifted teachers view their teaching as something more than work done for pay. Passion—a profound interest in the subject matter and the learners' intellectual development—is indispensable. Students, apt critics of teaching, respond to perfunctory, listless pedagogy with instant ennui. Conversely, animated teaching stimulates a response to the teacher's commitment.

Most students of the arts, seeking to develop skills, will at one point or another imitate an acknowledged expert. Many an aspiring writer has attempted to write a paragraph or two in the style of Hemingway. Mozart, it is said, mastered composition by recopying the scores of Bach. Legions of painting students have tried to produce, if only in fun, a canvas fashioned after Picasso or Mondrian. Such imitation of masterworks is useful because the replicative process provides analytical practice, helps to develop technique, and, in some mysterious way, seems to deepen one's intellectual grasp of the art form itself. The important thing, of course, is that the learner must know that the imitation is not an end in itself but rather a means of enhancing capability.

The point was made plain to me when, early in my career, I studied composition with Roger Sessions at Berkeley and John Vincent at UCLA. Each year UCLA engaged an eminent composer to serve as composer-in-residence. Graduate students in composition were invited to create a piece which, if deemed worthy, was performed in a mini-recital and then critiqued by the composer-in-residence. In the year that the distinguished American musician Aaron Copland was the resident composer, I was fortunate to have a viola sonata, composed for the occasion, selected. As it was performed by a fellow student, Mr. Copland sat at the piano bench reading the score.

When the playing concluded, I nervously joined him on the

bench and listened to his comments. A warm, extraordinarily gentle man, he indicated passages, here and there, saying such things as, "It would have been nice if you could have reemphasized the primary theme here," or, "The momentum was good until it began to drag a bit at this point," and, noting another place, "This was a rather lovely touch, here." Then, looking me full in the face, Mr. Copland said gravely, "The unfortunate thing, Mr. Rubin, is that Debussy did it first!"

Several years later, teaching in the public schools of San Francisco, I recalled this incident and tried to incorporate the principle in my instruction. I found that, having read "Memories of President Lincoln," my ninth graders could approximate a few lines of Whitman. Similarly, once high school students had studied *The Tempest*, the best of the lot could produce a surprising approximation of Shakespeare. I discovered, as well, that after my classes understood what historians do and how they went about their craft, I could provide them with a cardboard box, filled with artifacts from my attic, collected over the years—a restaurant menu, perhaps; an old newspaper; a hairbrush set of my father's; my high school year book—and, with relatively little coaching, they could write a page or two of history. Borrowing the wastebasket from the room next door, eighth graders could unpack the contents—a piece of gum, a girl's flirtatious note to a boy, three crumpled balls of paper, each with a false start to a composition—and, reasoning in the manner of an archaeologist, reconstruct some of the events which probably transpired in the other room. All of which suggests that, given a reasonable background, students often can learn a surprising amount by emulating the behavior of professionals.

There is a rough parallel, in this regard, with curriculum, if we take curriculum to embody both what is taught and how it is taught, and if we acknowledge the importance of linkages between specific disciplinary knowledge and general intellectual processes. Assume, as an example, that it would be useful to teach middle school students the economic principle of supply and demand, and to teach them, as well, the cognitive procedures which enable one to predict the economic consequences of changing conditions. An adroit teacher might accomplish both objectives by enabling her students to perceive the effects an exceptionally early Florida frost would have on the cost of orange juice the following spring. In this example, the subject of economics is akin to the artist's medium; the strategies of prediction are analogous to the artist's intent; and the teacher's ingenuity corresponds to the artist's creativity.

Artists, as a general rule, seek to illuminate human experience, to penetrate the outer veneer of events and accent their larger impact. In so doing, they must of necessity work within the limits of their media. Painters, for example, can readily convey a concern about corruption and greed in contemporary culture, at least to the degree that their skill, imagination, and perception permit. Dancers, in contrast, are bound by a medium in which emotional states—joy or sorrow—are more easily represented than cupidity. Whereas photography can deal with anything perceptible to the eye, architecture focuses, by and large, on particular human activity; and sculpture, in the main, uses the body to express conceptualizations. Artistic achievement, consequently, results from inevitable compromises between the restrictions of the art form itself, the subject matter, and the range of the artist's genius. Put another way, the quality of art depends upon the creative ingenuity with which the artist utilizes the resources inherent in the medium and upon the expressive power of the objective.

The scant attention we pay to teacher inventiveness takes a fearsome toll. In schools of art, originality and creative invention are presupposed and of capital importance. In schools of education, the usual emphasis is on prescriptive, prefabricated solutions to workplace problems. Much is lost, not only in the way of imaginative teaching, but also in a tragic abortion of the psychic benefits associated with fertile pedagogy. There is, first, considerable gratification in solving seemingly impossible dilemmas through inventive devices; and, second, the exercise of one's creative capacities carries its own intrinsic rewards.

While researching a book on artistry in teaching, I chanced to visit the classroom of a teacher in Ohio who had organized an intriguing six-week instructional unit in American history that harnessed the same trinity intrinsic to artistic endeavor: medium, objective, and creative ingenuity. The shipment of a needed set of textbooks, for some reason, had been delayed six weeks. To cope, during the interim, the teacher designed an approach wherein current events were taught through the daily newspapers (the medium); significant concepts were extracted, analyzed, and subsequently related to a historical precedent (the objective). A story on public outrage over higher gasoline taxes led to a discussion of taxation without representation which, in turn, was related to the Boston Tea Party. What made the unit possible, obviously, was the teacher's faith in her own ability to relate a current event to a historical one (creative ingenuity).

Elsewhere, I have written about the development of pedagogical intelligence.[1] The centerpiece of the argument is that inspired teaching comes not merely from a command of content and method, but also from a conditioned instinct for guiding learning. While contextual clues frequently influence instructional decisions, it is the reaching back into experience, the tacit interpretation of earlier encounters similar to the present, and the inferring of potential solutions which serve as the springhead of intuition. Pedagogical intelligence, hence, is the ability to facilitate significant learning, with maximal efficiency, under the circumstances that exist. It consists of a particular amalgam of aptitudes which can be cultivated and enlarged. The bottom lines of this hypothesis, self-evidently, are that teaching, at least in part, is an art form; that great teachers are artists in their own right; and that training in imaginative pedagogical problem-solving is an important linch-pin in curriculum delivery.

Knowledge and execution are distinct. One can recognize that something should be done, for example, but lack the ability to do it. Preservice training deals predominantly with knowledge. Teaching, in contrast, involves execution. Most of the important skills of teaching can be acquired only *in situ*—through direct involvement with the materials, artifacts, and environments of classrooms and through direct engagement with students. Moreover, the general rules of teaching often must give way to the specialized rules of particular subject matter. A useful device for teaching poetry, for instance, may be unsuitable for teaching paragraph structure.

No teaching method circumvents the need for expertness: it is not the tactic, but how well it is used, that matters. Good strategies used badly produce little of value. Conversely, a relatively poor method—bolstered by effective compensating mechanisms—may, on occasion, bring surprising results. It is becoming increasingly evident, moreover, that the constructive use of experience is a vital element in skillful teaching. Teachers, like artists, frequently rely on intuitive knowledge in making rapid decisions during the course of instruction. This intuitive knowledge stems from insight—gleaned through past experience—which repeatedly has been processed and internalized through reflection about classroom phenomena. For this reason, there is considerable danger in the assumption that imitating expert teachers will produce expert pedagogy. It cannot be. Imitation may enable teachers to emulate intelligent procedure, but it does not automatically produce excellent teaching. Skilled teachers consider a variety of factors in making instructional choices. What they do, in sum, fits the situation at hand. Replicating this behavior without regard for context offers no assurance of appropriateness. Thus, when a good technique is used at the wrong time or in the wrong way, the benefits are likely to be lost.

It is not what expert teachers do, but rather the ways in which they decide what to do—the ways in which they choose one action over another, using conditioned instinct to determine the best alternative—that makes the difference. These decisions stem from interpretation and analysis, from bringing lessons learned earlier to bear on the problems of the moment. If curriculum serves the teacher, as clay, metal, and wood serve the sculptor, the importance of creative impulse and inspired vision are hard to exaggerate.

If, then, artists achieve their goals by exploiting the expressive dimensions of their media, teachers perhaps can similarly use their talents to guard against excessive insularity of isolated subject matter, to resolve the clamoring assertions of the disciplines through ideas of central significance, and to embellish their teaching with the kind of originality, flair, and panache that artists bring to their projects.

Another curricular lesson from the arts stems, I suspect, from several common denominators that make it exceedingly difficult to assess the quality of a school program—or of a work of art—with anything approaching precision. When I was a student of musicology, I once was required to do a detailed analysis of Ravel's compositions. After days of study, I eventually was able to break down his harmonic structures, rhythmic patterns, and melodic preferences into atomistic fragments. I found, to my dismay, however, that a sharper understanding of the parts had destroyed the earlier pleasure of the whole. Before the onset of cognition, I responded to the beauty of his music with simple sensory pleasure. Afterward, although I had a far better knowledge of his craftsmanship, the sensory joy had diminished.

It is much the same with curriculum. We concern ourselves, as obviously we must, with the right substantive content, proper sequence, sound pedagogy, appropriate evaluation mechanisms, and so on. But, clearly, to judge a curriculum purely on the basis of its anatomy—the structure of aims, goals, subject matter, teaching methods, evaluation procedures, and the like—is to err. Although these elements create a scaffolding, what happens within the scaffolding matters more. It would be absurd to assume that anyone who used the same oils, palette, brushes, and canvas as Picasso could produce paintings of equal greatness. The excellence of a work of art or an instructional program depends upon something greater than the sum of these individual components.

Periodically, in my consulting, I am asked to identify the best instructional model or course of study in the country. Such questions are impossible to answer, of course. Two equally outstanding schools can have sharply different curricula; they accomplish their goals in varying ways because school quality is tied to purpose and heavily influenced by specific conceptions of the good, true, and beautiful in education.

There is, in this regard, a striking similarity in the problems of judging artistic and curricular merit. Neither, for example, can be described with any accuracy. A written course of study does not communicate the essence of a curriculum any more than the program notes of a Mozart violin concerto convey its elegance or the different aesthetic nuances it reveals when performed by Isaac Stern or by Itzak Perlman. Just so, a physics lesson taught by one teacher is not at all the same when taught by another. One cannot describe the parsimonious elegance of Mondrian or a vivid classroom discussion of human anguish in ways which capture their real quality: both must be experienced directly. Like the arts, curricula must be perceived in order to be understood.

Moreover, neither curricular worth nor aesthetic value can be proven: each is intangible. We can, obviously, verify whether a given instructional unit familiarizes students with the plot of Shakespeare's *Twelfth Night*, but we cannot with any exactitude assess the attitudes of mind, values, and human insight which may, or may not, have been generated. As with other abstractions, like moral goodness or ethical judgment, curricular and artistic quality defy precise definitions. And while rational analysis is useful, it does not result in definitive conclusions. Ultimately, the excellence of a course of education—or of a work of art—is a matter of judgment, rooted in the sense one makes of reality.

Nonetheless, works of art and works of curriculum both fall on a continuum of quality. In the arts, aesthetic merit derives, essentially, from a consensus of opinion—from the informed judgments of critics and knowledgeable consumers. Similar appraisals can be drawn with respect to schooling: in the case of curriculum, assessments are based on the responses of the learners themselves, the reactions of their parents, the achievement registered on standardized tests, and, in time, the kinds of humans students become when the lessons are over.

The merit of an instructional unit depends both on its pedagogical appropriateness and the mindset of the critic. I am frequently astonished, after a lecture, at the disparateness of student reaction. One student finds a particular discussion stimulating and meaningful while another regards it as much ado about nothing. I ask my classes to comment, occasionally, not on the content of the lecture, but rather on the ideas generated in their own heads. The results are sometimes astonishing: students tend to filter intellectual constructs through a sieve constituted by their own notions of what does, and does not, enlarge their capabilities. It seems reasonable to infer, therefore, that in evaluating curriculum and instruction, we would do well to look beyond content mastery per se and appraise, as well, what the learning has contributed to the students' general sense of what matters.

Choreographers, sculptors, poets, and composers derive their inspiration not only from the resources of their art form alone, but also from ongoing cultural phenomena which capture their attention. The resulting art, consequently, can be critiqued with respect to technique and thematic perception. Bach's *B Minor Mass*, as an illustration, was an awesome expansion of invention, taking musical syntax in unsuspected new directions, and a powerful portrayal of Christian adoration of God. Similarly, when we view Daumier's *The Third Class Carriage*, we are struck by the extraordinary use of light and dark, as well as by the hardships of travel suffered by the poor.

Our intrigue with intellectual ideas, like our infatuation with works of art, is tinctured by our ways of looking at the world and our private arenas of meaning. Currently, as the curriculum undergoes yet another cyclical readjustment, in deference to accountability and rigor, the quality of instructional programs is again being equated with student performance on standardized tests. While, to be sure, such evaluation is useful, it ignores the powerful lessons embodied in our responses to the arts and defines learning as a pound or so of accumulated fact, rather than as personal experience.

Judgments regarding the relative greatness of art are influenced, to a considerable extent, by personal values and preferences. Opinions regarding import and excellence are heavily laced with idiosyncratic conviction. William James observed, long ago, that "the philosophy which is so important in each of us, is not a technical matter; it is our more or less dumb sense of what life honestly and deeply means. It is only partly got from books; it is our individual way of just seeing and feeling the total push and pressure of the cosmos."[2] The appreciation of art, thus, is guided, not by absolutes, but by appraisals arising from biases as well as substantive knowledge. Evaluations of worth, in both art and learning, stem from reflection wherein passions and insights operate in tandem.

NOTES

1. *Journal of Teacher Education*, in press.

2. *Pragmatism* (New York: Longmans Green, 1922), p. 4.

3

HARRY S. BROUDY

The Role of Art Education in the Public School

In the early 1950s I tried to explicate a Classical Realistic philosophy of education, having worked through, and partially out of, a doctoral preoccupation with the James, Bergson, and Kierkegaard version of anti-intellectualism.[1]

The latter part of the book dealt systematically with the problems of value education in a series of chapters dealing with economic, social, recreational, associational, health, religious, moral, and aesthetic aspects of experience. I was surprised at how little I had to say about the aesthetic domain, especially as it pertained to the role of the arts in the curriculum of the public school. This led to some digging into formal aesthetics and speculation as to why art education and its role in general education received such casual treatment (or so it seemed to me) in the teaching of the philosophy of education. The concern was stimulated by my meeting with D. W. Gotshalk, the aesthetician, when I joined the faculty at the University of Illinois in 1957. Several years later I offered a graduate seminar in Aesthetic Education, which attracted twelve to fifteen students each year from various art media, as well as from teacher education curricula. The course was devoted about equally to the study of formal aesthetic theory and what has come to be known in the trade as "scanning," a method of systematically exploring the aesthetic properties of objects, especially works of art.

It became apparent, to me at least, that art instruction in the elementary grades consisted largely of demonstration lessons by an art specialist and reinforced subsequent practice sessions directed by the classroom teacher.

The purpose of the lesson was to develop some degree of skill in drawing or singing. The enthusiasm of the classroom teachers varied with their competence and confidence in producing works of art. Holiday art was very much in evidence and the periodic exhibition of the children's work edified the parents. Art and music were generally regarded as desirable adornments of life rather than necessities, especially for a typical public school population. Real achievement demanded talent, which, as might be expected, was unevenly distributed in the school population. It seemed obvious that, if art was to be studied as a standard component of the common school curriculum, it would have to be desentimentalized and delivered from its "*caviare* to the general" image.

To this end I harangued school people with articles about "'rt" being "the fourth r," the necessity of the arts in the curriculum, and the role of art in general education. I devoted my 1972 Kapppa Delta Pi Lecture to *Enlightened Cherishing*.[2]

These endeavors resulted in a number of projects in aesthetic education implementing some of these theories, notably in the work of Dr. Carol Holden, Nancy Roucher, and Michele Olsen in Decatur and Champaign, Illinois.

In 1975 a summer institute called "The Aesthetic Eye" was organized by Dr. Frances Hine, Art Supervisor for the Los Angeles County School Board, and supported by a grant from the National Endowment for the Arts. On the staff of the institute were Dr. W. Dwaine Greer, Dr. Gilbert A. Clark (both at the time working in South West Regional Laboratory), Professor Ronald H. Silverman of the California State College at Los Angeles, and myself.

This group became the nucleus of the staff of the Getty Institute for Educators on the Visual Arts in Los Angeles in the mid 1980s, the seed site for Discipline Based Art Education.[3]

Dr. Greer had worked on such a curriculum at the Laboratory, and the completed curriculum was subsequently acquired and distributed by Phi Delta Kappa. A revised version is being readied for distribution. Known as the SWRL curriculum, it was used in many of the Los Angeles districts organized by the Institute. Later, under pressure of complaints that other curricula were being shut out by the Getty enterprise, but which seemed to meet the DBAE requirements, some districts were permitted to choose alternative curricula.

THE DBAE CURRICULUM

The essence of the DBAE movement is that art education programs should use a written, sequential curriculum grounded in the disciplines of aesthetics, art history, and art criticism. Art production was to provide opportunities for understanding and appreciating art, as well as for acquiring some of the skills involved in its creation.

The project sent seismic reverberations, so familiar to Angelinos, throughout the art education establishment. Textbook authors, conventions of art educators, and assorted votaries of the art world were invited to discuss DBAE at national conferences. Evaluation teams were recruited to scrutinize the DBAE projects and, it sometimes seemed, to find fault with them. The Getty Center, for its part, encouraged the art education world to feel free to use curricula other than SWRL that could meet the DBAE requirements.[4]

The major complaints against DBAE have been that (1) it is too rigid, (2) it downplays production in favor of understanding and appreciation, (3) it threatens existing curricula and programs, and (4) it overintellectualizes art education by emphasizing academic subjects, namely aesthetics, art history, and criticism. According to many critics, it neglects or undervalues the emotional responses to making and viewing works of art.

As to the spate of criticism of the "disciplinary" emphasis of DBAE, it should be noted there is a difference between a curriculum being discipline-*based* and discipline-*constituted*. It is one thing to *derive* the content of the curriculum from the disciplines, but quite another to teach third graders the contents of aesthetics, art history, and criticism, albeit some exercises have been devised wherewith to introduce children to some of the concepts of these disciplines.

However, there are good grounds for helping teachers who are working on DBAE projects to become familiar with these disciplines, albeit the summer exposure to a few lectures in these fields is probably too little and come too early in the game. Certainly, some classroom teachers could benefit from courses for university credit in these areas.

Scanning has also been scorned as an oversimplification of the aesthetic experience and pedagogy. The SWRL curriculum and scanning have been the most frequent targets of the DBAE critics. To my mind, the DBAE emphasis on scanning is justified by the need for an aesthetic alphabet. It is a simple, well tested path to the systematic perception of aesthetic properties in the work of art. The evidence for the efficacy of scanning is wide and impressive, despite the disdain of some art educators for any pupil response to a work of art that does not throw the senses and glands into an aesthetic spasm.

I have yet to persuade a museum to 'bug' the paintings on one of its corridors so that comments made by the passing visitors could be recorded for study. From informally overhearing many of these comments, one draws the melancholy conclusion that the struggles of the artist to capture human significance in an image, what Suzanne Langer called a "portrait of feeling," are often not even noticed, let alone understood and appreciated. Scanning systematically provides the viewer—even the least sophisticated one—with a rudimentary but genuine access to aesthetic literacy—and literacy is the accepted route to mastery in virtually all other subjects of instruction.

Despite these criticisms, DBAE programs have been established at a number of sites in California, Minnesota, Nebraska, Florida, and Tennessee. Recently, the Getty Center received a national diffusion grant to help communities establish DBAE programs for teacher education in the arts. Dr. Greer is Director of the network.

THE ROLE OF IMAGERY IN LEARNING

The role of imagery in learning school subjects is a topic of immediate interest to educators, as indeed is any aid in this direction.[5] It can be shown that the teaching of language, concepts of various subjects of instruction, the values of a culture all depend on appropriate images for their comprehension. So simple a locution as "We worked around the clock" may be unintelligible to non-English speakers, even though a dictionary supplies them with the definition of each word.

The equal sign of mathematics requires the aesthetic category of balance, which, in turn, is the imagic root of equality and justice. More than fifty figures of speech were invoked by President Reagan in his last inaugural address, a veritable imagic vocabulary of patriotism.[6] But virtually every phase of our lives depends on imagery, on the inveterate activity of the imagination.

We do not need the skill of the painter or poet to imagine what "might be," and some of these "mights" turn into "coulds," "musts," and "oughts," the seeds of science, ethics, philosophy, and religion. Very early in the game it occurs to us that if one ice cream cone is delicious, a dozen might be even more so; and, by the same process, visions of possessing large numbers of sexual partners, servants, soldiers, and dollars may spur the effort to actualize them. What might be is the fuel of the human enterprise.

Imagination can expand the intellectual and spiritual horizons into the loftiest ideals, but it can also envision the vilest villainy. When one considers the reason given for the expulsion of Adam and Eve from the Garden, namely, the eating of the tree of knowledge and therewith of good and evil, one may speculate that the race had not only been shorn of innocence, but that it had discovered the power of what *might be*, what the human mind could imagine. Henceforth, this power would have to be policed by reason and self-restraint—qualities never in adequate supply.

It is the imagination that turned the simplest physiological needs into complicated systems of behavior, ideas, and values. Consider, for example, the matter of shelter, certainly one of the basic needs in the natural world of living things. Why doesn't taking shelter under a tree or in a cave supply the desired protection from the elements? Yet, over the centuries, the construction of shelter has become one of the major concerns of humankind, one that taxes the ingenuity and imagination. For it is by imagining what shelter *might* be that builders, masons, and architects first came into being and thereafter became necessary. Today we judge the genius of a people and a culture in no small measure by the buildings they have been able to visualize and construct.

Feeding, the ingestion of nourishment, is certainly a fundamental and primitive activity. But how long did it remain a simple physiological reaction to hunger pangs? It was probably not too long before feeding became related to what human beings imagined powers, natural and supernatural, had to do with food preparation, consumption, and its role in celebrations.

In the same vein, one might consider how the physical act of reproduction became involved with the numerous and varied ceremonies and customs designed to 'humanize' it. A physiological twitch was converted by imagination into romance, marriage, the family.

As might be expected, the images created by the imagination have become the stock in trade of the arts, for it is through art that what *might* be becomes available to the senses to be shaped into ideals that stretch the boundaries of reality.

It is only natural for a culture to use the arts to educate the young. From the earliest years, fairy tales and cradle songs are our tutors. Later, each generation continues and elaborates the aesthetic education of its members; adolescents who have not become connoisseurs in the shapes, colors, and sounds of their generation are doomed to misery. From then on, the benefits and penalties of adulthood are absorbed through imagic clues without formal instruction; the media and the workplace apprise the individual by way of imagery of what is desirable in speech, clothing, virtues, and vices.

We are told that "men sang before they spoke" and that they learned the language of water, fire, and clouds before they produced more formal and sophisticated language systems.[7] Indeed, it is difficult to imagine how the race survived unless they construed these images correctly most of the time.

I have noted, as many may have, that residences in middle-income neighborhoods often do not bother with a front door entrance that has some aesthetic pretensions—perhaps constructed with ornamental bricks, edged with flowers, etc. Indeed, for some residences the front walk is no more than a path from the garage hidden by shrubbery. It is the double car garage that confronts the passerby, with its bold, broad, concrete expanse declaring the economic status of the household.

This bit of architectural detail by direct imagery tells a complex social story, just as in an earlier era the elaborate front entrance and the driveway to the carriage house discreetly winding its path behind the mansion gave its social report. A bank, hotel, costume, voice, a store front sign informs us by its *appearance* about its function, its values, and often about its price. So do our speech, posture, dress, and demeanor 'speak' about our social status, formal education, economic niche, and not infrequently, albeit not always correctly, about our character.

Another and perhaps even more fundamental approach to the evaluation of general education—and especially of art instruction as a part of it—that deserves more attention than it has received is the successive reports on school performance. They give the impression that the school, especially the public school, is a miserable failure. The evidence cited are SAT scores and comparison with Japanese schools that produce remarkably superior results in these tested domains.

These dismal reports on schooling in the 'basics' of literacy and science have recently been augmented by the Bloom-Hirsch dismay at the public's ignorance of great books and high culture in general. This issue is especially important in designing and evaluating art education because art is expected to portray the highlights and deep shadows of the human enterprise. One wonders whether SAT scores on facts and figures, names and dates, problems in math and science will adequately reveal the effects of art instruction or the lack of it.

For a handle on this issue, one might think of the uses of schooling in four dimensions: the replicative, the applicative, the associative, and the interpretive.[8]

The *replicative* use is measured by asking the learner to reinstate responses studied and tested in school, such as names, dates, formulae, rules, and procedures. The *applicative* use asks for a solution to a problem the data and methods for which have been studied. The *associative* use of schooling manifests itself in the cluster of responses that has been accumulated since infancy from a wide variety of experience. The *interpretive* use covers much of what is commonly called "associative" thinking, albeit it is more closely related to the use of concepts to interpret a situation. I have dubbed the associative and interpretive resources the Allusionary Base.

A good deal of what is learned in general education functions in the allusionary modes long after the replicative and applicative uses decay from disuse. We have some empirical evidence from a series of case studies for this hypothesis (cf. *The Uses of Schooling*), but some simple tests can be used to confirm it. For example, individuals who have never studied Latin are very unlikely to use "breathing together" as a definition of "conspiracy" or "carrying across" of "transport," albeit they may all give adequate definitions.

This is no great matter in ordinary discourse, but in reading English poetry the images conjured up by the Latin or Greek roots of a term may make a lot of difference. Long after many of us can no longer speak or read Latin or Greek texts, these root images function interpretively. And the same may be conjectured about the interpretive uses of other subjects studied in school, the details of which one can no longer replicate or apply.

Art education relies heavily on this usage, which in a somewhat similar sense is called tacit knowing, or *thinking with* rather than *thinking of*.[9]

If this makes sense, we can better articulate what can reasonably be expected from a curriculum that is grounded in (albeit not consisting of) aesthetic theory, art history, and criticism, and conversely what a lack of such education would mean. This is so because the images of art are rooted in the primal gropings of the human mind to understand life itself. The sights and sounds of nature are translated into meanings, into signs of significance, and civilization proceeds from these beginnings.

ART EDUCATION AND THE CULTURE

Are we trying by means of art education to introduce-seduce the young to an art world composed of artists, museums, critics, etc., or has this *art world* produced values that can be realized—or at least adequately perceived—by the graduates of our public school?

This query dominates current discussion in philosophy, social science, and the arts. Is there a truth or an assertion of it that is not a reflection of the values of a particular culture or subculture? Critical theory insists on a negative answer. The Platonic supposition that human minds, by achieving access to the forms revealed by the dialectic of reason, can arrive at a vision of Truth is thus rejected as itself a function of cultural influences. Accordingly, the notion that 'great' art portrays 'great' truth is also rejected.

This impacts on art education in several ways, the most vocal being that feeding the young inhabitants of the classroom on art that is predominantly western, not only is unfair to other cultures represented in the school population, (women, Asians, Afro-Americans, and others), but also conceals the 'fact' that western culture is itself an interpretation of art and everything else by western values, and no more 'true' than any other interpretation.

If we accept the relativism urged upon us by 'critical theory,' what accounts for the persistence of the belief in the 'eternal' verities? What happens to the responsibilities for transmitting these verities? Is it to rid the schools of them? Is it to apprise the young that the 'great' truths are only the prejudices of particular cultures? Or is it to remove them from the curriculum entirely? Can we finesse the issue by systematically insisting that it is important to study the 'eternal' truths even though no such truths exist?

Another alternative is to recognize that there is a kind of truth to which logic is not relevant. It is the truth that is revealed and 'proved' by a leap of faith. The 'proof' that a Supreme Being endowed with supernatural attributes exists is the willingness of believers to bet their lives on the existence of such a Being.[10]

One may question the logical validity of such a belief, but one cannot question the sincerity of the believer's wager. It is an existential proof. In the history of human life, this leap of faith has left deep traces on a culture. Not the least of these are the images of faith in the reality of ideals recorded by the artist.

THE SPOORS OF HUMANITY

The record of this faith can be summed up in three portrayals of the human quest: achievement, justice, and compassion.

Achievement

Achievement is a pervasive theme of art. The artist celebrates achievement, whatever form it takes. The hero or heroine wins the race and thereby reinforces its value. The military contest is only one, albeit historically the most obvious one, for victory in this kind of race denotes power, which is self-validating. To the victor belong not only the spoils of material goods, but glory, honor, and self-esteem. This 'glory' is 'recorded' in the images of the hero portrayed in song, story, paint, and stone.

In our time, economic success is the dominant form of achievement. Control of material resources is the immediate reward, but it is accompanied by high social and civic status. Art contributes its portraits of economic power, and possession of esteemed works of art is among the most familiar indicators of economic success. The economic race has the aesthetic potential of all contests—high stakes, danger, courage. All contribute to the drama which invites the imagery of art.

In our time, achievement in the sciences, in scholarship, and in political life is likewise a theme for celebration. Prizes, publicity, and honors celebrate achievement. Here, as in other domains, it remains the business of the artist to portray the complex of feeling attendant upon winning the race and the rewards of victory.

Accordingly, art becomes an important and distinctive avenue to understanding achievement whether in conquering a continent, an enemy army, a secret of nature, or a tragic misfortune.

Justice

Achievement, however, has its victims as well as its victors. In every domain where the race is for scarce resources—military power, wealth, intellect—there are losers as well as winners. Sometimes the losers are destroyed, sometimes they suffer disgrace—always the losers are unhappy, but on occasion they complain bitterly that the race was unfair. By this, they usually mean unequal opportunity to win because the winner had unfair access to wealth or political infuence—in short, power. For instance, a winner in the military or economic race may give his friends, children, and associates advantages denied to other competitors, a head start, so to speak, in the next race.

The children and friends of the high achievers rarely go unrewarded. They do not start the achievement race on even terms with competitors less fortunate. When, therefore, one surveys the race for success, there appear inequalities which seem, and often are, grossly unfair—an uneven playing field. Hence arise the complaints of injustice and demands that justice—an even playing field—be restored.

The quest for justice, for fairness, thus becomes a pervasive quest in every epoch and produces its heroes. Those who battle injustice, real or imagined, have their victories and defeats. Art records, or at least portrays, the quest for justice—the battle with social evils of all sorts. The most familiar symbol of the quest for justice is the famous lady equipped with blindfold and scales. It is a simple, straightforward image that symbolizes an important aspect of the human quest.

The quest for justice can intersect with the race for achievement. It can become a contest among lawyers, judges, and legislators, and winning the race can bring the rewards of achievement.

Nevertheless, the dawn of the need for justice is a radically novel intrusion into the natural order. One does not find it in the life of plants and animals. Imbalance of power and success are ever present in nature, but not the resentment against it. In the world of tooth and claw one finds no righteous indignation, so characteristic of the impulse to justice. Plants and animals compete on the battlefield of nature, but the strong win out. Evolution proceeds without, one must suppose, any conscious resentment against the law of survival. Unlike the drive for achievement, the quest for justice requires envisionment of an ideal that the human imagination creates as a possibility and develops into a necessity—an ideal foreign to the subhuman battle for survival.

Art depicts the struggle in portraits of human behavior, demeanor, and emotion that clarify its nature as it occurs in human nature.

Compassion

The efforts of the human mind and spirit as expressed in the race for achievement and the quest for fairness are not, unfortunately, always successful. Despite the efforts in behalf of justice, the achievement race produces losers. Some lose because they lack the strength to compete; others, because of unfairness of the race. It is a rare society that escapes the problem of the chronic losers. Once more, the human mind seizes upon a sentiment and converts it into an imperative, an ideal that, so far as we know, is peculiar to human beings; the sentiment is pity; the imperative is compassion—a demand to help the weak, the unfortunate, the perennial victims.

The most familiar form of compassion is pity, but human emotions cannot for long escape the impulse to justify them by ideology—by a demand that the universe validate pity for suffering and therewith dignity of human existence.

This ideology posits a deity endowed with infinite power, wisdom, and compassion, one that may command worship. Religions may vary in their commands and the institutions for carrying them out, but they all demand a leap of faith that transcends temporal power and wisdom.

The leap of faith transforms experience, but on what grounds can one testify to its reality? Clearly, it is not the logic of science, nor the evidence of our senses. The evidence lies in another direction, namely, in a willingness to wager *everything* on its reality, despite all empirical evidence to the contrary—the blood of the martyrs. It is difficult, if not impossible, to doubt the genuineness of a belief when it inspires a willingness to die for it.

The role of art in portraying the phenomena and sentiments of religious faith is too familiar to require extensive discussion. It is not surprising that the domain of the holy attracts the imagination of artists and impels them to construct sensory surrogates of what transcends the senses.[11]

These three domains—achievement, justice, and compassion—one may say are channels for the artistic impulse to flow into our lives and to become a record of a culture. The images art creates thus constitute a distinctive type of information that communicates directly about the concerns of life. For they are images of experience in all its phases and moods—not photographic likenesses, not analytic discussions, but feelings made accessible by their portraits created by art.

This ability to portray feelings in images gives art its power to communicate the ineffable and to do so with a directness that no other medium can match. And it is the same power that makes art education a necessity rather than an interesting diversion from reality.

THE FUTURE OF DBAE

Despite the spirited criticism of the DBAE program, a grant to create a National Diffusion Network promises to encourage the expansion of the program. An increasing number of texts are emerging that claim to be consistent with the DBAE approach. It remains to be seen how genuine these claims are: the organizational apparatus of DBAE is easier to duplicate than its theoretical underpinning. Nor will it *really* reassure all art educators that a scholarly approach to art education will not stifle the romance that surrounds the artist, that it will not dampen the creative impulse in school children and their ability to express this creativity as proto artists.

The DBAE project may stimulate a reassessment of the role of the scholarly disciplines in schooling, whether social institutions in general and schools in particular have a special function in society or whether all functions are shared by all institutions. Although scholarly disciplines do from time to time merge their interests and research (e.g., chemistry and physics, sociology and anthropology), each discipline retains its distinctive methods, texts, authorities, and traditions.

The organization of the universities from their beginning tended toward specialization. When general education became institutionalized, schools faced the task of fashioning a curriculum that included selections from many disciplines. Art history and aesthetics, however, rarely broke into the "circle of studies," and art and music, like physical education, were regarded as activities rather than disciplines.

The DBAE stance, therefore, represents an effort to ground art education in its intellectual matrices, in which art production is only *one* of its components. Without the disciplinary background, the role of art in the culture cannot be understood, much less appreciated.

Given or taken that art education is a genuine function of the public school, what prevents its becoming so? Primarily the unreadiness of the classroom teacher to teach it. Can elementary school teachers become as competent to do so in the same sense that one expects them to teach the other subjects?

This is the crucial question, because if they cannot do so, not all the praise accorded the arts will make them regular members of the curriculum. They will retain the status of specialties, extras, so to speak, most easily dismissible when funds for art specialists become scarce. But why should not the regular teacher be able to teach art? Does such a teacher have special training in the other disciplines? The answer to these queries lies in how much of an artist the classroom teacher is expected to become and how teachable the 'language' of art can be made.

The DBAE curriculum is a positive answer to such queries. The Getty Institute's work in a number of sites in a number of states gives evidence that it can be done, especially if scanning is used to 'read' the aesthetic properties of the images that constitute art. If a written curriculum *based* on the aforementioned disciplines is constructed, and if classroom teachers are given the opportunity to become familiar with it, the plausibility of art becoming a fixture in the elementary school is very high.

The DBAE movement has been seen by some art specialists as a challenge to their role in art education. This can take several forms. It may be construed by some as a move to displace them altogether or to diminish their status in the public school art programs. A common attitude is that developing artistic skills does not require a DBAE approach—indeed, that such an approach is antithetical to the creative and expressive functions of art. To this objection it may be pointed out that at issue is the status of art in *general* education, not the proficiency of school children in art-making.

Experience in the districts where the DBAE approach has been used does not support the charge that 'production' is neglected nor creativity stifled. On the contrary, the confidence that the movement has engendered in both teachers and pupils in matters of art holds out the promise that aesthetic illiteracy may be on the way out—the first small step, but genuine nevertheless.

NOTES

1. H.S. Broudy, *Building a Philosophy of Education* (Englewood Cliffs, N.J.: Prentice-Hall, 1954). The citation of my own writing is to be explained by the fact that this essay sketches my own problems with the subject: those of a philosopher or an educator who is not an artist.

2. University of Illinois Press, 1972.

3. The Institute is one of the activities sponsored by The Getty Center for Education in the Arts, under the direction of Leilani Lattin Duke.

4. Cf. Margaret Moorman, "The Great Art Education Debate," *Art News* (Summer 1989): 124-131.

5. I have tried to spell this out in *The Role of Imagery in Learning* (Los Angeles: The J. Paul Getty Trust, 1987).

6. Ibid, 26, 27.

7. Cf. Alasdair MacIntyre, "Relativism, Power, and Philosophy," *Proceedings and Addresses of the American Philosophical Association* 59 (September 1985): 5-22; F. Dretske, Presidential Address, *Proceedings and Addresses of the American Philosophical Association, Western Division,* 26 April 1985, 23-24; and I. Berlin, *The Divorce Between the Sciences and the Humanities,* 2nd Tykociner Memorial Lecture (Urbana, Illinois, 1974). Indeed, according to Alasdair MacIntyre, the efforts to construct a universal language are thwarted by the lack of a universal imagery.

8. H.S. Broudy, *The Uses of Schooling* (New York and London: Routledge & Kegan Paul, 1988).

9. As used by Michael Polanyi in *The Tacit Dimension* (New York: Doubleday, 1966).

10. I have tried to explicate this notion in *Truth and Credibility—The Citizen's Dilemma* (New York: Longman, 1981).

11. Of course, some religions decry "graven images" that serve as surrogates for the deity, probably because they seem to threaten the supernatural character of the deity.

4

MADELEINE R. GRUMET

Curriculum and the Art of Daily Life

The problem with everyday life is that it is always the ground, rarely the figure. Except, of course, for Virginia Woolf's presence at Mrs. Dalloway's party and Mrs. Ramsay's table and the more recent writing of, say, Marilynne Robinson (1988) or Joan Chase (1983), doing the laundry, setting the table, bringing in the paper, taking out the garbage become autonomic processes: the respiration and digestion of the domestic body.

And yet, for most of us, the location of our earliest and most poignant experiences of fear and pleasure, disgust and comfort, boredom and excitement, was home. The emotions and relationships that formed the matrix of our desires and defenses were situated around the kitchen table or in the backyard. For me they are bathed in the fluorescent light of the 1940s, resonant with the sound of the radio, swirled and speckled like the linoleum on the kitchen floor.

The dailiness is hard to recover. Memory often records it only as a backdrop to the drama that interrupts it.[1] I think that I remember the kitchen of the apartment we lived in until I was ten only because I remember my mother standing at the kitchen sink, scrubbing clothes against a washboard and crying on the day that she learned my Uncle Bob had been wounded in Germany. An appendectomy frames my memories of the bedroom I shared with my younger brother, my father's tribute of flowers on the night table, my mother smoothing the covers and dealing cards for continuous canasta games when it still hurt to laugh. And I doubt if I would remember the dark hall and the door to our third-floor apartment if I had not regularly knocked over the milk bottles as I left for school, turning back to see the tide of milk and broken glass flowing across the marble floor.

But it is not only disorder that illuminates the dear order of the everyday. There are its ceremonies: the ritual embedded right in the center of daily life that says, "This relation, this way of doing things, this object matters." There was the heavy pearly satin bedspread that my mother would put on her bed when company was coming. Together we would fling the heavy spread across her bed, lining up the seams, sliding our hands under the pillows and tucking the satin under them. There were dinners, Rosh Hashona, Thanksgiving, and birthdays when the rose goblets and the bowl with the blue and golden grapes were brought out of the china cabinet. And these ceremonies were debated, constructed, and continually revised. "Should we use the goblets, Norm?" my mother would ask. She was short and the cupboards were high. Taller than she, I soon became significant. Soon it fell to me to arrange the cornucopia on the Thanksgiving table, arranging the grapes and pomegranates, the walnuts and dates and apples so that they cascaded out of the little wicker horn in a flood of plenty.

Now this process of selection, this determination that something matters, is the very heart of curriculum. The choosing and naming of what matters and the presentation of those values for the perception and engaged participation of others are the deliberations that constitute curriculum development. And we learn how to do it—or how not to do it—at home. Nevertheless, you will not find our homes—in Brooklyn or Columbus, Los Angeles or Pittsburgh—or our parents, for that matter, cited frequently in our papers as sources of what we know. For centuries home has been the place we left to go to school. Domesticity has always been denigrated as a source of knowledge, and because home, the place we all come from, is anathema to the academy, we wander through academic halls like vulnerable and bewildered exiles who speak a language nobody wants to hear.

The practical knowledge that we bring with us from home remains trapped in memory coded in images, sensory associations, stories, and emotions. Lodged in intuition, this practical knowledge is rarely extended to our work in the public world because it is rarely resymbolized through processes that encode it for reflection and translation to other settings.

The problem with practical knowledge is that we don't know we have it until the context where we developed it is changed. Then in a new place, seeing again the events, relationships, and configurations of the old, we experience *re-cognition*, recognizing the world we know and realizing that we know it well. When home and school are dichotomized into the private and the public, the female and the male, the infantile and the adult, the familiar and the strange, both students and teachers are cut off, isolated from the practical knowledge that is our real homework. Instead of recognizing what we learned at home and extending it and elaborating it in other forms, we deny it and relinquish a usable past.

This paper is a project of recovery as I remember and name the processes of ritual and transformation that constituted my family's domestic order. The things that we purchased, saved, made, and transformed, like the rose goblets or my grandmother's cameo, brass candlesticks or cut-glass bowl, are cherished and preserved. They are witnesses to the shared life. This collection of things, like the curriculum of great books or the canon, achieved value because it was intertwined with the daily passions, struggles, and attachments of people we care about. The ordering of daily life requires the aesthetic processes of symbolization, reinterpretation, the incorporation of alien cultures, objects, meanings, the blending and crossing of boundaries, the choosing of sacred objects, sacred spaces, secret names and jokes and curses and songs. These processes constitute the art and craft of curriculum as well.

Home Sweet Home

The aesthetics of everyday life do invite sentimentality. Reinforced by the recipes and four-page color spreads of *Good Housekeeping* and *Redbook*, by Bell Telephone commercials and Hallmark cards, the images and rituals that are known as home encode assent, continuity, and cohesion. Anne Douglas has identified the denial that embarrasses us, making us feel guilty when we indulge ourselves in sentimental emotion:

> Sentimentalism is a complex phenomenon. It asserts that the values a society's activity denies are precisely the ones it cherishes; it attempts to deal with the phenomenon of cultural bifurcation by this manipulation of nostalgia. Sentimentalism provides a way to protest a power to which one has already in part capitulated. It is a form of dragging one's heels. It always borders on dishonesty, but it is a dishonesty for which there is no known substitute in a capitalistic country. (PP. 11-12)

I confess that often in the early weeks of November, I, too, surrender to national nostalgia. With a guilty glance around, as if I were shoplifting or purchasing the *National Inquirer*, drawn to glowing photographs of preindustrial feasts, I flip *Good Housekeeping*, *Redbook*, and *Better Homes and Gardens* into the cart. Armed with their visions of home-baked breads, cranberry molds, latticed pies, and cornucopias, I rush home to put together a feast reminiscent of a time that neither I, my ancestors, nor anybody else, for that matter, has ever known.

It is a feast that compensates us for loss, as it celebrates the capacity to draw sustenance from a new and alien place. It is a feast that denies our fear of difference as it encodes the cooperation of alien cultures. It is a feast that denies our mobility as we shuttle back and forth to the airport: "All is safely gathered in, 'ere the winter storms begin."

Theories of Nostalgia

In the late 1970s the work of Dorothy Dinnerstein and Nancy Chodorow gave us other ways of understanding this nostalgia. Their books, Dinnerstein's *The Mermaid and the Minotaur* (1976) and Chodorow's *The Reproduction of Mothering* (1978), advanced the argument that when the primary parent of both male and female infants is a woman, adults of both sexes repudiate her and, with her, their earliest experiences of the world. For a man, the repudiation is lodged in gender identity, for maleness is achieved by denying his first identification with the human being who has cared for him most intimately, his mother. For a woman, the repudiation comes later in her development, for it is not bound to the structure of the ego and gender identity but develops as she turns away from her mother in pursuit of erotic heterosexuality. Bonded to the development of a gendered ego in the male, and to a gendered eros in the female, repudiation of the mother—the first identification, the first love,and the first relation to give the world and existence meaning—is a loss.

Sentimentalism, as Douglas describes it, is a way of denying that loss. In "Pedagogy for Patriarchy: The Feminization of Teaching," I have suggested that industrialization accentuated this loss as men were drawn out of home, away from the farm, and into urban centers of production (Grumet 1988). The splitting of the family and the exaggeration of gender differences that followed the decisive schism between reproductive and productive worlds were encoded in the sentimentalism that rationalized these changes. The cult of motherhood justified the domestic isolation of women and the feminization of teaching as well.

Multiple Meanings

But it was not only that. It is interesting to note that a cultural code or emblem can function simultaneously as rationalization, denial, accommodation, and resistance. Because the emblem stretches between the experience of the individual and the order of the public culture, it contains multiple registers and encodes meanings that are variations of each other, ofttimes contradictory.

The cult of motherhood was also a comfort if it provided metaphors that helped women who left their homes and their families, their own mothers and their own siblings, to establish a metaphorical link between those places and the classrooms of the common schools where they worked. False comfort, perhaps, if that maternal leitmotif served to disguise a desire to get out of the house, away from the family, into a world ordered to repudiate its arrangements and patterns. False comfort if it was merely a domestic decoration that embellished lonely days. False comfort if it led merely to the current conventions of home room, snack time, and teachers who, through their own effort and attention, try to compensate children for the impersonal system that controls their activity, compels their compliance, and labels their efforts.

The cult of motherhood and the feminization of teaching may also be seen as forms of resistance, subtle ways of undermining the project of schooling: the passage of children from their mothers' laps and kitchens to their fathers' offices and factories. In this case, using an emblem originally designed to rationalize an industrial economy and accommodate women to their new roles in it, women convert a false gesture into a real one. For a while the ungraded classrooms of the infant schools promised vivid actualization of the maternal ethic. These days the movement to empower teachers works to endow the sentimental myth with real power.

In a pluralistic culture, in a country always trying to forge a national character and loyalty from a medley of races, religions, and ethnicities, gender—a feature that all groups share in common—may be articulated and accentuated to establish roles and conventions that cut across regions and ethnicities.[2] "The Provider," "The Homemaker" are icons that speak for nobody but tumble out of magazine pages and flash by on billboards, flicker on TV screens, and occasionally show up for dinner. Resisting assimilation to these icons, we exaggerate traditions associated with the specificity of our backgrounds, articulated and projected to declare resistance to nationalism's inventory of gender stereotypes.

Living in Brooklyn, close to the synagogues where their fathers dovenned, my parents somewhat reluctantly observed traditional holidays. On high holidays, with measured decorum, the neighbors walked slowly by, dressed in fall suits and hats of autumnal splendor, deep maroons and navies, russets and suedes. Traffic still, the streets were quiet; most of the stores on the avenue, closed. Classrooms were almost empty.

Years later in upstate New York we would have to create the event that had come to the streets of Flatbush with the inevitability of the vernal equinox and the harvest, the agricultural moments to which they were tied. Having to make what had once been given, I, along with the exiles who shared my urban past, would struggle to reconstruct the meaning that had suffused our childhoods, encoded in the sound of our grandparents' prayers; the musty smell of the prayer books; the delicate, faded flowers and gold leaf on the holiday dishes; the carefully laundered tablecloth; the exquisite boredom of the long days when we were forbidden to play outside, to ride our bicycles, to wear our jeans, to make noise.

The forms changed, adapted to our circumstances, at once diluted and exaggerated, new chants, new foods, new melodies accompanied the lighting of the candles, the prayers over the wine, and the challah. For a few years, my daughter Amanda would always confuse Passover and Thanksgiving. Chicken soup and matzah balls and turkey and stuffing would blur in her childish anticipation, and I would worry that assimilation had indeed extinguished my past. Then I redoubled my efforts to light those candles, fry those latkes, buy the little chocolate figures of Judah Maccabee, and get the kids to temple on Friday nights.

I imagine that it was easier for my mother and grandmother, but perhaps for each generation the determination of the domestic tradition is as deliberate as I experienced it to be. We always imagine our own era to be more tumultuous and tentative than the ones that preceded it, and I have always suspected that the conviction that one's own time is more critical, threatened, or desperate than that of other centuries or generations betrays an ahistorical narcissism. What is more probable is that we fail to distinguish the world we received as children from the one we are responsible to create as adults. Because the world of our childhood was a decision for our parents, but a given for us, and failing to grasp the intentionality that directed the construction of what we found, we conflate domesticity with nature, mourn the loss of what felt natural, and imagine that we are the first ones to have to invent a way of life.

> The force behind the movement of time is mourning that will not be comforted. That is why the first event is known to have been an expulsion, and the last is hoped to be a reconciliation and a return. So memory pulls us forward, so prophesy is only brilliant memory—here will be a garden where all of us as one child will sleep in our mother, Eve, hooped in her ribs and staved by her spine. (Robinson, 192)

Finding ourselves always exiled, missing the curve and comfort of our mother's body, we collapse the domestic into whatever is complete and sufficient. I remember my parents' music. My mother vacuuming, with Beethoven's *Emperor Concerto* turned up high on the new stereo. My father singing "Old Man River," "Tit Willow." To this day the music of the thirties, my mother's renditions of "Beautiful Dreamer," "You Made Me Love You," and "Come to Me, My Melancholy Baby" make the tunes of my own adolescence—"Unchained Melody," or even "Yesterday"—merely futile imitations of real feeling. And only now, as I name my mother's melodies and remember her singing them, does it occur to me that they also signalled her sense of loss and longing.

Lest these memories reveal what no sensitive writer wants to confess—a happy childhood—let me point out that even those who grow up with an acute sense of lack feel entitled to remember what it is they have never known. The myth of home flourishes even when there has been little biographical evidence to support it. Not only does the myth romanticize, sentimentalize, and distort the relations and emotions associated with intimacy, it also erases the perception and memory of the effort and art that constructed our domestic experience.

In "Feminist Politics: What's Home Got to Do With It?" Biddy Martin and Chandra Talpade Mohanty (1986) celebrate the complexity that Minnie Bruce Pratt brings to the concept of home in her essay "Identity: Skin, Blood, Heart" (1984). The perpetual yearning for home is identified as a yearning for stability, for unity and invulnerability. Both Pratt and her readers, Martin and

Mohanty, explore the price of those comforts, the repressions and exclusions which purchase them and warn us not to create new "homes" under the name of feminism that repeat the sanctimonious clannishness of home. While anyone who aspires to feminist or humanist reconstructions of society must concur that reductive categorizations diminish both individual and collective identities, I worry that enlightened and open-minded feminists will replicate the denigration of domesticity that has characterized centuries of Western art, politics, and schooling.

Martin and Mohanty also express concern about the lure of the theoretical and the abstract that persuades us to ignore the situatedness of human experience, its ever-present material, concrete, political character. In *Bitter Milk* I have suggested that the lure of the abstract is echoed in the motives that men and women bring to the project of education. For we look to curriculum and schooling to deny the biological and cultural constraints that have limited our original relations to our own parents and to our own children.

Fleeing from their identifications with Mom, both men and women seek a school with an aesthetic that is different from hers, different from home. Compensating themselves for the inferential character of paternity, the fathers turn inference into preference, valorizing whatever is speculative and denigrating the actual, sensuous, and felt texture of existence. Seeking liberation from the symbiotic bonds of maternity, mothers relinquish their children to their fathers' schools and study and teach in them themselves, hoping to graduate with a credential for adulthood. When home is drenched in anxiety about identification, schooling is sought as a path to differentiation. What I hope to suggest in the home movies projected on the bare walls of this essay is that we recognize that home was also a place of conflict, of improvisation, of shifting loyalties and cultures, and that the unity that it presented was often the aesthetic achievement of men and women working to draw form out of the chaos of their own lives.

The Aesthetic Order of the Happy Home

Happy childhoods do not just happen. The comfort that is later inscribed as a fluid and lovely connection to the natural and social world is produced by the art of domestic order. There is a system of rising and sleeping, of greeting, of contact and privacy that orders the child's contact with the world. The better the system, the more artless it appears.

The renaissance concept of *sprezzatura*, originally coined to symbolize the apparent artlessness of the courtier who could master many arts but present his achievement as effortless (Blanchard 1955), is embodied in the grace and ease of the happy childhood. The careful balance of order and disorder, the planned and the spontaneous that distinguish arts of Zen, is found in the happy home. Tea Master Okakura Kakuzo cautions us that the ordered paths of the teahouse garden must be interrupted with scattered leaves and random pebbles (1979). So I would leave a Kool-Aid stain on the beige formica kitchen counter to remind us that this home was organized to support and not obliterate pleasure. These aesthetics are organized to have the constructed environment imitate the interplay of order and disorder that characterize our perception of nature. Clearly the danger of this domestic aesthetic is that it would disguise the cultural construction of home and of the roles and expression that its system allowed as natural, and thus inevitable, unalterable, and necessary. The tension between order and disorder is what Anton Ehrenzweig (1970) has identified as the special tension of art, as its organizations of space and time challenge the habitual order, figure-ground gestalt with perpetually new configurations. It is ironic, then, to realize that it is the ordering of homes less happy, perhaps, but more deliberately and intrusively constructed, that provokes the perception of a constructed domestic order, and with that perception the energy and purpose to actively redesign the life spaces of one's own world. I would expect that energy from the childhood friend whom my husband remembers, whose mother demanded that he remove his shoes before entering his own bedroom, so that he would not soil its white carpet. We often wonder whether he has extended those restrictions and boundaries into his own home or whether he and his family cavort over bare floors, sprinkling and tracking and dripping at will.

With effort and reluctance I also remember the tension that surrounded the family ceremonies and rituals of my childhood. I remember my parents' ambivalence and the ways we all played it out. There was always a struggle of some sort on the day we were to present ourselves at synagogue for the high holidays. We would always be late. One of us, my brother or I, would be sulky, tear-stained. Years later, I too would find myself yelling at the kids, blaming them for not being ready, for losing their dress-up shoes or sleeping too late, or chewing gum during the services.

When we look to art to guide teaching and curriculum we are tempted to talk of the influence of objects, of Henry James' novel *The Americans*, of Stravinsky's *Rites of Spring*, Picasso's *Guernica*, or Duerenmatt's *The Visit*. We forget the dining room furniture.

Poesis

It took months to refinish that old set. It had a mahogany finish. Clawed feet and globes embellished the legs of the table and chairs, curlicues graced the sideboard and the piano. My parents sanded it and antiqued the whole set months after we moved to the two-family house on Ninth Street. Months of work on evenings and weekends culminated in applying the gold paint that clung to the rim that framed the table and nestled in the curves of the china cabinet.

I do remember them making things. My mother fashioning baskets out of pasta for fried chicken, writing poems of praise for people's birthdays, gathering the other mothers to our living room where they worked at card tables writing a play about George Washington that my second grade class performed. My father using his experience as a ship fitter during the war to cut out a slip from white taffeta to be sewn into a ribbon dress that I had received as a hand-me-down from an aunt with an exotic wardrobe. All this was not accomplished without struggle, my father complaining that my mother was full of creative ideas that required his labor, my mother complaining that as soon as he became involved in a project he would take charge of its perfect execution, excluding the less adept—us—from the process.

And I remember them making up things. A great-aunt had sent us chocolate figures of Mickey and Minnie Mouse, Pluto, and Donald Duck. Hard dutch chocolate. Each night we would break a piece off, and, so dismembered, they ceremoniously disappeared. We were disconsolate until my father showed up with a bag of Hershey's Kisses which were quickly dubbed "Mickey Mouse chairs." Like Proust's memory of the madeleines, Mickey Mouse chairs return the memory of childhood's sensuous pleasure and of our complicity in our parent's capacity to rename the world so that it had special significance to us.

These are not, I know, extraordinary stories. I tell them at the risk of boring you. I imagine you have many stories like them and may be impatient with me for telling mine here and for expecting you to read them as if they were special, for designating this very conventional childhood as deserving narration in these scholarly pages. But here is our dilemma: When these accounts are omitted from our scholarship, when we look elsewhere, anywhere, for our sources, our reasons and motives, we perpetuate and exaggerate our exile. We deny that whatever it is we fear we have lost ever existed, and in that denial we cut the ground right out from under us. Unsure, refusing to speak what we know, and practicing the sounds and cadences of the canon—of standard English, les paroles, the basics, etc.—we try to connect children to a world that refuses to hear the songs of our own connections.

This disjunction is what Dorothy Smith has called "the ideological rupture." She defines ideology as "the ideas, images and symbols in which our experience is given social form not as that neutral floating thing called culture but as what is actually produced by specialists and by people who are part of the apparatus by which the ruling class maintains its control over the society" (Smith 1987, 54). The rupture, a concept that Smith draws from Marx and Engels, occurs when "ideas and social forms of consciousness . . . originate outside experience, coming from an external source and becoming a forced set of categories into which we must stuff the awkward and resistant actualities of our worlds" (55).

There is now an extensive, persuasive, and poetic literature that testifies to the exclusion of women's experience, and particularly of our domestic experience from the texts and glossaries that constitute the disciplines of knowledge. In literature, in sociology, in anthropology, in philosophy, psychology, history, physics, biology, political science, woman's standpoint is one which honors the material, concrete particularity of everyday life and honors the connection and intimacy between those who share the actual time and space of everyday life. The power of those who bear the babies and nurture them, who order the provision of food, decide what is clean and dirty, who wash the sheets and care for the aged is palpable. Repressed, this creativity has been repudiated by the myth of immaculate conception, the myth of menstrual contamination; it has been inverted into violence and destruction; it has been appropriated by abstract disciplines of knowledge, bureaucratic systems and the production and collection of things called property.

Public Words and Intimate Arts

The project of this book, the exploration of the aesthetics of curriculum, invites the sensuous particularity that we associate with women's experience. After all, that is how the symbolic systems of painting, music, literature, sculpture, and dance differ from discursive and scientific symbol systems. The art work, a form which, according to Langer (1953), expresses knowledge about feeling, does so in material, concrete, sensuous forms that rely on context and specificity and engagement for meaning. The sense of immediacy, of vivid, sensuous experience that we associate with the world we flung ourselves toward or recoiled from as children, is summoned by the artist who, using Ernst Kris' term "regression in the service of the ego," recovers the youthful intensity of the everyday world in order to reinterpret and challenge the meanings of the thematized and categorized world of adult experience (Kris 1952).

Women have access to our early experiences of self and world because we have not had to repress so decisively the way the world felt to us when we identified with our mothers. The emotional expressivity, attention to the particular, manipulation of the material, palpable, and sensuous objects and processes that sustain daily life constitute the labor of the women who keep house.

Now there are not too many curators bidding for that refinished dining room set. You will not find it in a corner of the Metropolitan Museum of Art cordoned off by a red velvet rope. To see my father's paintings, to taste my mother's cuisine, you must come to their home, to their tables, or, for my version, to mine. The art of domestic life rises to its surface and then is pulled along with its currents, beached in an attic, or buried in memory. The objects, the melodies, are sediments in the family's history of expression, of celebration, of struggle. They signify the process of making a shared life. And that is the process as well of the curriculum.

Objects of Desire

The politics of that process place it on a continuum that stretches between the old and the new, the fixed and the fluid, the imposed and the negotiated, the private and the public. And while there is an aesthetic to the everyday life of every domestic group, the experience of poverty, of wealth, of authority, of neglect can meld the relationships of objects and desire into an economy that extends into new lives and new families. Poverty can feed desire for objects always withheld, or grasped only in fleeting video images.[3] Never sufficient, even when present, it creates an appreciation of value that is always somewhere else, somewhere better. Wealth can situate value only in the past, condemning its children to conserve the achievements of another generation rather than determining their own. Affluence can replace a shared life with shared objects so that consuming is continuous and obsessive and obsolescence occurs even before the object has been incorporated into the life of those who have desired it.

The curriculum of our classrooms often expresses these economies. The fetish of the canon is fed both by poverty and by wealth: the former, by desiring that art that is other, and therefore better; the latter, by desiring only that sanctified by the authority of the past. And to the degree that our institutions of education express class differences between those who dispense knowledge and those who receive it, both the poor and the wealthy collude in the deification of the canon and the deadening of the curriculum. The bourgeoisie, terrified of poverty and contemptuous of wealth, attempts to solve the dilemma through obsessive consumption. Texts, facts, scores are devoured as credentials are inflated and value seeps out of the experience of education.

It was the project of *Bitter Milk: Women and Teaching* (Grumet 1988) to address another economy, the economy of nurture, and the politics of domesticity and to begin to trace their presence in the curriculum. For even if the workplace is our destination (and I'm not so sure it is), home is our place of origin. The deeply felt motives, and the ideologies most intricately intertwined with our bodies, feelings, and habits, are rooted there, pasted into photograph albums with crumbling black pages, held in objects that migrate with us—I have one of those dining room chairs in our bedroom—sustained in rituals that only appear to have no history: Mickey Mouse chairs initiated the snack time my own children clamored for before bedtime.

Languages for Lost Worlds

What we lack is a public language to speak of these old private things. School stands between the workplace and the home, a passage between the two. Language from the workplace is readily available. Already public, designed for dissemination, encoded in manuals, newsletters, commercials. and contracts, it is easy to appropriate to both the analysis and development of curriculum.

Language from home is harder to find. I apologized to you for mentioning Mickey Mouse chairs. They are not even romantic, lyrical images of domesticity. They are refugees from the newly developing Disney media that found shelter in our family. As representatives of the domestic they reveal its porous membranes, its vulnerability. They also, as I hope to show, suggest how domestic art appropriates the public form and transforms it into something particular and shared. Here, then, is the paradox that I want to consider: domestic languages transform the general into the particular, the external into the internal, the public into the private. That very process is the process of teaching and learning, as new phenomena and information are presented, cognized, and resymbolized so that they gradually become part of the student's experience. But the very politics and direction of the translation of the general to the specific, of the distant to the personal, reverses the direction that schooling takes, leading children toward the general, the abstract, the distant world.

For the remainder of this essay let me suggest how teachers may extend the rituals and processes of domestic knowledge into the analysis and development of curriculum. Women, who have had both the burden and opportunity to assume responsibility for the order of their homes, bring the complex aesthetics of daily life with them to their work as teachers. The task that lies before us is to provide a language that resymbolizes the knowledges that we have generated through the specific rituals of our domesticity so that it can inform the processes of curriculum development, negotiation, and teaching.

We start with narrative. It is necessary. It situates our knowing in time and place, and that is not only an artistic effect, for the knowledge which we would describe is intertwined with neighborhoods, errands, bicycles, antibiotics, and begonias. But then we read what we have written. We talk about it with other people. And in those interpretive acts we find the language link between what is specific in our tales and what is general. We need the general words that signal the specificity, complexity, transformations, and improvisations that constitute our experience. If we let that knowledge linger only in poetic memoirs, it will never penetrate the schemas that organize curriculum and teaching.

Words for the Middle

In *Bitter Milk* (1988), I argued that we needed to think of schools as middle places, mediating the worlds, values, relationships, and languages of the private and the public, of the worlds of home and workplace. In this essay I have tried to show how home itself is a mediating process as past and present, inside and outside, are transformed into the culture of the family. The processes of this construction of family life are, I have argued, primarily aesthetic, as they involve the development of expressive forms, linguistic, ritual, and material, that gather up and present the felt life of the family for its perception and negotiation.[4] Through the processes of specification, recontextualization, ritualization, internalization, improvisation, and shifting boundaries, pieces of the world are picked up and knitted into the fabric that blends community and identity. I offer these terms as candidates for a new rhetoric, one which resymbolizes our knowledge of the art of everyday life so that we can bring the creative struggle, the energy, and sensuous possibility of home into our classrooms.

NOTES

1. Daniel Stern (1989) points out that the early narratives of young children who have recently experienced some trauma rarely address the trauma itself but record instead the disruption in the daily routine of their domestic lives.

2. In her study of Catherine Beecher, Kathryn Kish Sklar develops the argument that links gender stereotypes to the national project to organize and pattern the social life of a new and developing industrial nation.

3. In *The Roots of the Ego*, Carl Frankenstein develops an insightful theory that relates the externalization of poverty to the cognitive style it fosters: an intolerance of ambiguity and vulnerability to pressures and values of the social world.

4. In *Everyday Cognition: Its Development in Social Context*, Barbara Rogoff and Jean Lave have gathered together essays that examine how children learn in domestic contexts. They offer language that generalizes from the transcripts of mothers and children involved in daily tasks. Terms like *scaffolding, proleptic instruction, proximal zone of development* emerge from their text as generalizations that stand for the complex and subtle ways that mothers and children interact with each other and their

environment. Nevertheless, these terms do tend to strip the interaction of time and place, and I suspect that the discourse of theatre and cultural anthropology may prove a richer glossary for the purposes of the language project that will link the knowing of home to what goes on in classrooms.

5

ROBERT DONMOYER

The First Glamourizer of Thought: Theoretical and Autobiographical Ruminations on Drama and Education

INTRODUCTION

There is a scene near the end of William Gibson's play *The Miracle Worker* (1957) in which Annie Sullivan, teacher of the blind and deaf Helen Keller, becomes exceedingly frustrated. The play's other characters are pleased with what Annie has done. She has taken a child who, at the outset of the play, was more like a wild animal than a human being and transformed her into an obedient, well-mannered, delightful little girl. In everyone else's eyes, Annie Sullivan is already a miracle worker. Annie, however, realizes that what she has accomplished is relatively insignificant when compared with the goals she had hoped to achieve. In a moment of great frustration, she turns to Helen and says:

> They're satisfied. Give them back their child and dog, both housebroken, everyone's satisfied. But me, and you. . . .
>
> I wanted to teach you—Oh, everything the earth is full of Helen, everything on it that's ours for a wink and it's gone, and what we are on it, the—light we bring to it and leave behind in—words, why you can see five thousand years back in a light of words, everything we feel, think, know—and share, in words, so not a soul is in darkness, or done with, even in the grave. And I know, I *know* one word and I can—put the world in your hand—and whatever it is to me, I won't take less! (P. 81)

The goals articulated in the speech quoted above are rather lofty, to say the least. None resembles a behavioral objective. None would be judged adequate by those who extol the virtues of measurement-driven instruction. Indeed, Annie Sullivan's poetic words would probably seem out of place in any curriculum guide in any school district in this or any other nation.

Yet I cannot help but think that the goals articulated by Gibson's Annie Sullivan should undergird any curriculum we count as educational. All such curricula should attempt to promote understanding, not merely mindless behaving; and all such curricula should be concerned with students' affective and aesthetic responses, not just with cognition narrowly defined. Curricula, in other words, should strive to put the world in students' hands.

Furthermore, I cannot help but think that the sort of passion and commitment embodied in the Annie Sullivan character matters at least as much as the teaching methods and the classroom management strategies discussed in such great detail in our professional literature.

It is no accident that Gibson's character relies on poetic language to articulate her goal, just as it is no accident that I have drawn upon Gibson's drama to suggest the sort of teachers required to achieve such goals. Some things cannot be said—or thought—with ordinary language, or even with the less-than-ordinary, jargon-ladened language of social science. To say (and think) certain things we must turn to the arts—to music, dance, painting, sculpture, and drama.

Drama seems especially important for those concerned with thinking about the world, because of all art forms it has the potential to be most lifelike. Laurence Olivier has called drama "the first glamourizer of thought." In saying this, I believe Olivier is referring to at least three potential contributions of drama: (1) its potential to add an aesthetic, visceral, feeling dimension to our thinking; (2) its potential to fill in the abstraction of thought with flesh and blood concreteness; and (3) its potential to make intensity, passion, and motivation a part of intellectual activity. Drama certainly has the potential to contribute all three of these characteristics to curriculum thought.

In this paper I will explain why I say this, why I believe drama should have a central role in the curriculum field. I will proceed in two ways. First, I will briefly review the arguments that have been made for thinking of the arts as modes of knowing. The form and tone here will resemble the form and tone of any traditional academic paper: arguments will be developed in a more or less linear way; appropriate literature will be cited; the emphasis will be on the theoretical, the abstract, and the impersonal.

In the second part of the paper, I will try to illustrate the abstract, theoretical ideas presented in the first half of the paper by taking an autobiographical tack and telling how these ideas have been made operational in my own work as a curriculum scholar. More specifically, I will indicate how drama—both theatre and its first cousin, cinema—have influenced my thinking, scholarship, and teaching in the curriculum field.

THEORETICAL PERSPECTIVES

For some time now, scholars within the field of education in general and the subfield of curriculum in particular have recognized problems with both social science discourse and social scientists' engineering orientation. Some curriculum scholars' critiques have been relatively straightforward and pragmatic. These critiques have focused on, among other things, the use of behavioral objectives in curriculum design, the use of operational definitions in research, and the role of measurement in evaluation. Scholars have argued, for instance, that behavioral objectives inhibit the development of creativity and productive idiosyncracy (Macdonald and Wolfson 1970; Eisner 1969, 1967); that operational definitions are inadequate because the meanings attributed to behaviors are normally far more important than the behaviors themselves (Cronbach 1975); and that measurement is problematic because, time and again, what we can easily measure matters least, while what matters most seems impossible to quantify (Parlett and Hamilton 1977; Eisner 1985).

Other critiques by curriculum scholars have been more deeply theoretical and also more grounded in value questions than in pragmatic concerns. Macdonald (1967), for example, employed Marcuse's (1964) concept of *technological rationality* to critique the discourse and engineering orientation of social scientists. According to Macdonald, technological rationality involves (1) abstracting aspects of the world, (2) using these abstractions to characterize reality, (3) using the characterizations of reality one has created for purposes of prediction and control, and (4) employing the powers of prediction and control to promote efficiency and effectiveness.

Macdonald suggested the problem here:

> The danger of using technological rationality in human behavior is that, in our desire to gain control, understand, and predict, we may (and perhaps already have) come to see ourselves as

> objects or the representation of these objects that we find useful for our purposes. (Macdonald 1967, 167)

> Gaining knowledge, then, is not quite the simple matter of mastery of man's statements about reality, no matter how well organized these statements may be for pedagogical purposes and social uses. The very form of man's symbols are creations of the culture in which he lives and predispose him to limit and shape his awareness of the "to be known" in the forms of his symbolic structures. Yet the abstracting of experience through symbolic form does not encompass all of what is to be known with reference to the statements of reality. (Macdonald 1966, 5).

At the same time scholars were critiquing the assumptions and language of social science, certain curriculum scholars began to look to aesthetics and the arts for inspiration and insight. Macdonald, for example, coupled his critique of technological rationality with the claim that curriculum theorists could be framework-oriented rather than engineering-oriented theorists. Framework theorists' concern is not with technological rationality, but rather with aesthetic rationality. Macdonald defines aesthetic rationality as the

> capacity to cope rationally with the world on an intuitive basis—to return to the world for insights which will enable [a knower] to transcend his [or her] present systems of thought and move to new paradigms (as Kuhn demonstrates, for example) or fresh perspectives. (Macdonald 1967, 167-168)

Elliot Eisner (1985) has suggested that we can never return directly to the world for insight. Like cognitive psychologist Ulric Neiser (1976), who has demonstrated that even the most rudimentary acts of perception are influenced by the knower's cognitive structures, Eisner has argued that all our knowledge of the world is mediated by the mind. Eisner, however, also adds that we need not limit ourselves to the mediating symbols employed by social scientists. The arts are also symbol systems which can encode aspects of reality which cannot be encoded by linguistic and mathematical form.

Eisner's basic line of argument is as follows: Every form of symbolization conceals as well as reveals; the linguistic and mathematical forms of knowing we have employed almost exclusively in the past, while useful for certain purposes, have not allowed us to talk about significant educational phenomena; the arts can expand both our ability to describe educational phenomena and our ability to 'think about' educational questions.

The work of curriculum scholars interested in aesthetic and artistic modes of knowing is supported by scholarship in other fields and disciplines. Eisner himself draws heavily upon the work of philosopher Susanne Langer (1963). He has employed Langer's distinction between representational symbols (symbols such as "cat" and "1+1=2," whose meaning is derived from conventional association, not through anything inherent in the symbol itself) and presentational ones (the sort of symbolization found in a painting, where color, shape, texture, line, and proportion interact to create and communicate holistically the painting's meanings), for example, and, like Langer, has argued that the latter type of symbol is more appropriate for symbolizing the realm of feeling.

While philosophers such as Langer have helped bring conceptual clarity to curriculum scholars' discussion of the arts as modes of knowing, the field of psychology has provided empirical support for the claims being advanced in these discussions. The work of Jerome Bruner, for instance, from his early *Essays for the Left Hand* (1962) to his recent *Actual Minds, Possible Worlds* (1986), supports the claim that there are two quite different forms of knowing. In his recent book, Bruner writes:

> There are two modes of cognitive functioning, two modes of thought, each providing distinctive ways of ordering experience, of constructing reality. The two (though complementary) are irreducible to one another. Efforts to reduce one mode to the other or to ignore one at the expense of the other inevitably fail to capture the rich diversity of thought. (Bruner 1986, 11)

Sociologists have made much the same point, though they also have emphasized social scientists' reliance on more artistic forms of knowing. In his delightful little book, *Sociology as an Art Form*, for example, Nisbet (1976) presents historical data to demonstrate the influence of what he (following Sir Herbert Read) calls "iconic imagination" on the field of sociology. At the outset of the book, Nisbet writes:

> Over and over, it seems to me, we are made aware in the history of thought of the primacy of the artist. I mean this in a double sense. Not only is the artist likely to precede the scientist in recognition of the new or vital in history—with a Blake castigat-

> ing the machine-driven factory long before anything but complacent acceptance had occurred to a social philosopher or scientist—but, in one and the same person, it is the art-element of consciousness that is likely to generate through intuition and other states best known to art, the elements we are prone to describe as science. (P. 8)

Sociologist Joseph Gusfield makes the same point with contemporary rather than historical references. In an article entitled "The Literary Rhetoric of Science," Gusfield (1976) asks why a research article, Waller's (1967) "Identification of Problem-Drinking among Drunken Drivers," which had had a significant impact on public policy, was, in fact, so influential. He demonstrated that while Waller went to great lengths to make his article appear to be the antithesis of rhetoric (a strategy Gusfield argues is itself a rhetorical device, and a particularly effective one at that), the recommendations for action which emerged from his study were implicit in the imagery conjured up by the language Gusfield used throughout the article.

Throughout the article Waller refers to his subjects as "drunken drivers"; even the title uses such terminology. More neutral terminology, however, could have been used. Gusfield notes, for example, that Waller might have chosen to describe his subjects as "drivers who get into accidents after drinking" or "drinking drivers." In choosing to label his subjects "drunken drivers," however, Waller foreshadowed and made tenable his conclusion that the problem of drinking and driving must be treated as a medical rather than a legal problem. The term "drunken driver" conjures up a pathological, out-of-control subject rather than a normal social drinker who occasionally errs and drives after drinking too much. While severe enough legal penalties can have an impact on the latter type of person, they are ineffectual on the former.

Lest one argue that Waller's "drunken driver" category was simply extrapolated from the data, Gusfield points out that in the study drunkenness was defined operationally by the legal definition of alcohol content of the blood. This definition, as Gusfield points out, in no way logically requires the emotion-filled terminology employed by Waller.

Gusfield argues, however, that the use of emotion-filled imagery is inevitable in research reports which have implications for action, for abstract definitions must be linked with common-sense images if meaningful action is to be engendered. "Science," Gusfield concludes, is inevitably a "form of action with meanings derived from its Art as well as its Science" (P. 31).

AUTOBIOGRAPHICAL REFLECTIONS

I am drawn to the work cited above in part because it helps legitimate who I am and what I do. I am a storyteller. I tend to think with images and communicate my thoughts in narrative form. In undergraduate school, philosophy and drama battled for my soul and, during my junior year, drama won. I encountered Anouilh's Antigone and found it far more interesting, far more compelling, far more intellectually satisfying than the treatises on civil disobedience I was reading in a course on political philosophy. I discovered, in other words, that drama permitted one to struggle with the same issues I had been struggling with as a philosophy major, but in drama the struggle was cast in flesh-and-blood terms rather than in the philosopher's abstract discourse.

The world of linear logic is not entirely alien to me, of course. After undergraduate school and after working for a time as an (often unemployed) actor, and later a teacher and school administrator, I went to Stanford University and received graduate degrees in political science and education. Needless to say, at Stanford I had to do more than tell stories. I have had to learn to make linear arguments, engage in theoretical discourse, and speak the language of social science. In short, I was forced to become 'bilingual.' The work cited in the previous section, however, reassures me that I need not be defensive about my more natural proclivities. Indeed, I believe they have served me well as a scholar within the curriculum field.

In the remainder of this paper I will indicate how my interest in drama has influenced my thinking, scholarship, and teaching. I hope this admittedly subjective, "n of 1" account will illustrate and help clarify the relatively abstract ideas reviewed in the first part of this paper.

Influence on thought. Thinking about education—or anything else, for that matter—requires the use of imagery. Theatre and film provide a storehouse of images with which to think about educational questions, and I have drawn from this storehouse frequently. At the outset of this paper, for example, I used William Gibson's play *The Miracle Worker* to help conceptualize both significant goals missing in most curriculum guides and significant characteristics of exceptional teachers normally not included in the literature on effective teaching.

Plays and movies need not necessarily be about education in order to influence thought about educational questions, however. As an academic in the field of education, my thinking has been influenced by a wide array of images from a wide array of dramatic works. Here I will focus on the influence of a few works, in particular the film *One Flew over the Cuckoo's Nest* and the play *Equus*.

The film *One Flew over the Cuckoo's Nest* was helpful when I was trying to understand philosopher Nel Noddings's conceptual analysis of the concept of caring. In her analysis, Noddings suggests that a defining characteristic of a caring relationship is *engrossment*, which she defines as

> a first-person condition in which the consciousness of the one-caring is focused on the cared-for. This engrossment induces a displacement of motivational focus from the one-caring to the cared-for. (Noddings 1981, 139)

Later she adds:

> Engrossment is the fundamental aspect of caring from the inside. When I look at and think about how I am when I care, I realize that there is invariably this displacement of interest from my own reality to the reality of the other. Kierkegaard has said that we apprehend another's reality as possibility. To touch me, to arouse in me something which will disturb my own ethical reality, I must see the other's reality as a possibility for my own. This is not to say that I cannot try to see the other's reality differently. Indeed, I can. I can look at it objectively by collecting factual data; I can look at it historically. If it is heroic, I can come to admire it. But this sort of looking does not touch my own ethical reality; it may even distract me from it. (P. 140)

Noddings goes on to distinguish between truly caring teachers and those who only appear to care. The latter may be consummate professionals. They may act in accordance with the dictates of research. They may even act in what they and others might judge to be the best interests of their students. Unless the relationship they have with their students exhibits the property of engrossment, however, teachers cannot, according to Noddings, be considered caring.

When I first encountered Nodding's discussions of caring and first tried to understand the distinction she makes between caring and non-caring teachers, I found the discussion quite abstract and the distinction relatively meaningless. Then I thought of Louise Fletcher's subtle yet stinging performance of Nurse Ratchet in *One Flew over the Cuckoo's Nest*. On paper, the Nurse Ratchet character is little more than a melodrama villainness. Fletcher, however, transforms Nurse Ratchet into a human being, the sort of pseudocaring professional Noddings tries to describe. With Louise Fletcher's performance in my head, Noddings's distinction was no longer abstract and academic. It had a flesh-and-blood referent and, consequently, it became clear and significant for me.

My second example involves a play, *Equus*. I remember sitting in the back row of a Broadway theatre watching Richard Burton play the psychiatrist in that play. (Burton recreated the role, less successfully, I believe, on film.) As Burton's character agonized over whether to use his professional prowess to transform a unique, passionate, but problem-filled young man into a passionless, ordinary, but relatively problem-free human being, I found myself reflecting, for the first time in any systematic way, on a dilemma of my own. From the time I began my career as a teacher of children in Harlem, children who were, somewhat like the youth in *Equus*, unique, passionate, and from the school's perspective, at least, problem-filled, I had felt a tension: Should I use my growing influence as a teacher to get children to conform and become functioning members of society, or should I encourage my students' uniqueness and passions and, inevitably, their problems?

Watching *Equus* did not provide answers to my dilemma, of course. The tension, in one form or other, is still very much a part of me. It is present every time I advise a doctoral student on whether to do a relatively conventional dissertation or to explore an interesting but quirky idea as part of dissertation research. The tension is also present every time I must advise a school system on whether to adopt a relatively loose curriculum which will allow for classroom serendipity or to adopt a less flexible curriculum which will meet the community's accountability concerns. Watching Richard Burton's psychiatrist struggle with a similar sort of issue on stage at least made me conscious of these professional dilemmas, and the level of consciousness engendered by Burton's performance was not only cerebral, but visceral as well. The visceral part of my new-found consciousness reassured me of the significance of my problem and encouraged me to keep struggling.

Other plays and films have been helpful in other ways: Ionesco's absurdist play, *The Bald Soprano*, in which people say absurd things and eventually speak only nonsense syllables, has helped me keep my academician's bias toward rational explanations in check when trying to understand organizational life. (The play has been especially useful when trying to 'make sense' of behavior at university faculty meetings.) The play *Waiting for Godot* has helped me better understand some of my empirically oriented colleagues who continue to expect science to provide answers to questions which, it is now obvious, science can never answer. Even a silly musical number in the film *Little Shop of Horrors*, in which a girl from skid row imagines that marriage to a fellow skid row resident will miraculously transform their lives into a series of 1950s clichés of suburban living, was useful in making sense of a graduate student's interview data about why some inner city high school girls became pregnant.

To summarize, images are the raw material of thought. For me, at least, theatre and cinema provide very rich raw material for thinking about educational phenomena and issues.

A potential problem. Before proceeding, I want to acknowledge and briefly address a potential problem with the sort of anological thinking just described: Whenever we use ideas and imagery from one context to provide insight and understanding about phenomena in another setting, we run the risk of distortion. Schools, after all, are not theatres, and students and teachers are not characters in plays.

I do not believe these facts represent insurmountable difficulties, however. To be sure, there is always a problem of distortion when we engage in the sort of analogical thinking I have just described, but such thinking cannot be avoided. As Nisbet and Gusfield demonstrate in work referenced above, even social science is rooted in iconic representation. At least when we are drawing our images from the obviously illusory realm of the arts, we should be under no illusions about the metaphorical nature of our thought.

Influence on scholarship. To the extent that images from cinema and theatre have influenced my thinking about educational matters they have also influenced *indirectly* my scholarly work in the field. On occasion the influence has been more direct and obvious. Once again let me focus on two examples.

The first example comes from my chapter "Generalizability and the Single Case Study," published in the book *Qualitative Research in Education* (1990), edited by Elliot Eisner and Alan Peshkin. The chapter focuses on the problem of generalizability which confronts writers of case studies. I develop an alternative way of thinking and talking about generalizability—one rooted in schema theory rather than theories of statistical sampling and deductive logic. Before doing this, however, I suggest why researchers' traditional conception of generalizability is no longer adequate. I also challenge the alternative conceptions of generalizability put forth in recent years by advocates of qualitative research. For example, I challenge Lincoln and Guba's (1985) notion of transferability.

According to Lincoln and Guba, findings from a case study can only be generalized (or, in their words, transferred) to another case if the two cases are nearly identical. To suggest that this assumption may be problematic, I employ a personal example involving drama. In the chapter, I write:

> Although the notion of transferability accommodates the problem of complexity, it still assumes that findings from one setting are only generalizable to another setting if both settings are very similar. My intuition suggests this need not necessarily be the case. . . .
>
> The research community does not currently have a language available to translate my intuition into linguistic form. Indeed, the point of the second half of this paper is to try to develop such a language, or, more precisely, to take an existing, widely accepted theoretical language and apply it to unfamiliar territory: the context of research utilization. Before proceeding with this task, however, let me try to give some sense of where I am heading by relating . . . [a] personal anecdote. . . .
>
> When I was in my early teens, I had an opportunity to see Arthur Miller's *Death of a Salesman.* Though the Willy Loman on stage and the adolescent who sat in the darkened theatre had little in common, I learned a great deal about myself that night. Despite the many differences between Miller's aging salesman and the adolescent who watched him—or possibly because of these differences—something, which in ordinary parlance could be called generalization, occurred. (Donmoyer 1990, 184-185)

In the chapter described above, references to drama played a relatively small role. In my second example, the role of drama is more central.

My second example involves a paper entitled "Pedagogical Improvisation" which was published several years ago (Donmoyer 1983). In the paper, I analyze what might be called improvisational, informal, or responsive teaching, and I try to suggest characteristics which may be necessary, or at least helpful, to make this sort of teaching work.

The first half of the paper is a description of an effective improvisational classroom. Even in the descriptive section there are allusions to drama. For example, in describing the teacher, Mr. Diemo, I indicated that he is a

> consummate theatrical performer. His voice sings with a velvet intensity; his movements seem almost dance-like. Even when standing still talking to students about their various activities, his hips mirror the emotion in his voice, springing or sliding or oozing from side to side as though under the influence of Bob Fosse's choreography. His arms and shoulders move too, often in broad, intense, expressively flowing gestures, not unlike the gestures of a French cabaret singer.
>
> Although Diemo is a skilled and energetic performer, this is clearly not a one-man show. Here everybody is expected to get into the act. His primary interest seems to be in getting people to think. In this context, thinking is a five-step process involving (1) defining the problem, (2) establishing criteria for solving the problem, (3) generating alternative solutions to the problem, (4) choosing the most appropriate alternative, and (5) evaluating the consequences of the chosen alternative. (Donmoyer 1983, 40)

References to drama figure even more prominently in the second half of the paper where an attempt is made to analyze Mr. Diemo's improvisational classroom and articulate characteristics which contribute to its success. The analysis presented draws heavily upon Viola Spolin's book, *Improvisation for the Theatre* (1963). This book presents Spolin's theory about how to develop improvisational ability in actors.

The analysis, for example, employs Spolin's concept, "point of concentration." In improvising in the theatre, Spolin argues, an actor must have something specific to focus upon. In an improvised situation involving two elderly characters, for example, the actors' point of concentration might be on communicating the character's age to the audience. Spolin (1963) argues that a point of concentration is necessary because it

> gives the control, the artistic discipline in improvisation, where otherwise unchanneled creativity might become a destructive rather than a stabilizing force. . . . It provides the student with a focus on a changing, moving single point ("Keep your eye on the ball") within the . . . problem, and this develops his [or her] capacity for involvement with the problem and relationship with his [or her] fellow players in solving it. (P. 22)

Spolin also suggests that a point of concentration can be compared to the rules of a game. A point of concentration, she argues, functions as a

> boundary . . . within which the player must work and within which constant crises must be met. Just as a jazz musician creates a personal discipline by staying with the beat while playing with other musicians, so the control in the focus provides the theme and unblocks the student to act upon each crisis as it arrives. (P. 23)

In my analysis of Mr. Diemo's classroom, I suggested that the five-step problem-solving process outlined in the above quotation from the descriptive part of the paper served as a pedagogical version of Spolin's point of concentration. Like the point of concentration in a theatrical context, it served as both a focal point which brings a degree of control to the improvisational classroom and as rules which guide the educational game.

I also suggested that a point of concentration in an improvisational classroom serves a function similar to the function served by objectives in a more traditionally structured classroom. I noted that advocates of behavioral objectives might even be tempted to think of a point of concentration as a lazy person's objective and then went on to suggest that such a characterization would be unfair:

> Certainly, a point of concentration can be thought of as a goal: Diemo wants his students to become adept at approaching problems rationally, just as basketball coaches want the members of their teams to become adept at playing within the rules of the game. His goal, however, is not the sort that can be translated into a behavioral objective. The rules in basketball

> do not prescribe specific player moves; similarly a point of concentration cannot dictate specific student behavior.
>
> Furthermore, just as it would be absurd for a basketball coach to cancel all further practices once his or her team demonstrates mastery of the rules of the game, it would be equally absurd for Diemo to believe his goal had been achieved when his students could apply the rationale problem-solving method in a particular situation. Problem solving is normally not the sort of thing one can or cannot do; rather it is the sort of thing one does more or less well, based to a large extent, on prior experience. Diemo wishes to provide a wealth of such experiences; his point of concentratIon provides focus and direction to these experiences without inhibiting spontaneity. (P. 43)

It is probably no accident that I had to go to the arts for a theory in order to make sense of Mr. Diemo's improvisational pedagogy. Theorists in the arts, such as Viola Spolin, have traditionally been, to use Macdonald's distinction (see above), *framework* rather than *engineering* theorists. Indeed, in the arts, ideas almost always serve a heuristic function. Styles of painting, for example, provide guidelines and boundaries, not dictates and templates. No two masters of impressionism, for instance, will paint in precisely the same way. Furthermore, it is expected that any painter working in any style will constantly expand the boundaries of the style in which one works. There is no greater sin in the arts than being a cliché or being redundant. Even the text of a play provides ample opportunity for an actor or actress to fashion his or her own interpretation. *Hamlet* is considered a great play, in part, because over the centuries different actors have been able to play the title role in radically different ways.

By contrast, as Macdonald's analysis indicates, theory in the social sciences has been seen as far more prescriptive than suggestive. Consequently, it was not very helpful in analyzing an improvisational classroom.

Influence on teaching. Drama also plays a role in my teaching of curriculum-related courses. In addition to using film (in a course in which students read Noddings's work on caring, for example, I show selected scenes from *One Flew Over the Cuckoo's Nest*), role playing, and sociodrama, I have also staged mini-theatrical productions in class. I normally do this, for instance, in a course called "The Changing American Elementary School."

This course examines current issues in elementary education. As part of the course, Lawrence Cremin's (1961) history of progressive education, *The Transformation of the School*, is used to provide an historical perspective on contemporary concerns. The miniproduction *America Montage*, which I stage as part of the course, consists of excerpts from literature and plays as well as folk songs which render, artistically, the ideas in the Cremin text. My purpose in creating the script and staging the production is twofold: to make the themes and ideas in the Cremin text more vivid and less abstract; and to model the use of the arts as modes of knowing and methods of teaching (one of the topics of the course is the changing conception of the arts in elementary education).

I stage the production with volunteers from the class. The production is staged simply as readers' theatre, hence there are no lines to memorize and no scenery to construct; we use only stools and ladders to stage the work.

The production opens with a choral reading of Frost's "The Land Was Ours Before We Were the Land's." Then various readings and folk songs are used to characterize how Americans saw themselves prior to the industrial revolution. Included in this section are an excerpt from *Huckleberry Finn*, the great American novel about a street-smart but unschooled boy; the rather violent folk song "The Banks of the Ohio"; a scene from *The Contrast*, the first American comedy which contrasts down-to-earth, common-sensical Americans with the pretentious "academic" British; and an excerpt from *Our Town*, with its portrait of a quaint, bucolic small-town life.

The midway point of the production is signaled by a people machine: One cast member comes forward and begins to make a simple movement and sound which he or she repeats in machinelike fashion. One by one, each of the remaining cast members joins in with his/her own movement and sound. When all cast members have joined the machine, it dissolves into a choral reading of Sandburg's "Chicago," which renders the exhilaration and enthusiasm which often accompanied industrialization and urbanization. Individual readings from Upton Sinclair's *The Jungle* then provide a stark contrast as do readings from Steinbeck's *The Grapes of Wrath*. Sandburg's poem "God Is No Gentleman" and a rousing choral rendition of the union song "Union Maid" present a collectivist orientation which contrasts sharply with Paul Bunyan's rugged individualism and which is reflected in the thinking of progressives characterized by Cremin as social reconstructionists. The production concludes with two poems by Langston Hughes.

Judging from many of my students' reactions to the production just described, I am not alone in finding drama a potent source of insight and understanding. Many of my students have commented that their understanding of the Cremin text is different and deepened after viewing or participating in the production. Some students, for instance, have commented that the rousing rendition of the song "Union Maid," featured in the final part of the production, provided the sort of visceral experience which helped them move beyond their ethnocentrically biased views of unionism. After the production, they could better understand how unions were perceived during the progressive era described in Cremin's history.

FINAL COMMENTS

In this paper I employed the distinction between engineering and framework approaches to theorizing. I have also suggested that theorizing in the arts—both the formal theorizing of people like Viola Spolin and the informal theorizing, the theorizing-in-the-concrete (Simon and Dippo 1980) of playwrights—is of the framework variety.

Implicit in the approach I have taken in this paper is one additional assumption: Theorizing about the relationship of the arts and education should also be approached from a framework perspective. Such theorizing both fulfills its function and becomes comprehensible only when it directs our attention back to the realm of real world experience.

The theoretical discourses about education and the arts which curriculum scholars have generated over the past several decades have undoubtedly helped sharpen the perceptions of individuals within the field of education, and these sharpened perceptions have undoubtedly enriched individuals' understanding of the theory. This dialectic between theory and experience has occurred largely at the individual, personal level, however; it has not had a prominent place in our collective, public discourse. With a few exceptions, books and journal articles about education and the arts have emphasized the theoretical rather than the phenomenological.

Here I have tried to rectify this situation in a small way by focusing on how one art form, drama, has impacted on my personal experiences in the curriculum field. I hope this focus will enrich our collective understanding of theory linking education and the arts. I also hope it will encourage others to share their experiences so that understanding at both the individual and collective levels can be further deepened.

6

MAXINE GREENE

Blue Guitars and the Search for Curriculum

To speak of the arts in relation to curriculum inquiry is, for me, to summon up visions of new perspectives and untapped possibilities. Curriculum has to do with the life of meaning, with ambiguities, and with relationships. And, yes, it has to do with transformations and with fluidity, with change. I choose to begin with Wallace Stevens's imaging of a blue guitar, with a metaphor for the imagination, one of many. The guitar player in the Stevens poem refuses requests to play things as they are. He tells his listeners: "Things as they are / Are changed upon the blue guitar" (Stevens 1964, p. 165). Later, as the poem opens to unexpected vistas, tensions, and particularities, the guitarist says:

> Throw away the lights, the definitions,
> And say of what you see in the dark.
> That it is this or that it is that,
> But do not use the rotted names.
> How should you walk in that space and know
> Nothing of the madness of space,
> Nothing of its jocular procreations?
> Throw the lights away. Nothing must stand
> Between you and the shapes you take
> When the crust of shape has been destroyed.
> You as you are? You are yourself.
> The blue guitar surprises you. (P. 183)

Shape, yes, breaking with the "crust," the fixity, and finding your own.

This has to do with knowledge as well, the perspectives offered by the knowledge and understanding we want to make accessible to newcomers. Elizabeth Bishop, in "At the Fishhouses," compares knowledge with the cold water of the sea, "icily free above the stones . . ." She goes on:

If you should dip your hand in,
your wrist would ache immediately,
your bones would begin to ache and your hand would burn
as if the water were a transmutation of fire
that feeds on stones and burns with a dark gray flame.
If you tasted it, it would first taste bitter,
then briny, then surely burn your tongue.
It is like what we imagine knowledge to be:
dark, salt, clear, moving, utterly free,
drawn from the cold hard mouth
of the world, derived from the rocky breasts
forever flowing and drawn, and since
our knowledge is historical, flowing, and flown. (1980, 65-66)

It struck me early that the languages of imaginative literature disclosed alternative ways of being in and thinking about the world. There were not only the fairy stories early on; there was Charles Kingsley's *The Water Babies* (which I did not originally realize was the work of someone outraged by the mistreatment of child laborers) and there was Kenneth Grahame's *The Wind in the Willows*. Before I was able to enter into Lewis Carroll's *Alice in Wonderland* and *Through the Looking Glass*, James Barrie's *Peter Pan* was a climactic discovery for me. The metaphor of flight through an open window towards what was called "Never-Never Land" gave me some hint of what imagination could do before I ever learned the word. I believe I found William Blake's "Songs of Innocence" in those days as well and began to suspect something about the ways in which organized authority and power slammed shut such open windows, cast shadows on the "ecchoing green."

Then, however, there was Louisa May Alcott's *Little Women*; and, like countless other girls, I found a role model in Alcott's Jo March. She concocted a Gothic melodrama for a bleak family Christmas during the Civil War. Breaking with Victorian exemplars, she invented open spaces for herself and even a kind of swashbuckling language. She managed to do all that while remaining loyal and loving, bravely responsible for those around, as she chose herself to be reader and writer, someone who *demanded* to be free. More challenging, more perplexing than Jo, of course, was Nathaniel Hawthorne's Hester Prynne in *The Scarlet Letter*, to which I was introduced some time later and which I have kept rediscovering ever since. It was not so much her adultery that fascinated me, or even that extravagant letter

A. It was the emancipatory thinking she engaged in when ostracized and living on the outskirts of town. Having "habituated herself to such latitude of speculation," she looked from an "estranged point of view at human institutions, and whatever priests or legislators had established; criticizing all with hardly more reverence than the Indian would feel for the clerical band, the judicial robe, the pillory, the gallows, the fireside, or the church" ([1850] 1969, 217). She began also to question the condition of women in her time. "Was existence worth accepting, even to the happiest among them?" she asked herself, in the conviction that it was not and would never be (Hawthorne [1850] 1969, 184). Hawthorne, of course, made the point that her life turned from passion and feeling to thought in her terrible solitude, as if she could not be womanly and speculative at one and the same moment. It took me a while to realize that she did achieve a reconciliation when she returned to New England at the end and spent the rest of her life comforting and counseling women suffering "wounded, wasted, wronged, misplaced, or erring and sinful passion" (275) and wondering who would be the prophetess of the new order to come. Slowly, I came to realize (experiencing the "bitter" taste of knowledge) that the novel presented an insoluble problem, and that there could be no knowing what 'side' its author chose to take. On the one hand, there was the necessity on the part of a free, thoughtful, sexually alive woman to break with the rigid forms of theocracy and to challenge everything the elders took for granted. On the other hand, there was the importance of membership, even in an inhuman community. The recognition that there was no clear answer, that there could be no final resolution of the tensions involved, made me begin to understand the ways in which engagement with literature feeds into interrogation. Reading, working to achieve works of fiction as meaningful within my own experience, I found that the questions remained forever open. I could never, never be sure.

The "as if," the imaginative vision launched me then—and continues to launch me—on quests I hope will never cease. I am constantly reminded of Walker Percy's *The Moviegoer* when I think of that and of the moment when "the idea of the search" occurs to the narrator:

> What is the nature of the search? you ask.
> Really it is very simple, at least for a fellow like me; so

> simple that it is easily overlooked.
> The search is what anyone would undertake if he were not sunk in the everydayness of his own life. This morning, for example, I felt as if I had come to myself on a strange island. And what does such a castaway do? Why he pokes around the neighborhood and he doesn't miss a trick.
> To become aware of the possibility of the search is to be onto something. Not to be onto something is to be in despair. (1979, 13)

This connects, for me, with Mary Warnock writing about the connection between imagination and education (1978). She associates the capacity to imagine with the sense "that there is always *more* to experience, and *more in* what we experience than we can predict." She goes on to say that, without some such sense, "even at the quite human level of there being something which deeply absorbs our interest, human life becomes perhaps not actually futile or pointless, but experienced as if it were. It becomes, that is to say, boring. In my opinion, it is the main purpose of education to give people the opportunity of not ever being, in this sense, bored; of not ever succumbing to a feeling of futility, or to the belief that they have come to an end of what is worth having" (1978, 203). The despair Walker Percy's narrator was talking about was surely linked to the feeling of boredom and of futility as well. The search involves a consciousness of what is not yet, of what might be; it is the "more" we cannot predict.

The view of the castaway is not unlike the view of the stranger, which (for me) also arouses imagination. Becoming aware of the ways in which particular novels (or poems, or plays, or short stories) defamiliarized my experience, I came to see that the taking of odd or unaccustomed perspectives can indeed make a person 'see' as never before. I think of those fictional voyages—Ishmael's in Herman Melville's *Moby Dick*, Marlow's in Conrad's *Heart of Darkness*—and how they enabled me to select out certain aspects of my existence I felt but could not name. To confront "the whiteness of the whale" in *Moby Dick* was to be able to identify a number of figures against the ground of my lived life. What, after all, do I have in common with someone who, having felt a "damp, drizzly November" in his soul ([1851] 1981, 2), decides to go to sea as a sailor? And what with someone who links whiteness with "a dumb blankness, full of meaning—a colorless, all-color of atheism from which we shrink" (198)? What do I have in common with someone who has lived in the midst of the "incomprehensible" and the barbaric, and who is moved to say sardonically to his interlocutors on the River Thames, "What saves us is efficiency—the devotion to efficiency" (Conrad n.d., 221)? Or with the same man explaining how he had to look out for snags in the river, for signs of dead wood that might have ripped apart his steamboat? And then: "When you have to attend to things of that sort, to the mere incidents of the surface, the reality—the reality, I tell you—fades. The inner truth is hidden—luckily, luckily. But I felt it all the same; I felt often its mysterious stillness watching me at my monkey tricks, just as it watches you fellows performing on your respective tightropes for—what is it? half-a-crown a tumble—" (254). Male views or not, they made me *see* in the sense Conrad explained when he wrote his famous preface. He said it was the writer's task "by the power of the written word to make you hear, to make you feel—it is, before all, to make you see. That and no more, and it is everything. If I succeed, you shall find there according to your deserts: encouragement, consolation, fear, charm—all you demand—and, perhaps, also that glimpse of truth for which you have forgotten to ask" ([1897] n.d., ix-x). A few lines later, he went on to speak of a vision that might awaken in the heart of the beholders "that feeling of unavoidable solidarity; of the solidarity in mysterious origin, in toil, in joy, in hope, in uncertain fate," which binds human beings to one another and to the visible world.

I think that fictions like these were revealing my stake in the human condition, helping me reveal the ground of my being—which is also the ground of learning, or reaching beyond where one is. It took some time for me to confront what it signified to be excluded, on some level, as a woman from the steamboats and sailing ships where I imagined myself aboard. It took the perceptions gained from Charlotte Perkins Gilman's "The Yellow Wallpaper," Kate Chopin's *The Awakening*, Virginia Woolf's *Three Guineas* and *A Room of One's Own* to move me into confrontations, concrete confrontations with exclusion, indifference, contempt. I needed that mad vision of the women creeping out of the wallpaper in the Gilman piece, as I needed my own indignation before Edna's shortsightedness in *The Awakening*, my ambivalent indignation at her suicide. I, after all, was lending these people my life; I was, through my reading, allowing them to emerge in my consciousness and, by so doing, to transform it, as social scientific accounts or even psychological ones would never do. Tillie Olsen came later, and Maya Angelou, and Marge Piercy, and Margaret Atwood, and Toni Morrison; and I began, for the first time, seeing through many women's diverse eyes.

I wanted to see through as many eyes and from as many angles as possible; and I believe I deliberately sought visions for a long time that might enable me to look from the other side of the looking glass, to begin to feel what Alfred Schutz called the "multiple realities" or "provinces of meaning" that mark lived experience in the world. For Schutz, "it is the meaning of our experiences and not the ontological structure of the objects which constitutes reality" (1967, 230). We have begun only recently to recognize the constriction of our interpretations due to gender and ethnic exclusions, to our denial of the dialogical, of what Mikhail Bakhtin called the "heteroglossia" that deepens "as long as language is alive and developing" and becomes most evident in literature (1981, 272). To hear the languages of *The Brothers Karamazov*, the indeterminacies, the openness, is to break (as Bakhtin said) with "the hegemony of language over the perception and conceptualization of reality" (369) and open the way to all kinds of changes. To read William Faulkner's *The Sound and the Fury* and to move from Benjy's idiot voice to Candace's, Jason's, Quentin's, Dilsey's is to recognize the inconceivability of a stable "objective" world. Benjy loved three things: "the pasture . . . his sister Candace, firelight" (1946, 19), and largely in their absence. Yet his interpretation, too, like the interpretations of those who laugh and those who take a "carnavelesque" view, must be taken into account as what is called "reality" is variously achieved.

Ralph Ellison shocked me into a new awareness of this when I read his *Invisible Man*. At the start, the narrator says that the invisibility to which he is referring "occurs because of a peculiar disposition of the eyes of those with whom I come in contact. A matter of the construction of their *inner* eyes, those eyes with which they look through their physical eyes upon reality" (1952, 7). Yes, I saw before very long that the "construction of their inner eyes" was a function of and a response to a racist society and that an education for reflectiveness might play a part in altering such dispositions. It cannot be done by emphasizing categories, abstract formulations, or prescriptions of any kind. The particularities of the world revealed by Ellison—public arenas, offices, bars, tenement stoops, Sambo dolls, light bulbs, paint cans, an oily piece of filed steel (with "a heap of signifying wrapped up in it" [336]), a manhole cover, the arch of a bridge, an underground room—offer the reader a context in which reinterpretations can be made and significations read.

A *New Yorker* writer wrote recently:

> Ambiguous and unpredictable, details undermine ideology. They are connective. They hook your interest in a way that ideas never can. If you let in the details of some aspect of life, you almost have to allow that aspect to be what it really is rather than what you want or need it to be. And yet details are also mysteriously universal. If fiction is news, it's largely news about the details of other lives, but if fiction has a vital interest for people, it's because in those details they somehow get news of themselves. The readiness to be interested in the details of lives unlike one's own is a profound measure of trust. Resisting details is usually an expression of xenophobia, of some insecurity or shyness, of a need to keep safely to oneself. (1989, 23)

Without some knowledge of connective details, it is extraordinarily difficult to overcome abstraction in dealing with other people. A fearful oversimplification takes over: in the blankness, we see only 'Russia', 'student movement','ethnic minorities.' We are likely to chart things in terms of good/bad, white/black, either/or. We become pawns of a Manichaean allegory of good and evil. Primo Levi, the late chronicler of Holocaust experiences, once reminded us that popular history and the history taught in schools are influenced by this Manichaean tendency "which shuns half-tints and complexities; it is prone to reduce the river of human occurrences to conflicts, and the conflicts to duels—we and they, ... winners and losers, ... the good guys and the bad guys, respectively, because the good must prevail, otherwise the world would be subverted" (1988, 151). For Levi, it was altogether important for people to realize that no one existed in an entirely different zone of ethics than the ones responsible for the Holocaust or any other violation of humankind. To think otherwise is to impose a wholly false clarity on history, to rid ourselves of ambiguities and paradoxes, to simplify hopelessly. Yet this is what is done, more often than not, when the past is unrolled for children to see. Our forefathers emerge, in consequence, as untainted by greed or the lust for power; our victorious generals appear untouched by battlefield brutality, by suffering or betrayal; our democratic representatives appear untarnished by prejudice or deceit. Those on 'our side' are good in a manner that is unqualified; 'they' are evil in the total void of good.

Whether it is Shakespeare's Lear, George Eliot's Dorothea Brooke, Henry James's Isabel Archer, no figure in serious imaginative literature is free from "half-tints and complexities"; each has a multiplicity of voices contesting within; each, even at Lear's advanced age, is in the making. Literature, therefore, always has the potential to subvert dualism and reductionism, to make questionable abstract generalizations. Moreover, it has the capacity continually to frustrate readers' expectation of some final harmony or coherence. Wolfgang Iser, in *The Act of Reading*, has spoken of the ways in which people still cling to classic paradigms where reading is concerned: they seek out hidden meanings; they yearn for revelations of a symmetrical, unified, complete totality in the literature they read (1980, 13-15). At once, they recognize that the traditional norms no longer hold and that we can no longer posit an objective system to which our ideas and fictions 'correspond.'

Iser and other exponents of reader reception theory speak of the aesthetic experiences reading can make possible; and they do so in a manner that, for me, illuminates the relation between the arts and curriculum inquiry. As did Jean-Paul Sartre (1965, 43-45) and John Dewey (1934, 52-54), they emphasize the exploratory and productive *action* required of the reader or percipient. If curriculum is regarded as an undertaking involving continuous interpretation and a conscious search for meanings, there are many connections between the 'grasping' of a text and the gaining of perspectives by means of the disciplines.

For Iser, readers grasp texts by engaging with sentences as those sentences are situated within particular perspectives at various moments of reading. If the text at hand is Virginia Woolf's *To the Lighhouse*, the reading viewpoint wanders between Mrs. Ramsay's perspective to Mr. Ramsay's, between young James's and Lily Briscoe's, between the student Charles Tansley's and the background point of view, between the fragmented vision in "Time Passes" and the vision of outsiders choosing to become readers of Virginia Woolf. These perspectives continually challenge and modify one another. Foregrounds change with backgrounds; associations accumulate and produce new experiential possibilities. In the course of all this, readers work to achieve the work as meaningful and, at once, as an aesthetic object. Iser, in

Deweyan mode, describes transactions between readers' presences to the text and their habitual experiences, which recede somehow into the past. The aesthetic experience at once transcends that past experience. Discrepancies found during readers' efforts to create patterns in the process of reading become significant. Lily Briscoe, unmarried woman painter, "sees" the seafront Hebrides world quite differently than does the analytic Professor Ramsay. Both viewpoints are at odds with those of the various children, and with that of the aged poet, or that of the lighthouse keeper. Such phenomena may make readers conscious of the inadequacy of some of the patterns or interpretations they have produced along the way. They may become self-reflective. Iser writes: "The ability to perceive oneself during the process of participation is an essential part of the aesthetic experience; the observer finds himself in a strange, halfway position: he is involved, and he watches himself being involved. . . . The resultant restructuring of stored experiences makes the reader aware not only of the experience but also of the means by which it develops. Only the controlled observation of that which is instigated by the text makes it possible for the reader to formulate a reference for what he is restructuring. Herein lies the practical relevance of the aesthetic experience: it induces this observation, which takes the place of codes that otherwise would be essential for the success of communication" (134).

This, for me, holds implications for a conception of curriculum, as it does for learning itself. The approach to reading suggested challenges subject-object separations. Not only is there no presumption of an objectively existent "world" to be uncovered. The reader becomes entangled with Virginia Woolf's thoughts and perceptions; and once that occurs, the same reader finds herself/himself conscious of questions and concerns buried in her/his ordinary experience. Something is brought into the foreground, then, which in some way alters the background consciousness against which the themes of the text are being pursued and its meanings gradually achieved. There is, for example, a well-known dinner party scene at the heart of *To the Lighthouse*. Mrs. Ramsay has arranged the dinner to satisfy her own needs for order, stability, and (perhaps) control. The conversation has been going on; twilight has given way to darkness outside.

> Now all the candles were lit, and the faces on both sides of the table were brought nearer by the candle light, and composed, as they had not been in the twilight, into a party round a table, for the night was now shut out by panes of glass, which, far from giving any accurate view of the outside world, rippled it so strangely that here, inside the room, seemed to be order and dry land; there, outside, a reflection in which things wavered and vanished, waterily.
>
> Some change at once went through them all, as if this had really happened, and they were all conscious of making a party together in a hollow, on an island; had their common cause against that fluidity out there. (1962, 114)

For me, and for certain other readers, the idea that social life and even civilization are human creations in the face of nothingness may have been buried in ordinary experience of the world, never quite confronted. To confront them here, in the midst of a rendering of a cultivated British family's dinner party in the country, is to come upon something unexpected and, at the same time, shattering. In the novel itself, the passage prepares in some way for the intermediate section called "Time Passes," the period of the Second World War, of death in childbirth and death on the battlefield, of "the chaos and tumult of night, with the trees standing there, and the flowers standing there, looking before them, looking up, yet beholding nothing, eyeless, and thus terrible" (156). It is not that I learned anything altogether new. I was made to *see* what I had not particularly wanted to see; and, once seen, it moved me to summon energies as never before to create meanings, to effect connections, to bring some vital order into existence—if only for a time. It made me recall Maurice Merleau-Ponty writing, "Because we are in the world, we are condemned to meaning" (1967, xix) and, on the next page, "We witness every minute the miracle of related experiences, and yet nobody knows better than we do how this miracle is worked, for we are ourselves this network of relationships . . . True philosophy consists in relearning how to look at the world" (xx).

It was in large measure because of insights like these that I included works of literature in my classes in the history and philosophy of education, as well as (more or less recently) in aesthetics. The importance of imagination increased for me as I saw that it is a capacity not solely for reaching beyond to the "as if" or the "not yet" or to the "might be." Imagination, as Virginia

Woolf once said, "brings the severed parts together" (1976, 72); it breaks with the humdrum and the repetitive; it brings integral wholes into being in the midst of multiplicity. Not insignificantly, it makes metaphor possible. Cynthia Ozick, in a recent book, *Metaphor and Memory*, tells of being asked to address an assembly of physicians. Like many doctors, they were said not to have seen the connection between a patient's vulnerability and their own unacknowledged susceptibility. "The writer, an imaginer by trade, will suggest a course of connecting, of entering into the tremulous spirit of the helpless, the fearful, the apart. In short, the writer will demonstrate the contagion of passion and compassion that is known in medicine as 'empathy', and in art as insight" (1989, 266). Associating imagination with "inspiration", for which they had no use, the doctors were irritated and demanded "plain speech." The writer, pondering the connections between poetry and inspiration, metaphor and inspiration, recalls that she had wanted to tell something else about metaphor: "I mean to persuade the doctors that metaphor belongs less to inspiration than it does to memory and pity. I want to argue that metaphor is one of the chief agents of our moral nature, and that the more serious we are in life, the less we can do without it" (270). This is reminiscent of Conrad's words about solidarity; both comments have to do with relationality, reciprocity, mutuality. It is difficult for me to teach educational history or philosophy to teachers-to-be without engaging them in that domain. How else are they to make meaning out of the discrepant things they learn? How else are they to see themselves as practitioners, working to choose, working to teach in an often indecipherable world?

The ability to take a fresh look at the taken for granted seems equally important; without that ability, most of us would tend to remain submerged in the habitual and the routine. We would scarcely notice, much less question, what has appeared perfectly 'natural' throughout our life histories. We would, therefore, be almost incapable of reflective critique. Although it may be the case that certain newspaper and television disclosures, public events like assassinations, things whispered in corridors and on street corners can shock people into a kind of awakeness, the arts have a power distinctive from that of random messages and incidents. Arthur Danto has reminded us that literature may be viewed as "a kind of mirror, not simply in the sense of rendering up an external reality, but as giving me to myself for each self peering into it, showing each of us something inaccessible without mirrors, namely that each has an external aspect and what that external aspect is. Each work of literature shows in this sense an aspect we would not know were ours without benefit of that mirror: each discovers . . . an unguessed dimension of the self. It is a mirror less in passively returning an image than in transforming the self-consciousness of the reader who in virtue of identifying with the image recognizes what he is. Literature is in this sense transfigurative" (1985, 79).

To realize that the works of literature Danto and the others of us have in mind were deliberately created to communicate a particular vision or perception of, or feeling about, or insight into some dimension of the human reality is to come in touch with what has been called the "conversation" going on "both in public and within each of ourselves" (Oakeshott 1962, 199). Today many of us think of a contextualized conversation or dialogue, open to increasing numbers of voices. Moreover, having learned from Michel Foucault about the significance of chance and discontinuity in the history of thought (1972, 231), choosing contingency over the false clarity the arts help us combat, we want to release persons for a transfigurative initiation through our curricula. With a sense of the incompleteness and the perspectivism gained from encounters with the arts, we may be more likely, also, to discover transformative dimensions in what we do.

There are numerous examples of adventures into meaning that might provoke learners to learn for the sake of repairing deficiencies in their social world as well as becoming different in their personal lives. I have always been struck by Sartre's point in *Being and Nothingness* about what it takes to move people to transformative action, the education and intelligence it requires as well as the ability to break with immersion. When we are immersed in our situations, he wrote, we cannot take heed of the failures and lacks that mark our economic or political realities. "It is on the day that we can conceive of a different state of affairs that a new light falls on our troubles and our suffering, and that we decide that these are unbearable" (1956, 435). Doctrinaire or explicitly revolutionary literature is not needed. I have tried to talk of the literary works of art that have the capacity to move readers to look beyond the actual, to imagine alternative ways of being alive. In his book on literature, Sartre said that a work of art can become both a gift and a demand. "And if I am given this world with its injustices, it is not so that I might contemplate them coldly, but that I might animate them with my indignation, that I might disclose them and create them with their nature as injustices, that is, as abuses to be suppressed" (1965, 62). That indignation, he insisted, was a "promise to change." Works like Toni Morrison's *Beloved* surge up in my consciousness, works that talk in particular and searing terms about (in Morrison's case) slave children who are sold away from their mothers, but that appeal to our indignation about any violation of children and ought to lead to a promise to change. There are the anti-war books present and past; Nadine Gordimer's *Burger's Daughter* and other renderings of *apartheid*; *The Diary of Anne Frank*, Elie Weisel's novels, Primo Levi's; novel after novel exposing discrimination against women or against minorities in this country. If they are attended to as created worlds, achieved in the ways described, the experiences they open to informed awareness cannot simply be self-enclosed, miseducative, complete unto themselves. As Herbert Marcuse (1978) put it, it may be "intensified to the breaking point," especially if the world appears as it does for Baby Suggs or Sethe in *Beloved*, for a prisoner in Auschwitz, for a woman taking responsibility for the wounded children after the Soweto uprising in South Africa. Such persons "experience the world demystified," said Marcuse. "The intensification of perception can go as far as to distort things so that the unspeakable is spoken, the otherwise invisible becomes visible, and the unbearable explodes. Thus the aesthetic transformation turns into indictment—but also into a celebration of that which resists injustice and terror, and of that which can still be saved" (Marcuse 1978, 45).

The art form I have been focusing upon is imaginative literature, in part because so many literary works remain of such importance to me in my life and teaching, and so inexhaustible when it comes to explorations of how and what they mean. I might say similar things about certain theatrical works and films, with the reminder that they also render illusioned worlds, to be entered only when imagination is released and beholders are ready to lend them their lives. Film art, particularly, may be of special relevance today because of the importance of the visual and the growing familiarity with the language of visual images. A recent instance of the power of film and the richness and complexity of the world it can make visible is Spike Lee's *Do the Right Thing*. What with the renewed upsurge of racism in America's cities and with the ubiquity of 'explanations' and diagnoses, a film of this order can be a living argument for what a work of art can do when compared with discursive or descriptive talk. Set in the Brooklyn ghetto, populated by a diversity of distinctive personalities (including an Italian pizza store owner and a Korean couple who run a grocery store), the film makes present a range of vital and deprived lives, as it does a range of perspectives on how those lives are experienced and what ought to be done. It ends, as it must, with no resolution—with a quotation each from Martin Luther King and Malcolm X upon the screen. Viewers are left with disrupted categories, with numerous particularities in their eyes and minds, with unresolved tensions, with relentless ambiguities. If they are informed at all about what it signifies to engage with film, to perceive it as something other than photographed 'reality', they are left with huge and provocative questions. These are the kinds of questions that can be refined only by sensitive inquiry, by dialogue, by connectedness, and by reformulation within the framework of what Dewey called social inquiry. At once, and strangely, viewers are left with an expanded vision, with a consciousness of wonder and the pleasure only attainable when living beings lend their lives to works of art and bring them into being in their own experience.

It must be made clear that the languages and symbol systems of the arts differ measurably from one another and cannot, as Nelson Goodman made so clear, be translated into one another. For him, however, "we have to read the painting as well as the poem, and that aesthetic experience is dynamic rather than static. It involves making delicate discriminations and discerning subtle relationships, identifying symbol systems and characters within these systems and what these characters denote and exemplify, interpreting works and reorganizing the world in terms of works and works in terms of the world" (1976, 241). For him, too, we do not engage with art works to find representations of or copies of an objectively existent world; but they have the capacity to enable us to see more, to discover nuances and shapes and sounds inaccessible without them.

In my changing encounters with the visual arts over time, I found particularly important the recognition that paintings ordinarily emerge after a long dialectic struggle between a painter and his medium. John Gilmour, for one, has made startlingly clear (in part through reminding us of Henri Matisse's *The Red Studio*) how enlightening it can be to realize that paintings emerge in a context of meanings and that the "artist's concern with the subject of his painting parallels the philosopher's quest for self-understanding" (Gilmour 1986, 16). Struggling for significant responses to problems arising in his own life and work, the artist's attempts "to make sense of the world through the created pictures reflects a *cultured* vision" (18). To realize this, to understand that meanings here develop in cultural contexts as they enable us to view the world *in accord with* what is presented by Picasso or Matisse or any other pictorial artist, is to open ourselves to new disclosures. Also, it is to be moved to make new interpretations of the paintings, the world, and of ourselves. Merleau-Ponty once made the point that the meaning of what any artist is going to say "does not exist anywhere—not in things, which as yet have no meaning, nor in the artist himself, in his unformulated life. It summons one away from the already constituted reason in which 'cultured men' are content to shut themselves, toward a reason which contains its own origins" (1964, 19). This can only mean an originally perceived landscape and a background of sedimented, changing meanings. In encounters with paintings, too—pictures met *as paintings* and not as illustrations or representations—the search can be urged to go on. The meaning, not solely for the artist, but for the beholder as well, lies ahead.

Coupled with the contextualized quest for meanings in the domains of painting ought to be the consciousness that, as John Berger has put it, "seeing comes before words. It is seeing which establishes our place in the surrounding world; we explain that world with words, but words can never undo the fact that we are surrounded by it. The relation between what we see and what we know is never settled" (1984, 7). Beyond that, there is the need for critique of paintings, especially those used for mystification and those treated as holy relics, beyond the reach of ordinary persons. For Berger, if we were to begin to learn more about using the language of images, we would be able "to define our experiences more precisely in areas where words are inadequate. . . . Not only personal experience, but also the essential historical experience of our relation to the past: that is to say, the experience of seeking to give meaning to our lives, of trying to understand the history of which we can become the active agents" (33).

That idea seems to me to feed directly into what is important about curriculum inquiry and, in some manner, to sum up much of what is important about the arts in relation to curriculum. Not only do we feel the importance of releasing students to be personally present to what they see and hear and read; we are reminded of the need for them to develop a sense of agency and participation and to do so in collaboration with one another. I am reminded of Alfred Schutz's consideration of "making music together" as a kind of paradigm for social relationships and social intercourse. He spoke of a "simultaneity" created by the flux of the musical process, a coming together of the composer's stream of consciousness and that of the listener. This sharing of another's flux of experiences in inner time, he wrote, "this living through a vivid present in common, constitutes ... the mutual tuning-in relationship, the experience of the 'We', which is at the foundation of all possible communication" (1964, 173).

To conceive the arts in relation to curriculum is, for me, to think of a deepening and expanding mode of "tuning-in," of communication. There have to be disciplines, yes, and a growing acquaintance with the structures of knowledge; but, at once, there have to be the kinds of grounded interpretations possible only for those willing to abandon "already constituted reason," willing to feel and to imagine, to open the windows and go in search. The search—sometimes rigorous, sometimes gay—ought to be accompanied by the sound of a blue guitar.

II

GEORGE WILLIS AND WILLIAM H. SCHUBERT

ILLUSTRATIONS:
Reflections on the Arts by Educational Inquirers

"As readers begin the second part of the book, Bill, let me briefly explain what we mean by entitling this part 'Illustrations: Reflections on the Arts by Educational Inquirers.' We had suggested to the authors of these chapters that they consider how the arts in general, certain artistic genres, or some specific works of art have influenced them personally and how these influences on their personal lives have also influenced how they define—no, how they actually live—their professional lives. The suggestion assumes, of course, that there are close connections among the arts, the personal world views of educators, and educational practice. Unfortunately, these connections do not seem to exist for all educators, but for those educators within whom such connections do exist—well, those educators seem to be reflective inquirers into the very nature of education largely because of the reflectivity encouraged in them by their experiences with the arts. They seem to strive for understanding in the fullest possible senses. In any case, that seems to be what has happened in the lives of the authors of these chapters. The illustrative examples they present from their own lives seem to confirm our assumption. So the title of this part of the book indicates merely that its chapters contain examples of educators reflectively inquiring about the influence of the arts in making them reflective inquirers in the first place."

"I agree that is what these chapters contain, George. Their authors certainly seem to understand curriculum and teaching more fully than do educators who hold more conventional epistemologies. However, I do wish to raise a question about the degree of emphasis you seem to place on the arts as the source of reflectivity in people's lives. As important as the arts are, it seems to me there must be other sources of reflectivity itself, even though reflectivity may be picked up and heightened by experience with the arts.

"For instance, I think back to the sources of meaning in my own life during my early days as a student of education at a small liberal arts college in Indiana. I was consciously trying to develop my personal philosophy, a set of beliefs that would guide me as a person and a teacher. This was a process of personal reflection that I had begun with a good friend or two in high school. I think even then, without knowing it, we were addressing life's great mysteries and events. Yet, in the small town I grew up in (probably not unlike that of some of the readers), there was little exposure to the arts in any extensive way. My first real experiences with the arts came in college, after I had begun to be reflective. It was then that I read the likes of *The Tempest*, *Billy Budd*, and *Antigone*. Only then did I look to the arts for insight into the project of building my philosophy."

"I see what you are driving at, Bill, but you have qualified one of your key statements. You said that in the small town you grew up in there was little exposure to the arts 'in any extensive way.' Did you not have some limited but real experiences with the arts then, even if those experiences were not quite with all that, in college, you found the arts could be?"

"I see what you are driving at, George, and it is true that I have often thought that I did, in fact, experience aesthetic sensibilities in profound ways—if not the arts directly in a formal sense—in my home town. In this light, I recall the countless hours that I spent in imaginative games and stories with my parents, relatives, and friends throughout my childhood and youth. Coupled with these far-reaching imaginative experiences was a constant exposure to a family who tried to determine the good and worthwhile in their daily encounters. They exhibited a kind of subtle ethical awareness wherein that which is good and right to do is determined in part by an aesthetic sense. It is true that you could say I believe during my early years I was experiencing a kind of personally and socially constructed folk art that gave me a kinship with the then unexperienced world of more public art I met in college. Perhaps that is much the same as what Madeleine R. Grumet has suggested about the artistry which can be found in daily living."

"Then in this book we are suggesting that what counts as art can arise from many different sources and take many different forms?"

"Yes."

"And that the test of art is not primarily the form it takes, but the quality of the aesthetic sensibility and the reflectivity which it tends to engender?"

"Indeed."

"And that aesthetic sensibility or personal reflectivity leads out into actions in the public world?"

"Quite correct, George, and all that certainly seems borne out in the many different kinds of art referred to in the chapters throughout this book and in the influences the authors feel the arts have had on their personal and professional lives. Especially those chapters in this, the second part of the book may be read in any order, we agree, for each is a self-contained, personal example of the experiences of its author with the arts in some form. However, several of the chapters at the beginning of this part of the book do seem to describe the same kind of general aesthetic sense which I believe permeated my life as I was growing up, even before I became aware of the arts in a formal sense."

"That is because we have chosen to begin this part of the book with chapters that focus more on the qualities of experience engendered by the arts in general than on the specific influences of any particular form of art. Even so, Bill, I think later chapters more tightly focused on specific forms still convey the same aesthetic sensibility that we have maintained is the heart of reflective inquiry.

"We begin these reflections with chapters by Arthur W. Foshay on how the arts may engender transcendent experience, by James Henderson on what he calls 'native experience' (often, but not exclusively, inspired by Native American art), by Wanda T. May on experience she describes as 'lingering,' and by Ann Lynn Lopez-Schubert on how several forms of art awaken artful possibilities in the experiences of children. One art form she emphasizes is music, which becomes the major theme carried over into the next chapters by Gail McCutcheon on Mozart's *The Magic Flute*, by Kenneth Kantor on rock and roll and popular culture, and by José R. Rosario on jazz. The following chapter by Ted T. Aoki on both sound and movement segues into Susan W. Stinson's chapter on dance, and the theme of visual arts continues in the next series of chapters. This series begins with Landon E. Beyer's chapter on both song and film and includes chapters on film by William Ayers and Michael W. Apple. Francine Shuchat Shaw's transitional chapter, which includes film but focuses on other forms of visual arts, leads into three chapters primarily on painting, by Elizabeth Vallance on Mondrian, by Janet L. Miller on Picasso, and by William F. Pinar on Pollock. The remaining chapters of the book are on literary arts. These begin with chapters on poetry by Nelson L. Haggerson and Delese Wear. Three chapters on drama follow, by Richard Butt, Noreen B. Garman, and William H. Schubert. These are followed by chapters on children's literature by Max van Manen and Joel Taxel. This part of the book concludes with chapters on science fiction by Noel Gough, on novels by Alex Molnar and George Willis, and on literary nonfiction by Thomas E. Barone."

7

ARTHUR W. FOSHAY

The Arts and Transcendence: An Autobiographical Note

I was fourteen years old. Coming from my English class to the high school auditorium, I took my place in the balcony for the regular midweek assembly program. It was customary for William George Alexander Ball, the music teacher (who had studied with Sir Arthur Sullivan, and never let us forget it), to begin matters by leading the high school orchestra in an overture. The babble ended as he raised his baton and began "The Poet and Peasant." A strange thing happened to me. My classmates, the auditorium, my sense of time and place, all disappeared from my consciousness. I was completely absorbed in the music. My world, for the time being, consisted entirely of the sound of the orchestra and me. When they ended the piece, I had a distinct sense of 'coming to.'

I had learned to play a piano arrangement of that music, but I had never heard an orchestra play it. I noticed after that day that whenever the orchestra played, no matter what warhorse, I was transfixed in the same way. (Remember, warhorse music gains that status because it requires less effort to understand than some other music, and because it is good of its kind.)

This was the first of what became on reflection a series of such experiences that seemed to grow from one to another. I shall recount some of them here, and indicate where serious reflection on them has taken me.

In the same high school auditorium, I attended a piano concert given by Percy Grainger, the composer of "Country Gardens" and other well-known music. To this day, I remember Grainger," with his mop of red hair, playing from his collection of English country dances during the second half of the concert. Once more, everything vanished except Grainger, the concert grand that had been brought in for the occasion, and me.

Time passed. I don't remember having had the experience again until I was a senior at the University of California. This time, having been prepared by a class lecture by Prof. Caldwell, I had my first encounter with the poetry of William Blake—his "Tyger." I was in the cavernous Cal library reading room when I came under Blake's spell. I don't know how long it lasted, but once more I had the feeling of 'coming to' when I put the book aside. But there was a new dimension to the experience this time. I came away from the poem with a greatly enlarged sense of myself—as part of a vastly larger sphere of being. This was for me a new way of encountering great poetry. I remember having had a similar experience when I first read of Satan's fall in "Paradise Lost."

A few years later, when I made a kind of literary pilgrimage to Europe, I visited Chartres Cathedral and came upon the famous stained glass window, *Notre Dame de la Belle Verriere.* The window 'took over.' The Lady gazed at me through the ages in timeless beauty. I, too, felt timeless and placeless, lost in a universe much larger than the actual world around me. When I 'came to,' I found the curator of the cathedral sitting next to me, and he very kindly talked at length with me, excusing my schoolboy French, about the window, about Henry Adams (whose *Mont St. Michele and Chartres* I had read before leaving home), and about the cathedral.

Again, standing at the back of the San Francisco Opera House, I heard Melchior and Flagstad in *Tristan.* I had been introduced to Wagner by a close friend who was devoted enough to have memorized the entire Ring. He had told me a little about *Tristan und Isolde.* Even then, however, I was not prepared for the effect on me of the performance of the "Liebestod." I was transported into a larger sphere of being, in which I glimpsed the unity of Love (or Life) and Death. Once more, I was unconscious of where I was, of the passage of time, even of the two overweight people on the stage. It was the transaction between me and the performance that took me out of myself.

The first time I saw Picasso's *Guernica*, I was driven into myself, with a new realization of the vastness of human experience. Here was pure panic, which I had never experienced. My own existence took on a new dimension. At an Association for Supervision and Curriculum Development (ASCD) convention in Los Angeles, the Pasadena High School choir, without warning, burst into Handel's "Hallelujah." The power of the music jerked all three thousand of us to our feet. I still wonder how many in that group felt as I did.

A much more intense event of this kind led me to think seriously about these experiences. It took place In Rome. I had joined a sight-seeing group, and the guide had taken us to a small, elegant church near the center of the city. Inside the church, we had separated, each going his own way. I went round the altar and came upon Michelangelo's *Moses*. The feeling of tension between me and the statue was almost palpable. Moses, having just come from God, glared at his people, confronting their human frailty. The tablets fell from his hands. Everything about him expressed pure shock. I was confronted, not with the marble statue, but with the disillusioned Moses himself. When I 'came to,' the tour group had left, and I took a taxi back to the hotel.

In the taxi, I fell to wondering at my own behavior. Not recalling the earlier experiences I have described here (I had paid no particular attention to them, and none to their common qualities), I thought that this behavior was not like me. It certainly did not correspond to my picture of myself as a somewhat imaginative, somewhat methodical professional. But it had happened, and I knew that somehow I was the better for it.

What did these experiences have in common? Did they have any meaning for anyone else? Were they a part of human experience in any broad sense? If they were, did they have any meaning for the curriculum, my chosen field? These questions lingered in my mind for several years.

In 1972, I bought a harpsichord and began the battle with its difficult eighteenth century literature. In the midst of this, I heard—really heard—the Bach *Brandenburg No. 5*, which contains a cadenza that fully realizes the instrument. This time, I resolved to give my questions some systematic attention.

Not to my surprise, I found that others had preceded me. What I had undergone corresponded closely with what Maslow calls a "peak experience," and what several theologians call the "spiritual," sometimes "mystic," experience. The experience was always transcendent; that is, it always had an enlarging effect on the individual who had it. At Benjamin Bloom's suggestion, I read Epstein's *Masters: Portraits of Great Teachers* and found in these accounts that the great teachers consistently went beyond the subject matter they offered. They often put what they taught in an enormously large, even cosmic, context. Bloom had found (and reported in his *All Our Children Learning*) that an occasional student reported having had a peak experience in class. Could that be made more likely in school?

I had made a model of the curriculum field that later became my "Curriculum Matrix." In it I proposed, as the purposes of education, growth in six dimensions of human experience: the intellectual, the emotional, the social, the physical, the aesthetic, and the spiritual or transcendent. These were offered in the descending order of our knowledge about them: we know most about the intellectual dimension of human experience, and least about the transcendent or spiritual. For a person to achieve full self-realization, or, in Maslow's term, "self-actualization," it would be necessary, I thought, to grow in all six dimensions. I resolved to test the matrix by taking the least understood dimension—the transcendent, or spiritual—and searching for it where it was least likely to be found: in mathematics. If I could find the possibility of this experience in that field, it seemed likely that it could be found lurking in the other parts of the curriculum, and that if it could, we ought to seek it out in ordinary instruction.

I found that mathematicians (though not math educators) had already pursued this aim. Cantor, who had developed set theory, had 'tamed' the concept of infinity by rigorously applying one aspect of his theory with mind-boggling results. Every actual set, he reasoned, is a subset of a larger set. "Ordinary" infinity may be taken as a set; hence it is a subset of a larger infinite set, and ultimately one is confronted with an infinity of infinities. Similarly, the concept of an asymptotic curve, which forever approaches its base but never touches it, was likened by one mathematician to the human quest for perfection—in one's life, in government, in the arts. One vision of life is that we forever pursue unattainable goals, as if we were on an airplane that continually approaches a landing, but never touches down.

The development of non-Euclidian geometry during the nineteenth century opened whole new vistas of logic, as did Gödel in 1931 when he demonstrated how the concept of recursiveness made it possible for some hypotheses to be incapable of ordinary logical proof. The idea was applied by Douglas Hofstadter in his popular book *Gödel, Escher, Bach*, in which he demonstrated how the concept operated in graphic arts and in music. (The application to music is to the canon, which folds back in on itself. Perhaps Pachelbel's *Canon* is the best known of these.)

There are other instances in mathematics. The idea of proof, formalized by Euclid, is one. If my geometry teacher, Mr. Siegrist, had made it plain to me that proof was the central concept in the course, and that it was *plane* geometry, not the geometry of the curved universe or the spherical world, I would have done better. The independent invention of zero in China, in India, and by the Mayans, all in the same century, is of itself a wonder. Perhaps children could be brought to sense the wonder if they recapitulated the invention. Mathematics is truly a majestic field when looked at this way.

I have become convinced that transcendence lurks in every part of the formal curriculum, and that it can be found in the other parts of the offering, too—the technical subjects, the school culture (that is, the customs, the expectations, the values projected by the institution), and in sports and other public performances that are usually a part of school life. It doesn't come free, however. If we wish to make the experience of transcendence in school learning more likely, we will have to learn to plan teaching in depth. Transcendence requires knowledge, or it will remain latent or unrecognized. The difficulty with much instruction appears to be that the curriculum stops short, offering only a superficial acquaintance with the symbol systems and manipulative paradigms associated with a field, leaving the larger meanings unexplored.

There is more to the arts than transcendence, of course. In the case of music, there are interesting parallels with other forms of knowledge: the succession of forms since ancient times; Broudy's aesthetic questions of form, technique, sensory impact, and expressed meaning; the relationship between technical inventions and basic discovery; the relationship between what is expressed in music and what is otherwise expressed in science, the other arts, and even in politics. In these remarks, however, I have chosen to focus on the meaning of this one aspect of the musical or arts experience.

Our knowledge of how to take advantage in education of the transcendent experience has only just begun. It is impeded by our cultural reluctance to acknowledge that such experience deserves serious attention, since it is not obviously rational. The fact that the experience exists does not of itself imply that it belongs in school. However, there are a few people who now ask that we attend to that possibility. I have already mentioned

Benjamin Bloom, who replicated some of Maslow. More recently, Nel Noddings and Paul Shore, in *Awakening the Inner Eye*, have studied intuition and related phenomena rigorously. They offer interesting examples of how these experiences may be induced in mathematics and other school subjects. In 1978, Irving Morrissett and I edited *Beyond the Scientific: A Comprehensive View of Consciousness*, which contains essays by Thomas Kuhn, Maxine Greene, Ronald Lippitt, and others, as well as some speculations of my own.

These books have so far attracted very little notice. One can only hope that this significant dimension of human experience will soon receive the attention it deserves.

8

JAMES HENDERSON

Native Experience: An Inspiration for Curriculum Leadership

I have always been drawn to a certain aesthetic experience of nature. This experience is beautifully expressed by Henry David Thoreau in a book I first read as an undergraduate. Thoreau writes:

> But alone in distant woods or fields, in unpretending sprout-lands or pastures tracked by rabbits . . . I come to myself, I feel myself grandly related. . . . This stillness, solitude, wildness of nature is a kind of thoroughwort, or boneset, to my intellect. This is what I go out to seek. It is as if I always met in those places some grand, serene, immortal, infinitely encouraging, though invisible, companion . . . (Porter 1967, 154).

The aesthetics of being "grandly related" and of conversing with an "infinitely encouraging, though invisible, companion" are integral to Indian or Native American cultural traditions. Consider what it means to experience nature as a *native*. You feel neither separate from nor dominant over the life around you. You perceive yourself as part of a complex, mysterious, and sacred tapestry. Though you must eat to stay alive, you recognize your connection with other living things—even with what you eat. In fact, in good Native American fashion, you may even thank the spirit of what you eat for sustaining your life. Lame Deer, a Sioux medicine man, states, "Now we are one with the universe, with all living things, a link in the circle which has no end" (Lame Deer and Erdoes 1972, 107).

I have explored and contemplated many different artistic evocations of native experience, from Hopi Kachinas, which are doll-like "symbolic representations, in human form, of the spirits of plants, animals, birds, places or ancestors" (Bahti 1982, 39), to such classic Native American literature as *Black Elk Speaks*.

I recently attended the First Annual Rainbow Warrior Music and Arts Festival in Sante Fe, New Mexico, a twelve-hour celebration of music, poetry, philosophy, and dance performed by Anglo-American, Native American, Latin-American, Afro-American, and African artists. The festival's program contained this inspirational statement:

> It is our belief that human life is a gift through which the creative power can be known and expressed. This aspect of human existence is manifested in all cultures via their unique mythology, ceremonies and arts. The purpose of the Rainbow Warrior Music and Arts Festival is to honor and share these diverse expressions and to celebrate our common creative source.

This statement celebrates a new way of moral being—a connected, caring, and dialogical way of functioning as a planetary citizen inspired by the beauty of life. Humanity may have a long way to go to make this statement a reality, but I think it's a worthy educational challenge. I find the metaphor of "rainbow warrior" to be quite apt. Rainbows are dramatically multicolored and inviting, yet ephemeral and ethereal. They cannot be concretely touched since they recede as they are approached, and warrior consciousness is required when the envisioned journey contains formidable obstacles. Such is how I experience the challenges of curriculum leadership today.

Though my curriculum work has been inspired by Native American art, my inspiration has been tempered by three existential themes. I was raised as a white middle class American. I understand the paraphernalia of middle class existence: achievement-motivation, competitiveness, other-directedness, task-orientation, material acquisition, and narcissism. I recognize that people can be cunning, manipulative, dishonest—that they are readily caught up in win/lose scenarios; and I comprehend the fascination with soap operas and how someone like Ronald Reagan could become president of the United States.

But I was raised by a mother and father who were both teachers. I understand the value of growth, problem solving, pluralism, intrinsic motivation, caring, and social consciousness. I recognize that people can open their hearts and give to others—that many people instinctively support the underdog; and I comprehend indignation over social injustice and how someone like John Kennedy could become president of the United States. I was also raised in a transitional age. I understand the value of critical consciousness, deconstruction, postmodernism, irony, and irreverence. I recognize why people challenge authorities and question traditions, and I comprehend why President Bush is invisible and Vice President Quayle is a feather in Garry Trudeau's *Doonesbury* cartoon strip.

Since my experience of Native American art is neither simplistically inspirational nor romantic, but is rather tempered by the "heteroglossia" (Bakhtin 1981) of modern existence, I feel particularly moved by artists who are inspired by native experience but who are also sensitive to the ambiguities and conflicts of American society. Eliza Gilkyson is one notable example. She is a songwriter and singer, and one of her albums is entitled *Legends of Rainmaker*. One of the cuts on this album is "Children in the Wilderness." In this song she describes a diverse world of people seeking love and liberation on a damaged, war-torn, and power-hungry planet. Her song is neither fatalistic nor cynical but is, rather, an evocation of hope and a celebration of life amidst the beauty of nature. This type of music is quite meaningful to me since I interpret native experience—the Thoreauian feeling of being grandly related in the dance of life—as an inspiration to enter the struggles of modern existence with optimism and hope. Yes, there is a Darwinian struggle in nature, but there is also an uplifting presence. Yes, there are great struggles in our society, but there are also untold possibilities.

In particular, native experience serves as my inspirational touchstone for three social aspirations. I can envision a future society where people feel more connected to one another. This is a society where people deliberately create "public spaces" (Greene 1988) to solve problems together and where power is interpreted as collective empowerment. Greene writes: "Power may be thought of, then, as 'empowerment,' a condition of possibility for human and political life and, yes, for education as well" (1988, 134). I was a swimming coach for many years, and I understand the power of feeling connected. Part of the art of coaching is the cultivation of team spirit. When swimmers experience themselves as an important member of the team, a feeling grows that "there is nothing we can't do together." This results in a tremendous group dedication to excellence.

I can envision a society that understands the power of caring. As Noddings (1984) so elegantly states, to care for another is to help that person discover his 'best self.' She writes that "we must see the cared-for as he is and as he might be—as he envisions his best self . . ." (Noddings 1984, 67). But what is this best self? Clearly, it is subtly different for each one of us. For a teacher to be sensitive to the best self of each student, he or she must take the time to listen carefully to each child's innermost yearnings. Native experience is, for me, a time of careful listening; a time of contemplation; a time to feel the uplifting possibilities in my life—possibilities which are always directed towards contribution, towards a strengthening of the bonds that tie people together.

Finally, I can envision a society that understands the beneficial consequences of ethically based reciprocal dialogue. Like Thoreau, I find native experience a time to converse with an "infinitely encouraging, though invisible companion." This 'conversation' has a certain quality. It is respectful of uniqueness but based on a sense of relatedness. It is tolerant of individual interpretation but in a context of ethical awareness. Habermas attempts to conceptualize this quality of discourse, particularly in his *The Theory of Communicative Action*. Bernstein (1985) provides a concise analysis of the historical context of Habermas's project:

> Socrates in his words and deeds embodies the basic conviction that there is a type of self-reflection that can free us from the tyranny and bondage of false opinion (doxa). Habermas is also in the Socratic tradition in linking self-reflection with dialogue. For it is only in and through dialogue that one can achieve self-understanding. If dialogue is not to be an empty impotent ideal, then a transformation and reconstruction of the social institutions and practices in which dialogic communication is embedded becomes a practical imperative. (P. 12)

I agree with Habermas's project. We must find a way to integrate a meaningful dialogical praxis into our social life.

Unfortunately, Habermas is trying too hard to conceptualize the nature of this dialogue.[1] There is a mysterious quality to ethically-based reciprocal dialogue. There is a reason my native "companion" remains invisible. I can be inspired by a grand and immortal presence, but I cannot know this presence with certainty. My native dialogue is open, but it cannot be positivistic. I must converse with a sense of humility. This is what I find missing in Habermas's sophisticated analysis of dialogical praxis. I admire his articulate moral sensitivity, but where's the humility? I experience a subtly grand and serene dialogue in nature—it has a certain refined, playful, and far-reaching aesthetic; but I don't fully understand it. I am uplifted, but I cannot conceptually know what uplifts me. This much my companion tells me by remaining invisible.

Returning from the heights of native experience to the realities of the historical world, I am immediately struck by the dialectics embedded in my three aspirations for a better world; and I recognize these dialectics in my own life as well as those around me. I continually feel the struggle between solidarity and narcissism, between giving and self-seeking. In countless ways, I am reminded everyday that my work in a university is highly individualistic and competitive. Professors operate autonomous classrooms. Taking time to develop a common frame of reference with one's colleagues is a low priority. When one faculty member wins at the merit pay game, someone else loses. When one researcher gets an article accepted in a refereed journal, someone else doesn't.

My professional life also involves a continuing struggle between strategies of standardization and an ethic of caring. As an instructor, I encourage students to engage in inquiry because a caring, "best self" orientation requires this mode of learning. But this instructional approach is shocking to most students. Almost all of their learning has been carefully managed through predetermined instructional and performance objectives. They don't know how to inquire. They need help. I respond to their needs by developing curricula that provide them with initial structured guidance on how to inquire, particularly with reference to an ethic of caring. Some students don't accept my invitation to inquiry: they were raised on a management diet, and they want things to stay that way. Many of my teacher education colleagues exhibit a similar conservatism, though in more subtle ways. They are comfortable managing students, even while quoting John Dewey and studies on teacher empowerment. They easily overlook the inconsistencies of their position. It's not surprising to me that such people readily interchange the terms, "teacher education" and "teacher training."

I struggle every workday to find a way to engage in an ethically based reciprocal dialogue. This is a most difficult and time-consuming challenge. We live in a society where traditionally based moral principles are crumbling. I have no problem with this state of affairs. As I wrote earlier, I welcome social transition. But not at the price of a lack of public ethics. Not at the price of a shallow Reaganism—an off-shoot of the Social Darwinism of the nineteenth century where the rich prey on the poor because they are the 'fittest'.

Over the past three years I have developed a preservice seminar for elementary and secondary education students that is guided by the above three aspirations and their associated dialectics. This seminar has the following sequence:

1. An interpretation of teaching excellence, which has been inspired by an ethic of caring (Noddings 1984): an *inquiring* approach to *problem solving* as a member of an *interpretive community*.
2. Case examples of two teachers who practice this type of expertise.
3. Interpreting your professional needs: four general strategies that have been inspired by an ethic of caring.
4. Inquiring into active problem solving with the help of a general model of problem solving and four historic variations: how shall you interpret "active problem solving"?
5. Inquiring into instructional problems with the help of a general model of reflective instruction and four historic variations: how shall you interpret "reflective instructional leadership"?
6. Inquiring into classroom discipline problems with the help of a general model of reflective classroom community leadership and four historic variations: how shall you interpret "reflective classroom community leadership"?
7. Inquiring collaboratively: peer teaching with model based peer coaching and collegial coaching.
8. Deliberating over your professional growth: interpreting your problem solving strengths and limitations.
9. Case analysis: practicing an inquiring approach to problem solving as a member of an interpretive community.
10. The politics of inquiry: why are professional problem solving communities "at risk" in most schools today?[2]

I have been pleased by the students' positive response to this curriculum sequence.[3] Generally speaking, students are willing to take up the struggle of sustaining an ethically aware, collegial praxis. I tell students that this type of professionalism is time-consuming and difficult. If it was easy, it probably would have already been done or at least packaged by some astute educational entrepreneur.

I owe much to my background in native experience. It has been a constant source of inspiration as I have gone about the challenge of translating visions of a better future into concrete curriculum activities. And I owe much to the artistry of Henry David Thoreau and traditional Native American artists such as Lame Deer who have helped me appreciate the moral significance of native experience. But, perhaps most pertinently, I owe a debt of gratitude to artists such as Eliza Gilkyson who have provided me with insight into how to synthesize native sensibility with modern-day reality. To me, the point of studying and contemplating native awareness is not to learn a traditional tribal dance or a new folk rock song, but to find inspiration for a new way of ethical being in an open, nontraditional, pluralistic, and shrinking world.

NOTES

1. For a good critique of Habermas's idealism, see Rorty, R. (1985), "Habermas and Lyotard on Postmodernity." In R.J. Bernstein, (Ed.), *Habermas and Modernity* (161-175). Cambridge, MA: MIT Press.

2. This ten-step sequence is scheduled to be published by Macmillan in 1991 under the title *Becominq an Inquiring Teacher: A Caring Approach to Problem Solving*. J. Henderson is principal author; C. Melnick, M. Koerner, and T. Barone are contributing chapters to the text.

3. For an analysis of student reactions to the seminar sequence, see Henderson, J. (1988), "An Ethic of Caring Applied to Reflective Professional Development," *Teaching Education* 2 (1), 91-95; and Henderson, J. (1989), "Positioned Reflective Practice: A Curriculum Discussion," *Journal of Teacher Education* 40 (2), 10-14.

9

WANDA T. MAY

The Arts and Curriculum as Lingering

I linger because something is provocative, unusual, pleasant, or jarring in a time or place that feels like it needs to be grasped, prolonged, fully experienced, and understood. I take advantage of time and place, risk personal ridicule and punishment, and am able to recognize mundaneness for what it is and recoil from it temporarily. Lingering means making room for myself and reflecting upon my relation to the world and what it means to be in it. I have learned to create occasions for myself and others to linger by locating and recognizing the significance that lingering has had for me personally.

Most often, my lingering has involved direct encounters with various forms of artistic expression—specifically, visual arts, music, and poetry—and the social contexts and predicaments in which these occasions for expression occurred. I learned to linger and came to appreciate the promise and power of it primarily through my early school experiences, informal social contacts outside of my family, and experiences that preceded teaching. In the following examples, I link these early experiences to my view of curriculum inquiry. Understanding the personal significance of my encounters with the arts, the nature of my lingering, and what I learned from lingering best illustrate how my view of curriculum has emerged.

First grade lingering at the sandbox. I learned about lingering from Miss Dorf, my first grade teacher, who repeatedly slapped my arm with a ruler for my lingering too long at the sandbox when it was math time. The smell of new books and crayons was intoxicating, the stretch of blank tablets and drawing pads and the possibilities of sand, irresistible and compelling. Color and form needed to be there, my interpretations of the world, my stories, fingerprints, diagrams, experiences, and understandings that words could hardly convey. Thus, at age five, I learned what counts as legitimate school knowledge, experienced the disjuncture between authentic and artificial experience, and realized that aesthetic interests and expression in school most often are undesirable, if not punishable.

To be meaningful, curriculum inquiry exposes and critiques dominant ways of knowing presented in the school curriculum which are considered more legitimate than other powerful ways of knowing. It critiques the negative effects of such a narrow focus for real persons. And it vividly describes and illuminates what students learn about the world, themselves, and others through aesthetic ways of knowing, building a more convincing argument for lingering in the formal school curriculum than thus far has been presented. Finally, such inquiry pursues what students find authentic and aesthetic, and why. This requires our granting students—no matter their age—their own voice and 'expertise' in choosing and making sense of their experiences. It requires more space and time in the curriculum to linger so that students experience various ways of knowing and are better able to distinguish and choose for themselves between the memorable and the mundane, the meaningful and the mindless.

Fourth Grade Lingering on Linda's Handwriting. In the fourth grade, I learned about lingering from Linda. I emulated Linda's handwriting for a short time because of its aesthetic qualities. She kept three No. 2 pencils, sharpened them frequently, and prepared each point by rubbing them on an angle so that she could write with perfectly thick dark lines in an equally perfect, loopy, backward slant. The teacher permitted Linda's back-slanted style because her work was neat, consistent, and effortful. No matter how sticky the temperature, lengthy the task, or peculiar the subject to calligraphy (long division!) Linda hovered meticulously over her papers, tongue matching her pencilled formations in action, beads of sweat on her forehead, in absolute concentration, perfecting her art, sticking with it all year.

Linda was content in her expressive technique, oblivious to peer envy or graphic imitations all around her. I couldn't maintain the slant, the pressure of embossing so that a page could be read like Braille from the other side as it curled slightly from hard work and a sweaty palm. Instead, I developed skill in writing backwards—first practicing the alphabet over and over, finally writing secret notes penned as rapidly and flawlessly backwards as forwards. I got the idea from Linda's textured writing. Linda seemed interested in the surface, 'right-side' features of her work.

I was more impressed with the less obvious 'back side,' the embossing, the secrets and possibilities therein.

I pursued writing backwards because I hated math and dittoed assignments that were incredibly boring with so few requests for full sentences, illustrations, imaginative story plots, or hypothesizing. Somewhere in the busy schedule of fourth grade, I found time to develop my writing skill without Miss Marsh ever knowing. To this day, whenever I am near a chalkboard and wish to provoke others to linger, to have them stumble over the taken-for-granted, I write backwards: "Until you have seen a thing *other* than the way it is, you have not seen it at all." My statement feels as profound today as it felt in the fourth grade when I expressed it to Pete, who was clever at creating and cracking secret codes. However, this was one he didn't figure out without some explanation. "See, it *looks* like real writing. Then, you pick it up. You say, 'This isn't *real* writing!' So you don't try to read it and throw it away. But it's real writing after all! There's a message. You can say anything you want! Only people who love cracking codes will try to figure it out and be able to read it!"

While originally I found Linda's form of lingering aesthetic in the formalistic sense, I extended this lingering to the active construction of meaning. I saw the power of messages and multiple meanings. I recognized that human expression connotes more than surface features or elements, and that those who wish to make meaning must be curious, attentive, and active constructors of meaning. As in the arts, curriculum has provocative and connotative dimensions related to the active construction of meaning(s) by those involved in teaching, learning, and policy making. It requires our looking beneath and beyond surface features and appearances, particularly of those messages we ourselves create—not just the texts of others. Linda had no idea what her efforts provoked in others, nor how rich our interpretations and spin-offs were. We also made many assumptions about Linda's motivation and perceived benefits without questioning or clarifying these.

Neighborhood Lingering. Neighborhood play was both an imitation and antithesis of school. It highlighted what was present and absent in our curricular experiences. The woof and warp of our neighborhood drama could not be predetermined, woven, nor understood without enactment. School assignments were not homespun experiments nor evolving, unpredictable scenarios.

"Playing school" in the backyard was developed as confidently and predictably as it existed in reality. "Teacher" gave A-pluses to superbly obedient students who could answer "2 + 2" and write their names neatly. All questions would be answered confidently and rewarded. When enacted, the brief school scene was the familiar, rusty anchor that tethered our airy, far-flung, neighborhood action. The colorful balloons of our imagination contrasted sharply with the dead weight of our strings. The more visible and extended conflicts developed in jungles, outer space, Hollywood, and dank oppressive caves where lingering was lighter and longer, our time together suspended, buoyant, tugging us upward and away from the everyday—from school and its submerged anchors with bumpy barnacles, its predictable ends.

Neighborhood play and its unfolding dramatic episodes suggest several things with regard to curriculum matters. First, adequate curriculum inquiry cannot exclude enactment. Curriculum is the dynamic interaction of persons, artifacts, and ideas in a particular context over time—it is not a script. It has no formulaic and definitive beginning, middle, and end. An adequate account of curriculum acknowledges this interaction, the fluid and subtle shifts of characters and their roles, and the ambiguous and often uncertain outcomes of what participants derive from both creating and participating in the drama. Secondly, the relationship of home and school, work and play, must be fully explored in order to make adequate sense of students' school experiences. Had my teachers seen me in neighborhood action, they may have understood me better and helped me make more meaningful connections between academic and vernacular experiences. They would have noticed my proclivity to organize without coercion, my sense of humor and adventure, my creative but plausible turns in stories and twists in character development. As a "good" student, however, I "followed directions well" and remained anonymous.

Finally, enacted curriculum often lacks imagination, playfulness, and improvisational features. It allows few divergent narratives to unfold and evolve naturally over time, and rarely is time given to students' imagination, thoughtful reflection, or group development and active negotiation of ideas. In the dramatic unfolding of our inventions and stories, valuable truths about ourselves, subjects, and our situatedness can be unearthed and shared. Lines blur between fact and fiction, reality and fantasy, more nearly reflecting our human condition in dramatic social context. Curriculum inquiry needs to encourage creative invention and reflection upon these inventions in social and historical context. I speak not only of preschool-to-university classrooms, but of the discursive-practices in the curriculum field. Fortunately, some of us are imaginative and courageous, leading others to the sandbox. Unfortunately, most of us continue to follow institutional codes of conduct, get good grades in deportment, and no one knows—including ourselves—what makes our individual stories unique and worth telling. We play school, remain anonymous, and wonder why we feel alienated.

Fifth Grade Lingering with Tempera Paint and Mr. Moe. I am good at lingering because I was one of the fortunate four in fifth grade selected to paint a six-foot vertical mural of tempera bells for the school's Christmas program. We lingered on this project exceedingly long, cleverly making it take an entire day—even when the paint protested and flaked up in layers around 10:00 a.m. We learned much about creating convincing excuses for why we weren't finished; symmetry of form; how pleasant creamy tempera paint is when mixed just right; how some paint stinks like rotten eggs (wondering why); how red and green mixed together make brown; how intense and delightful some blues are, quite perfect for steely bells; how to experiment and make green when there is none; where the janitor's (Mr. Moe) hidden sink was, and how forceful the water flowed there compared to the restrooms; and that Mr. Moe's boiler-room space had a cozy braided rug, a rocking chair, a thermos, a vase of fresh flowers, and a photo of his wife and three children.

I learned about the essence of lingering—how it feels to be free from routines and fractions, off on a deserted stage where the smell of fabric and old wood suggests other unlived-in places—like attics. Attics and stages are where rare opportunities and life's earmarks lie buried silently like treasures till you spy them, manipulate them, wonder about the past, your situatedness in the present, and your connection to anything or anyone else memorable. From the above, I learned that lingering has a *memorable* quality; therefore, *much* can be learned from lingering. I understood lingering as politically negotiated and worth fighting for because of its memorable qualities. Ten-year-old students are capable of negotiating what they want to learn with much success—even for only one day out of the year.

Students learn many things that we might *want* them to learn (if not more), but we fail to ask them what they are learning. We provide few diverse opportunities for them to learn through their own observations and questions. I am convinced that in the above episode, my teacher had no academic objectives in mind. Painting tempera bells was time off for good behavior—not for talent or learning. However, we questioned and learned much that crossed disciplinary boundaries and transcended "time off," had someone thought to ask us. Further, we learned many things from the hidden curriculum. Mr. Moe became a real person to me—no longer a school fixture like paper towels and powdered soap. I now knew things about Mr. Moe that my teacher did not and was incensed when she asked Ted to "go get Mr. Moe to mop up Cynthia's vomit, and tell him to hustle and shuffle."

Sixth Grade Lingering on Poe and Poetry. Mrs. Filber's college-aged daughter taught me about lingering in the sixth grade. In her one-time visit to the classroom, she dramatically recited Poe's "The Raven." This was my first encounter with the power of poetry. I realized that some authors create with different intentions and authority than textbook authors. I realized that the arts need and love performers, that all arts deserve an audience, that one can be actively engaged and immersed as audience, and that there is a difference between entertainment and engagement. Mrs. Filber's daughter never spoke of this, nor did Mrs. Filber. However, I learned this from one occasion, one poem's lilting meter, rhyme, and mystery.

Language holds and spews meanings like cattail seeds, whether next to a sunny pond in July or in the dark envelope of night when things are not all that clear. Like the hidden messages of backward writing in fourth grade, poetry offered a new window on texts and meanings, particularly when it was spoken aloud. Somehow, the printed and spoken texts were connected in more significant ways than I had realized. The fact that Mrs. Filber's daughter had committed this poem to memory did not go unnoticed either. Some persons derive so much pleasure from poetry that they obviously read quite a bit of it and are willing to commit some poems to memory. How independent Mrs. Filber's daughter was—she could conjure up this poem at any time in the future, enjoying it again and again! I would now look up "The Raven" in the library and read it for myself. I would look for other poems by Poe. I would discover Emily Dickinson, all on my own. Beginning in my late teens, I would begin writing my own poetry—volumes of it over the years.

Curriculum inquiry needs to acknowledge unusual events in the everyday life of schools which might be extraordinarily meaningful to students for a variety of reasons. The impact of programs such as "artists-in-schools" on students' perceptions of the arts or their place(s) in the arts has not been examined seriously. We have not asked the most penetrating questions. What sense do students really make of these rare encounters? This episode makes me reconsider what it means to be actively engaged in learning—despite the appearance of student passivity. It reminds me of oral traditions lost or distorted in our postmodern culture. Where and how are worthwhile stories in our culture(s) passed on from elders to youth? What has taken the place of cave campfires, deep starry nights, and legends that illuminate the human condition and jar our complacency?

Lingering with Beatrice's Predicament. Beatrice taught me about lingering as an artist and woman when I was about thirteen years old. I babysat for Beatrice and Joe, who had five children, and I spent a great deal of time in their home up the street. How Beatrice had time to create wispy, light, pencil-and-pastel sketches of her children, I'll never know. Even though we never 'drew' together as mentor and novice, it was Beatrice who introduced me to pastels, drawing human faces from life. She taught me that some lines were less important than others and could be omitted altogether with great effect, that skin contains a range of colors, and that one can be creative with inexpensive supplies (grocery bag paper). Delicacy, transparency, innocence, and quiet could be depicted in the faces of children where there was much tension in a home.

Beatrice taught me about trapped and abused housewives who dream of art or interior design as an escape to self-proclamation—which, in reality, carried Beatrice nowhere but through the day, day to day, always a precarious inch from her husband's tyranny. I lingered with Beatrice, witnessed artistic expression that virtually no one else would see, and reassured her that she should spin her dreams and act upon them. I learned about human spirit, hope, and feminine sacrifice from Beatrice, a flowering weed persisting in hard concrete.

Often at 1:00 a.m., waiting for Beatrice and Joe to return home, I would sneak in their bedroom closet, pore through her photo album, stare transfixed at the perfection of her image as a bride and airline hostess (when beauty was the primary criterion for selection). I'd think long and hard about what it meant to be an airline hostess, the irony of Beatrice now being a kiwi (or flightless bird, as the former attendants now called themselves). What did it mean to be so beautiful, a woman on the wing, to fall in love? How could she have known that this dapper, handsome man would be a monster? How could a person be intensely isolated and married? Be a kiwi and fly? "If I could draw faces as well as Beatrice and could show how beautiful she is, I'd do a portrait of her." However, it would have taken a Beatrice to capture Beatrice's beauty.

What a quandary I put myself in, lingering week after week, talking with Beatrice and tending babies, studying the photo album, Beatrice's face, her predicament! Knowing Beatrice made me sensitive to gender and equity issues: women's seeming 'absence' in a male-dominated art world; the tension of women's lives between home and work; gendered roles and inequities in the bureaucratic layers of schools; different expectations and opportunities for girls and boys, minorities and whites, wealthy and poor, the powerful and powerless; women teachers' images of themselves as decision makers and curriculum developers; using autobiography, journal writing, letters, drawings, poetry, music, and conversation to illuminate and reflect upon our collective beliefs and social situatedness.

Curriculum inquiry must acknowledge a gendered profession, women's historical moments, and their contextual ways of seeing and caring. 'Scholarly' inquiry must involve persons—no matter their age, race, position, or gender—in sensitive talk that promotes active and shared inquiry which does not perpetuate powerlessness and silence. Those who perceive only flow charts, MBOs, textbooks, simple solutions, and omit the names of live, feeling persons in talk of their work need to be confronted with seeing things 'backwards,' contextually, problematically, and in all their complexity. They need to learn how to linger.

Adolescent Lingering. In high school, lingering became powerfully personal and political—as significant as my feeling unspecial in the context of adolescent conformity and cliques. The art and music rooms were safe harbors for exploration, self-expression, competence, skill building, and developing an identity—a vision of myself in the context of all others in an unknowable life that loomed ahead of me like a primordial mist on the horizon. The contests over school schedules, turf, and subject matter emerged as shared understandings and realities. I never skipped economics to loaf, but rather to work on an art project or practice piano. My art and music teachers participated in this conspiracy and gave me space to become (and valuable written excuses).

Lingering in high school required moods defined and excused by myself and others as the down side of an artistic temperament, distinct from all my peers who had comparable hormonal surges, I'm sure. It was in the arts, however, that who I was, what I did and did not do, what I liked/disliked, what I stood for, how I felt, and how I interpreted the world and my experiences took public shape. As the muddled puddle that I was stopped shimmering and moving once in a while, I could pause to look at me. I saw someone who loved the arts and was the better for it. Lingering was immortalizing our tentative, narcissistic selves in plaster masks with straws stuck up our noses—not only to breathe during the procedure, but to remind us of our mortality, our sacrifice to artistic expression as we lay prone on tables feeling the heat of the plaster setting, its weight, the weightiness of it all. What artists do for their art! How special they are—I am!

Lingering occurred when I heard my biology teacher play Chopin and Debussy before vocal music period began, recognizing the multidimensionality of individuals and questioning why some people taught biology—or taught at all, for that matter. Miss Peterson played piano passionately and sensitively, and few people in school knew it. I was one of the privileged. Yet she approached the dissection of a cow's eyeball dispassionately. I marveled at this contradiction and wrote about it. What about music was merely technical and matter-of-fact? What about biology, beautiful and passionate? By lingering in biology and Beethoven, I recognized the connection of subjects, feelings, and forms of representation. I realized the power of depiction, connotation, form, abstraction, organized sound, subtlety, and detail. I appreciated variation through the study of evolution and trying to teach myself to play Mozart. I sought connections that most teachers said were unrelated and only confused matters. Yes, the trilobite might remind you of an Egyptian scarab, and the geological contour map, God's fingerprint on a clay sphere; but can you label the parts for the test? Where in the school curriculum could I record and express these metaphorical connections?

College Lingering in Figure Drawing. After excursions into nursing and volunteer work on playgrounds and in mental institutions (where I discovered art and music were the least authentic both to the arts and those there), lingering emerged in prolonged undergraduate study where I decided to major in visual arts while working full-time at the newspaper as a layout artist, a magazine art director, and later, an artist and puppeteer in public television. Gil was my major instructor in studio art. I learned about painting with a limited palette like the old masters, working from dark to light with only four or five colors and a prepared sepia-toned canvas, rather than white—a marvelous secret preserved and handed down through the ages. Empathy for the beleaguered, tortured, misunderstood, and ostracized artist was indelibly reinforced by others' vicious treatment of Gil for his suspected homosexuality and known alcoholism.

Figure drawing in Gil's classes exemplified provocative pedagogy. "Now, sketch with your opposite hand, do this one as if you were underneath the model, try this one in five seconds, do this one without lifting your pencil or looking at your paper, draw the mirror image, let's combine some of these figures into an interesting composition." Gil helped me find muscles and movement, give weight to line, understand Leonardo's notebooks and his versatility across disciplines and time. (Leonardo even wrote backwards!) Gil helped me soar beyond the present and trite experimentation, anchoring me to a lived history, a place in time, a continuation of human experience through the arts coupled with reflection on my own development. Gil helped me see art beyond myself while helping me see my place in it as artist, viewer, and critic. His challenges—along with those of printmaking, philosophy, psychology, history, and doctoral studies in curriculum—reminded me of writing backwards, of seeing things other than the way they were, of locating subtleties I might have easily overlooked had no one challenged me to look.

From lingering in these particular university courses, I learned that questions were more important and provocative than answers. I sensed a profound difference in expectations among educational levels. I became angry and despaired over what I had missed for twelve years, much the way an adolescent turns on her parents and accuses them of being real people, for having unforgivable flaws in parenting. Shouldn't elementary and secondary schools also deal with profound questions and ideas rather than trite, forgettable answers like the seven major rivers of Brazil? Curriculum inquiry needs to attend more to adults' low expectations of children and the disjointed vertical articulation of students' experiences over their years of schooling.

Commercial art paid my bills, while fine arts—exhibiting, museum-going, and formal study—gave my life personal meaning and pause for thought. Although I entered jurored shows and won awards, I detested competition and thought it contrary to the creative spirit. Although I was a paying member of two arts organizations, I never belonged to this membership of full-time artists who did not have to work eight to five outside their studios like me. Although I loved sidewalk art shows, I hated insensitive public comments like, "This is beautiful. Do you have one in green, because my living room is in green?" or, "Could you put a dress on this nude?"

Curriculum inquiry must acknowledge various cultural and sociopolitical contexts to which schools are oddly linked and embedded. These would be the parents of my students to whom I would be teaching the arts. These would be the reviewers and critics of district-wide school competitions and exhibits. These persons would not fully understand teaching, commercial art, and fine arts as professions, nor would they understand how all of these endeavors could be complex and fulfilling. Yet, these people were realistic litmus paper tests beyond the shelter of my studio and classroom. I learned much about what I needed to say and do as artist and future teacher, within the classroom as well in the communities I tried to serve.

Lingering in Teaching. Still working full-time, I went back to school in the evenings to obtain elementary certification. My early love of children, anger over missed and stolen opportunities in K-12 schools, remembering the personal power of human expression I conjured up as a child, and the few but remarkable teachers who fostered my artistic interests and understanding all contributed to this career decision. I chose elementary education because that is where I missed the arts most profoundly and looked hardest for it as a youngster. That is where I felt the largest abyss between school and home, work and play, boredom and joy. Elementary school held the greatest possibility for making powerful connections across subjects, time, home, and school because of its more amenable structures. I could visualize myself creating opportunities there, grasping unexpected moments and connections with kids, trying to make things memorable.

Fortunately, I taught in an open-space school where experimentation and faculty decision making was encouraged and rewarding. Not only did students have more encounters with the arts per week, the interdisciplinary curriculum was created thematically and team-taught with fluid schedules and varied settings for teaching and learning. The school population and communities served were diverse and challenging. There was much to be learned about negotiating roles, goals, methods, and schedules; taking an active role in professional decisions that helped shape the entire school community; and creating a unique school curriculum based upon shared, progressive interests in the face of a tidal wave of conservativism in the district. The principal knew how to linger and understood the importance of sandboxes for students and teachers.

Teaching gradually became the primary vehicle for my creative expression. It was—and still is—fraught with persistently interesting questions and puzzles regarding what students ought to learn, want to learn, why, and how. Each group is a canvas of possibilities, our ideas constrained only by the finite dimensions of the surface and trying to match our tools and materials to what we wish to understand and convey. Teaching lets me create encounters that help educators make important connections. It challenges me to help teachers appreciate themselves as learners in their past and present, and to see their own learners more vividly, as the true subjects of the curriculum.

My courses involve journal writing, visual representations and projects, dramatic episodes, choices, group work, soul searching, critique, and defensible ideas in light of ethical consequences. I incorporate a historical perspective to help students locate themselves in the flow of time and determine where they have been, wish to go, and why. I challenge students with visual, musical, and literary forms of representation and assignments, encouraging them to see things "other than the way they are," as well as the way they seem to be—the truths in what we believe and how these beliefs and values are constituted and revealed in all forms of expression and professional activity. These representations allow persons to express ambiguity, paradox, and complexity when the linear and denotative features of academic discourse obscure and limit. They confront educators with why such expression is both painful and pleasurable; why most recognize lingering as memorable and embrace it, but some cannot; and why, when we share our multiple interpretations, we find ourselves profoundly creative and unimaginative, fair-minded and prejudiced, unique and alike, trapped—yet free.

Research means lingering in classrooms for long periods of time with kids and teachers, trying hard to reclaim myself there as teacher, student, and friend. It is looking for uniquenesses and connections among lives, disciplines, ideas, and cultures, context to context. It is the continuous search for what others find memorable. Lingering is poring over fieldnotes, transcripts, curriculum documents, and texts that are codes to be cracked, poems to be enjoyed, subtleties and form to be teased out and understood in the dense texture of this symphony called education. It is watching the drama unfold and wanting to participate as actor and audience. It is the desire to speak in first person, to be the author of my own story, to help others write their stories.

Lingering is the compelling need to draw, build, and transform what I understand—to return to the sandbox, blank sketch pad, Mr. Moe's braided rug, Beatrice's kitchen, Miss Peterson's Debussy, my first one-woman exhibit, and elementary classrooms and their neighborhoods. Lingering locates the memorable in curriculum; it transcends time, place, and person.

10

ANN LYNN LOPEZ-SCHUBERT

Wondrous Possibilities: On the Value of an Artful Setting in Childhood

I was born into a home rich with art and music. My father was a celebrated pastry chef and teacher of chefs. He created pure wonders spun of sugar and imagination; many of his creations were the centerpieces of celebrations and found their ways to the pages of *Life* magazine and Chicago newspapers. Sculptures of chocolate, sugar, buttercream, marzipan, and ice filled the senses. My birthday was always wondrous because of the love and the beauty fashioned into my father's cake for me. The ribbons, swirls, bows, and flowers which he spun from molten sugar with his bare hands on cool slabs of marble I encased in a place of honor in my room to admire long beyond the gifted day.

In the year that I entered the first grade my father made the suggestion that I bring a cake to my teacher on her birthday. It was the most breathtakingly beautiful thing my teacher and classmates had ever seen. They all looked at the cake as though they had never before seen a cake, and we talked about the cake, my father, his style, his techniques, his other work, and looked and looked again for quite a long time. Mrs. Foster, our teacher, deeply moved by the tribute and our genuine interest, allowed the discussion to go forward for quite some time before she finally cut the cake and distributed pieces to the class members whose sadness at seeing the cake broken into pieces was overcome by that first heavenly taste. Needless to say, through my father's artistry I found myself in a very happy state. The events of that day filled our senses and imaginations in a way that revisioned our experience of things we had come to see as ordinary. A birthday cake had become a work of art so moving that thirty hungry six year olds chose to study, admire, and discuss it at length and be forever changed through coming into contact with it. This was an experience unparalleled in that first grade year. I imagine that no cake would ever be the same for my teacher or my classmates. Each would be seen in the light of the wonder my father had created through the cake and the majestic curiosity inspired by that autumn afternoon. I resolved to continue to strive to learn to awaken emotions, visions, souls; to fashion wonder, connection, curiosity, growth, and sheer joy as my father was so able to do.

My father also enjoyed painting, which he learned from his mother. My grandmother, who lived upstairs, loved to paint largely on china and porcelain. I loved the work they made and relished watching them work. Everything was approached with such vitality and vision. My interest was welcomed, and I was taken into the world of creation as they each spoke aloud the thoughts that directed the work. Ideas, perspectives, technique, feeling were all brought to speech so that I might share in them. I was invited to try, to make suggestions, to offer commentary, to feel, to question, to engage my experiences, to practice, to see, to create, and, through the creative process, to awaken and involve the essence of my being. When I went forward with projects of my own, my father was always there with tremendous enthusiasm, support, and concrete as well as inspirational suggestions. Really, really looking at things and ideas carefully and seeing them for what they are and what they might become, trying to capture a bit of imagination, finding techniques to give form to vision, reaching for words and other media to share the development of ideas, emotion, and growth were some of the things I came to value through these times.

I also came to value music. Our home was filled with music throughout the day. My parents both loved to sing, to play, to listen to and talk about all types of music. Their facility with music made it seem as significant and as easy as breathing. There was a song for every occasion and if there wasn't then my family would create one. My mother and her sisters created scores of compositions and parodies for family gatherings and I am hard pressed to remember any of the wonderful weddings, outings, parties, reunions, funerals, or other special or ordinary events to be without the fulfillment of music. The music touched us, awakened our spirits, brought us together to share of ourselves through the power of aesthetics, and to revel in the depth and fundamental essence of experience. The music allowed us to communicate with and through one another that which would have remained unspoken and perhaps unrealized without its essential power. That aesthetic experience provided us powerful and unique ways in which to be touched and communicate made me resolve to search out and engage it, to be open to it, and to find ways in which to help others find their spirit awakened, visions expanded, and abilities developed through its power.

My mother has always had the ability to play music by hearing the melody without the benefit of seeing the printed score. As a young child I thought that this was the only way that people played an instrument, and I was encouraged to try my ear and hand at finding and creating sounds from various instruments. Before long I found it to be quite a simple thing to play in the way my mother did. No mystery was made about it. And yet it was like magic: not the celebrated magic of an illusionist or a side show actor but a genuine magic which is like sharing in love, participating in birth, wondering in the mysteries of death and life, growing in friendship, expanding in understanding, awakening ideas, finding trust, growing in competence, amazing in the resilience of body and spirit, or exhilarating in a thunderstorm, the majesty of the sea, the seasonal changes, and the ecological cycles of nature. Music theory in India holds that if music is played and experienced in its fullest, the deities are given form and Nirvana is actualized for the duration of the harmonies. To feel the anger in "Why Do the Nations Rage . . ." from Handel's *Messiah*, the exhilaration in "Jauchzet, Frohlocket" from Bach's *Christmas Oratorio*, the depths of despair and the promise of hope in Beethoven's Ninth Symphony, the passion in "Bamboleo" by the Gipsy Kings, the despair in "Fast Car" by Tracey Chapman, the danger in "La Calma Que Precede a la Tormenta" by Ruben Blades, or the stability and splendor in the "Rodrigo Suite" from Handel's Harp and Lute Concerto: this is magic, and I found it essential to be a part of it. I loved to be near an instrument as someone played. I yearned to hear the stories of who had found which piece or song especially dear; I understood more of who they were and grew in who I could be. I discovered that much could be touched and uncovered through music that would otherwise remain hidden or buried. There were vulnerabilities to expose, risks to take, feelings and sensibilities to discover and explore. I believe that these dispositions are an integral component of education generally and that the rewards available through musical experience can make one more receptive to experience, discovery, learning, feeling, growth, education in other areas.

When my parents started my formal musical education I frustrated and amused my teachers by insisting that they pay attention to the variations which I had developed. Unfortunately, they lacked imagination and imposed rigorous instruction with an adherence to strict rules of performance, carefully following the received curriculum. The classes of technique and theory were better than most, I suppose, and I retained and grew in my love of music despite those private lessons. It was the consistency of high quality, authentic, supportive, creative, emotional musical experiences outside of the formal classes that saw me grow. Reflecting upon this remembrance, I find evident that curriculum and instruction in music—the arts in general—can suffer from the same emptiness and rigidity as other areas of study if the soul and imagination of the teacher and student are left idle. Such lifeless instruction can be clearly detrimental. My parents' gift of music, through their example, talent, and love, and their ability to inspire and to be imaginative and vulnerable, provided a wealth of experience and enjoyment unable to be squelched.

Adding to the wealth of musical experience as a young child was the wonder and magnificence of belonging to choirs and ensembles. To make music with others moved me out of myself to the experience of a community joined, cooperating, sharing their souls as well as talent to create a vision, an encounter with art much larger than believed possible. The joy and enticing nature of group performance led me from a preschooler in cherub choir through adult days in the senior choir. In those times, through the medium of music, the vision and love of our choir director, Paul Schade, the artistry of the composers, and the talent and fellowship of the choir members, I found that the whole is greater than the sum of its parts. This led me to a resolute belief in the strength of community action guided by artistic vision, talent, and love, and it drew me ever closer to music as an integral part of my being.

Worlds of musical possibilities continued to be opened to me as a growing child through the devotion of my dearest aunt, Doris. She has always been an ardent lover of the arts and found ways to encourage my aesthetic experiences and performances, and she included me in her visits to Orchestra Hall to commune with the Chicago Symphony Orchestra, to the ballet, to concerts in the park, to galleries, to the theater, to the cultural perspectives available through the art, dance, stories, traditions, and music of a country's folk, and to become transfixed and transported through the artists of the Lyric Opera of Chicago. I discovered that these things were not the exclusive domain of the monied and privileged. Art belongs to, and finds expression in, people of all walks of life and should be accessible to all. The bejeweled and fur-laden donors in the box seats were equalled in their experience to those dressed simply and seated in the last row of the uppermost balcony of the auditorium. What I discovered is that the arts can give expression to what is similar about our being in the world and opens possibilities for sharing that are not perceptible elsewhere. Unfortunately, not every one has an Aunt Doris to bravely lead them to this realization. I know that there need to be more ways to facilitate participation in the arts by people from all walks of life. Without the music lovers in the rafters, a great deal of the heart of the audience would be missing, thus lessening the authenticity of experience for all and bringing a moribund nature rather than a vitality to the performance. In a similar way, curricula must find ways to be inclusive. It should seem little wonder that students, in record numbers, are leaving school early, finding solace in drugs, authenticity in the experience of conception and childbirth, and vitality in violence.

Vitality is what I have always loved about the dance. Here conception, time, space, sound, dimension, emotion take form through the human figure. Dance for me has always been extraordinary. From my days as a young child I can remember the sheer joy of being an expression of the music. To be a dancer was one of my dreams, and I think I was not alone in this. My sister recently confided that it was her dream, too, and she added that she thought it must have been every young girl's dream in the early fifties when we were growing up. We both started our formal dance training as preschoolers and found ourselves still making the after-school pilgrimages to the dance studio as we ended our high school days. I only loved dancing more through all of this. And not just in the dancing school, but dancing with friends, at school dances, in dance club, in cheerleading routines, at recitals, at performances, alone, in my imagination. The love of dance inspired me to learn more, to seek out instruction, to practice, to experiment, to improvise, to create, to imagine, to grow, to share, and to teach.

I cannot forget the desire, anticipation, admiration, vulnerability, and trust in the eyes of the little girls who were in the first dance class I taught. It was a look that I often saw in my elementary school students, though many had become so disappointed, disillusioned, and distrustful from other experiences that it took some time, imagination, and care to find them hopeful once again. They knew that we were about to share something incredible and magical. We were going on a journey together; a world only previously imagined would be opened to them. We were going to become art. We were going to make dreams become clearer and go forward to envision even more wondrous realities. I promised never to disappoint the trust, the art, or the spirits. To keep alive the disposition and vitality which was represented by the look in their eyes seems the goal of every educator and all who would be involved in curriculum.

This is the same look I see in our daughter, Heidi. She has been a dancer and musician from before her birth as far as we have been able to discern. Relatively quiet in my womb, I first felt her stir at a performance of Wagner's *Lohengrin* at the Lyric Opera. On our regular visits to listen to the Chicago Symphony and the Lyric she became very animated to the sounds of the music: dancing, we said. Wagner's *Ring* cycle greeted her on her arrival home from the hospital and she continued her attachment to opera as the only melody to soothe her on long car rides was the "Triumphant March" from *Aida*.

Her musical aptitude and dancing continued as she began singing and recognizing melodies as a toddler, amazing people by noticing the differences between major and minor keys and requesting pieces such as Mozart's *Eine Kleine Nachtmusik*. As a six year old she composes songs, picks melodies out on musical instruments, and can do things such as listen to a soundtrack from a movie and recount every mood and detail which it underscores. She has been surrounded with a love of music, an environment rich in material to facilitate listening to and making music, resources from which to develop music, and love, fellowship, attention, imagination, and technical as well as spiritual support in her musical endeavors.

In dance we have tried to provide a similar situation and she has continued to develop in this area as well. From her first days I danced with her in my arms with sheer enchantment and joy. When she was able to walk she began dancing on her own, and before long our toddling Heidi had discovered the magic of the *Nutcracker* Ballet. She first attended a performance of the *Nutcracker* Ballet (choreographed by Ruth Page) at the age of two. She sat enchanted and throughout the performance occasionally nursed to keep up her energy. Upon her request, we must have watched our videotape of that ballet at least one hundred times during the years she was two and three. Each watching provided higher levels of artistry to her and deeper levels of understanding of technique and emotion. She reenacted the ballet after each watching and many times simultaneously with the videotape, always careful to adjust her lighting, provide explanatory comments, and gather her costumes and props. In a short period of time she had been to several more full length ballet performances including *Swan Lake, Cinderella, Sleeping Beauty, Romeo and Juliet,* and several more iterations of the *Nutcracker*. Others in attendance would often approach us and ask just how old Heidi was, marvelling at her attention, comportment, and apparent love of the ballet. Interestingly, the authentic engagement of interest, imagination, and spirit were found somewhat lacking at a performance of the "Stars of the Bolshoi Ballet" which we attended last year. The performance was replete with technical and athletic skill but seemed lifeless due to the lack of a live orchestra and an engagement of technique without spirit. Too often, 'canned' experiences lacking in spirit but supported by technique are made available to students generally. In the end, it seems that there are few who recognize the difference between the curriculum that is authentic, living and filled with the essence of the participants and the curriculum that is repressive, moribund, created by professionals who are so removed from the environment and moment during which the learning is to be brought to life that even a teacher's virtuoso performance for willing and vulnerable students is apt to fall short of authenticity.

Searching for the authentic, our dancer (Heidi) studies other forms of dance as well as ballet. She is engaged by almost any dance that is made available and attempts to model it and expand upon it. We have learned, through her periodic lectures, that certain music inspires a particular type of dance in her and that her love of dance, technique, imagination, and artistry can only grow through a continued engagement. From the vibrancy of *Flashdance* and *Dirty Dancing*, to the passion of flamenco dancers, to the enduring vitality of Celtic dancers, to the splendor of the ballet, Heidi's repertoire continues to develop and grow. Her brother and our son, Henry, seems to be as intensely and naturally attracted to music, dance, and art as Heidi is. Henry is joy incarnate when dancing, singing, making up or recognizing melodies, and experimenting with instruments and media of the visual arts. At two years of age he too surprises people with requests of the overture from Mozart's *Marriage of Figaro* so that he may perform with Heidi a dance they have termed sneaky and elegant. We anticipate his first full-length performance of the *Nutcracker* this year will open even more wondrous possibilities for him and for us all. And isn't the ultimate goal of all who are interested in art, education, and curriculum the development of wondrous possibilities?

11

GAIL McCUTCHEON

Curriculum and *The Magic Flute*

When I tell people of my love of opera (no matter which one), they look at me aghast. "It's not in English!" they say. "What! A bunch of fat ladies standing around screeching in foreign languages?!" Indeed, what could anyone see in opera and its connection with the real worlds of curriculum? In other words, what's a nice person like me doing in a place like this?

As Bill, Chris, Dana, Corrina, Dallene, Lois and other of my friends of childhood and my brother John were reading the all-about books, biographies of sports figures, *Heidi*, *Lorna Doone*, *Kidnapped*, *The Swiss Family Robinson*, and *Treasure Island*, I read those, but was also reading books that housed between their covers the stories of *Carmen*, *Aida*, *The Flying Dutchman*, *Madame Butterfly*, and *La Bohéme*. On those slick pages full of tiny print and colorful, small paintings, those stories came alive. Their music filled the house and my head as my mother played records, the piano, and an old pump organ. None of us liked school much, but we loved to read and escape into books.

My friends' fantasies were peopled with Lorna Doone, Babe Ruth, Kit Carson, Heidi, Ben Gun, Long John Silver, Dr. Lindsay, and their associates; mine were populated with Senta, the Flying Dutchman, Mimi, Tosca, Carmen, Madame Butterfly, and their friends. Of course, we also shared baseball players and cowboys as heroes. My friends didn't know the operas, so we usually played baseball or cowboys.

Later, I married. My first husband played clarinet during summers with the Sante Fe Opera. Dream of dreams! I'd never seen a live opera before. As his wife, I could attend free, and did. Here, I saw my childhood friends and met new ones. Opera in Sante Fe was intimate, real, and beautiful. While I saw many, I never missed a performance of *The Magic Flute*, which is indeed magic, and music and magic comprise its language (whether the words are in German or English).

Here, as in curriculum, different actors tell different stories, yet they interweave to tell one very complex story, and the interweaving and sensemaking occur only through the active mental efforts of the audience in operas, of students and teachers in the case of curriculum. So, in the beginning of the opera the Queen of the Night is an awesome but "good" heroine. As the opera progresses and we meet Sorastro, who also seems "good," we start questioning the actual goodness of the Queen of the Night (who's in conflict with Sorastro for their daughter, Pamina, and for control of their subjects through the darkness of night or through the enlightenment of day). We interact with the text of the plot and change our minds. In curriculum work, many characters also interact—textbook authors, administrative policy makers, state policy makers, teachers, and students—to develop their personal versions both of truths such as goodness and of a story line (whether about literature, mathematics, economics, the arts, sciences, social studies, or whatever). Students have to interrelate these stories to make sense of the complex whole just as an opera audience does. Like the Queen and Sorastro, administrators and developers of curriculum materials don't seem to know whether control through the darkness (ignorance) or self-enlightenment for teachers is a better course of action. That is, the Queen of the Night (perhaps like some administrators) would just as soon keep her subjects in the dark about matters, whereas to lead "the good life" Sorastro (perhaps like other administrators) would have his people strive for enlightenment through knowledge. A current controversy in curriculum concerns this: Do we wind up with an excellent curriculum by controlling teachers through scripted programs (such as Distar), or do we work toward teachers' becoming self-emancipated and thereby excellently redeveloping the curriculum as they enact it? Just as the audience of *The Magic Flute* must concentrate attention on understanding occurrences (not typically in English), so must students and teachers concentrate and be mentally active.

The Magic Flute is different each time I see it. I suspect that sometimes this difference is because of my previous experiences and my mood. But I also believe it is objectively different in different performances. Ingmar Bergman's movie version[1] brings the opera to people through his casting, charming costumes, and staging. There is an intimacy here. These are people we can meet anywhere, from the audience we see during the overture to the performers on stage. They sing with English subtitles. They smile, cry, eat, drink, laugh, and show feelings the rest of us have. I'm close enough to see Princess Pamina's scars and blemishes and Prince Tamino's fillings in his molars. I hope Prince Tamino finds Pamina and they survive the three tests. I hope the Queen of the Night doesn't persuade Pamina to kill her father, Sorastro. He's a good guy. Papageno is foolish, but I hope he finds his Papagena and they will be happy together (as the song goes, raising lots of little Papagenos and Papagenas). I see these people backstage playing chess, perusing a comic book or the music to *Parsifal*, readying themselves for the next scene and peering out at the audience, perhaps somewhat nervously. They're real people I could see anywhere, not aloof, fat screechers. Sometimes they even want me to sing along, and they hold up the words. What a delightful 134 minutes! It is a joyous celebration of Mozart and I am filled with wonder everytime I experience it, just as I am filled with awe watching masterful teachers enact the curriculum or groups complexly developing a curriculum. The ideas and experiences are different, but the feelings of wonder, glee, and awe at the masterful excellence are the same.

Sante Fe has a wonderful intimacy. I can see the sun set across the desert through the back of the stage. Later, the sky gets black and stars shine down on us. I think they're happy to be here. The stage is near me and the audience is small. We wear comfortable, warm clothes and later we bundle up in small blankets. It gets cold in the desert at night! The costumes are wonderful and magical. The Three Ladies have gossamer wings. The serious songs and humorous ones are cheek by jowl on the stage and in my mind. Music fills the air, and because it's a live performance, a sense of immediacy is here, unlike the movie version. It's clearly a fantasy, with its panpipes, dragon, lustful Monostatos, three boy-spirit guides, Papageno's magic glockenspiel that plays autonomously, Tamino's magic flute, enchanted forest animals, a good/evil queen, a handsome prince, a lovely princess, and other characters, but it's here on stage in front of my eyes and around my ears. This is real hi-fi and it has 3-D pictures! It is very accessible, magic, and enchanting.

At the Metropolitan Opera in New York City, I wear a gown and enter more formally. I sit properly, smile, and clap at proper places (my grandmother would be proud). A chandelier glistens down on me, but perhaps less happily than Sante Fe's stars. This is a performance, and I feel less attached to the opera. It is a huge house full of tuxedoed and begowned people. Furs wrap, jewels glitter, and people pose. The magic's missing here. Magic isn't for begowned, fur-wrapped, bejewelled, betuxedoed adults. You can't play when you're gussied up. But you can hear and watch. Somehow, it's more distant than is Ingmar Bergman's movie (even though that version is "canned"). But opera it is. The Queen of the Night is powerful. She sings with precision. Pamina, Tamino, Papagena, and Papageno seem young, yet are beautiful performers. There's no doubt here that these people are technical wonders, and there is magnificence in that, but not magic.

The curriculum is probably also different each time it is enacted, and the differences among its received stories for different students may be because of their different prior experiences and their moods as well as differences because Teacher A using a set of curriculum materials enacts the curriculum differently from Teacher B and because classroom settings (like opera houses) differ.

Opera and curriculum are also alike because both call for qualitative thinking in order to answer the question, "What's going on here?" Qualitative thinking (whether about *The Magic Flute* or a curriculum development project) has several dimensions. One of these dimensions is epistemological, where I wonder, What is this thing? Another is ontological, which asks, What is the meaning of this thing in the world? Ethics and moral issues enter here. Yet a third is cosmological, where I wonder, What is the meaning of this in the broader order of things? Like human life elsewhere (such as in curriculum development committee meetings and classrooms), life in an opera is three dimensional, constantly changing through complex interactions among lives, which may explain why records and radio broadcasts of operas simply don't work. These changes are communicated through words (whether sung or spoken), actions, and dress. Perhaps this is one reason why Americans wish to have operas performed in English. If I'm experiencing an opera only musically, the language doesn't matter, for the voice is but a human musical instrument. But if I want to understand the drama and story as well, I have to understand the words so I can interpret what is transpiring in front of me; because it takes my active mental effort to do so, I need to have as much data as possible in order to understand by immersing myself in it.

The only way I've found to understand either is to immerse myself in their nature: in opera, the qualities of the music, actions, and stories; in curriculum, the words, actions, and stories. I have to be mentally active whether it's about the Queen of the Night and Sorastro or about a team of educators developing a curriculum. I have to watch, listen, and feel, but I also have to be mentally alert. I have to be alert for surprises, so definite preconceptions are harmful. I'm responsible to make sense of it, developing the story and patterns as I watch, listen, feel, and partake of and consume the experience.

Further, qualitative thinking calls for an interplay between thinking about the general (such as the overall theme and story of *The Magic Flute* or themes in a curriculum development project or a teacher's enactment of it) and the specific (such as an aria by the Queen of the Night, a shift to minor key or a specific teacher's comments and other acts). The general and the specific inform one another, whether I am experiencing *The Magic Flute* or a curriculum setting, when I wonder what's going on in this version of the opera or in this curriculum setting and how that occurs. When writing about the curriculum setting, I have to communicate that interplay between the general theme and specific details, for these specifics comprise the evidence of the general theme and convey its life and meanings to readers.

Both opera and the curriculum are scripted to a certain extent, but each enactment is different because of individual differences in experience and mood among members of the audience and differences from performance to performance related to the setting, the performers (principals, orchestra members, and chorus in opera versus teachers in the curriculum), leaders (conductors and stage directors versus administrators), and materials (costumes and props versus computer programs, textbooks, workbooks, and audiovisuals). Lucia Popp[2] as Queen of the Night virtually xylophones through the arias. Her bell-like clarity and precision are powerful. How can Pamina possibly resist her demands to kill Sorastro? In *Amadeus*[3], on the other hand, we see the Queen of the Night metamorphose from Mozart's nagging landlady. She is heavyset and fearsome, a powerful harridan rather than an equally awesome power resulting from precise, bell-like singing. The Queen of the Night's arias are probably the most beautiful ones in the mezzo-soprano literature. In a curriculum development meeting, people are often talking simultaneously about different matters. Part of *The Magic Flute*'s music consists of trios of the Three Ladies who serve the Queen of the Night and other ensembles singing individual but musically harmonious songs. This is displayed in a libretto by writing the words each sings, but enclosing them in huge brackets to denote that they are sung simultaneously. Initially, it looks confusing, but by examining it closely—whether in the curriculum setting or the opera—one can see the relevance the separate texts have to the whole story.

Clearly, in the case of *The Magic Flute*, an opera company has the opportunity to work with an outrageously excellent script when they enact it. Curriculum, though, is more a dialogue than a script. Teachers are not Queens of the Night singing arias; rather, they redevelop the curriculum by teaching it. Indeed, in this case a metaphor of improvisational jazz is probably more appropriate to use in considering the work of teachers vis á vis the curriculum. When a teacher knows the theme of "Green Dolphin Street," for instance, s/he is able to reconfigure it into an appropriate variation. This also means that more work is needed when teachers conceive of teaching the curriculum than is needed when mezzo-sopranos follow the Queen of the Night's role. Perhaps because curriculum work is so much more complicated than singing *The Magic Flute*, I can (sadly enough) think of no curriculum that is as excellent as that opera. While in Santa Fe, singers of the opera seemed very excited about singing it. They talked with smiles and excitement about their roles in particular and the opera in general. Few teachers seem as excited to be teaching their curricula as were these singers to be singing *The Magic Flute*.

The metaphor also breaks down because teaching and curriculum work aren't fruitfully conceived of as teacher or curriculum developer as onstage performer or director of the action. Rather, a teacher's role also calls for perceiving oneself to be an audience for students who are on the stage; likewise, neither a teacher nor a curriculum developer is the director of actions, but rather provides teachers with materials and/or suggestions from which they are likely (and should be encouraged) to depart to redevelop the curriculum. This is because teachers' theories of action may not be consonant with the curriculum developer's conceptualization of practice, so classroom management, instructional strategies, content, and its organization may differ.

Similarly, while teachers might somewhat direct students' actions, teachers also need to understand students' departures from what was expected. However, a good opera director is also aware that when s/he hires a particular singer for a role, the singer may perform it in a way different from, and perhaps better than, the way the director conceived of it. So, for instance, Lucia Popp's Queen of the Night is very different from Roberta Peters's version of it, just as Teacher A's version of second grade science differs from Teacher B's, even though both use the same opera script or science curriculum.

In another sense, though, opera and the curriculum are connected in that both many singers and teachers get 'stage jitters' before a first class session or an opening as they wonder, Will my audience (students) enjoy this? Will they like me? Do I know this well enough to get it across to people who aren't familiar with it? Typically, once underway (whether *The Magic Flute* or a class), singers and teachers get so involved in what's happening that they lose their initial nervousness, as they interact with the other performers and reactions of the audience/students. Sometimes the jitters return, though, such as when a famous music critic or one's supervisor enters the scene.

Both *The Magic Flute* and the curriculum are an emotional and intellectual experience requiring mental involvement for understanding. Because a great deal of this probably flows out of our autobiographies, even a nice person like me can be in a place like this—be it *The Magic Flute* or a curriculum setting.

NOTES

1. Ingmar Bergman (producer), *The Magic Flute* (Bel Canto. Paramount home video #2351).

2. W.A. Mozart, *The Magic Flute* (Otto Klemperer, Conductor. Angel Stereo #SCL-3651).

3. *Amadeus* (HBO/Cannon Video #PTVF2997).

12

KENNETH KANTOR

"Deliver Me from the Days of Old": Rock and Roll (Etc.) as Liberation

The title comes from Chuck Berry's classic "School Day," chronicling the in- and out-of-school curriculum of the late fifties and early sixties. The line is less well known and cited than "Hail hail rock and roll!" from the same song. But it is perhaps more significant, in promising not simply an escape but a *deliverance* from the old, outdated, and meaningless. It speaks of a profound spiritual alternative to the mundane and irrelevant details of school life. That is what this narrative is about.

I want to present my story in two parts. The first is "The Record," referring specifically to the idea of a song, but also more broadly to the historical record of a period of time in which various aspects of popular culture had a great effect on me. In using the present tense, my intention is to capture the immediacy of a 45 rpm single—short, sweet, and sensuous. The second part is the "Record Review" (or a review of the historical record), a reflection of the particular kinds of influences these media have continued to exert on me since that time, especially as a teacher, teacher educator, and curriculum theorist.

THE RECORD

It is the Eisenhower Cold War era, and I am coming of age. The times, and the music, are bland, sentimental, untroubled (at least on the surface): a ballad by Patti Page or Perry Como, the Chordettes lulling us to sleep with "Mr. Sandman." America has suffered the traumas of World War II and Korea, and seeks peace and stability in the corporate image, the man in the gray flannel suit. As a teenager in that period, I'm not impressed; I want something more visceral, more funky.

Record buyers are shifting from 78 to 45 rpm, a slower speed certainly, but more compact and dangerous; you can put a whole stack of them on the turntable and just let them pump away at your soul. The Top 40 stations are beginning to play Fats Domino with his exotic New Orleans renditions of "Blueberry Hill" and "Blue Monday," Buddy Holly and the Crickets vibrating in "Peggy Sue" and "That'll Be the Day," Jerry Lee Lewis sliding furiously up and down the piano with "Whole Lotta Shakin' Goin' On" and "Great Balls of Fire," Little Richard shrieking outrageously "Gonna rip it up!" I am also listening intently to the "girl groups"—the Ronettes, Chiffons, Shangri-Las, Chantels, Crystals—treading the thin line between innocence and sexiness. Their lyrics offer pledges of devotion ("Baby It's You") and loyalty ("He's not a rebel—no no no—to me.") And late at night I discover even more esoteric "race music" at the mysterious far end of the radio dial, on a black-operated station playing rhythm and blues, and doo-wops by groups with names as smooth and classy as their sounds: the Paragons, Eldorados, Flamingos, Harptones, Cadillacs.

Back at the mainstream frequencies, the disk jockeys and record producers and station owners have become aware of the appeal of black music to the white teenage market. So they make it palatable to that audience by having Pat Boone sing Little Richard's "Tutti Frutti" and Fats Domino's "Ain't That a Shame" in enunciated tones that strip the music of its driving inner force. Or they promote the Crew Cuts' stiff, sanitized version of "Earth Angel" to capitalize further on the soulful rendering of the song by the Penguins. All in the name of respectability, and money.

And, of course, there is Elvis, who has earned his credentials by listening to and emulating black musicians at the Apollo Theater in Harlem, and who stirs up suppressed desires in the raunchy "Hound Dog" and taunted "Heartbreak Hotel." He eventually appears on our family black-and-white TV screen as a guest on the Ed Sullivan Show, but only from the waist up. I become aware of the subversiveness of that gyrating pelvis, as the older white generation does not yet wish to acknowledge the lower half of the body. It will remain for Chubby Checker and the Twist (and to some extent Ray Charles's "What'd I Say") at the turn of the decade to bring the masses out onto the dance floor to shake it up.

Two other artists excite me especially, and help to bridge the gaps between black and white musical tastes. One is Sam Cooke, his silky voice trained in gospel choirs, who provides that warm slow dance feeling in "You Send Me" and "Bring It On Home To Me." And I respond to the plaintive message of "Wonderful World":

the struggling student ("don't know much about history") who seeks a way to gain the affections of his true love by becoming an A student.

The second is Chuck Berry, who plays guitar in his inimitable, driving, bluesy style, asserting the universal themes of love and sex and freedom and success, but in a lighter, less threatening manner than Jerry Lee Lewis or Little Richard. "Johnny Be Goode" tells the story of the young man from the backwoods who earns fame and fortune by becoming a rock star. "Roll Over Beethoven" asserts the triumph of the contemporary over the classical ("and tell Tchaikovsky the news"). "Rock and Roll Music" further sets forth the credo of the era. And "School Day" sharply contrasts the banality of the classroom—the mean-looking teacher and the drudgery of school subjects—with the joyful escape at three o'clock to the juke joint. This is true deliverance, from the sad routine of the school day, from the oppressive days of old, to a place where the body and soul can find their true expression.

I experience in this music, then, that most powerful of combinations: freedom *from* the boredom of everyday existence, especially in school, and freedom *to* feel something primeval and to express that feeling in dance and song and physical action. My parents' and teachers' disapproval, of course, makes it all the more seductive.

Other songs depict for me, too, the vicissitudes of school life. The Coasters relate the woes of Charlie Brown, the class clown and troublemaker, who calls his English teacher "Daddy-O" and gets caught shooting craps in the boys' gym. Ricky Nelson is "waitin' in school," for nothing much, it seems. And the Four Freshmen sing wistfully about the joys and sorrows of "Graduation Day." These songs are a far cry from what will be the angry screams of the late 1960s in Alice Cooper's "School's Out for Summer" ("School's out forever") and Pink Floyd's "Another Brick in the Wall" ("Teacher! Leave those kids alone").

I find some inspiration, too, in a few television shows. When Giselle MacKenzie and Snooky Lanson can no longer legitimately sing Top Ten songs, "Your Hit Parade" gives way to "American Bandstand," with Dick Clark presiding benignly and appreciatively over the sock hop. My heroes become a gang of Philadelphia kids, with names like Pat, Tony, Fran, Bob, and Justine, who stylishly dance the Jitterbug, Cha-cha, and Stroll, and rate the latest recordings ("I give it an 85. It's got a good beat—you can dance to it."). I am particularly impressed with one 17-year old dropout who tells Dick that he earns enough money as a mechanic in a gas station to buy seven to ten records a week. Why bother staying in school, I wonder.

Two other TV shows appeal to my longing for the unconventional. One is "Your Show of Shows," with Sid Caesar, Imogene Coca, Carl Reiner, and Howard Morris acting up in improbable and manic skits. I laugh hysterically when I see a group of visiting royalty in an open touring car suddenly driven into an automatic car wash, maintaining their glum poker faces while sheets of water assault them from all sides, or when I see Howard Morris as Uncle Goopy clinging desperately to Sid Caesar's leg on a "This is Your Life" send-up. The second is the revolutionary "Ernie Kovacs Show," which paves the way for "Laugh-In" and "Saturday Night Live." Kovacs is a comedic genius well ahead of his time, the master of the optical illusion. He shows us a succession of strange characters emerging from a bathtub, or a man placing pieces of fruit on a table and watching them slide across and off the edge. I enjoy this world in which things are not as they appear; I appreciate Caesar and Kovacs because they are risk-takers, turning tradition on its head and poking it a few times for good measure.

Finally, there is the venerable *Mad* magazine, taking satiric aim at all forms of phoniness and hypocrisy in politics, the media, schooling. My friends and I read it religiously, learning valuable lessons in crap detecting. I especially like the parodies of TV shows and movies, and the features which comment pointedly on generational differences. The follies of both my peers and elders are exposed without partiality or sentiment; the laughter helps to ease the tension between us.

RECORD REVIEW

Somewhat later I was delighted to see a tribute to *Mad* written by Richard Reeves ("Mad Magazine: Witness for the People," in Hugh Rank, ed., *Language and Public Policy*; Urbana, IL: National Council of Teachers of English, 1974). Reeves praised the magazine for being one of the great teachers, fostering in young people a much-needed skepticism toward propaganda, manipulation, and deception in the larger society. *Mad*'s editor and founder, William Gaines, expressed his worry that such praise might cause the magazine to be taken too seriously. Other examples come to mind. *Rolling Stone* magazine now has a Rock and Roll Hall of Fame, recognizing the performers who established, maintained, and developed the art form. In Chicago, the Museum of Public Broadcasting honors television pioneers. These represent important attempts to give credit where credit is due, but they also serve to institutionalize popular culture, a contradictory phenomenon, I think. Additionally, they remind me that I am getting older. One of the advantages of aging, though, is the opportunity it affords to reflect on one's personal history, and to identify themes and patterns, if not direct influences.

"Since feeling is first," as e. e. cummings began one poem, let me begin with feeling. What I found in rock and roll music and irreverent comedy and satire was a means of giving vent to my emotional and physical being that was not typically available at home or school. I didn't consciously analyze this culture for its social and political messages (the sexist elements bother me especially now); I simply took part because it attracted me.

In my professional life, I have instinctively resisted the pretense of objectivity and the disconnection of the mind from the body and spirit. A case in point: while supervising student teachers at the University of Georgia, I was required to evaluate them using a performance inventory, consisting of a checklist of behaviors that supposedly represented good teaching. The instrument was flawed in many ways, not the least of which was its dispassionate, value-neutral façade. At a time when I was striving to develop a sense of trust among student teachers, the evaluation scheme intruded, creating suspicion and barriers to honest communication. When we complained, we were advised to "play the game." All the wrong lessons: a fitting target for *Mad*, I would suggest.

In retrospect, what I was searching for in my 1950s adolescence was the *counter*cultural: those elements that resisted and challenged white middle class safety, politeness, indifference, ethnocentricity, and asexuality. Rock and roll helped to teach me the value of resistance and the need for oppositional states, especially between generations. I feel fortunate to have taught high school English in the late 1960s, when students were engaged in moral conflicts over civil rights and the war in Vietnam. Some of them began underground newspapers to express their views on these issues as well as on what they saw as the repressive nature of their schooling. A few of these student writings appeared above ground, too, as in the school literary magazine for which I was the advisor; the tributes to Martin Luther King in the 1968 issue were particularly moving. Even as a sympathetic adult, however, I found I could not always offer consolation or reconciliation, as my students needed to test out their values against those of their elders. The music changes, even though sometimes I wish it wouldn't.

I try to resist this kind of conservatism. My views of teaching and living need to be accepting, generous, inclusive, pluralistic, democratic. In graduate curriculum courses which I currently teach, we examine critically the "cultural literacy" of Allan Bloom and E. D. Hirsch. Recently I shared with students Hirsch's list of "what every American needs to know," and asked them to identify names, places, and events important to them but missing from the list. We noted, as have others, that the list is conspicuously lacking in references to minorities, women, and "nonmainstream" groups generally. It also contains few names of rock and roll artists or television stars; William Gaines would likely feel upset if he were to find his name included. Expanding the list, as Hirsch has attempted to do, does not resolve the problem; the values remain condescending and elitist, the pursuit remains trivial.

In his brilliant and enlightening critique, *The Death of Rhythm and Blues* (New York: E.P. Dutton, 1989), Nelson George decries the loss of soul in black music, accompanying the movement of blacks to the middle class, and reflected in the 'crossover' songs of Whitney Houston and even, at times, Aretha Franklin. Perhaps he is suggesting that what we need now, in these days of designer clothes, glitzy shopping malls, disco and New Age music, Reaganomics and George Bush clichés is a deliverance *to* the days of old, not in the sense of a return to racism, sexism, elitism and xenophobia (we have plenty of those diseases to go around), but in the sense of feeling, creative tension, and cultural diversity that we were building before we were anaesthetized by the constrained "cultural literacy" of the 1980s. In the spirit of rock and roll lies the genesis of an alternative curriculum.

13

JOSE R. ROSARIO

On Thinking as a Sacred Act, Coltrane Jazz, the Inaccessible, and Curriculum

I can still remember when and how I first experienced the music making of John Coltrane. I recall the scene often, always like a Van Gogh impression: arriving home from school one day—don't know exactly when—to hear my sister mention a package, what she thought was a record from some record club. I never actually do see the image of my sister when I recall this moment—only me in a shadow-like living room, in motion yet somehow still, putting the record on, remembering the record club I had in fact joined (for the free albums). The club was insisting I listen to the "selection of the month," something called *Ballads* by someone named John Coltrane, and on a label[1] that meant very little to me at the time, for I knew only Tico, Fantasy, Verve, and Alegre—labels famous for Latin (what others now call Salsa) and Latin Jazz. The record played, and I was lyrically moved by the undulating lines and phrases of the musician's tempered saxophone. His tone, unmistakably different, seemed natural in color and liberating in its effect. There was something of the sacred and the mystical in what I heard.

John Coltrane was not the first (as far as I can tell) to move my sensibilities by showing me what Jazz could be. By then, Symphony Sid had been doing what he could to shape my taste. Over the radio, Sid's Latin was always fun but rarely charming (in shamanist sense), unless, of course, he happened to play—which was extremely rare—*santeria*. Much more charming (in shamanist sense again) was the Jazz, two compositions in particular: "I'm in the Mood for Love,"[2] a J. McHugh/D. Fields composition sung by King (Mr. Jazz) Pleasure; and "A Song for My Father,"[3] composed and performed by the underrated but highly influential (listen to Cecil Taylor, for example) Horace Silver, without whom Art Blakey's Jazz Messengers were never the same after he left. King Pleasure's scatting (improvisational singing?) and cascading melodies spoke to my adolescent dreams and wishes. There was a world in Pleasure—sometimes sensual and sometimes sexual, but always real and poetic—certainly to be learned, but more importantly to be explored.

Horace Silver's "A Song for My Father" also disclosed a world—not sensual or sexual, but mystical and holy, something to adore, to bless, and preserve. That too was charming. Neither song, however, ever lingered long enough to alter my view of what it meant to think. It took Coltrane's lyrical intonations to connect me to the Dolphic densities and sacred mysteries of Jazz and thought. His sinuous tenoring set the tone for my particular relationship to thinking as a sacred form. Coltrane allowed me to see and experience Jazz as Adorno, perhaps too tied to his own creative force (*la burguesa?*), could not: as a *window into being*, a passage to that highly illusive, and fundamentally aesthetic, lived and sometimes experienced quality on which Heidegger worked so (metaphysically) hard to language out.

But somehow the particular sense for thinking I acquired from the Jazz making of Coltrane fell victim to my transition to Madison, Wisconsin, and it was by chance, it seems, that I came to regain it. I was visiting, on a Sunday afternoon, I think, a fellow student from Cincinnati, a friend—a very good friend, as a matter of fact—when one of his sweater salesmen showed up as we talked, and I was introduced to him: a very gentle and amiable person named Jim Bullware (as I heard it, not as I learned it).

Jim needed a ride, so we took him home. In between, we talked, about what I don't recall, but, upon arriving at his flat, he invited me in for a glass of wine. I looked at Richard, and Richard looked at me and said: "Go ahead; I'll pick you up on the rebound." He was dropping someone else, as I recall.

I sensed my world transforming when I saw Jim take off his shoes just outside the door to his flat. Following his lead, I began to remove mine. Not until both of our acts were finished did Jim open the door, and, when he did, I could see as well as feel why. The soft lighting, dark colors, and carefully-arranged furnishings conveyed the sacred tones, which quickly struck my lost sense for Coltrane Jazz and the aesthetics of what it meant to think.

After drinking wine and picking chicken, Jim suggested music. We moved to the elegantly simple and religious-like living room and on the floor by the stereo system I saw it: the unforgettable face of King Pleasure on a record cover. "What would you like to listen to?" Jim asked in his gentle and quiet way. "That," I think I said, in my own tempered tone.

We did not listen long. But the little I heard was enough to fill the emptiness of those early Wisconsin days. I felt blessed again, with no remorse for not being at the dorm, where earlier I had agreed to be, to encourage white students to support black students in their struggle for rights.

I moved out of Adams Hall not too long after meeting Jim, and began listening again to John Coltrane, through whom I also got to know Ayler, Dolphy, Taylor, Giuffre, Sun Ra and many, many other Jazz makers too numerous to mention.[4] Jim I was unable to visit again. After running into him three times on campus, I never saw him again. Approximately two years after the visit to his flat, I learned from a fellow student teacher who had known him that he had died in Boston the year before from an overdose. I remember thinking in sadness, as she told me the news, what those few sacred moments we spent together on a Sunday evening had meant to me, and whether it really mattered that I had never come to know for certain the correct spelling of his name, which I had heard but not learned.

II

It is much clearer to me now why the Jazz making of Coltrane could be so liberating to thought. For Coltrane, Jazz was not just a different, entertaining, and highly technical way of making, arranging, and toning sound. It was a *sacred* and *liberating* tool, a way of exploring the spiritual, of transcending the profane and connecting oneself and others to inaccessible being. With Coltrane, jazz as entertainment gave way to Jazz as sacred act.

A Love Supreme,[5] *OM*,[6] and *Kulu Sé Mama*[7] are good illustrations of what I mean. All three works are concerned with celebrating the sacred as a universal condition or principle, not as a particular religion, dogma, or creed. Coltrane uses these works as opportunities for creating musical spaces which are intended as spiritual contexts where prayer, meditation, and ritual can be experienced *through* sound as particular ways of relating to the sacred in the world. In each work, Coltrane draws on different sacred forms to create the solemn contexts. In *A Love Supreme*, for example, the reliance is on Christianity; in *OM*, it is on Hinduism; and in *Kulu Sé Mama*, it is on Afro-Creolism.

The liberating tendencies of these and other works (*Meditations, Expressions*, and *Cosmic Music*, for example) came from Coltrane's radical approach to making Jazz. Coltrane's thoughtful invention frees the soloist to play either *vertically* (chordally) or *horizontally* (melodically) to create a kind of "flexibility-within-unity." Ira Gitler termed the style "sheets of sound" because of its multinote quality and the textural density it conveyed.[8] Built on the intellectual advances of other Jazz makers (Sydney Bechet, Charlie Parker, Thelonious Monk, Miles Davis, George Russell, Eric Dolphy, Ornette Coleman, Sun Ra, Cecil Taylor, and others), the innovation was put to good use in *Ascension*,[9] which is one, long, sustained improvisation that alternates group improvisations with individual solos.

In *Ascension*, only the ensemble passages, which were written as usual with notes and time values, and the order of soloing, which was designed to maximize changes in texture and prevent similar instruments from following each other, had any structure. The other sections were purposely left to each musician's interpretation by providing only pitch designations grouped in sets of four without time values. Since the lack of a set tempo prevented the use of a given bar to signal the changes to the musicians while performing the piece, a number system was used. The raising of one finger meant improvise on the first set of notes; the raising of two meant improvise on the second set; and so on. In retelling a story of how a traditional Persian carpet is made, Martin Hollis captures the reasoning behind Coltrane's improvising ways:

> A traditional Persian carpet, I am told, is woven on a mesh of threads placed upright between the master weaver and his minions. The minions hook coloured wools through the mesh on command, without seeing or knowing the pattern. He orchestrates, but not by working to a blueprint. Even if the commands could be precise enough, it would not be in the spirit of the business. The weaver conjures up the design as he goes along, by giving rough guidance and turning its results into something original and unique.[10]

Coltrane's reconstruction of the Jazz form went beyond improvisation to include changes in timbre and rhythm as well. The example here is *Africa Brass*.[11] In this piece, Coltrane frees himself of chords, and avoids the usual 3/4 and 4/4 rhythmic pattern by drawing on African rhythmic lines, which he tries to duplicate by using two basses. While one bass keeps a steady pulse throughout the piece, the other improvises. He also uses an instrumentation highly unusual to Jazz: a trumpet, four French horns, alto sax, flute, bass clarinet, tenor sax, two euphoniums, piano, drums, and tuba. In combination with the two basses, this radical blending of instruments works to expand the constraining tonal boundaries of monorhythm Jazz. *Africa Brass*, like a lot of other Coltrane music deeply rooted in the African tradition (e.g., *Kulu Sé Mama, Selflessness*, *Liberia*, and *Dahomey Dance*, is a colorful landscape of open sound, rich in polyrhythms and tones, and tempered by a steady drone.

III

Coltrane Jazz opens thought to thought. The music makes us think about those orders of knowledge and meaning (the religious, the aesthetic, the intuitive, the tacit, the so-called qualitative, and so on) that for some reason or other simply defy direct access. To grasp in any meaningful way these inaccessible forms (what I prefer to call *invisible being*) requires that they be approached *indirectly* through some kind of mediating process or experience. The way Coltrane came at the sacred in Jazz is one example. How Johann Friedrich Herbart, John Dewey,[12] and Harold Rugg[13] in curriculum making approached certain orders and textures of meaning offers others. In the case of Herbart, the way to moral being was through "an aesthetic revelation of the world," which was in turn obtainable through certain knowledge forms (for example, Greek and Roman history and Homeric mythology); a way into the act of knowing, in the case of Dewey, was through the basic "occupations" of our predecessors (cooking, building, gardening); and in Rugg, the route to imaginative creation was "a program of designed movement" (namely, choreography and dance). Perhaps the Herbart example is the one that comes closest to Coltrane's.

Herbart's own concern with moral being led him to see curriculum as liberation. The perspective defined the role of the curriculum maker (the teacher) in mediating and transcendency terms. The principal objective of teaching, that is, was to create passage to an aesthetic and moral experiencing of the world by providing a setting in which there could be intellectual movement "upwards" and "outwards" (Coltrane's vertical and horizontal improvising?). The movement upwards led to the *supersensuous*; the movement outwards, to the *actual*. Over time, increasing knowledge of the two would produce revelation of the beautiful and, hence, passage to the good. Herbart summarized it this way:

> While then through the reading of poets and historians, through growing knowledge of men, through moral and religious discourses which help to digest the previously collected material, the moral distinctions become sharper, observation of shades of character and the estimation of their distances by a moral measurement become rectified, and the elements of the practical (moral) idea of God gain increasingly in clearness and dignity thereby; – during all this there develops on the side of knowledge the concept of nature in increasing sharpness of outline, as the system of forces and motions, which rigorously persistent in a course once begun forms for us a type of law, and order, in sharply defined proportion . . . He goes forth to meet Providence, he seeks himself to join in her care for the race, he hears the summons to continue that which is begun, he realizes that theodicy is left to the actions of men.[14]

In the curriculum making of Herbart, as in the Jazz making of Coltrane, thinking liberates thinking. The focusing of thought on the inaccessible weakens the prevailing notions of thought as thought is required to take on sacred character. Thinking as skill, conception, or inquiry is made to make way to thinking as ethic or value, to what Francis Schrag calls "the virtue of being thoughtful":

> The thoughtful person avoids both impulsive and stereotyped responses because he or she is wont to do so. Thoughtfulness becomes instinctive, but it is not blind or mechanical since it derives from an appreciation of its own value ... Learning to be thought*ful* is *not* learning to perform a particular action nor is it acquiring a method of obtaining a particular result; it is developing a 'second nature' which transforms heart and mind.[15]

That there is no direct access to this "second nature" is not just the lesson of Herbart and Coltrane, but of others, such as Dewey and Rugg, as well. Only through the right settings, circumstances, and experiences can we pass into what it means to be thoughtful. The immense difficulty here for curriculum making, as well as for all other forms of human activity, is that the creation of a right context for promoting thoughtfulness itself depends on the act of being thoughtful. Are we trapped? The answer depends, I think, on how thoughtful we want and will to be. Political preferences and the concern for methodological and technical rigor cannot be allowed to dampen or limit our responsibility to be thoughtful. Attention must also be paid to aesthetic values and moral sensibilities. But more important still is the central role that freedom must play in the act of thought, which is perhaps the most important lesson to draw from Coltrane: without liberty to improvise, to be ourselves in exploring fully the limits and dimensions of our voicings, thoughtfulness is virtually impossible.

Very telling in this connection is Coltrane's fond response to the needling he often got from Miles Davis for having the reputation of taking such very long solos (sometimes over an hour) on the bandstand. "Why you play so long, man?" Miles would ask. "It took that long to get it all in," Coltrane would answer. Indeed, what else could he say? In Coltrane's world, the making of Jazz is an exercise in veneration, a sacred act whose enactment truly depends on the ability to improvise free of imposition and constraint. That is what, for me at least, makes his music making such a powerful metaphor for what it means to think, not just in curriculum but in life in general.

NOTES

1. Impulse Records A-32

2. United Artists Jazz 14012

3. Blue Note 81518

4. For an introduction to the music of these artists *see* Leroi Jones, *Black Music* (New York: W. Morrow, 1967).

5. Impulse Records A-77.

6. Impulse Records A-9140.

7. Impulse Records A-9106.

8. *Down Beat*, October 16, 1958, pp.16-17.

9. Impulse Records A-95.

10. Martin Hollis, *The Cunning of Reason* (Cambridge: Cambridge University Press, 1987), p. 47.

11. Impulse Records A-6.

12. John Dewey, *Experience and Education* (New York: Macmillan, 1938).

13. Harold Rugg, *Imagination* (New York: Harper and Row Pub., 1963).

14. Johann F. Herbart, *The Science of Education and the Aesthetic Revelation of the World* (Boston: D.C. Heath & Co., 1893), p. 75.

15. Francis Schrag, *Thinking in School and Society* (London: Routledge, 1988), p. 80.

14

TED T. AOKI

Sonare and *Videre*: Questioning the Primacy of the Eye in Curriculum Talk

I Skate in Tensionality; I In-dwell in Music

It happened during a lingering Canadian winter of 1987. During a rare television sitting, I was lured by a Canadian Broadcasting Corporation episode in which Barbara Frum interviewed Brian Orser, a Canadian figure skater of some note. Experiencing something that might speak to curriculum, I wrote in my personal notebook my interpretation of the interview I had just seen and heard. Under the title, "I skate in tensionality; I in-dwell in music," I wrote the following:

> On March 12, Brian Orser touched many of us when he, standing tall on the podium, eyes uplifted, unabashedly allowed tears that welled up to roll down his cheeks uncontrolled as the swell of "O Canada" resounded through him. He was being crowned in Cincinnati as the men's world figure skating champion.
>
> In an interview with Barbara Frum the day after, Brian was asked about his experience of the 4½ minutes of his free skating number. "How calm were you as you were skating?" Frum asked.
>
> Brian answered, "No, I was not calm. Calmness was not what I wanted. I was in tension—in a good tension that surged throughout my whole body." Then, he spoke of the practice sessions geared to allowing him to experience different forms of tension, firmly regarding that skating well means not the presence of calmness or tranquility but rather the appropriately tensioned in-dwelling that allows his body and soul to resonate well with the surface of the ice, with the music, with the spectators."
>
> His remarks remind me of Daisetzu Suzuki, a noted Zen master, who spoke of Nature in the following way:

> "It is not a sense of . . . tranquility that must be seen. . . . To seek tranquility is to kill nature, to stop its pulsation, and to embrace the dead corpse that is left behind. Advocates of tranquility are worshipers of abstraction and death."[1]
>
> These remarks give voice to Brian Orser's words on good tensionality which speak to the shimmering pulsation, vivifying animation that is experience when it is attuned aright with the world.
>
> When later in the interview, Barbara Frum commented how in his performance his skating seemed to reflect well the shift in mood of the music, Brian responded,
>
> "When I skate well, as I feel I did in my number, I become the music. I do not skate to music as if it were outside of me. I become the music. My skating is the music."
>
> In my view Brian speaks not from the world wherein subject and object are twin poles. His is a world beyond such fragmentation; his is a world in which his very being shimmers and pulsates, a world in which his skating sings, a world in which he is the skating. (Penned, March 17, 1987).

I linger in this story and allow myself to be drawn into four themes that echoingly call upon me.

Theme 1: To Be Alive Is to Experience Tensionality. In our North American tradition, we tend to appropriate tension negatively. We seem to succumb to an urging within us to reduce it or even to eliminate it. For example, in our pedagogic practice, teacher stress is regarded as a debilitating form of tensionality, something we ought to, if we can, demolish or diminish. Yet, listening to Brian Orser, we sense that to be alive is to be in some kind of tension and that to be tensionless, like a limp violin string, is to be dead. To be alive humanly, then, is to be in appropriate tautness such that sound resounds well. Tensionality and aliveness seem to be kindred human modalities.

As curriculum people interested in resonance between teacher and students, the question seems to be not so much the issue of presence or nonpresence of tensionality in pedagogic relationships, but more so the question of the quality of tensionality.

Brian Orser practiced, so he said, striving so that his entire body could be alert to different experiences of tensionality. In the midst of action that is skating, he seemed to be seeking forms of embodied tensionality that know resonance with the surface of the ice, with the music, and with the spectators (so-called). Such a knowing known bodily seems vastly different from rational knowing that knows action only derivatively as application. Indeed, Orser's seeking is for something fundamentally different. He is not calling for a letting go that diminishes the habituated think-and-do modality; rather, he is calling for an attunement such that thinking and acting simultaneously inhabit his body—indeed, embodied thinking which by diminishing the hold of the habitual allows the coming into being of ecstatic tensionality that is Brian Orser when his skating truly sings.

Theme 2: Towards Inspirited Curriculum. In our story, Orser said, "'When I skate well, . . . I do not skate to music." He was saying, so it seems to me, that he does not find music distanced from him, outside of him. Rather, as he said, he becomes the music.

Here, I am reminded of The Elementary Fine Arts Music Curriculum in British Columbia wherein we find voiced a two folded attunement to curriculum given as two strands:

Strand 1: "The learning about music strand" urging "a study about music and the role of music in society past and present," and

Strand 2: "the living in music strand wherein children are actually involved with music through the activities of singing, listening, playing, etc."[2]

Strand 1 is attuned to the positivistically inclined, intellectually visual world of music, including what we typically call the abstract theoretical and technical in music. Strand 2, on the other hand, is attuned to lived experiences wherein teachers and students are called upon to live in music. Although in this curriculum guide, the text calls upon teachers to consider the coexistence of these two strands, something more is being said unsaid. There is an implicit layeredness of the two strands when we listen to the curriculum guide as it leans on an excerpt from Plato: "Education in music is most sovereign because more than anything else, rhythm and harmony find their way into the secret places of the soul."[3]

We sense that Strand 2 is the existential ground that makes Strand 1 possible. That in curriculum discourse there is explicit interest in touching the soul is excitingly satisfying.

The two folded texture of music in the British Columbia Music Curriculum allows curriculum workers another thought. It alerts us to possible misguidedness of any curriculum that seeks univocity, the call of a single voice given to abstractive generalizability, province-wide or state-wide.

Recently, Wendell Berry,[4] concerned about abstract global talk, pointed to the futility of global thinking that univocalizes thoughts-in-the-abstract. Abstract voices, he said, cannot hear the concrete voices of the situationally lived. Necessarily, indifference begins to reign. Necessarily, abstract life leads to a half-life, soulless life. Centralized curriculum given to univocity floats in air. It is a futile preoccupation because it is indifferent to situated voices of teachers and students. Our British Columbia Music Curriculum, by advocating two strands, avoids the half-life, nourishing instead voices that flow from the human soul.

Theme 3: Opening up to Sonare. In the Orser story is the comment: "Brian speaks not from the world wherein subject and object are twin poles; his is a world in which his skating sings." Likewise, in the B. C. Music Curriculum, we noted an interest in in-dwelling in the midst of music.

Listening to the foregoing carefully allows us to become thoughtful of how we may have become beholden to the metaphor of the I/eye—the I that sees. The notion of the objective world we are so familiar with assumes the nexus of subject and object in which the prime connecting mode is observation with the eye, the key to understanding the scientific-instrumentalist posture assumed by so many curriculum workers. We fail to see how we are caught and held within the metaphor of *videre* (to see), speaking mainly of what eyes can see. We revel in words such as *images*, *perceptions*, *sights* and *insights*, *visions* and *envisionings*, and phrases such as "illuminations that allow us to see more clearly".

I wonder if in our enchantment with the eye there does not lurk a danger of too hurriedly foreclosing the horizon where we live as teachers and students. I am reminded of Ludwig Wittgenstein, who late in his life as scholar taught school so he might be nearer to understanding how students come to understand language. He spoke of how in the West the world of language has come to overemphasize and overrely upon visuality, thereby diminishing the place of other ways of being in the world.

Could it be that the time is right for us to allow *sonare* to dwell juxtaposedly with *videre*? If, indeed, we as earth dwellers are interested in heeding the call of *humus* in the midst of which we humans dwell, might we offer ourselves to listen to its soundings and resoundings, to the tone of sound, perhaps even to the tone of silence, which some say is the mother of sound? Could it be that in *sonare* is found a way to be in the midst of sound in silence? Or to be in the midst of the sound of silence?

Theme 4: Sonic Polyphony: Beyond Harmony. In the B. C. Music Curriculum we noted its appeal to Plato, who said, "Education in music is most sovereign because more than anything else . . . rhythm and harmony find their way into the secret places of the soul."

Harmony, as Plato, an early metaphysicist, understood it, is a fitting together, a con-c(h)ord, a synthesis of sounds—a sonic univocity. In our Western tradition we are given to a notion of harmony as a goodness that is thought to be in accord with that which is natural and true. But could it be that such an understanding of con-joining is a reflection of our caughtness in our own creation, a metaphysical notion of oneness, a harmonic oneness?

Recently, I heard Edwin Dumas, a music teacher in British Columbia, speak of contrapuntality in certain of Bach's fugues. Speaking to curriculum-oriented people who, like me, are non-musicians but fascinated with the notion and sound of the contrapuntal, he had us listen to the contra-ness of five lines of a fugue. Edwin pointed to a sonic realm in which five lines co-exist in polyphonic tensionality, whose openness within its own space contrasted sharply with the closedness of synthetic harmony.

Could it be that within this sonic texture the belonging together of Orser's skating "with the ice, with the music, with the spectators" could be understood as a polyphonic tensionality? Could it be, too, that the belonging together of the two strands of the B. C. Music Curriculum might be understood not as harmonic unity but rather as polyphonic tensionality? Could it be that such an understanding allows us to let go of our inclination to totalistic, harmonic wholeness and to open us to the threshold of a space which, like a frontier, acknowledges both the limits of the *is* and the openness to the stirrings of sounds yet silent?

Lingering Notes

Currently, I am in the midst of reading a manuscript entitled *Toward Curriculum for Being: Voices of Educators*.[5] It sparkles with the voices of five university educators who have been in conversation about curriculum and pedagogy for four years. In it are narratives of these educators in their hermeneutic effort who insistently opened themselves to the realm beyond generalizable, abstractive knowings. In these writings, they searched for embodied knowings that disclose insights. With such interest, their discourse frequently relied on images that depend on sightings of the eye. But, over these years, increasingly, we find their discourse relying on metaphors that pertain to the ear, reflected in wordings such as "listening to callings," "seeking attunement," "finding resonances," "the tonal quality of voices." Their discourse began to reflect both the world of sight and the world of sound.

In their search for an understanding of curriculum for being, they immersed themselves in the notion of "personhood." Could it be that in their search for the ground of being, consciously or unconsciously they found resonance with the original etymological understanding of the word *person* as *per* (through)/*sonare* (to sound)—reminiscent, as we have already noted, of Wittgenstein's questioning of modernism's fidelity to the primacy of the visual.

Another note. The manuscript resounds with five voices. In my endeavor to understand these voices, I became more mindful of what I heard as I read. I became sensitive to the polysonic lines of these voices. I began to understand these voices not so much as a melding of these voices in a concert of closure, for I sensed a distinct resistance in their voices to closure. Rather, they seemed to celebrate openness to openness. I liken these five voices not to a symphonic harmony of oneness, but, as in Edwin Dumas' interpretation of a Bach fugue, to a sonic polyphony of five lines in contrapuntal interplay, in a tensionality of differences.

A polyphonic curriculum that decenters *videre* by allowing a legitimate place for *sonare* might indeed be a way to help us in a curriculum venture that attempts to find fresh meaning in emerging curriculum discourses.

A final note. A forgetful academic being that I am, in my musings about *sonare* and *videre*, I have already forgotten what Wendell Berry told us about how the abstract tends to lead us to a forgetfulness of our human beingness as teachers.

Almost blushingly, I seek to re-touch the earth, mindful that like Brian Orser and others, I, too, am an earth dweller. So as earth dweller, I respond to the call of Mary Wilke, and in responding, I in-dwell in her prose poem, "All I Wanted Was to Sing"[6]:

When I was in first grade
I loved to sing.
When it was my turn, I'd stand up
and sing clearly and happily,
thoroughly enjoying myself.
My teacher declared me singing champion . . .

Why did something as innocent and joyful
as the music of small children
have to be turned into a contest?
The voices should have been
sources of joy, not pride or shame.
But my first grade teacher thought
that my talent should be brandished
in front of my peers . . .

My joy became a mixture
of pride and shame,
and as time went on
shame overshadowed pride . . .
My teacher was the one who wanted
a champion;
all I wanted was to sing.

ACKNOWLEDGMENT

"All I Wanted Was to Sing" is reprinted by permission of the author, Mary Wilke.

NOTES

1. This saying by Daisetzu Suzuki, a noted Zen master, is quoted in Rolof Beny, *Japan in Colour* (London: Thames and Hudson Publishers, 1967.), p. 8.

2. T. Aoki, "Understanding Forms of Curriculum Balance in The British Columbia School Curriculum", a report commissioned in 1987 by The Continuing Education Department, School District #44 (North Vancouver, British Columbia), under the terms of UNESCO Contract, "National Case Study on Distribution and Balance of The Content of General Education." These excerpts describing the two strands of the music curriculum are found on pp. 11 and 12.

3. The Ministry of Education, British Columbia, Canada, *The Secondary Music Curriculum/Resource Guide*, 1980, p. 1.

4. Wendell Berry, "The Futility of Global Thinking" (*Harper's*, September 1989). The article itself is an adaptation from "Word and Flesh", a commencement address given at the College of The Atlantic in Bar Harbor, Maine.

5. The manuscript referred to, *Toward Curriculum for Being: Voices of Educators,* is in preparation for publication. The five voices are those of Dr. Louise Berman, Dr. Francine Hultgren, Dr. Jessie Roderick, Dr. Dianne Lee, and Dr. Mary Rivkin, all associated with the University of Maryland. (Albany, NY: SUNY Press, In Press)

6. "All I Wanted Was to Sing" is from Mark Link, ed., *In the Stillness is the Dancing* (Niles, Ill: Argus Communications, 1972), p. 53.

15

SUSAN W. STINSON

Dance as Curriculum, Curriculum as Dance

I was a dancer and dance educator long before I thought of myself as a curriculum theorist. It was only after many years in dance that I seriously began asking questions that took me outside my original field, questions that eventually led me to a study of curriculum theory and practice. Today I walk in both worlds, but they are intertwined for me. Dance gives me a center, a place to start from; curriculum is the continuing journey.

When I say that dance gives me a starting place, this recognizes my awareness that all insights, including those in curriculum, begin with personal knowledge—what we know 'in our bones.' It is reflection on this personal knowledge that allows us to extend our boundaries and make important connections to the world. For example, I know in my body that my shoulders will go where they belong if I release them, allowing them to widen; proper alignment is not attained by pulling one's shoulders back or holding them down. My study of body therapies has led me to marvel at how the body is constructed, so that a dancer's job becomes to understand the internal connections and release into them, not to control natural impulses. This is a dramatic change from the relationship to my body that I first learned in dance, where it was an adversary to overcome. Such knowledge is not just for the dancer in me. When I reflect upon it, and ask, "What does this mean for me as a person in the world?" I recognize that it also tells me about other relationships we attempt to control. *Control* is as much an issue in curriculum as it is in dance: we fear that institutions, as well as bodies, will not work without control. From my dance experience, I know that understanding relationships, and releasing into them, provides an alternative to control that allows, rather than inhibits, movement and growth. This knowledge guides my thinking about curriculum and teaching, as I seek to find relationships to my students that allow us to work together without my attempting to control them.

For a time, I thought that my 'body-level knowing'—images on which I could reflect—was a characteristic peculiar to dancers. I remember feeling so affirmed when I read that Einstein's ideas first came to him as "visual and kinesthetic images" and the words came later (cited in North 1973). I am convinced that the origination of ideas takes place on a sensory level: we see or feel an idea first, and then form it into a language. Until knowledge takes on form—the symbols of a language—we do not know what we know, but the store of sensory experiences like the ones I have from dance is a necessary prerequisite.

When I speak of sensory experience, it is not the same as mere activity. To sense myself moving is different from just moving. In fact, this sensory awareness is a primary difference between dancing and other forms of movement: to dance is not just to move, but to sense oneself moving.

I am no longer a dancer in the way I was when spending six to eight hours a day in studio or theater; today I spend little more time moving than most adults. But now I recognize that each moment is an opportunity to experience myself dancing, if I choose to shift my consciousness in that direction. As I tell my students, dance is not so much a matter of what we do as how we do it. When I walk, reach, turn, rock a child, hug a friend—I am not only doing, but sensing. Sensory awareness is the raw material from which metaphors are made. Perhaps metaphors come more readily to artists, not because they are innately creative, but because they immerse themselves in the sensory.

Metaphors are important not only in the arts, but in curriculum theorizing. Over the years I have affirmed for myself Jim Macdonald's belief that metaphor is at the root of curriculum theory. Theory speaks of relationships—and relationships are not just a matter of abstract language. I think back to a curriculum theory course I took with Macdonald during my doctoral program. He had described for us a number of commonly used metaphors in education: the empty vessel (to be filled with knowledge), the garden (in which students are the flowers to be cultivated by teachers), the factory (in which students proceed along an assembly line of learning). The assignment given was to come up with a metaphor of our own. Immediately into my consciousness came the concept of *improvisation*, a central part of my dance experience. Improvisation—creating movement as one goes along—is ordinarily based on a clear theme (such as meeting and parting) or structure (such as a rhythmic pattern), or otherwise comes with specific limits or ground rules (such as the requirement to stay in constant contact with at least one other dancer). The responsibility of the participants is to be open to the movement that develops, rather than trying to control it or make it go in a predetermined direction, and to stay constantly aware of and sensitive to other participants. The structure provides boundaries, but within those one expects surprises and discoveries. Sometimes even the boundaries change. Improvisation seemed to me then, as it does now, an apt metaphor for a process in which teachers and students engage together with mutual respect for each other, and lesson plans provide only a structure within which all participants can make meaningful discoveries.

But when I look back at my description of improvisation, I am aware that I know much more of improvisation than I have written or could write. As Polanyi (1966) reminds me, we know more than we can say. When I thought of improvisation as a metaphor for education, I did not just think in words. It was all that I knew of improvisation on a body level that generated the connection for me: recollections of joyous times in improvisation groups with my peers, for the pleasure of dancing together; alone times in the studio trying to generate movement material for choreography; threatening times, taking the risk necessary to improvise in front of critical teachers and peers. It was such visual and kinesthetic images which allowed me to find the connection between dancing and education, and which allowed my metaphor to appear.

I became most aware of the significance of sensory awareness in generating metaphors when I was working on my dissertation (Stinson 1984). I was dealing with the relationship between the ethical and the aesthetic dimensions of human existence as they related to dance education—an abstract topic indeed. I was trying to figure out my conceptual framework, but all of my attempts felt like empty words, disconnected from what I cared about so deeply. Following a suggestion from my advisor David Purpel, I began to write short pieces about moments that seemed important in my life. These were stories, full of sensory language that reminded me of the whole experience they were describing. Some were stories of dancing. Others came from my life as a child, a mother, a student, a teacher, a friend. All were moments I had lived, experiences embedded in my body but accessible to consciousness. As I tuned in more and more to such experiences, my awareness of even everyday activity was heightened. One day, still searching for the elusive framework that would reveal what my dissertation was 'really' about, I returned from a long walk (trying to 'clear my brain') and lay down to rest—and became acutely aware of how I perceived myself and the world differently when I was standing compared to when I was lying down. Within moments I knew my framework, which was based upon a metaphor of verticality (the impulse toward achievement and mastery—being on top) and horizontality (the impulse toward relationship and community—being with). I sensed how being horizontal felt passive and vulnerable and the return to the vertical made me feel strong and powerful, important insights as to the holds these impulses have over us. Once I had identified this dual reality in my own body, I recognized it in the work of others: Bakan (1966), who spoke of agency and communion; Koestler (1978), who referred to self-assertion and integration; and Fromm (1941), who wrote of freedom and security. But until I knew it 'in my bones' I did not know it; I was unable to think creatively with the concept and see it in relationship to the issues with which I was dealing.

I am convinced, then, that we can think only with what we know in our bones; sensory awareness is the clay, and thinking forms the clay. (I have also experienced art-making in this medium, or this metaphor probably would not have arisen for me.) Yet the clay cannot form itself. The forming process is the acting on sensory awareness to create ideas in symbolic form, whether the form is art or curriculum.

The process of giving form to ideas is similar for me in curriculum and in choreography. Thinking is a dance; ideas have shape and weight, and I first feel connections between ideas as energy. Sometimes I start with assembled data or materials, as I have done in my recent work (Stinson, Blumenfeld-Jones, Van Dyke, 1990) involving in depth interviews with young women, regarding the meaning their dancing has for them. From pages filled with their words, I sought patterns of relationships (which I could sense before I could explain); this is akin to choreography when one begins with the improvised movement of dancers, then structures and extends that movement to make a dance. Other times I start with nothing concrete—only my own images or impulses—and have only myself with which to develop them. In this case, facing empty paper is like facing empty space in a studio: there must be an engagement in the process before having a really clear idea of what the outcome will be. It is only once pencil meets paper that the curricular ideas take form. In both choreography and theory, form and content develop simultaneously: I do not know fully what an idea is until I have found the appropriate symbols for expressing it, whether those symbols are in movement or words.

This awareness helps me in guiding graduate students in dance through the various theory courses I teach. Some of these students, with well-developed skills in dance, are beginners in terms of conceptualizing and developing their ideas in written form; many are also fearful of the process and doubt their verbal abilities. Use of the choreographic model not only gives them confidence, but guides their way over what increasingly begins to feel like familiar territory.

In addition to providing the intimate knowing that is the raw material for ideas, and a model for the forming process, my experience in dance has made certain ideas in curriculum seem like friends I already knew. When I read Elliot W. Eisner's suggestion that one might evaluate education through a process similar to art criticism (1979), it made complete sense to me. Maxine Greene's work has been a frequent companion, not only because of her frequent use of images from the arts, but because she sees the kind of engagement one ideally makes with certain works of art as a model for what ought to be happening throughout the curriculum (Greene 1978). This has fueled my own work in thinking about the aesthetic dimensions of curriculum (Stinson 1985). And Madeleine R. Grumet's references to body (1988) resonate deeply with me. Jim Macdonald's important piece "A Transcendental Developmental Ideology of Education" (1978) is another example, affirming the awareness I had, from dance, of the significance of transcendent experience. He used further language familiar to me when he wrote that "The aim of education should be a centering of the person in the world" (Macdonald 1978, 112). While many of my peers found this a very abstract statement, I knew the meaning of centering on a body level; it was only a matter of extension to sense what Macdonald meant when he used the term.

I had the pleasure of serving as a guest lecturer in Macdonald's special course entitled "Personal and Social Transcendence," in which personal transcendent experiences in the arts provided a model or a guide for imagining new possibilities—"how things might be"—in education and in the world, and imagining oneself as a creator in and of the world. It is at this point—when speaking of the link between personal and social transcendence—that I must acknowledge the limits of my dance experience, as well as what it contributed to the person that I am. My education in dance taught me that I am strong and creative, but only within the walls of the studio or theater. Dance can be so satisfying, and make one feel so whole, that it is easy to use it as an escape from a difficult and often dangerous world. Once I admitted I was using dance as a way to escape, I considered leaving the field entirely, because it began to seem too trivial in the face of the 'big problems of the world', and, in fact, was riddled with its own problems. Now I recognize that dance does not have to serve as my final destination, but in fact can be a launching pad into the world.

In addition to sometimes serving as an escape, dance, like anything else, can begin to seem like a fixed entity, rather than a human creation which can be changed. My recent listening to the voices of young dancers (Stinson, Blumenfeld-Jones, Van Dyke, 1990) has affirmed my own experience that it is all too easy to reify dance as something one must fit into as it is, if one wishes to take part at all. Dancers tend to see only how dance creates them; they have a harder time recognizing that the dance world is something that we make and that, therefore, it can be remade. Recognizing this phenomenon in dance helps me realize why it is also hard to remember that society is similarly a human construct. This is one of the many ways in which dance is a microcosm of the larger world; it gives me a laboratory, so to speak, in which I can identify both problems and possibilities that also exist in society.

Dance is like any other human activity, holding both possibilities and limitations. It is only when we recognize the latter that the former can be fully realized. Therefore I find it necessary to be a critic as well as a supporter of the arts in education and of the aesthetic dimension in education. The arts can make us more conscious, or can anaesthetize us to the world outside; they can be a way to find ourselves or to lose ourselves. Attending to the aesthetic dimension can make us more human or less so, depending upon what we mean by the "aesthetic dimension." Today my work in curriculum is grounded in dance but not limited to it. My writing relates to curriculum in dance and to aesthetic dimensions of all curriculum. Dance helps me to recognize what often gets left out of curricular language (transcendence, wholeness of body/mind/spirit) and to appreciate such ideas when I meet them. Dance is the home to which I return for the nourishment of sensory awareness that becomes the raw material of ideas, and for insights into the process of forming ideas. Dance is the laboratory which helps put social and cultural problems into terms I can recognize. It is a magnifying glass for finding myself and a lens for looking at the world. This does not imply for me that one must dance in order to be able to do curriculum, but that it is important to educate the senses, including the kinesthetic sense (which comes from the nerve endings in muscles and joints), as a critical component in thinking. The arts, including dance, are needed in education as an important source of sensory awareness and understanding of form. Yet such understanding should not stop with itself. Educators must help students build bridges between personal and social experience, and recognize that the arts have been most important throughout human history as a way to understand the world and oneself in it. Hopefully, the arts can then help students discover their thinking/feeling/doing selves that can go back out into the world, better able to make sense of what they experience there and to do something about it.

16

LANDON E. BEYER

The Arts and Education: Personal Agency and Social Possibility

The arts held an important place in my personal life long before an interest in curriculum issues became a focus of my professional endeavors. Both in terms of the creation of works of art (earlier centering on music and poetry and later on photography, film, and environmental aesthetics) and in their appreciation, the arts have been a source of fascination, meaning, and insight. The most difficult aspect of writing this essay has, in fact, turned out to be limiting my focus to one or two examples of art works that have affected my understanding of curriculum issues and the nature of inquiry in the curriculum field. Any such essay must also include, unavoidably, some indication of the affects of such works on my understanding of what it means to live a decent life. I seek, then, to indicate, through one or two examples, something of the range of aesthetic meaning, personal impact, and social vision which the arts are perhaps uniquely suited to provide. After thinking about possible choices for a considerable time, I choose two interrelated works—one of which is a song within the other artwork, a film—that illustrate how the arts at their best have affected my perceptions of curriculum matters and, hence, of what sort of personal and social worlds are possible.

I first saw *The Women of Summer* a few years ago during an annual meeting of the American Educational Studies Association.[1] It had a profound visual/aesthetic and personal/political impact on my views of education and teaching as well as furthering my understanding of the dynamics of gender, class, race, and ethnicity in American social life. This film documents the reunion and celebration of a group of women who were enrolled in the Bryn Mawr Summer School for Women Workers in the 1920s and 1930s. Among the powerful stories and images conveyed in the film, I was especially taken by the reminiscences of one of the students who recalled her participation in demonstrations surrounding the trial and execution of Sacco and Vanzetti. These reminiscences were punctuated by the song, "Two Good Arms," performed in the film by Holly Near and Ronnie Gilbert. For me, the meaning of the events chronicled in "Two Good Arms" was extended when I heard it performed by its composer, Charlie King, at a small gathering of social and political activists in Peoria, Illinois, during the spring of 1989. It brought back some of the central messages of *The Women of Summer*—the importance of historical consciousness and continuity, of social struggle and political solidarity, and of individuals who manage to create and live within genuine communities.

The Bryn Mawr program provided an opportunity for working class women—many of whom were factory workers who subsequently became union organizers, actively involved in community and political projects—to experience something of the kind of educational experiences that would otherwise have been unavailable. Perhaps more importantly, the sort of education these women demanded, and at least partially attained, illustrates what teaching and curriculum inquiry might mean for us within our own contemporary settings. I have shown this film to undergraduates probably a dozen times since I first saw it, and I always find it an inspirational, moving, and humbling experience from which I learn a great deal with each viewing. I worry about the occasional viewer who seems not to be alternately moved to laughter, tears, and anger.

The women attending the reunion openly share their personal and political motivations for attending the summer sessions, and the effect their educational experiences had on them during the ensuing half century or so after their participation in the program. They also recount their deep self-doubts about enrolling in the summer school initially. As working class women whose own public school educations were frequently short-lived and of less than outstanding quality, trying to survive the economic blight of the years just before and during the depression, they were led to blame themselves or doubt their own abilities. Looking forward to a work life consisting of factory labor that offered little personal fulfillment and few avenues for creative and social action, and a personal life dominated by an exclusionary emphasis on patriarchal relations within the family, the idea of attending a "seven sisters," private, elite college seemed remote and daunting indeed for many of these women.

The educational experiences they constructed for themselves were directly related to their past lives; their interest in political, economic, and social issues that arose within that context and in the context of contemporary U.S. society; and the prospects for restructuring personal and social realities. Classes formed around concerns that were central to these women, together with the input of faculty from a variety of backgrounds who tended not to be constrained by artificial academic boundaries that so often separate disciplines, methodologies, and people. The film brilliantly captures the dynamic interconnections between the personal and the political, education and social justice, and historical and contemporary ideas and possibilities. One woman recounts looking through a telescope for the first time, and how that view of the stars allowed her to see their relevance to her life and to nonpossessively claim them for herself; another former student talks about the plays and skits the students put on, as the film projects visual images of those plays, which illustrated the conflicts between capital and labor, worker and supervisor; another participant discusses the importance of poetry in her life and in the summer school programs; and other women discuss their and faculty members' involvement in political activities, demonstrations, and local strikes. The development of personal control over their lives both at Bryn Mawr and later is powerfully conveyed through these women's recollections.

One of the contemporary events that was of intense concern to many students was the trial and death of Sacco and Vanzetti. Some of them attended demonstrations that conveyed their outrage at the "system of justice" that convicted these men, and participated in vigils that marked their death. The personal anguish felt by students during these events, and their sense of loss, determination, and struggle, is captured in the song, "Two Good Arms," performed at the student reunion:

> Who will remember the hands so white and fine
> That touched the finest linen, that poured the
> finest wine
> Who will remember the genteel words they spoke
> That named the lives of two good men a nuisance
> or a joke.

Chorus:
And all who know these two good arms
Know I never had to rob or kill
I can live by my own two hands and live well
And all my life I have struggled
To rid the earth of all such crimes.

Who will remember Judge Webster Thayer
One hand on the gavel, the other resting
on the chair
Who will remember the hateful words he said
Speaking to the living in the language of the dead.

Chorus:
And all who know these two good arms
Know I never had to rob or kill
I can live by my own two hands and live well
And all my life I have struggled
To rid the earth of all such crimes.

Who will remember the hand that pulled the switch
That took the lives of two good men in the service
of the rich
Who will remember the one who gave the nod
Or the chaplain standing near at hand to invoke
the name of God.

Chorus:
And all who know these two good arms
Know I never had to rob or kill
I can live by my own two hands and live well
And all my life I have struggled
To rid the earth of all such crimes.

We will remember this good shoemaker
We will remember this poor fish peddler
We will remember all the strong arms and hands
That never once found justice in the hands that
rule this land.

Chorus:
And all who knew these two good men
Knew they never had to rob or kill
Each had lived by his own two hands
And lived well

And all their lives they had struggled
To rid the earth of all such crimes
And all our lives we must struggle
To rid the earth of all such crimes.[2]

Hearing Charlie King perform this and other songs to a small group of social activists earlier this year added another level of meaning to the song, and to the struggles of the Bryn Mawr students. This was partly the result of the lyrics and music themselves—the images of immigrants who were guilty by association, of questions regarding what and which people are worth remembering, of the necessity of seeing our own work as allied with the struggles of others. In addition, the words and music of King's performance became instantly connected for me to the pictures of Sacco and Vanzetti that had been included in *The Women of Summer*, thus providing another connection between the concert and the film. Charlie King's own stories and songs, and his obvious determination to combine a commitment to social justice with the arts at a considerable economic sacrifice (who would agree to perform a concert for fifty people in Peoria?), provided other examples of the connectedness and passion that had been apparent in the film.

One of the things that continually impresses me about the characters in *The Women of Summer* is their very concern for, and awareness of, the social and historical contexts of their actions as workers, women, and students. They evidenced an increasingly uncommon concern that a sense of historical consciousness be conveyed to contemporary and future students and educational institutions. The women in the film clearly see themselves as people engaged with a much larger set of issues and actions, interconnected with both people and events who preceded and will follow them. This contextualization of both personal and social life—the connectedness of people and the struggles that animate and give meaning to their lives—is something that I strive to convey to my own students, and that has been a central concern in my own understanding of issues in curriculum and teaching.

The film ends by having the alumnae sit for a portrait, with one woman providing a narration. In these final remarks, the narrator acknowledges the passing of many of the former students, "one by one," and wonders if future generations will continue the work that they took over from their own foremothers and forefathers. It is a touching moment that exemplifies the historical ties they feel and that we might share with our own students. Together with the opening lines of "Two Good Arms," it pushes us to consider again which things we remember and are worth remembering, the communities of people and ideas of which we are a part, and the sort of commitment that must be made if our own educational undertakings are to make a difference.

One of the central issues that many of us in curriculum have been wrestling with recently concerns the split that can often be seen by those who recognize an independent social or institutional structure that is to some extent determining and those who accentuate the importance of personal agency and autonomy. This issue is expressed in different ways (structural influences/autonomy, critical theory/existentialism, conceptual analysis and autobiography), and arises in a number of contexts (the classroom, research agendas and styles, various educational and philosophical schools of thought). Within the curriculum field, this division is the familiar one that separates some neo-Marxist scholarship from some writing of a more mythico-poetic form. Both personal antagonisms and conflicting analyses have sometimes developed as a result of this split between structural and personal emphases.

This is not a new finding, of course, and many people in the field have sought ways to bridge the conceptual and perceptual gap that separates the various advocacy groups that have formed. In fact in the past few years there have been many well-intentioned attempts to heal the wounds that have developed over time along these lines. My own teaching has recently centered on undergraduates who are preparing to become public school teachers. I have tried to help them see that while there are real material and ideological constraints on what counts as legitimate activities in schools and elsewhere, and while the origins of many current issues have historical, social, and political roots and rhizomes that often become quite entangled, these constraints are not impermeable nor indestructible. As people who work and struggle together we can make a difference. At the same time, it is equally important for us to realize that as individuals working alone and together, we are capable of creating spaces for educative work that is transformative, both personally and socially.

Here, it seems to me, the arts at their best provide examples of this unification of personal voice and social power. They provide testimony to the force of the individual self and to the kind of communal transformation in which the self is realized and simultaneously heightened. To see teachers as more or less caught in a web of structural constraints beyond their control, or as individuated professionals operating from a knowledge base that ensures a disengaged competence in students, is to deny our role as moral agents engaged in the recreation of ourselves and our worlds. *The Women of Summer* and "Two Good Arms" are insightful, moving reminders of the contexts within which individuals live and work, and of the remarkable accomplishments of which we are capable when we see our lives as directly connected to those who came before and those who will follow us and when we see our actions as dedicated to the common good.

The current political and social context is far from an ideal time in which to help further the critical analyses of curriculum issues in which I have been involved. Both domestic and foreign affairs work against the kind of critical, reflective, contextualized view of education and schooling I seek to develop with my students. It is easy, at least occasionally, to wonder if this sort of work makes a difference, and to devolve into self-doubt and even, from time to time, cynicism. *The Women of Summer* and "Two Good Arms" are personally inspirational for me, even as they illustrate the distance between much of what currently is and what has been and might be again. That sense of creative tension, ambiguity, and even melancholy seems to me a central part of what the power of the arts consists in, as they provide new ways of understanding ourselves and our worlds, and our possible selves and worlds. The two works only sketched here provide, to my mind, excellent examples of this power of the aesthetic form.

ACKNOWLEDGMENT

The words of the song "Two Good Arms" by Charlie King are printed by permission of the composer.

NOTES

1. "The Women of Summer," produced by Suzanne Bauman and funded through the National Endowment for the Humanities, is

available through Filmaker's Library, 133 East 58th Street, New York, NY 10022.

2. Charlie King, "Two Good Arms," copyright 1977, PIED ASP MUSIC (BMI), performed by Holly Near and Ronnie Gilbert on *Lifeline* (Emeryville, California: Redwood Records, 1983).

17

WILLIAM AYERS

Camera Obscura: An Encounter With War at the Movies and a Personal Journey through the Flickering White Light

We have a nine-year-old, the middle of three children, who steadfastly refuses to go to the movies. Oh, he's seen a couple of films in theaters—*The Muppet Movie* and part of the first *Indiana Jones*—but he watches from the back of the house, and he exits regularly to regain his courage. It's not that he dislikes films—he likes going to a friend's house to watch them on television, or going to his grandparents' to see a video. He loves hearing his brothers talk about even the most gruesome films, and he often joins in the discussion, describing nuance and detail as if he had actually been there. But *being there*, sitting in the large, dark room and watching those huge, bright images, is simply too much for him. It is altogether too real, and it frightens and overwhelms him. As he himself told us, "The movies swallow me."

The movies swallowed me when I was a kid, too, but with a difference: I was an eager victim. I got into the movies and the movies got into me. As a young person the lowest rating a film ever received on my personal scale was "Worth Seeing," and it had to be pretty dismal to sink that far. With my uncritical mind, my enthusiastic eye, and the inevitable box of popcorn perched on my lap, I was at the movies each and every week.

Because I grew up in the late forties and the fifties, a lot of what I remember of those Saturday afternoons are war films. *Flying Leathernecks*, *Sahara*, *The African Queen*, *The Bridge on the River Kwai*, *Casablanca*, *From Here to Eternity*, *The Audie Murphy Story*, *Mister Roberts*—these were among my favorites, each receiving my highest rating, a "Must See," and each making a powerful impression on my understanding of people and the world. World War II was a large part of the context of growing up in those years, and the reality of war was brought to me on film. War was, to my mind, what the movies said war was: heroic, romantic, sometimes difficult, sometimes funny, but always *exciting*.

From the dull ordinariness of my growing up, war was a welcomed event. After I was swallowed by war at the movies, I played at war with my friends on a dirt hill near my house or, later, in an elaborate variation of "capture the flag," a team game that ranged from the lake by the high school to the forest preserve on the other side of town. I carried my gun, a short stout stick, across my chest as I ran to battle, and I heard echoes of the movies as I dived for cover or overwhelmed an enemy machine gun nest. I was powerful in war, just like the heroes in those movies, and killing and being killed was sanitized and safe, just like on those Saturday afternoons.

The cinema helped to shape the play, and the play became a lens through which to view the films. With John Wayne, Old Blood-and-Guts, I fired my machine gun at "Japs" as I raced up a hill on some obscure Pacific island to plant a shredded but proud American flag. With Montgomery Clift, the working-class hero, I surveyed the wreckage at Pearl Harbor with a troubled look in my eyes and said, "They're pickin' trouble with the best army in the world." And with the regal Henry Fonda—Mister Roberts—I ached to be riding west across the Pacific, into the action.

I shared Mr. Roberts's pain when he felt that the war was ending and he couldn't get to it. What could be worse? Without war he could never prove himself, and we could never prove ourselves. We could never really experience the fullness of life, never fall in love, have buddies, overcome adversity. We could never become men if all we ever did was raise a family, work at a job, participate in a community's life. We needed war. Poor, sweet Mr. Roberts, the most decent guy in the navy, but not yet a real man, not until he had the opportunity to kill. I choked and cheered with millions of other boys when Mr. Roberts finally got his wish: he went to war and became a man—a dead man. And when Henry Fonda became a man, the timid Jack Lemmon became a rebel, ripping crazy James Cagney's palm tree out of its bucket and pitching it overboard. The sailors cheered and so did we. Everyone was empowered, a little more grown up, a bit more manly. Ah, war.

One summer morning when I was about ten, at an age when war play was fading as a central preoccupation but becoming a man was more an obsession than ever, the calm and quiet of our neighborhood was shattered by the sound of sirens. Ambulances and fire trucks rushed up our street, converging on the house directly across from ours, and I ran barefoot with my brothers and sister to see what was happening. Kids from everywhere crowded the lawn and we were thrilled to have serious-looking police officers telling us to stay back. I was giddy, excited, and happy, joking and rough-housing with friends, and I was gripped by a fresh, tingling feeling, an incipient sexual stirring at the expectant scene. Within moments a surge of firefighters spilled through the front door hoisting a stretcher with a bloody body flung upon it. It was John, a boy just eight years older than I, and he had blown his brains out with a handgun. One firefighter was holding John's mother, who lurched and heaved after her son, her face as red and contorted as his, her voice unrecognizable in its wailing. I got sick and became drained and weak, confused and guilty. John, I found out later, didn't want to go to Korea. He felt isolated in his opposition, a misfit without a community of care and concern. He was high-strung, I was told, and must have been temporarily insane. Nothing temporary about it, I thought, and that was the end of innocent killing for me.

This was an unwanted lesson in death, and it played against a backdrop of war at the movies, war for domestic consumption, war for boys growing up. It was years before I understood the significance of unleashing the nuclear nightmare on an Asian nation, for example, or learned about the domestic internment of the Japanese; it was years before I discovered that the U.S. consistently refused to accept Jewish refugees from Europe, or grasped the ways in which every aspect of the domestic political landscape—the New Deal and the popular front, for example, various openings to the left and then the overwhelming and successful right-wing push—were shaped and misshaped by war. Those lessons, too, were costly; they were long in coming, but that is another story.

I confess that my rating scale for films hasn't changed much. It still ranges from "Worth Seeing" at the lowest end to "Must See" at the highest. A film gets a six on a ten-point scale simply for flickering by on the big screen. But there is a difference. Today lots of films are worth seeing in order to understand ourselves and our culture more clearly, to examine what messages we are being sent, or what shit we are being asked to eat. A film like *The Big Sleep* is now a "Must See" because it so powerfully articulates the rewriting of an insurgent moment in our collective history. In other words, while my rating scale hasn't changed, my disposition of mind, my stance, and my reasons have changed significantly. I still bathe regularly in the flickering white light, but I no longer get swallowed by the movies and I no longer swallow what I'm fed. Today I urge other viewers, including my own children, to become critical readers of cinema, to search for the subtle messages and the hidden curriculum, to uncover the subtext, to sort through the complex and multiple meanings, and to recover the full significance of what moves by.

My own first lesson in cinematic text and subtext was when I discussed the anticapitalist classic *Bonnie and Clyde* ("What do you do?" "We rob banks.") with my very capitalist father and found that he, too, loved the film, but for him it was a gangster classic. Even more jarring was my discovery that one of my favorite anti-war films of the seventies, *Patton*, was one of Richard Nixon's very favorite war films ever, and that he showed it regularly to guests at the White House. To me *Patton* was the story of a megalomaniacal general bent on destruction and self-destruction, a clear parody of patriotism, and a cautionary tale on the dangers of glorifying war. To Nixon, I discovered, it was the story of a true American patriot, a man of courage, wisdom, and erudition, and it was a story of men in battle, a tale of sacrifice and triumph. Slowly I realized that both were true, that it was all there and that whatever sense the film made depended on the particular attitudes, experiences, and autobiographies that reached out and met the film. In a sense this is the result of the Hollywood business ethic: make entertainment that means all things to all people and create, therefore, a huge paying audience. But more important for me was a rediscovery about the importance of interpretation and the ways in which reality has meaning for a person. It made me less dogmatic, I think, less certain, less willing to insist that my viewing of a particular film or novel or event is necessarily the clearest or the truest. It opened me to multiple interpretations and layered meanings.

War films can never be the same for me, not after the experiences and events of the sixties and seventies, but as I look at the enormously popular Vietnam War films, I realize that not much has changed for the film makers or the war makers. They are a bit more sophisticated, perhaps, subtle in new ways and with new technologies and gripping special effects, but the messages are frighteningly familiar, and the text and subtext are broad enough to drive a truck full of paying movie-goers through.

In the Vietnam War film we discover once again that war is hell. In Michael Cimino's Academy Award Winning *The Deer Hunter* the horrors of war are internal as well as external, and in Francis Ford Coppola's *Apocalypse Now* the horrors of war take on comic book proportions, all gaudy and fantasmagorical. *Platoon*, Oliver Stone's Academy award winner, gives us war through the eyes of an American foot soldier, and what we see is exhaustion, boredom, tension, bugs, blisters, fear, snakes, rain, oppressive heat, and sudden explosions of searing violence followed by the sight and smell of death.

In these films war is still a passage to manhood, and it is still a contest of good guys versus bad guys. Of course, in the jungle things get murky, and the bad guys can then turn out to be crazy Americans like Colonel Kurtz or Sergeant Barnes, and the good guys are always gripped by angst, but the larger point remains: war is an event in which the forces of good confront (and triunph over) the forces of evil. It's all so neat, so Hollywood!

The problem from an anti-war perspective is that "war as hell" can be read in a variety of ways. It can certainly tap an anti-war impulse, but it can as easily increase our admiration for those who have encountered war—indeed, it can make us long for a similar passage in our own lives. It can focus our collective attention on the human and ecological waste of war, or it can comfortably reinforce a view that Americans should not fight land wars in other countries, that distant wars should be fought from the air and from the sea, or by natives armed and supported by American dollars, all minimizing American casualties.

In *Democracy and Education* John Dewey argued that it was never enough to teach people the horrors of war, because that is not reason enough to make peace. Dewey argued for an emphasis on "whatever binds people together in cooperative human pursuits and results". And this is where the "war is hell" motif in these films is completely inadequate. In *All Quiet on the Western Front*, the classic anti-war novel from World War I and the work from which *Platoon* at least is in part derivate, the pivotal scene occurs when, in the midst of chaos, death, wreckage, and horror, the young German soldier, pinned down for a day in a foxhole, picks through the belongings of the Frenchman he has just killed and realizes that his enemy is just like him, a humble working man with a family, a trade, hopes and dreams like his own. He already knows that war is hell; what he discovers is that the young men who fight the wars are blinded to their common pursuits, common problems, and common enemies by mystifications like nationalism and patriotism. Again, from an anti-war viewpoint failure to make a human connection to the 'enemy' is where contemporary war films prove disastrous.

In virtually every film, Vietnam is portrayed as a kind of hell on earth. Scenes of its color and its lushness are all from above and afar—its soft and yielding beauty is seductive, but Vietnam sings a siren song, luring the innocent to wreckage, captivity, and death. Up close, Vietnam is heat and dust and, well, the opening line of *Apocalypse Now* is, "Saigon . . . Shit!" Vietnam is routinely referred to as "the worst place in the world" or "the asshole of the world," a place completely lacking in contour or depth, a scene that is at best gratuitous to the three-dimensional Americans, and at worst an overgrown jungle prison. There is a pervasive sense of American innocence, of Vietnam as a quicksand that seizes and traps the simple misstep and sucks helpless victims into itself.

The Vietnamese are similarly rendered nameless and faceless. They are "gooks" or "slopes" or "Charlies," and they are part of the danger, a background like the rats, the trees, the unmapped roads, the obscure jungle paths. The Vietnamese are pathetic victims, ridiculous clowns, duplicitous villagers, relentless hordes. Vietnamese women are dangerous booby traps, amoral and inscrutable: in *The Deer Hunter*, for example, a Vietnamese prostitute begs Nick to screw her even though her child is in the room watching; Nick, of course, is revolted and refuses. Nowhere are there Vietnamese who are effectively raising their children, thoughtfully defending their country, or sensibly speaking about their work or their hopes or their dreams. The Vietmanese people are, in fact, central to what makes the place so awful.

All of this leads to a comfortable and appealing rewriting of the history of war and of Vietnam. In *The Deer Hunter*, history literally stands on its head as Cimino uses the most memorable popular images of the war to tell a different story: here it is the Vietnamese who put the Americans in Tiger Cages, who commit the My Lai massacre over American objection, who encourage unwilling Americans to rape and pillage, and who play a deadly game of Russian roulette with life itself. It is, of course, the Vietnamese who regard human life as cheap, who know no constraints, who move with no understandable motives, who are endlessly barbaric, mindless, and manipulatable. One remembers forty-two volumes of the Pentagon Papers and the revelations of a bipartisan foreign policy that was deliberate, willful, and consistent, and a domestic corollary based on manipulation, obfuscation, and lies. One remembers an active, energetic opposition that broke free of the hawks-doves debate over technical and legal issues and put forth instead a position that humanized the Vietnamese and opposed imperialist aggression in principle. And one weighs the awful risk of living with a forgotten history, in a place where war is not understandable and, therefore, not avoidable, and in a time when killing lacks contactual knowledge, when everyone both knows and doesn't know, and when every soldier and citizen, then, is a potential Kurt Waldheim.

A central part of what we do as teachers and curricularists must be to peel away layers of mystification, levels of understanding and perception, to reveal other means of seeing and alternative ways of knowing. Art can help, opening our eyes to other worlds, to broader scenes, to different choices, to criticism and alternative. But works of art must be subject to critical scrutiny, too, to readings of text and subtext, to interpretation and thoughtful analysis. If we are to be true to our calling and fully present to the demands of our times, we must recognize the larger historical and social processes that influence human thought and action, and we must critically account for those processes in our interactions with students. Things like war and movies and much more cannot really be kept from classrooms; perhaps instead they can become a conscious starting point for critically understanding the world as it is, and as it might be, but is not yet.

It is twenty years since the Tet Offensive—the decisive moment in the Vietnam War, the moment when the American defeat was sealed although there would be years more of killing and destruction to come—and I am walking beside the Vietnam Memorial in Washington. I remember images of Tet: a girl burned by napalm running naked down a highway, a suspected Vietcong being summarily executed in the street, the American CIA fighting to retake the U. S. Embassy in downtown Saigon. I focus now on a nine-year-old girl with pigtails here at the memorial, crying. Why? Her mom is about forty and she is touching a name on the wall and she is crying too. Is this her brother? First husband? Childhood sweetheart? What does it mean to the girl in pigtails? There are flowers and notes and artifacts left everywhere along the wall. Two men are making rubbings for a long line of people, solemnly locating a name, holding the delicate white paper to the wall, and transferring the image from wall to paper. The wall is a living drama. It seems to grow out of the ground, and the names of the dead are animated by all the human motion and action taking place around them, because of them. It is sad and moving to walk along the wall, to feel the emotions swelling out of that ditch. It goes on and on, and still there are no Vietnamese names here.

Vietnam is the kind of event that shows us to ourselves. Like Hiroshima or the Holocaust or the gulags, it shows us things about being human, some of which we don't want to know and don't want to see. We live now in a post-Vietnam world, as well as in a post-Holocaust, post-Hiroshima world. We must see beyond the obscuring lenses if we are fully to take responsibility for that fact. We now live in a world marked by genocidal warfare and irregular warfare, psychological warfare and economic warfare, a world that has known desert warfare, guerrilla warfare, mobile warfare, mountain warfare, naval warfare, aerial warfare, open warfare, position warfare, bacteriological warfare, chemical warfare, underground warfare, nuclear warfare, and so much more. Standing against it all is simply peace. We know too much of precariousness to allow ourselves to be lost in indifference or narcissism; it is our task, rather, to become intensely aware, powerfully related to one another and the space we share, proactive in creating a world without war.

18

MICHAEL W. APPLE

"Hey Man, I'm Good": The Aesthetics and Ethics of Making Films in Schools

Those of you who are familiar with my work—from *Ideology and Curriculum* and *Education and Power* to *Teachers and Texts*—may know that I approach educational issues in a way that is different from many other educators.[1] Rather than seeing our task as finding efficient ways of getting students to learn the knowledge already selected for the curriculum, I have urged us to ask *whose* knowledge it is in the first place. That is, I have asked us to take very seriously the intricate connections between what we teach in classrooms and the unequal relations of power in the larger society. Power, of course, is both social and personal. It not only signifies one group's attempt to dominate another; it also refers to a person's ability to help *create* the social conditions and meanings that make life more fulfilling.

These are not only abstract issues. They influence nearly everything I do as an educator, especially in the courses on curriculum development that I teach. Here I try to deal practically with questions of power and the production of personal meaning.

I do not approach the issue of curriculum design as a technical problem to be solved by the application of rationalized models. Rather, following a long line of educators from Dewey to Huebner, I conceive of curriculum as a complicated and continual process of environmental design. Thus, do not think of curriculum as a 'thing,' as a syllabus or a course of study. Instead, think of it as a symbolic, material, and human environment that is ongoingly reconstructed. This process of design involves not only the technical, but the aesthetic, ethical, and political if it is to be fully responsive at both the social and personal levels.[2]

I want to stress one of these elements in this brief essay. While I do not believe that its importance overshadows the others, it is so necessary that I cannot conceive of curriculum design going on without integrating its concerns into the very heart of the process. Here I refer to the aesthetic.

If curriculum is in fact a *design* problem, then by its very nature it is an aesthetic act. In many ways, it is more like painting a picture than building a bridge. Because of this, and because of the fact that most educators have themselves been 'trained' to use behaviorally oriented technical models in approaching curriculum problems, it is essential that we recapture the aesthetic sensitivity that has been socialized out of all too many teachers and administrators. Oddly enough, it is in one of the most technically oriented parts of designing environments—the use of technology itself—that I believe the ethical, the political, and especially the aesthetic nature of curriculum design can be illuminated. What I do in a course entitled "Elementary School Curriculum" can serve as a case in point. Here I stress not the usual ways technology is used in classrooms, but its personal and aesthetic possibilities to do different things in schools. The focus is on film making.

Elementary Curriculum is filled with an entire range of people—teachers, administrators, social workers, librarians, full-time graduate students inside and outside of education, with many of these being from outside the borders of the United States. Almost none have had any 'formal' experience with the relationship among aesthetics, technology, and curriculum. By the time the semester is over, nearly three quarters will have engaged in film making.

We tend to think of technology in education as something of a 'better mousetrap.' Given a process/product curriculum model that says that education is good if it gets us from point A to point B efficiently and cheaply, technology simply becomes one more means to get prechosen knowledge into the heads of students. Films are seen as better than dry text material or a lecture. Goals don't change. Only the means do. Film, in essence, becomes one more 'delivery system.' The teacher sends; the student receives.

If we think of film not as a 'delivery system' of prechosen messages, but as a form of aesthetic, political, and personal *production*, our entire orientation changes. If we think of it as a way people help produce their own visual literacy, this too forces major shifts in our perspective as well.

Just as written literacy has its own 'grammar' and its own politics[3], so too do forms of visual literacy. And just as the exploration of writing as a creative act leads to self-production, so too can the exploration of the possibilities inherent in each aspect of visual production lead to the uncovering of alternate ways of making meaning both individually and collectively.

I choose working with film for a number of partly overlapping reasons. One is to engage students in my Elementary School Curriculum class as soon as possible in a process that demonstrates, in action, the connections among symbolic, material, and human resources in an environment. At its most practical level, making films requires reflections on this. Second, and again on a very practical level, I want to demonstrate how curricular areas in the elementary school can be integrated together through, say, film projects. Art, music, mathematics,science, language arts and reading, and so on can be made sensitive to each other as each is brought to bear on making the film. The linkages here to the "project method" are self-conscious. Third, I want to illuminate how technology is not simply one more way to get from point A to point B in classrooms, but *inherently* offers more ethical, aesthetic, and political possibilities that can go well beyond what now exists in so many classrooms. It enables us to do very different things that can expand the range of literacies and their grammars that teachers and students are able to work with. Finally, as I mentioned earlier, one of my aims is to reawaken that very sense of aesthetic possibility in teachers, to enable them not to be 'connoisseurs' of the 'art' of teaching but to engage in aesthetic (and political) production itself by actually making films singly or collectively.

Two kinds of film work tend to dominate. The first involves using 16mm film, but not at all in the way we usually employ it. What I am decidedly not interested in is 'instructional film'—you know, the content-laden and often oh-so-deadly presentations on the agriculture of X put out by commercial firms and publishing houses. Instead, the focus is on student aesthetic (and often political) production. Here, 16 mm film is not seen as 'containing' already decided content, but as something of a moving canvas through which students themselves create meanings. This is done by either bleaching old 16 mm film (literally unrolling it and dropping it in a bucket of household bleach to remove all of the previous images, thereby leaving transparent film as a result) or buying white film leader which usually comes in boxes of one hundred-foot lengths. These blank or white lengths of film are then drawn upon. One can create relatively intricate animations by drawing pictures frame by frame on the film; or Jackson Pollock-like effects of color, line, and shape can be created by simply using magic markers to go down the film relatively randomly. When put to different kinds of music (usually simply by playing a tape during the showing of the film, but sometimes with more elaborate attempts at synchronization), the effects can be quite startling.

The second style of film work involves the use of 8 mm film. Given its size, this film is not written upon, but instead is used in the camera itself to create animations, political statements (examples include a film made by middle school students against the stringent dress code of their school, anti-pollution statements, and feminist images), or simply interesting visual effects by exploring what one can do with slow and fast motion, single frame release cables, zoom lenses, and so on. Once again, the focus is not on creating Hollywood-like artifacts, but on playing (in the richest sense of that concept) with the medium to explore its grammar. The fact that this is usually done cooperatively, with small groups of students in my class or with groups of elementary and secondary students in schools working with people who are taking Elementary School Curriculum creates a collective experience that is important in and of itself.

I want to take one concrete instance of film work that grew out of the class, one in which two students who had taken the class and I decided to work together to see if film making as an integrative and personal form could make as much of a difference in real children's lives as we thought it could. We believed the best way to test this out was to go into an environment that was 'difficult.' The three of us had all taught in inner city schools and two of us had experience in working with some of the hardest-to-reach kids, those involved in the corrections system. We asked if we could come in to one of the state-run juvenile corrections institutions, a school for girls that had a reputation of being a tough place but where we had enough contacts and support from a teacher there to make access possible.

We walked into the most difficult cottage on the grounds. Twenty-two young women aged fourteen through seventeen, many of them adolescent girls of color, confronted us. They were there for a multitude of reasons—running away, prostitution, drugs, theft, and so on, all those labels the juvenile justice system affixes to the troubled children of the poor, disenfranchised, or oppressed. One thing was very clear immediately. This was a group of tough kids. Both words are important here—toughness and kids. There was no doubt that these adolescents *were* angry, difficult to reach, and mistrustful (sometimes for very good reasons). Yet the toughness covered up their fragility. These were often children inside, wrapped up in bodies that belied, had to bely, the fear and confusion and feelings of lack of self-worth inside.

Having worked with kids like this when I was a teacher and youth worker in the inner city schools of Paterson, New Jersey, I already had some understanding of what these kids felt and an unromantic appraisal of what they were capable of doing to themselves and others. We began by showing two films by Norman McLaren, the noted Canadian film maker who had, in essence, pioneered many of the cinematographic techniques that had influenced me. We explained to the girls the kinds of things that could be done with film and spent some time discussing and demonstrating how this could be done by showing other films that students such as themselves had made. Since most of these films had been accompanied by music that the kids liked, the atmosphere began to loosen up. Combining the joking yet still serious manner that we had each developed in working with kids, we answered their questions and then handed out lengths of film and brightly colored magic markers, making it clear that they could easily get more material if they needed it.

Of the total group, eleven began working. The theme they chose was simple yet so evocative—school. What started out as an activity that was seen by them as an excuse not to do "school stuff," shortly became totally engrossing as the girls got into the project.

Soon everyone, *everyone*, was deeply involved. Magic markers were shared. Comments and criticisms that were meant to help, not to cut down someone, were given by the kids to each other. Jokes and laughter, sighs and grimaces, calls for assistance, words of satisfaction and frustration also filled the air. It was at times noisy, at times remarkably quiet. It was the controlled chaos that organizes and reorganizes itself when kids are deeply involved in doing something that is playful and yet utterly serious to them.

At the end of the morning all the segments of film—some of which were now quite long—were collected and spliced together. Each girl took a turn at splicing her section into the larger film. And then we watched it. It was funny, immensely creative in places, and often brutally honest about their perceptions of schooling. Because of this, it may also have been threatening to some of the people who were on the staff.

The film had to be shown multiple times, as each girl had to see and resee her part of it and as each cottage had to be brought in to see it as well. The excitement was visceral. The sheer sense of competence, of having done something that was lasting and that proved to the world that "I am worth something 'cause *I did this*," was palpable. There were cooperative discussions among the girls about how to improve each other's sections. Plans were made about what to do next time, ones that were sometimes too elaborate, but showed a personal and collective spark that had been missing throughout all the prior school experiences these kids had been involved in at the school. Many of the girls grabbed the books I had brought in about animation, making 'write on' films, etc., and after reading them passed them on to others in preparation for the next film we would do together. We were turned on and so were the girls. They were *ready* to go further. They *wanted* to read and discuss. This was one of those occasions when the 'teachable moment' had expanded to such an extent that so much more could be integrated into it. Their pride in themselves, enthusiasm, and their growing sense that they, who had been labeled "stupid" for so long, had real yet untapped resources and talents—all this provided ideal conditions to go on and do even more serious things.

And then it died.

We were informed that, while this was interesting and "seemed to involve the girls and to keep them out of trouble," it was in essence a frill. They had to get back to their remedial reading and 'life-skills' classes, ones the students tolerated at best and often dismissed as irrelevant, boring, or, and again I quote, "bullshit." We then had to face the kids, to tell them it was over, to face their disbelief and their anger and the return of the cynical expressions that we had seen before we started the film work.

A group of youth who had been so beaten down in classrooms and had learned to hate school and had learned not to trust a system that seemed to have little to offer them, and hence had built impenetrable walls between their intimate feelings, hopes, and dreams and the institutions in which they lived, had removed large chunks of that wall. They let their defenses down and trusted some white teachers. Doors into themselves were opened. Talents were uncovered. Joys and possibilities were made visible, only to be once again denied.

There is a scene in Herb Kohl's book, *36 children*[4], where one of his students, a boy named Robert, comes back to see Kohl. Robert had been told he was stupid. Yet in the course of a year, he had been transformed in Kohl's classroom, had learned to trust himself, had learned that he was talented in that sixth grade classroom. The next year he went on to another school, another teacher, and was shattered. Nothing had really changed. It was boring, alienating, and repressive, perhaps worse for Robert now that he had experienced the very possibility of difference. He was angry at Kohl. How could Kohl have done this to him? How could Kohl have allowed him to drop his defenses, defenses that had enabled Robert to survive the numbing experiences of a schooling process that daily denied his very being as an individual and as an African American? Wouldn't it have been better just to leave him alone? In essence, it was like allowing a nearly starving person to sit at a food laden table for one night and then locking her or him out on the other side of the door from then on. Wasn't this simply unethical?

Many issues could and should be raised about this experience in film making in hind sight. Were we too naive? Should we have involved administrators and educational staff more directly from the beginning? Did we think through all of the possible effects and contingencies? Add to this the multitudinous issues surrounding the usual questions of bureaucracy and educational reform and we could spend many hours detailing what went wrong and the should-have-dones that arise from this episode. But through it all, one question remains. It haunts me. It provides the concluding story I tell each and every time we complete the weeks on technology, aesthetics, and curriculum in Elementary School Curriculum. The question is so simple to state, yet so damnedly torturous to resolve. Should we have done what we did? Should we have opened these young women up to the sense of what they could do, to reawaken hopes and a sense of self-worth, only to have the door slammed shut again before we and they could go further and build upon these initial awakenings?

Yet, there was this Christmas card that came in the mail five years later. It was from one of the girls of that cottage, Ramona. She had been one of those who was most excited by the experience of making the film. She had nearly cried when she saw her portion of it, a lengthy section in which she had painstakingly drawn a school burning down, a group of children playing basketball, and a segment in which multicolored rods and dots seemed to dance around each other. She had been positively glowing. This was *hers*. As she had put it, "Hey man, I'm *good*!"

Ramona was now working as a commercial artist and wanted to write to let me know. "You probably won't remember me. I did that film stuff at [the cottage] with you. I hope you like this card. I designed it."

I am still tortured by the experience of making films with those girls. In that one week, we did succeed, often well beyond what we had expected. Yet, hadn't we also failed? Hadn't we reawakened hopes and senses of self-worth that, of necessity, again had to be partly repressed by the girls in that cottage, only to fail them again? But then there's Ramona. Would she have been successful without the experience we helped create? Don't we have an ethical and political duty as educators, even when we can't change the entire range of one's school experiences, to struggle to make each single experience as personally meaningful and politically powerful as we can? Ramona's letter helps, but still I wonder. I'll leave it up to you to decide.

NOTES

1. See Michael W. Apple, *Ideology and Curriculum* (New York: Routledge, revised edition, 1990); idem, *Education and Power* (Boston: Routledge, ARK Edition, 1985); idem, *Teachers and Texts* (New York: Routledge, 1986).

2. See, for example, Dwayne Huebner, "Curriculum Language and Classroom Meaning," in James B. Macdonald and Robert R. Leeper, eds. *Language and Meaning* (Washington: Association for Supervision and Curriculum Development, 1966); and idem, "The Tasks of the Curricular Theorist," in William F. Pinar, ed. *Curriculum Theorizing* (Berkeley: McCutchan, 1975).

3. See Colin Lankshear and Moira Lawler, *Literacy, Schooling and Revolution* (Philadelphia: Falmer Press, 1988); Janet Batsleer, Tony Davies, Rebecca O'Rourke, and Chris Weeden, *Rewriting English* (New York: Methuen, 1985); and Allan Luke, *Literacy, Textbooks and Ideology* (Philadelphia: Falmer Press, 1988).

4. Herbert Kohl, *36 Children* (New York: Signet Books, 1967).

19

FRANCINE SHUCHAT SHAW

Blocks and Film and Other Media: The Aesthetics of Inquiry and Understanding from the Inside Out

THEMES

One of my former colleagues used to encourage me, mostly in jest, to spend my next sabbatical editing my university memos. At various sorts of gatherings he would bring this up and always managed to reach consensus among others there who were frequently on the receiving end of what actually was (and is) a continuous stream of messsages—ideas, proposals, critiques—-all having to do with goings-on, real or imagined, in our community. It's true, I do love to invent, to develop new ideas and ways of approaching problems, to look around and underneath to figure out things, to imagine what if, and I usually find it next to impossible to keep my thoughts to myself. All the better if I get a response or two from kindred spirits who will participate in the journey, to start a new project or tackle an old problem in a new way. I am clearly most content when I have in mind new ideas or fresh ways of thinking and in hand some tools—a pad of paper and a pen, a blank screen on my MacIntosh with "Untitled" as the running head, a video camera in front of a long and unpredictable day, or a stack of tapes at my editing console where I will weave together a new script of images and sounds—tools with which to inquire and experiment, express and communicate, in an original sort of way. For many years I have sensed a similar kind of creative and critical energy in my educational video students, and before that in my documentary film students, for whom I have found that my most important job is to provide the adaptable tools with which, and an environment of experimentation and community in which, they can discover, investigate, and act on the issues and problems they find most salient.

We all have such dispositions that evolve through and characterize our personal and professional experience, connect one arena to the other, and surface persistently in both. I view these as biographical themes that we seem to get stuck on at some point in our development as individuals and social beings. These themes serve as windows for the way in which we see the world and define our purposes in it. They serve as filters, drawing us selectively to certain situations and causes rather than others, and they drive our conduct and actions.

Being conscious of these themes permits us to be more thoughtful about, and critical of, our world views and the underlying interests and intentions that motivate our beliefs and our conduct, both personal and professional, especially as these affect others and our many relationships. But often we lose track of our biographical themes, getting caught up in daily events that crowd out reflection. When we drift away and become dissociated from home base, we take on what belongs more to others and give up thinking carefully, creatively, and critically for ourselves. Frequently it takes a new and profound experience, often an aesthetic experience, to bring us back. If it is compelling enough, and if we take the time to examine why, such an experience can illuminate our themes and the reasons and ways we have expressed them over the long haul.

I began to have such an experience five years ago, an experience of observing, in a progressive school environment, the freedom of creative and critical inquiry and experimentation, expression, and communication in young children. These children, aged two to seven, were learning about their world through a process which is, as Lucy Sprague Mitchell (1928) suggested, akin to the method of the artist and the scientist: a spiralling cycle of direct experience through investigation of original questions and interests and active expression and communication of these through first-hand interpretation and representation. As my observations intensified over these five years, engendering an aesthetic experience both direct and vicarious, what had seemed new and novel began to strike old and long-held chords. Observing these young artists/scientists at work made perfectly salient to me one theme that has been responsible for significant decisions I have made, positions and directions I have taken. This theme is the importance of a particular ground for knowing and understanding, for original inquiry and experimentation, and for expression and communication in a community in which individuals engage their creative and critical spirit through independent and collaborative work. I can best elaborate this theme by sharing some of my observations and interpretations of the ways in which children take charge of blocks and other raw construction media to make their mark on the open spaces of experimental progressive classrooms.[1]

THE BLOCK CITY

> Along one wall are shelves full of blocks—hundreds of them. In a corner are small shelves crammed with toy people and animals with miniature barrels, boxes, pieces of cloth, string and inumerable [sic] other useful and adaptable objects. Still other shelves hold boats, trains, airplanes, trucks, fire engines and derricks—all made by children. The floor is empty and inviting, flooded with sunlight.
>
> Into this room troop eighteen children, all of them approximately seven years old. Within less than an hour a transformation has taken place. On either side of a central avenue rise buildings. Here is a six story apartment house with a school and hospital close by. Stores of all kinds display their wares . . . A busy city lies spread out on the floor. . . . We find that the average child of seven in our school is a mine of information on a great variety of subjects. He has begun to coordinate information, to relate things to each other and to think about these relationships . . . he has learned in the most natural way by seeing, questioning, discussing, and reconstructing. With blocks and through play he has been working out whatever he has grasped of the world. (Murray 1945/1978, 37-41)

Experimental progressive classrooms are workshops in which curriculum and pedagogy develop from the children's experience of using adaptable media according to their own purposes. As small naturalists with a keen curiosity about all they observe and experience, the fives, sixes, and sevens find the most compelling channel for working out their purposes in the building of the Block City. The Block City is the children's interpretation and representation of the world they live in, and their use and detailing of it are investigations and dramatizations of how they believe this world works and the people in it live. For young children, and the artist and scientist as well, this process is most compelling when it centers on interests and questions original to—not imposed upon—them. In the Block City, the children express and extend the daily ordinary and extraordinary experiences they find most significant, as well as the observations they make on frequent group trips planned around their interests, by building and acting out their own versions. They draw on, and eventually come to value consciously, information "they have gained by their own efforts, firsthand, often unconsciously" (Pratt 1948, 30). The cycle continues, leading to a wider circle of questions with greater focus, keener observations and research, and more complex and usable interpretations and representations.

The children rebuild the Block City from a new plan every week or two in an enormous expanse of time and space, characterized by a mood of expectation but undivided by others' purposes and undefined by others' imperatives. For this project, the children require materials that will adapt to their intentions and schemes, respond to their ideas and variety of approaches, and invite them to translate what they have taken into themselves into concrete forms which they can then comprehend and judge in their own ways. The walls are lined by shelves well-supplied with media that are unstructured in nature: unit blocks, paint, clay, wood, cloth, and paper of many kinds. Easels and a woodbench with accessories are nearby, and in cubbies are stored small materials like pulleys and battery sets, tape, scissors, staplers, and writing tools. Ready-made models are limited to the most versatile, such as boxes and simply detailed people and animals, sized appropriately for typical block structures. These media and materials are the tools with which the children inquire and experiment, express and communicate. These they press into unlimited service in the interest of knowing their physical and social world, thinking about relationships within it, and understanding their roles and responsibilities in shaping it. Strikingly apparent is the absence of single-use materials that limit investigation and adaptability and, as well, commercial toys that prescribe their own use and prompt "leaning back exclusively upon facts gathered by other people and thinking done by other people" (Mitchell 1928, 217). As Mitchell (1928) wrote, "Any subject that interests children is appropriate for them if they can find tools for handling it as a first-hand situation, and if they can find media for first-hand output. My conception of a teacher's work is to try to provide for the children situations for this first-hand intake and media for this first-hand output" (217). As the children find few distractions and directives here, it becomes their custom to look to themselves and to each other to begin, and, once they have, there is plenty of work to do! There is no scheme for which their open-ended tools cannot be made to work; returning to investigate and use them again and again, the children's resourcefulness and self-reliance expands with their growing first-hand knowledge of the world, their original ideas, and personal interests. The children develop a history of thinking and building, independently and together.

Individuals or pairs of children begin separate structures that will become part of the Block City, following an early Monday morning group meeting during which they devise a basic plan and make commitments to work on the aspects they choose. They create the apartment buildings, fire stations, bakeries, plumbing factories, and parks they have experienced as participants or observed as spectators. The river painters have appointed and equipped themselves, and they arrive to hold a quiet debate about what floor space to use. Soon others gather to ask whether they will paint the East River or the Hudson, and the bridge builder dashes in, recognizing that where she will work and which bridge will be needed depend on the answer to this question. The teacher discusses directions with the assembled group, and, when east and west are settled, the river painters get to work on the Hudson, because it will not disturb access to the block shelves. The children begin to set up challenges, first for themselves and gradually for the group, in a community of perspectives that differ and converge and expand. Their inventions with tools are frames for finding the content within themselves and thinking about it on their own level.

The parts begin to fit into the whole. The children seem to be driven by a strong belief in their own internal maps, a desire to clarify their ideas for themselves, and a need both to express and to connect these. They gather materials and exchange information in order to refine their constructions, as is pertinent to individual schemes and the ways in which their relationships are developing in the larger city. The individual's play "links him with that of other children and his job becomes a contribution to a bigger scheme, often involving an entire group" (Murray 1945/1978, 42). As relationships in the Block City take shape and the children begin to use their own and each other's constructions, needs and problems arise that fascinate and absorb them. They find enormous satisfaction in the discovery of problems and in knowing there is a job to be done. An apple orchard is ready to ship, but the road out does not extend far enough across town to reach the market. Where are more road builders; the job is too big! The bakery has its kitchens on the first floor and its store on the second, but, as a customer discovers, a stairway has yet to be built. Where is the World Trade Center from what has now become the George Washington Bridge? Signs must be made.

Such discoveries prompt the city builders to critique their own and each other's constructions. The children respond by making endless changes, searching out what they do not yet know, calling on other children for advice, adding detail with other adaptable tools at the ready—all toward a more adequate representation of their schemes and purposes. Loaves of bread for the bakery are made of clay, in proper scale and lined up in baker's dozens. Each child's "person" is woodworked into simple shape and detailed by crayon or small nails. Unconstructed pieces of cloth are wrapped as clothing, used for rugs or taped up as wallpaper. Red cubies become apples, a bit too large, as the children note, but they will do if a truck large enough to carry them can be built or found. Vehicles are made of wood by the children, and those stored on shelves for such occasions are borrowed by anyone who needs them. The unit blocks serve many purposes beyond city structures themselves: butteries are lined up to fence off the children's playground in the park; boat shapes are made easily with a middlie-brickie-squarie stack and a half-butterie on top, and more complex boats are fashioned with interior spaces for people and cargo; ascending stacks of brickies lined up and topped with ramps lead to a high stack of curvies that circle around to the bridge entrance. The bakers, who decide to replace their stairway with an elevator for people in wheelchairs, gather a small pulley and a supply of string, and a child who knows a lot about making pulleys work is called to the scene. A swimming pool is constructed from a large boxtop, blue paint is used for the water and white for depth lines and numbers, and a diving board is made of cardboard pieces connected by a hinge—found on a visit to the big woodshop downstairs—for bounce. The pool builders paint a sign showing a mermaid and "Pool Open," and soon others arrive for a swim. Paper is indispensable. It is torn and marked for money. The librarians, who cut, fold, and staple it into books, now want a print shop on their second floor, and more building, and eventually writing, begins. An aquarium needs whales made of paper taped to cardboard, the owners decide, and they are off to the library to find a picture that will help them to get the shape just right. One Monday morning a child suggests that the group needs a *Block City News*, and this leads not only to a newspaper office—a structure that grows more complex through use over many weeks and at the hands of many builders—but also to new ways of working together, the experience of collecting, writing, delivering, and reading their own news, and to reflections on continuity and change in Block City life. The children are reconstructing their world in a democracy in miniature.[2]

This social project of idea testing and sense making is fiercely compelling for children in charge. The impetus to take risks, assert, and experiment with their imaginative lives is intensified by the spirit of community purpose, and the drive to raise questions of how and why is extended by the spirit of critical exchange. With adaptable, unstructured media to help them inquire and experiment, express and communicate, the children create a web of relationships through which they begin to establish and understand themselves and their responsibilities in the world. As the children come to recognize their own and others' resourcefulness in giving ideas a tangible form they themselves can judge, dependency gives way to interdependency, impulse to initiative, control to negotiation, the need for praise to satisfaction in the work itself. This weekly ritual is never just the same, and the children never leave on Fridays unchanged by it; for it grounds and prepares them for new and closer, more purposeful observations and experience in the real world to check and test what they have discovered in the Block City, and it draws them back in to use what they have found and figure things out all over again.

HOME BASE

Why did I find the Block City so compelling, and primarily in a personal way? Somewhere between childhood and graduate school I must have gotten stuck on the theme that runs throughout these classrooms—due not at all to lived experience and awareness of it, but rather as a growing and silent but forceful reaction to its antithesis. Throughout that period, most of my general cultural experience and surely all of my educational experience could be characterized as a long, arduous process of looking outward and taking on what belonged more to others—determining others' expectations and trying to meet them, getting ahold of authoritative ideas and trying to learn them, looking to others for decisions and trying to follow them. The drive to find my own voice, to work on and experiment with original ideas, to discover and express my own interpretations, to think creatively and critically in a community of independent thinkers was an undercurrent I had glimpsed pushing up through the cracks but ignored. The ironies of graduate school, however (it was the early 1970s in English education), pushed me to my limit: while saturated daily and nightly, in classes and coffee shops, with Freire's critique of banking education, graduate school was the ultimate banking experience. In education, we were being banked and banking ourselves in order to prepare to eliminate banking! And in the English Department, of course, it was also business as usual, regardless of the tenor of the times. While the content of our conversations had changed profoundly, the form of our conduct and relationships had not. We had simply replaced old heroes with new ones and otherwise, culturally, remained much the same. Finally these contradictions must have been plainly before me, and I was bursting at the seams.

Block City observations gave me perspective on this and on the moment I turned to look in a different direction. I enrolled in a film making course—remember that film in the English classroom was something of a bandwagon at that time—but with an interest in student film making rather than in the use of ready-made films in the curriculum. What I found there seemed to be, from the perspective in which I was most seasoned, an entirely upside down, inside out way of looking at the world, one more congruent with my long running but silent theme. Here we were encouraged to begin with our own critical interests and purposes rather than to defer to others' priorities, and to examine and experiment with our own individual and collective interpretations rather than begin and end our inquiries with the mastery, adoption, and imitation of others' ideas and methods. So, the 'teacher's agenda' that ostensibly brought me to film making was actually more of a personal one, involving the need for first-hand creative and critical inquiry and experimentation, expression and communication as the starting point for knowing and understanding, an agenda I believe I shared with most of my fellow students there at that time, who may have been pivoting in the same direction for the same reasons. Working at times independently and at others as an ensemble, we constructed our versions of the situations and issues most salient to us, a solid ground for wider inquiry. With the adaptable tools of filmmaking in hand, we were turned upside down to investigate and interpret the world from the inside out and, in ways nearly identical to the children responsible for the Block City, to discover and challenge our own voices and to negotiate our diverse views in an environment characterized by community purpose and critical exchange.

These experiences and the banking dynamics they have the capacity to undo have held me in film and video—for myself, my students, and their students—and have, as the Block City made forcefully clear, broadly shaped my perspective on curriculum and teaching, for which Mitchell's (1928) passion for *making young geographers instead of teaching geography* is among the strongest of metaphors. This perspective derives from a progressive view of the purpose of schooling that Pratt expressed this way:

> Most people considered their education finished when they finished school. But it seemed to me that a school's job was quite the opposite—not to finish, but to begin education. A lifetime is not too long to spend in learning about the world. A school's function could become that of developing in children the kind of thinking and working attitudes which would enable them to take over their own future growth. . . . It seemed to me that a school's greatest value must be to turn out human beings who could think effectively and work constructively, who could in time make a better world than this for living in. (Pratt 1948, 18)

NOTES

1. My observations were done at The City and Country School in New York City, established first as The Play School by Caroline Pratt in 1914 and a leader since that time among American experimental progressive schools. Examples of Block City work in this paper are drawn from observations of Groups IV, V, VI, and VII (four through seven year olds) between 1984 and 1989.

2. When Caroline Pratt's book, *I Learn From Children* (New York: Simon and Schuster, 1948) was translated into Chinese, it was given the title, *A Democracy in Miniature* (Hong Kong: Platitude Press, c. 1955).

20

ELIZABETH VALLANCE

Mondrian as Metaphor: Mondrian, Museums, and Curriculum Work

Looking back, it now seems clear that my professional life-to-be was shaped when, as a college freshman, I walked into a dormitory lounge and saw a fellow student reading an enormous book. I asked her what it was. It was "Janson," the *sine qua non* textbook of art history courses, and my acquaintance was studying art history, a field I only barely knew existed. "Is it hard?" I asked, and she said, "Yes, but it's wonderful." The next semester I took Art History 101. I continued in my social scientist ways, studying psychology and psycholinguistics and later getting a doctorate in curriculum studies. But it was Art History 101 that changed my life.

"Is it hard?" scarcely seems the wisest question to ask in making a professional decision, but that was the second time I'd used it, and both answers guided choices that later turned out to be significant. The first had been several summers before, just before eighth grade, when a phone call from the high school offered me a choice between Latin and French; assured by my mother that French was easier, I chose French, a decision which years later led to a teaching stint in France, in turn guiding me into education. I'd selected French only partly because it was easy; it was also a language that worked in real life, which had some appeal. To my credit, I chose art history because it was hard but worth it, and I stayed with it because it proved literally to be an eye-opener. Both "Is it hard?" queries led me to languages I had not known before.

The visual arts are not a language most of us are comfortable with once we have mastered the skills that school more normally rewards. We educators may be learning ways to rectify this gap in how we teach children, but in general we are not well informed about how to look at art, and art is a foreign territory. Graduating from a good suburban high school, I had not heard of art history before starting college (save from an exotic distant cousin passing through town one evening); in my job at an art museum now, I encounter adults every day who are for the first time trusting themselves to learn how to look. My job is to make this task accessible and rewarding. I know it can be done. I myself am a believer, a person who never got art history out of her system despite majoring in more 'practical' things: I took course after course as an undergraduate, created a graduate minor in American Studies that was mostly art history, actually read art history in my free time, applied for admittance to an art history master's program years after receiving my doctorate (the graduate advisor, assuring me that many grown-ups were as hopelessly smitten as I, admitted me to the program, but scheduling constraints kept me from pursuing the coursework).

Clearly my present position, applying curriculum development skills to the mission of a public art museum, is perfect. But it's unusual—a tiny fraction of art-obsessed curriculists will end up in such positions, so the question is that of how the visual arts pertain to my official designation as a curriculum specialist. How can art enrich curriculum inquiry?

The visual arts, and the experience of learning about art in museums, have enriched my own approach to curriculum inquiry in at least two ways, and I'll outline them here. I'll call them the metaphorical and the lived. The first refers to a lesson I learned from Mondrian, actually from an exhibition of his work. The second refers to my own work as a museum educator.

MONDRIAN AS METAPHOR

It was in Paris, in 1969, that I saw at a museum (whose name I now forget) an exhibition of the works of the early twentieth century Dutch painter, Piet Mondrian. I 'knew' Mondrian as many of us do, as the painter who painted black-on-white grids with little rectangular dabs of primary colors here and there: I knew 'a Mondrian' when I saw one, and I was willing to look at lots of them. But I hadn't known (not having majored in art history) that he had started out as a relatively traditional—if modernistically inclined—landscape painter, before he discovered Cubism and evolved his own rectilinear style. The story of his progression from landscape to his well-known grids is a story told in trees, and in recent years I have done slide lectures ("Did You Know Mondrian

Did Landscapes?") on this subject. It is easy to show, in slides, how Mondrian gradually abstracted his large leafy trees into increasingly horizontal-and-vertical patterns, simplifying colors into shades of grey, organizing the picture plane into stark but graceful grids, eventually dropping all visible reference to the natural world. The progression is a clear and powerful one, and it never fails to provoke at least a few startled gasps from a general audience to whom this story is as new as it once was to me.

We are accustomed to knowing artists from their most mature, most complete periods, and to describing them in those terms when using their work as examples for anything we might need them for. We appreciate, that is, the final complete form that the artistic idea has taken, much as we appreciate the final form that any idea takes. The progression of any *written* idea, of course, from its initial form through its various stages of development, is hidden to all but the author and a few trusted editors. But the evolution of Mondrian's style from landscapist to Cubist, recorded in enduring finished pictures, gives us a complete document of change, recording the evolution of ideas from beginning to final form. I hadn't worked out all these insights as I re-entered modern Paris after seeing that exhibition, but the experience haunted me then and has stayed with me. I now can see that Mondrian's story offers a visual metaphor for something I have long appreciated in curriculum making and in intellectual discourse: a clear line of development. I will argue in these few pages that Mondrian's work, and especially his record of growth in composition and in the use of color, works as a metaphor for clear argument and, therefore, for good curriculum development.

Years after that encounter with Mondrian's trees, and holding a brand new doctorate in curriculum studies, I was talking with some fellow curriculists, wondering what exactly were the skills we could say we had in our profession. Some of my colleagues were instructional designers, confident in their ability to describe and guide all curriculum development situations in terms of boxes and arrows; I knew I was not an educational technologist. I finally concluded that my curricular skills were analogous to editorial skills, to the ability to shape written argument to its tightest and most cogent form and create a product with a clear and compelling sequence from beginning to end. It seemed to me that the coherent development of ideas, the basis of all good editing (I had been an editor for years), is the core of a strong curriculum and the hallmark of the process of curriculum making. A well-developed idea results in a clear and powerful (even if simple) structure of some kind, and I realized that my strongest compliments in assessing a work of curriculum discourse included words like *clear*, *cogent*, *tight*, *articulate*, *well-paced*, *clearly demarcated*, and other testimonials to clear organization (all the opposites to muddled, thick, directionless, vague, and other less pristine qualities). It came to me rather suddenly that Mondrian's 'Mondrians' exhibited all these qualities, and that the story of his arriving at his mature style was itself a clear, directional, smoothly paced tale. I seek clear pictures; I want to avoid the thick, dense, unilluminating jargon that is rife in our field; I seek evidence of a problem clearly defined and cleanly solved. Mondrian seems to meet all these criteria.

I say this while fully realizing that Mondrian is rarely what I want to see when I enter an art museum. I gravitate to many things depending on my mood and my purpose: I may prefer the soft colors and diffused sunlight of the Impressionists, or the rich shadows of the Dutch Baroque, or the bold spareness of contemporary art, or the haunting shadows of tribal objects from Africa. Mondrian's rationality isn't always sufficient, and he's never been my favorite artist. But when rationality and order are what I seek, Mondrian comes to mind as a metaphor.

I look for clearly developed argument all the time in my work as a curriculist. I apply this standard in editing drafts of educational materials, in critiquing rehearsals of public talks by our summer interns, in assessing the sequence and scope of programs for grant proposal purposes, in reviewing manuscripts for scholarly journals, in reviewing paper proposals for professional meetings, in assessing the effectiveness of program planning meetings (indeed of any meeting): in all these cases I tend to seek a clear progression from beginning to end analogous to what I most appreciate in the story of Mondrian's trees. There are times, of course, when I must be lenient, and when my standards become less clear and more admitting of rich, dense confusion, when the confusion of unformed ideas incompletely expressed may be rewarding for its own sake. Not all argument can or should always be as clear as Mondrian's trees eventually became. Still, it's a metaphor I return to time and again. We can all compare our work to Mondrian's.

LIVING WITH THE VISUAL ARTS

It is my good fortune to be combining my rather strict training in psychology and curriculum studies with an obsession that has stayed with me since Art History 101 twenty-five years ago. Doctoral work at Stanford allowed me to begin synthesizing the problems of educational planning with the concepts underlying art criticism, but doctoral work comes to an end and real-life professional positions take over. In my case, I moved quickly into administration, a not illogical extension of curriculum planning but one that mystified my more theoretically bent colleagues; for years I actually had fun doing such things as planning statistics courses for nurses in the hinterlands of Kansas, for the program planning aspects of such work can be rewarding to a hardcore curriculist even if the actual content remains a mystery. But the rewards of the curriculum development process, I discovered, are ultimately not as great as those of communicating a body of content one actually cares about. I began seriously to envy my colleagues who worked in 'real disciplines' such as English and history; my forays into the art history master's program were symptoms of this malaise. Finally the amazing W. K. Kellogg National Fellowship Program anointed me as a Fellow and gave me released time to study, to read, to interview people working in the arts, all in the name of my particular project on "the hidden arts curriculum of small towns"—another clever synthesis of professional training and deep-seated convictions. The three years of the Kellogg Fellowship gave me many things, including a broad background on American social history, public arts policy, and art history, but especially the confidence to pursue a job opportunity listed with an organization I had joined on Kellogg Funds. I took this position at the end of my stint as a Kellogg Fellow, making the kind of career zigzag that the Kellogg people encouraged.

My work is now officially and exuberantly tied to the visual arts, and to making the arts inviting, accessible, and enriching to as broad a population as possible. The Saint Louis Art Museum is a publicly funded museum, one of the first: "Dedicated to Art and Free to All" is carved in stone above the doors, and it has a long tradition of excellence and breadth in providing art education programs to the general public. Our mission is to help to make the museum and its collections and special exhibitions as public a resource as possible. In administering my portion of that mission, I apply many skills directly transferable from other positions not at all arts-related: staff recruitment and supervision, budget development, curriculum deliberation, lots and lots of memo and report writing, chairing meetings, public speaking. But now it is all about art, or at least all about an institution dedicated to art; the focus on a content area so important to my own convictions about what is crucial to human enrichment has made all the difference. As a curriculist operating in a setting whose content is what I now would select were I to major in a 'real' discipline, I find I am even better focused on problem solving, a bit more patient with the inevitable mistakes and setbacks, a lot more concerned that the programs be truly excellent—not only because one should run excellent programs, but also because a very good art program can help others to make the leap that I stumbled onto in a freshman dormitory lounge. A very good program can change people's lives, and the art museum setting is a place where this can happen daily. Being part of it is the most rewarding curriculum job I can imagine.

This enthusiasm for both the content and the process of curriculum work is something I encounter in virtually every museum educator I have met, though most do not describe it as curriculum work. The same enthusiasm is apparent in any good teacher, of course, but perhaps what distinguishes museum educators as an especially lively breed is the excitement of working every day, and exclusively, with the real raw data of their fields: with original works of art, as well as with 'students' who, by being in the building at all, have evidenced some interest in the subject. This aspect of museum education—the generally eager audience—is a blessing we experience virtually every day, in working with audiences that have made some effort to leave other obligations to be here. It also skews our efforts somewhat; it can lead us to forget that the art museum audience is not a representative cross-section of the population and that we must work doubly hard to attract the broad profile that schools and their mandatory nature can expect. As a result, art museums and museum educators in particular tend to develop enthusiasms for things that more traditional educators can safely ignore: zip code distributions of our audiences, marketing surveys of the population outside the museum, visitor surveys, good 'signage' and other user-friendly aspects of a welcoming museum, tracking of publicity devices to identify the most effective approaches. On the whole, these are not skills taught to curriculists in graduate school, though some with more statistical backgrounds than I might have a head start. On the whole, these are concerns developed out of a commitment to our discipline and to reaching our audience. They are the subject of unending discussion among museum educators at professional meetings, for museum education is an intensely practical field. I have mastered much new art-historical content in the process, of course, but of more generalizable importance to other curriculists is that odd phenomenon of cultivating skills I never needed before (audience surveys and the like), simply because I now care so very much about my programs being good. I have never once heard a museum educator ask whether the field really exists; it must be a question peculiar to curriculum theorists.

How, then, do the visual arts affect my present work as a curriculist? They are the subject of all my programs. They present a kind of literacy, a means of access to the human experience, that I believe the public needs—and enjoys, when the doors begin to open. They are the *raison d'être* of the institution that pays my salary. They are the basis for a ceaseless flow of clever program ideas from our staff members for students of all ages (preschool through senior citizens). They are a constant challenge in our search for ways to package both instructional materials and live programs in ways that will be rewarding to as many people as possible. They inspire my staff and me in surprising and delightful ways. And our commitment to making the visual arts accessible to a broad public—not merely to scholars and other believers—keeps us honest and direct in our own communication of what we have learned about art. My commitment to the public has made a bigger difference in the directness and clarity of my own public lectures than many years of presenting at professional meetings of curriculists could ever do; our lecturers, speaking to a general audience, are better than many professors at talking about art. There is something terribly real-world about museum education—at least as real-world as the traditional classroom, but rendered even more demanding by the fact that our students need not come and need not stay. They vote with their feet. The success of every program we offer depends on our ability to help students learn to translate from the peculiar and unfamiliar language of the visual arts into their own experience and idioms.

For this curriculist, at least, coming home to a subject matter that is central to her own enthusiasms as a student has provided a sense of focus that was otherwise unavailable. I think my experience may say something about the importance of a commitment to subject matter, generally, in curriculum work.

I must mention one other area of 'living' with the visual arts. I have been a serious photographer for many years, making some quite wonderful images that were remarkable enough to others to have resulted in some exhibitions, awards, and sales. These official acknowledgements of my 'good eye' have been fun, but the true rewards of photography are always in the moment when I am framing a strong composition. I know no other moment quite so enriching and quite so *right* as when I am looking through the lens at a shot I know will be good. My best work is in color, odd 'found' compositions juxtaposing objects that are together by chance in interesting patterns and color contrasts. I have done portraits; I have done weddings; I have duly documented my travels. But my best work is simplified, abstracted, almost not recognizable for what it 'really' is. One of my favorite photos involves cables and grips against the side of a large white grain elevator. I entitled it *A Prairie Mondrian.*

21

JANET L. MILLER

Reflections of Picasso's *Guernica*

I first saw Picasso's *Guernica* when I was a junior in high school. As I stared at the huge painting, I felt as though life itself had been squashed, twisted, contorted—destroyed for reasons that I neither understood nor could forgive. I remember that I felt frozen by this painting, unable to speak even after I had moved back and away from the canvas, in retreat from the pain that emanated from Picasso's vision of the wanton destruction of war. As I struggled to make sense of the electric light bulb hanging above the shredded newsprint and the convoluted forms of humans and animals, the sounds of my friends' voices and the explications of our guide remained muted to me, and I was aware only of my bewilderment and the immensity of my outrage.

As our group was gently nudged into movement by our class chaperones, I recall that, even as I was able to slowly reenter the chattering world of my peers, I was pondering the intensity of my reaction to *Guernica*. However, as we made our way through the crowds at the Museum of Modern Art, I was not even dimly conscious of the changes that had immediately and irrevocably taken place in my ways of seeing my own and others' lives. What I primarily felt at that moment, but could not articulate, was that all the color had been drained from the world.

Earlier, as my friends and I had lurched up and down the aisles of the train that was meandering through the hills of Pennsylvania, hauling us on our junior class trip from Pittsburgh to New York City, we had laughingly prioritized our tourist stops and had made pacts with one another about seating arrangements on the myriad bus tours that had been arranged for us. This was a first trip to New York City for most of us, and we were excited about seeing the lights of Broadway and Times Square. I knew that we would be touring the museums, too, and I looked forward to actually seeing some of the paintings that our teachers had discussed in our art and English classes. However, as we voted on our absolutes for this trip, the mandatory snapshot poses for our group included waving from the crown of the Statue of Liberty and hugging one of the New York Public Library stone lions. Art was something that our teachers had put on our itinerary, something that we would talk about in class on our return, and, although I secretly was pleased about our museum stops, I also was caught up in being a New York City tourist. As I giggled through our whirlwind tour of the city, and even after we had left the Museum of Modern Art, I could not have anticipated that the force of my response to one particular painting would mark a turning point in terms of my understanding of the connectedness of the arts to my work and my life.

Before I saw *Guernica*, painting, for me, had been removed from the everyday, existing as images, color, and light melded together as representations of life as it should or could be, and hanging on walls of museums located miles from the south hills of Pittsburgh where I lived. As a child growing up on the cusp between the steel mill towns and the burgeoning suburbs of Pittsburgh, I always looked forward to our "art and music" field trips into the city or to the galleries in Shadyside or to the exhibitions and concerts at the University of Pittsburgh or what was then Carnegie Tech. I remember that, even in fourth grade, when the emphasis among my friends was on kickball games and bike rides after school, I loved clambering onto the school bus to be carted off to the symphony or the planetarium or the museums. Returning home, amidst the singing and jostling of my fellow classmates, I sometimes tried to envision myself within the frames of the paintings that we had seen of bucolic landscapes or of serene dignitaries whose portraits appeared to attest to their importance and bearing in the world. Such paintings represented a life foreign to me, appealing in its apparent serenity, beauty, and dignity, yet separated from my world not only in dimensions of time and space, but also in terms of wealth, power, and circumstance.

Always, as we returned from these outings, the school bus would lumber past the steel mills as it rolled us away from the city, crossed the Liberty Bridge and returned us to the south hills. Often, on darkening winter afternoons, we could see wavering red skies as molten steel was dumped down mountainous slag heaps. Some of my friends waved at the steel mills as we bounced by, sending symbolic salutes to their fathers who worked the night shifts. And as the driver wedged our bus into its parking place next to the school gate, those paintings that I had viewed during the afternoon at the museum faded, replaced by the gray air and the familiar faces of the people who lived and worked in my neighborhood. Art was remote for me, distanced by the idealization of form and content to which I had attributed its function, even as a fourth grader.

Although I continued to be drawn to art and music, by my junior year in high school I knew that I wanted to become an English teacher. Literature was at the center of my academic interests, and I thought that I was lucky to have been able to decide so easily and quickly on a career that seemed as natural to me as breathing. What could be nicer than getting paid for loving to read and sharing that love with one's students? It was easy to be a high school romantic.

In my junior year, too, I began to learn more about the paintings of the Impressionists, in particular. I was influenced by my favorite high school English teacher, who could quote extensively from Longfellow, Poe, Emerson, and Irving but who also introduced us to the verse of Whitman and Dickinson and Lanier and to the regionalists and realists. Miss Beidler talked about these authors as among those who revolutionized the forms and intentions of literature in the United States, and she often would make connections among painters and musicians whose works represented similar challenges to notions of a romantic idealism or an aesthetic purity. Although I was interested in these challenges, I was connected to words, to written expression, as the primary means of creating meaning and eliciting response from others. I was learning about literature as a discipline, as a separate entity, and although Miss Beidler made countless connections for us, way before interdisciplinary studies and response-centered curriculum had hit the high schools, I still saw my art and music classes as auxiliary in my awkward attempts to interpret the meaning of life. I, of course, felt confident that this was the primary function of literature and, by extension, of the English teacher. I was sure that novels and poems and short stories and plays were the direct connections to Truth, and I was just as certain that there was Truth to be found, if one could just learn how to interpret those symbols.

What's scary about all of this is that I continued to learn about literature and its functions and its genres in this segmented and definitive manner throughout my college years as an English major. And, as I began to teach eleventh and twelfth grade English, just as I had hoped to do since my junior year in high school, I could feel in my teaching the further splintering of the disciplines into discrete subject matter areas. As an English teacher, I was expected to emphasize my students' mastery of factual details, such as the elements of a short story or the parts of speech or the characteristics of a tragic hero (nevermind the heroine). My colleagues and I all taught furiously, as if in a race to cover the canons before they could yet again enlarge and encroach upon our established grade-level content. We also taught as though there were one agreed upon interpretation of *The Scarlet Letter*, the main choice for a novel selection among all the eleventh grade English teachers in my department who were preparing their students for the New York State Regents exam.

Throughout my college studies, I felt that there was more to literature than the facts surrounding its creation or the categories into which we constantly placed each selection. And, as I taught high school English, I constantly wondered how Miss Beidler had found the room in her curriculum to even mention the connections that she saw among music, art, and the literature that we were studying at the time. I attempted to juggle the demands of a curriculum conceived as a set of predetermined objectives for my high school English students to achieve and my own need by now to make my own connections among works of art and the circumstances of everyday life. I also began to wonder how I might possibly encourage students to make their own connections, given the structures of schooling that encouraged them only to replicate mine. And I thought of *Guernica*.

After that junior class trip to New York, I had spent many hours talking with Miss Beidler and my classmates about our reactions to *Guernica*, which, of course, were varied in their intensity and focus. I chose to read more about the Spanish Civil War and tried to figure out Picasso's political stance and learned more about the historical circumstances that impelled Picasso to paint *Guernica*. I did this research, not as an assignment, but as a form of questioning about my own passionate response to the painting. I did not especially want to know in what period of Picasso's work we might classify this particular painting, or what techniques he borrowed or rejected from Cubism in order to create his angry and anguished response to the destruction of a small Spanish town and its people. Still, I think that I fell back on the traditional ways that I already had learned were means to understanding because I did not know how to trust my own responses.

But even as I pursued these traditional routes to knowledge about myself as well as about the circumstances that evoked Picasso's painting, I found myself remembering foremost my reactions when I saw *Guernica* for the first time. I knew, after that encounter with Picasso's reaction to the senseless murder of innocent people, that words were not necessary to evoke or to express response not only to a work of art, but to a human condition. Painting no longer was remote for me, no longer distanced from my world. *Guernica* had shattered my limited ways of seeing, had forced me to consider new ways of looking at life, had thrust into my consciousness different angles from which to view, to encounter, to confront the forces of competing visions of the world.

And now, when I teach curriculum to graduate students who, as teachers themselves, constantly are confronted with conceptions of knowledge as fixed and immutable packages that they are to dispense to their students, I think of *Guernica*. How might I encourage my students to conceive of curriculum as myriad and changing experiences and constructions of, as well as responses to, the particular intersecting historical, cultural, political, and social contexts in which they teach? What works or forms of art might enable them to effect their own questions and connections among the themes and intentions of our work together? What connections can we make together that might impel us beyond merely expressing ourselves or responding to others' creations and move us into examinations of the power structures and languages that constrain us? What new and equitable arrangements might we create through our examining of the taken-for-granted and our own envisioning?

These questions now drive my teaching of curriculum, but they began as unformed wonderings years ago, evoked by my bewildered yet impassioned response to Picasso's *Guernica*.

22

WILLIAM F. PINAR

The White Cockatoo: Images of Abstract Expressionism In Curriculum Theory

> "The aesthetic function of curriculum replaces the amelioration of the technological function with revelation."
> —Madeleine R. Grumet

The effort to understand the aesthetic character of curriculum has taken several turns. First, the significance of the arts to the general curriculum has been researched (Broudy 1988; Eisner 1985). Second, the aesthetic notions of knowledge acquisition and of thinking have been elucidated in order to suggest frameworks—frameworks contrasting with those associated with mainstream social and behavioral science—for understanding students' effort to understand and master the curriculum (Padgham 1988; Rosario 1988). Third, conceptions of artistry, articulated by artists themselves, have been linked with conceptions of curriculum (Padgham 1988). Fourth, the relation of art to society has been studied to provide an aesthetic agenda for curriculum (Beyer 1988). Finally, notions associated with the arts have been utilized to provide conceptual tools for teaching, researching and evaluating curriculum (Eisner 1985; Grumet 1976; 1978). In this brief piece I will reflect on the painting of Jackson Pollock to suggest what it might imply for understanding curriculum as an aesthetic text.

Pollock

Jackson Pollock is generally regarded as one of the brilliant, if not the most brilliant, American painters of the century, certainly the most brilliant and well-known abstract expressionist (Frank 1983, 7). The paintings which draw me most intensely are the so-called 'poured' or 'drip' paintings, by-and-large painted from 1947 to 1950. As you know, his work was controversial, and generally treated negatively in the lowbrow press: *Life* magazine likened it to wallpaper and necktie designs (it also described Pollock's pouring method as "drooling"), and as late as 1956, just before his death, *Time* displayed its philistine wit in characterizing Pollock as "Jack the Dripper" (Frank 1983, 7). Pollock's life, which began in Wyoming and ended in an automobile accident on August 11, 1956 on Long Island, was a troubled one, plagued by psychological problems he had difficulty articulating. (He underwent therapy, including Jungian therapy; indeed, he once characterized himself as a Jungian (Frank 1983, 31).) His life was further complicated by a severe case of alcoholism. Of his life it has been said: he "lived at a maximum pressure, mental and physical" (Robertson 1960, 147). Lee Krassner Pollock, his wife, an accomplished painter herself, is credited with prolonging his life and assisting his career.

For a film about his work made in 1951, Pollock described his work in this way:

> I don't work from drawings or color sketches. My painting is direct . . . The method of painting is the natural growth out of need. I want to express my feelings rather than illustrate them. Technique is just a means of arriving at a statement. When I am painting I have a general notion as to what I am about. I can control the flow of paint: there is no accident, just as there is no beginning and no end. (Namuth and Falkenberg 1951)

This directness and direct relation to his 'need' led one commentator to describe Pollock as a hero of "inarticulate spontaneity," a man who "painted his autobiography," who broke down the barriers between art and life (Frank 1983, 83).

Breaking down the barriers between curriculum and life, in a very general way, describes phases of my own work. When I first entered the field as a graduate student in summer 1969, I was astonished by the obsession with the 'technical' in curriculum development. The absence of life as lived in its psychological, political, and cultural dimensions made curriculum a blank canvas. My first study, "Sanity, Madness, and the School" was an effort to portray—from perspectives inspired by the recently deceased R. D. Laing—"life in schools," emphasizing the unspoken, unseen, but seemingly inescapable experience of losing oneself in school. Much of the work that followed attempted to elaborate strategies of 'working from within' which might support affirmative and transformational educational experience (Pinar 1972).

I was concerned all along with 'getting it right,' but hardly 'right' in the mainstream social science sense of obtaining results which are measurable and visible to any observer. That 'lowest common denominator' view of research leads one, it seems to me, to say the obvious (only the obvious is visible to everyone) and to say it simply enough to so that, indeed, 'everyone' can understand it. I cannot imagine any field progressing with such a principle firmly in place. (Certainly art could not; neither could physics.) Fortunately, curriculum has escaped these epistemological *cul-de-sacs* of mainstream social science—for the time being at least.

Early on, Pollock abandoned realism or representational painting (Rohn 1987, 122), which I would link loosely to mainstream empirical or statistical research—and to some forms of ethnography (Pinar 1988). Relinquishing realism allowed Pollock to become more self-conscious about the very process of painting, the generation of each stroke or line, a self-consciousness which led to stunning visual results (Rohn 1987, 122). In an infinitely more primitive way, leading to an incomparably more modest result, I have explored the uses of autobiography in the effort to comprehend curriculum, devising the method of *currere,* which allowed one to become more self-conscious about the 'strokes' and 'lines' etched into the personality by curricular experience (and vice versa). My point here is to suggest to you that the processes in which Pollock was engaged, processes that begin with the relinquishing of so-called realism or representationalism and end in abstract dynamics of color, shape, and texture, allow us to see anew and to understand anew. Such is the high purpose of art, and such is the high purpose of scholarship in curriculum. The point of curriculum scholarship is, I suggest, not to prove a point, not to inculcate a dogma, not to create techniques that will work anywhere, anytime, with anybody. Rather, the point of curriculum study can be conceived of as a search for vision, for revelation that is original, unique, and that opens the knowing and appreciative eye to worlds hitherto unseen and unknown.

Representational scholarship

The projects on which I work now (1990) tend to be 'representational' in nature. For instance, the introductory text on which William Reynolds, Wen-song Hwu, and I labor is, in fact, intended to be judged as representational. We are attempting to summarize and organize major curriculum discourses on behalf of the beginning student. We are working to make the book accessible and comprehensible. Indeed, we hope that when this book appears even the Tylerians in the field will acknowledge that it represents a comprehensive picture of the curriculum field today. A second and third project, the phenomenology-poststructuralism collections Bill Reynolds and I are editing, are efforts to organize those discourses. In addition to phenomenological and poststructuralist scholarship, these studies will include genealogical studies. Our intention is to represent those discourses faithfully, including their histories in the curriculum field, organizing them to increase their accessibility to a wider audience than hitherto has tended to appreciate them.

The collection of essays I recently edited with Joe Kincheloe on the South was perhaps more 'expressionist' than representational, or so I expect a majority of Southern readers will judge. In my essay, I tried to portray the South as it is, although I suspect a minority of Southerners would recognize themselves in this portrait. My central thesis is borrowed from literary historian and theorist Lewis Simpson, who argued that the South suffers from the repression of memory and history. Naturally the repressed tend not to recognize themselves; to these readers the essay will appear 'abstract expressionist.' Another project, a collection of essays on mathematics education which I am coediting with Linda Brandau, represents an application of notions in curriculum theory to mathematics education, and in so doing suggests a reconceptualization of that field. Specifically, we envision mathematics education in all of its 'lived' complexity. This is a vision of an 'embodied' mathematics, one that is dynamic, interpretative, political. On an imaginary continuum with representational scholarship at one end and abstract expressionist scholarship at the other, this project occupies a location closer to the latter end than the other projects I have described.

Abstract expressionist scholarship

Pollock paintings remind me, however, that I am drawn to a next phase of work more direct, more intellectually experimental and revelatory than 'representational' scholarship permits. To illustrate what this order of scholarship might be like, I refer to Pollock's 1948 *White Cockatoo.* Any of the so-called drip paintings would illustrate my point I suppose, as would several paintings in preceding (for instance, *Male and Female 1942*) and subsequent (for instance *Number Four 1952*) phases of his work. I am, however, particularly fond of the *White Cockatoo*, the utter originality of its color, shapes, movement, its general dynamism. As I see it, the cockatoo is in flight in this painting, not only in space, but in time as well, as if the painting were a time-lapsed photograph. Further, the very boundaries of the 'object' cockatoo are in motion, as they would be, visually, if the bird were in flight. Recalling Pollock's identification with Jung's work, we imagine that the cockatoo symbolizes flight and motion, and—from the bird's perspective—everchanging landscapes of colors, textures, motions, smells. I see the fecundity of the jungle in this painting, especially the jungle's complexity, its irrationality, its fullness. From the complexity of the jungle is refracted the complexity of the 'perceiving mechanism': the bird, the painter, the viewer. In phenomenological terms, subject-object interrelationalities are painted here.

The *White Cockatoo* abstracts curriculum in this sense, the sense akin to what Daignault terms "translation" and Grumet describes as "the middle way." For me these phrases can refer to the senses of perspective, motion, and time, senses articulated by phenomenology and perhaps even more pleasingly revealed by art. Pollock's paintings convey the postmodern movements of immediacy and dissociation, absence and presence, the simultaneity of complexity and simplicity, not just life against death, but life *and* death, including death in life. Pollock's life was deathful, and in his death his life became celebrated. These themes and movements are imaginable in the *White Cockatoo*.

My modest version of the *White Cockatoo* will be an effort not to paint, but to write of this maelstrom of experience, a maelstrom that often appears as still on the surface as a Louisiana pond in summertime, concealing the turbulence underneath, and the struggles to survive the suctions of educational institutions. The organizing image of this work will be not a bird, but a young man named Torless. His story is told in Robert Musil's *Young Torless*, a 1906 novel of *fin de siècle* Europe in which the stern formality of a military school functions as a foil to the sadistic sexuality of three of its students. Of course, the sense of foil is on the surface, as the sadistic sex practices of the characters can be viewed as having been 'produced' in complex ways by the repression of the school. In this novel is the opportunity to show motion where there is apparent stillness, sexuality where there is sublimation (indeed repression), learning in the face of bureaucratism, love surviving amid fascism. The 'bird' who takes flight in this jungle is the young Torless.

The challenge will be to write this portait nonrepresentationally; that is, to write an essay that is not 'about' *Young Torless* or sado-masochistic homosexuality or militarism in pre-Nazi Germany. The challenge will be to write an essay that inhabits the space between the novel and our world, that is sufficiently boundaried and interesting to merit the status of being its own distinctive object. I think Jacques Daignault's essays achieve this status. Their layers of complexity, including the ways Daignault illustrates his arguments in the structure of his writing, enable that scholarship to become its own translation and its own object. Madeleine R. Grumet's work achieves this status, albeit with different themes and methods than Daignault's. The supreme pedagogue, Grumet teaches us to see what, and as, she sees. To attempt nonrepresentational, 'abstract expressionist' scholarship is to attempt these orders of writing, writing that aspires to, and at times exemplifies, the revelatory function of art. Such scholarship, like Pollock's *White Cockatoo*, takes flight, widens the eye, and reveals anew the world which comes to form through our imagination, our labor, indeed, our lives.

23

NELSON L. HAGGERSON

A Poetry of Curriculum Inquiry

As both a poet and a critic of poetry, I have, with Dilthey, come to the conclusion that a poem can be "a form of spiritual nourishment which brings to expression other wellsprings of the life in which we move" (Palmer 1969, 22). A major part of my professional life for the past forty years has been curriculum, curriculum inquiry, reconceptualizing curriculum. Poetry, particularly my own, has provided the spiritual nourishment which has allowed me, as a curricularist, to thoughtfully approach curriculum work. Two articles which manifest outcomes of that thoughtful approach to curriculum inquiry are "Reconceptualizing Professional Literature: An Aesthetic Self-Study" (Haggerson 1986), a case for aesthetics, as well as logic, being used as a criterion for assessing professional literature; and "Reconceptualizing Inquiry in Curriculum: Using Multiple Research Paradigms to Enhance Curriculum Study" (Haggerson 1988), which argues for multiple approaches to curriculum inquiry in order to gain optimal understanding. In this chapter I explore some poems which served as wellsprings for those thoughtful approaches to curriculum inquiry.

In my doctoral work, which ended in 1960, I had done intensive study into comparative philosophies of education and how they contributed to curriculum development and inquiry. The philosophies I studied, even pragmatism, as I interpreted it then, could be systematically compared as to the nature of humans, the nature of knowledge, the nature of values, the nature of reality, and then 'applied' to curriculum development or evaluation. In my third college teaching position after completing my doctorate, I had opportunity to teach and do research with doctoral students. It was then that I came face-to-face with the meaning of existentialism as it affected/effected curriculum and inquiry. I was baffled. It wasn't written about in understandable terms for me, it didn't fit into the 'comparison' box to which I had become accustomed. At the same time, I was experiencing a kind of midlife emotional crisis, and I sensed that several of my doctoral students were in a similar position. After listening to one student for several hours, I found myself exhausted and in a state of utter frustration. My mytho-poetic proclivities which I had experienced in my undergraduate days took hold of me, and I began to write poetry again. "Authenticity" (Haggerson 1971) is a revised version of the poem I wrote in my state of being at that time:

Authenticity

Aware of your freedom?
Know the choice is yours?
But what of the responsibility?
The price of your knowing?

Anguish!

What of your life, then?
Full of choices, full of responsibilities.
What are your choices?
What are your responsibilities?

You choose your friends, your lovers.
Yea, you take a job and a place.
But what of the taking?
What of the living, the loving?

Be the friend philia or erotica?
The lover, spouse, companion?
What responsibilities the friend, the lover?
The listener, the teller, the father, the satisfier?

The job. What meaning has it?
Financial, intellectual, altruistic?
What does its fulfillment impose upon
Friend, lover, spouse, children?

The place. A location for sinking roots?
A place to live, to work, to serve?
Can it fulfill without imposing on
Job, friend, lover, spouse, children?

Among all of these you are condemned to choose.
The choices you make determine your essence.
The choices you make determine your morality.
The choices you make determine your beauty.

Whatever you choose makes a difference.
Whomever you choose makes a difference.
But what difference does it make?
What difference make?

The choices may not be easy
For the consequences may be dire.
The joys in selecting
May become sorrows in doing.

Be it known, however, that whatsoever
Or whomsoever you shall choose
The choice is yours and in so being
THE CHOICE IS YOU!

To make these choices
To recognize these responsibilities
Is to become human
Is to become authentic.
(1971, 26-27)

The poem was published in an anthology, which gave me some feeling of being a poet and gave me the courage to share it with friends and students. I received responses in both the form of questions and of comments. "You don't mean that 'the choices you make determine your essence,' do you?" "Surely you mean, your essence (nature) determines your choices!" "Yes, your choices determine your essence, that is what I mean." I had made the giant leap in understanding existentialism: *the choice is you!* That notion of choice now permeates all of my thoughtful curriculum work. Surely, choice making was in my experience of everyday living, surely it was part of my tacit knowledge, my being, my mythic life; but in the poem it became explicit, it was recognized as the wellspring of the life in which I move. So, what other insights and understandings did it bring forth?

This poem and others I wrote during the same period of time, published in a book of poems entitled *To Dance With Joy* (Haggerson 1971), became curriculum for my curriculum course. They were forms of self-expression for me and provocateurs for students to write their own curricula in poetic forms. One of the opportunities (objectives) of the curriculum course, and all of my courses, is "to do a creative project which is both self-reflective and manifests insights into the field of curriculum theory and inquiry."

Furthermore, I discovered in "Authenticity" that a poem is, indeed, self-expression. While I thought I had written the poem about my student's dilemma, I discovered it was really about my dilemmas. The fascinating understanding that comes with writing or reading good poetry is that while it is really about the author, it also is about the author's essence, which may be very much like that of other human beings. The reader or listener, then, picks up the essential meaning, identifies with it; the poem becomes a form of spiritual nourishment for both the writer and the reader. A good poem has both particular and universal aspects.

This insight led me to a quick and profound understanding of the notion of "naturalistic generalization" in qualitative curriculum inquiry. Proponents of the concept of naturalistic generalization say the research report should be written with such depth and clarity that it acts as a "vicar" (Stake and Trumbull 1982) which provokes vicarious experiences in the minds of the readers of the research. I have had such profound response to the poems in *To Dance With Joy*, including "Authenticity," that I, as both writer and poetry reader, view my good poems as vicars, as research reports, and as naturalistic generalizations. I made a case for poems being naturalistic generalizations in "Reconceptualizing Professional Literature" (Haggerson 1986), mentioned earlier in this chapter.

In my earlier curriculum inquiry years, I became preoccupied with the irreconcilables in curriculum philosophy. The curriculum is either the experience of the learner or it is systematized knowledge which consists of abstractions in the language of the teachers and scholars. The basic assumptions of those two positions were, in my mind, irreconcilable. However, my poetry led me to another conclusion. That conclusion is that when viewed from wholistic, systems, ecological, organic, or spiritual perspectives, the irreconcilables have a place; I could now view them as being 'both/and' rather than 'either/or.'

Cassirer (1946), in *Language and Myth*, found himself in a similar quandary with regard to language and myth; that is, he depicted language and myth as irreconcilable without an art form, particularly lyric poetry, to put them in wholistic perspective. He wrote about it as follows:

> But there is one intellectual realm in which the word not only preserves its original creative power, but is ever renewing it; in which it undergoes a sort of constant palingenesis, at once a sensuous and a spiritual reincarnation. This regeneration is achieved as language becomes an avenue of artistic expression. Here it recovers the fullness of life; but it is no longer a life mythically bound and fettered, but an aesthetically liberated life. Among all types and forms of poetry, the lyric is the one which most clearly mirrors this ideal development. For lyric poetry is not only rooted in mythic motives as its beginning, but keeps its connection with myth even in its highest and purest products ... Word and mythic image, which once confronted the human mind as hard realistic powers, have now cast off all reality and effectuality; they have become a light, bright ether in which the spirit can move without let or hindrance. (Cassirer 1946, 98-99)

A poem I had written before reading Cassirer bridged the irreconcilable gap between curriculum as language and curriculum as image (experience) for me; it makes Cassirer's point, too. The poem is called "Oneness":

> The oneness of it all is
> A house of many mansions,
> Multiple levels of consciousness,
> Numerous degrees of caring, and
>
> Infinite individual personalities ...
> Juxtaposed in dynamic relationships
>
> called a
>
> UNIVERSE
> (Haggerson, 1971, 97)

The mythic experience out of which this poem came was a "bright ether in which the spirit can move without let or hindrance." Oh, that we could so integrate our curriculum! Unfortunately, our poetry teachers, who have the greatest potential for integration, for the most part do not allow themselves this curriculum 'coup'.

In recent days I have done and mentored several of what Douglass and Moustakas (1985) have called "heuristic inquiries" in curriculum. Heuristic inquiry begins with an 'immersion' into the situation, usually your own. Having explicated that immersion experience, the researcher moves into the 'acquisition' phase in which the literature, other studies, and others' experiences are studied to give perspective to the researcher on the case at hand. Finally, after analysis, interpretation, and evaluation, the researcher arrives at the 'realization' phase in which understandings take place. Those are written up in a research report. Sometimes the reports take the form of a story, a poem, or an essay. Two of my recent heuristic inquiries had to do with multiethnic, multiracial situations (and me as researcher). "Pluralism" and "Hey, Lady!" (Haggerson 1971), poems written after earlier multicultural experiences, gave me insights which allowed poignant perceptions and perspectives of the recent studies.

Pluralism
or
Outsiders (Inside)

We entered the barn-like room
The only ones from our ethnic group.
"I feel like an outsider, do you?"
"A little, but lets stay, we are
Just strangers, just strangers . . ."

Music filled the hall. We danced, we
All danced. We all perspired, moved in
Rhythm with the music, the beat . . .
"Excuse me." "Ok." "Hi there."
"You dance well. I didn't know . . ."

"Twelve o'clock! Where has the time
Gone? I forgot about being an outsider."
"We aren't even strangers. How many
Have accepted us! We speak the same
Language. We dance, dance with joy."

(1971, 97)

I only have to imagine myself as a naturalistic researcher going into a culture I want to understand, but from which I am different, in order to appreciate the contribution of these poems to curriculum inquiry. To gain those understandings I need to find conmonalities. Once I have learned their dance, and can dance with joy, I can understand. But as a researcher I have sometimes failed to understand that they who are being studied may want to know me, too. This kind of research is interactive; it demands much more of the researcher than the stereotyped objectivity or even subjectivity. A student of mine was shocked by a comment from one of her subjects. She came to me in tears and told her story. I put it into a poem which has served as a heuristic for other naturalistic researchers.

The naturalistic curriculum researcher has many choices to make regarding her role, as is so poignantly illustrated in:

Hey, Lady!

Hey, lady! How come you're so kind,
know us so well?
How come you care when others don't,
accept our dirt, our dogs, our stares . . .
You come back when its late,
ease pain caused by others.

But hey, lady! How come we don't know you?

You think we don't care?
You afraid to be loved, afraid
of getting hurt?
Maybe if you stopped for us to know you
Somebody down the road wouldn't
get your attention. Maybe?

But anyhow, lady, whatever
pushes, pulls you . . .
I wish it would stop and
you'd let us know you.
Hey, lady! What you think?—feel?

(1971, 83)

And so poetry, for me and for many with whom I have worked, "is a form of spiritual nourishment which brings to expression other wellsprings of the life in which we move" (Palmer 1969). It is for those of us whom William F. Pinar (1988, 8) calls "mytho-poetic" curricularists, a means of self-expression and self-revelation, a way to express our mythic lives in figurative language, to maintain the richness of our sensual experiences and at the same time to provide a heuristic for others' and our own future inquiries. Poetry is, for us, both substantive and syntactical as we thoughtfully approach curriculum inquiry.

24

DELESE WEAR

Poetry and Curriculum Inquiry

"Let others boast pages they have written,
I take pride in those I've read."
Jorge Luis Borges, "A Reader"

Introduction

I write this essay to describe my personal engagement with poetry and how this engagement helps me to think. For here, I am not concerned with the current theoretical preoccupations with structuralism or deconstructionism or other esoteric examinations of 'the text'. Rather, I revel in the naked poems themselves and describe my intimate, intuitive, and immediate reaction to several I like enormously, and illustrate how these poems have provoked me to confront decisions and relationships and questions in my various lives. In other words, I have personalized the *content* of these poems which have moved me "to see . . . dimensions of [my] experience and aspects of [my] lived world"[1] I wouldn't have noticed otherwise.

Moreover, the poems I have selected illustrate what the reading of poetry might mean to curriculum researchers. I use the content of the poetry to illustrate the four themes of *wonder*, *ambiguity*, *seeing*, and *action*, described below where I have generously used the poems themselves to illustrate each.

Wonder

The first theme, *wonder*, characterizes a world view described by poet and, perhaps, the reader of poetry. It is a belief in the incompleteness of knowing, a belief that rejoices in the quest for knowledge, however partial. Diane Wakoski states it outright, that "Poems come from incomplete knowledge. / From the sense of seeing / an unfinished steel bridge / That you'd like to walk across."[2] Denise Levertov acknowledges this elusive searching for truths or answers, always subject to change:

Two girls discover
the secret of life
in a sudden line of
poetry.

I who don't know the
secret wrote
the line.
. . . .
        I love them
for finding what
I can't find,

and for loving me
for the line I wrote,
and for forgetting it
so that

a thousand times till death
finds them, they may
discover it again, in other
lines

in other
happenings. And for
wanting to know it,
for

assuming there is
such a secret, yes,
for that
most of all.[3]

Ambiguity

A significant part of wonder includes the second theme, an ability to tolerate, even to be at ease with *ambiguity*. In his *Letters to a Young Poet*, Rilke gently urges a young poet to "have patience with everything unresolved in your heart and to try to love the questions themselves as if they were locked rooms or books written in a very foreign language."[4] May Sarton's poetic response to this same theme includes the belief "that to become / A great, cracked, / Wide open door / Into nowhere / Is wisdom,"[5] which suggests to the curriculum investigator that the answerable questions, the counting, the sorting, the pre- and post-testing, the experimental groups—doors to *somewhere*—offer only partial answers. Knowing that knowing is always incomplete frees the researcher to pursue the knotty questions which elude many investigator's modes. Such a transformed researcher wears a different garment than before, according to Erica Jong:

I put on my poetry suit.
The prose falls away
like a dream I cannot remember
the images unraveling like threads
in a cheap dress, sewn in Hong Kong
to feed the hungry mouths
of sweat-faced Chinese children.

Now I am in my poetry suit.
I zip myself into it,
pink as flesh, tight as the suit
I was born in, & looking
seamless as a perfect poem,
gleaming as the golden fleece,
slim as a stripper at the Crazy Horse Saloon,
transparent as silk stockings,
& smelling of jasmine & tea rose.

But what was that old perfume
I left in the pocket,
that old cotton ball soaked
in Bal a Versailles,
that yellow glace glove
which lacks a mate,
that fine cambric handkerchief
brown with dried blood
from an old nosebleed.

Even poetry, pure as nothing
but snow or music,
drags life along
in its hidden pockets.

Oh for an art
that is not made of words
with all their odors
& discretions.[6]

The poet, by trade, and the curriculum researcher, by cultivating, perhaps, revelry for the multiple layers of language, are drawn to "words that sing . . . soar and descend." The South American poet Pablo Neruda describes his love of words in his *Memoirs*:

> I bow to them. . . . I love them, I cling to them, I run them down, I bite into them, I melt them down. . . . I love words so much . . . The unexpected ones . . . The ones I wait for greedily or stalk until, suddenly, they drop. . . . I run after certain words . . . They are so beautiful that I want to fit them all into my poem . . . I catch them in midflight, as they buzz past, I trap them, clean them, peel them. . . . And then I stir them, I shake them, I garnish them, I let them go. . . . Everything exists in the word.[7]

The curriculum researcher, like the poet who knows the inherent, uncertain, and uncapturable nature of language, can delight in this same nature of the language he or she encounters in curriculum inquiry. Similarly, the investigator who doesn't squirm in the face of uncertainty might be apt to *see more* and to *see differently*, the third theme.

Seeing

As Annie Dillard writes in her essay on seeing (the same Dillard who sees a spider in the corner behind the toilet—and writes about it),

> The literature of illumination reveals this above all: although it comes to those who wait for it, it is always, even to the most practiced and adept, a gift and a total surprise. I return from one walk knowing where the killdeer nests in the field by the creek and the hour the laurel blooms. I return from the same walk a day later scarcely knowing my own name. Litanies hum in my ears; my tongue flaps in my mouth Ailinon, alleluia! I cannot cause light; the most I can do is try to put myself in the path of its beam. It is possible, in deep space, to sail on solar wind. Light, be it particle or wave, has force: You rig a giant sail on solar wind. Hone and spread your spirit till you yourself are a sail, whetted, translucent, broadside to the merest puff.[8]

Katha Pollitt describes phenomena persistently ignored by the quantitative eye, and the possible high investment/low yield nature of an archaeological dig, a metaphor of great significance to the curriculum researcher:

> You knew the odds on failure from the start,
> that morning you first saw, or thought you saw,
> beneath the heatstruck plains of a second-rate country
> the outline of buried cities. A thousand to one
> you'd turn up nothing more than the rubbish heap
> of a poor Near Eastern backwater
> a few chipped beads,
> splinters of glass and poetry, broken tablets
> whose secret lore, laboriously deciphered,
> would prove to be only a collection of ancient grocery
> lists.
> . . . .
> Pack up your fragments. Let the simoon
> flatten the digging site. Now come
> the passionate midnights in the museum
> basement when out of that random rubble you'll invent
> the dusty market smelling of sheep and spice,
> streets, palmy gardens, courtyards set with wells.[9]

Similarly, Miller Williams tells us to "notice everything: / The stain on the wallpaper / of the vacant house, the mothball smell of a / Greyhound toilet. / Miss nothing. Memorize it. / You cannot twist the fact that you do not know"[10]; William Carlos Williams describes cold plums and red wheelbarrows; Linda Pastan notices line breaks on highways. The poet *sees* what most of us only glance at, and writes of "what has no life / unless he gives it life / with words."[11] Immersion in poetry, then, can help us to see the taken-for-granted, or as Sarton portrays it, thanking not the light, but rejoicing "in what we see / Because of it. / All things are made new."[12]

Action

Obviously, curriculum researchers cannot merely ask questions or mull endlessly over hypotheses or methodological issues. Or just read poetry. Action is necessary, hopefully *reflective action*, the fourth theme. Here, if the reader of a poem is prompted to see his or her surroundings in a new way, so might he or she be energized to consider curriculum phenomena from a new perspective with a more critical awareness bound for action. Nikki Giovanni writes that

> poetry is motion graceful
> as a fawn

gentle as a teardrop
strong like the eye
finding peace in a crowded room
. . . .
a poem is pure energy
horizontally contained
between the mind
of the poet and the ear of the reader
if it does not sing discard the ear
for poetry is song
if it does not delight discard
the heart for poetry is joy
if it does not inform then close
off the brain for it is dead [13]

Pablo Neruda also writes of this poetic nudging, of what he calls his "poet's obligation":

to whoever is not listening to the sea
this Friday morning, to whoever is cooped up
in house or office, factory...
or street or mine or dry prison cell,
to him I come, and without speaking or looking
I arrive and open the door of his prison,
and a vibration starts up, vague and insistent
. . . .
so that, wherever those in prison may be,
wherever they suffer the sentence of the autumn,
I may be present with an errant wave,
I may move in and out of windows,
and hearing me, eyes may lift themselves,
asking, "How can I reach the sea?"[14]

Poetry, then, can evoke thought and press one to action: theory-building scholarship, perhaps; inquiry into the previously unexamined; or new examination of the taken-for-granted. Action, in this sense, encompasses all the previous three poetic themes of wonder, seeing, and ambiguity and is a reflective outgrowth of these perspectives. Something, it seems, can happen in that wondrous electric space between the mind and the written word which urges us to *move*.

Summary

I have taken the reader through what has been my reading of some poetry which has influenced the way I think. This, in turn, has influenced the way I approach curriculum: I believe I do so more reflectively; I try to see more comprehensively and minutely; I am less uneasy with incompleteness; I think I am more compelled to act on my beliefs.

I have not meant to suggest that poetry is the only medium which can release the researcher to such an awareness. Rather, it is only one of many discursive and nondiscursive forms of the arts and humanities which has the potential to do so. Walker Percy, a writer who has given me hours of discomforting pleasure, goes even further in his claim that

> the vocation of the artist, whether novelist, poet, playwright, film maker, can perhaps be said to come that much closer to that of the diagnostician rather than the artist's celebration of life in a triumphant age. . . . one of the tasks of the serious novelist is, if not to isolate the bacillus under the microscope, at least to give the sickness a name, to render the unspeakable speakable. Not to overwork the comparison, the artist's work in such times is surely not that of the pathologist whose subject matter is a corpse and whose question is not *what is wrong* but *what did the patient die of*? For I take it as going without saying that the entire enterprise of literature is like that of a physician undertaken in hope. Otherwise why would we be here? Why bother to read, write, teach, study, if the patient is already dead?—for in this case the patient is the culture itself.[15]

Another physician-writer, this one poet John Stone, knows this and told his students in a commencement address/poem, "Gaudeamus Igitur" ("therefore, let us rejoice"):

> For there will be the arts
>   and some will call them
>   soft data
>   whereas in fact they are the hard data
>   by which our lives are lived
> For everyone comes to the arts too late
> For you can be trained to listen only for the oboe
>   out of the whole orchestra
> For you may need to strain to hear the voice of the patient
>   in the thin reed of his crying
> For you will learn to see most acutely out of
>   the corner of your eye
>   to hear best with your inner ear [16]

About this same John Stone and multiple perspectives, of which poetry presents but one, Maxine Green has written that

> John Stone's poem, "He Makes a House Call," from *In All This Rain*, may have been written by the man who is a cardiologist, perhaps the very cardiologist who was present at his father's surgery; but even though poet and surgeon are the same human being, the experiences and the reports can never mesh. Whatever Dr. Stone was asked to write down in the hospital, on the other hand, possessed no greater or no lesser truth than what we find in his poem. The domain was different; the protocols were different; the cognitive style was different. Each perspective, like each utterance, was irreducible.[17]

Likewise, I have proposed here, we can find no greater or lesser truths in the best of curriculum scholarship than what we can find in a first-rate poem, or any fiction for that matter. Both have much to tell us that is important.

ACKNOWLEDGMENTS

Excerpt from "With Words" from *The Motorcycle Betrayal Poems* by Diane Wakoski, published by Simon & Schuster, 1971. ©Diane Wakoski. Reprinted by permission of the author.

Excerpt from "The Secret" from *O Taste and See* by Denise Levertov. ©1964 Denise Levertov Goodman. Reprinted by permission of New Directions Publishing Corporation.

Excerpt from *Letters to a Young Poet* by Rainer Maria Rilke, translated by Stephen Mitchell. ©1984 Random House. Reprinted by permission of Random House.

Excerpt from *The Magus* by John Fowles, revised edition and forward. ©1978 John Fowles Ltd. Reprinted by permission of Little, Brown & Company.

Excerpt from "Of the Muse" from *Halfway to Silence* by May Sarton. ©1980 W. W. Norton. Reprinted by permission of W. W. Norton.

"The Poetry Suit" from *At the Edge of the Body* by Erica Jong. ©1979 Erica Mann Jong. Reprinted by permission of Henry Holt and Company, Inc.

Excerpt from *Memoirs* by Pablo Neruda, trans. Hardie St. Martin. ©1976, 1977, Farrar, Straus and Giroux, Inc. Reprinted by permission of Farrar, Straus and Giroux, Inc.

Excerpt from *Pilgrim at Tinker Creek* by Annie Dillard. ©1985 Harper and Row. Reprinted by permission of Harper and Row.

Excerpt from "Archaeology" from *Antarctic Traveller* by Katha Pollitt. ©1982 Alfred A. Knopf, Inc. (first appeared in *The New Yorker*). Reprinted by permission of Alfred A. Knopf, Inc.

Excerpt from "Let Me Tell You" from *Halfway from Hoxie: New and Selected Poems* by Miller Williams.©1977 Miller Williams. Reprinted by permission of Louisiana State University Press.

Excerpt from "Poetry" from *The Women and the Men* by Nikki Giovanni. ©1970, 1974, 1975 Nikki Giovanni. Reprinted by permission of William Morrow and Co., Inc.

Excerpt from "The Poet's Obligation" from *Fully Empowered* by Pablo Neruda. ©1967, 1969, 1970, 1975 Alastair Reid. Reprinted by permission of Farrar, Straus and Giroux, Inc.

Excerpt from *Diagnosing the Modern Malaise* by Walker Percy. ©1985 Walker Percy. Reprinted by permission of Faust Publishing Co.

Excerpt from "Gaudeamus Igitur" from *Renaming the Streets* by John Stone. ©1983 The American Medical Association (first appeared in the *Journal of the American Medical Association*, volume 249, number 13, April 1, 1983). Reprinted by permission of the author.

NOTES

1. Maxine Greene, "Toward Wide-Awakeness: Humanities in the Lives of Professionals," in *Literature and Medicine: A Claim for a Discipline*, ed. D. Wear, M. Kohn & S. Stocker (McClean VA: Society for Health and Human Values, 1987), p. 7.

2. Diane Wakoski, "With Words" from The *Motorcycle Betrayal Poems* (NY: Simon and Schuster, 1971), p. 103.

3. Denise Levertov, "The Secret" from *O Taste and See* (NY: New Directions, 1962), pp. 21-22.

4. Rainer Maria Rilke, *Letters to a Young Poet*, trans. Stephen Mitchell (NY: Random House, 1984), p. 34.

5. May Sarton, "Of the Muse" from *Halfway to Silence* (NY: W. W. Norton & Co., 1980), p. 61.

6. Erica Jong, "The Poetry Suit" from *At the Edge of the Body* (NY: Holt, Rinehart & Winston, 1979), pp. 27-28.

7. Pablo Neruda, *Memoirs*, trans. Hardie St. Martin (NY: Farrar, Straus & Giroux, 1976), pp. 53-54.

8. Annie Dillard, *Pilgrim at Tinker Creek* (NY: Bantam, 1974), pp. 34-35.

9. Katha Pollitt, "Archaeology" from The *Antarctic Traveller* (NY: Knopf, 1981), pp. 21-23.

10. Miller Williams, "Let Me Tell You" from *Halfway from Hoxie: New and Selected Poems* (NY: Dutton, 1973), p. 61.

11. Wakoski, *The Motorcycle Betrayal Poems*, p. 105.

12. Sarton, *Halfway to Silence*, p. 61.

13. Nikki Giovanni, "Poetry" from *The Women and the Men* (NY: William Morrow Co., 1970), n.p.

14. Pablo Neruda, "The Poet's Obligation" from *Fully Empowered* (NY: Farrar, Straus & Giroux, 1975), p. 3.

15. Walker Percy, *Diagnosing the Modern Malaise* (New Orleans: Faust Publishing, 1985), pp. 3-4.

16. John Stone, "Gaudeamus Igitur" from *Renaming the Streets* (Baton Rouge: Louisiana State University, 1985), p. 23.

17. Maxine Greene, "Toward Wide-Awakeness: Humanities in the Lives of Professionals," p. 10.

25

RICHARD BUTT

In the Spotlight of Life: Dramatic Expression as Emancipatory Pedagogy

I have turned to the arts in the last ten years, particularly dramatic expression, for insight, imagination, and understanding as a form of emancipatory pedagogy. How I came to see dramatic expression in this way is the focus of this story. Bearing in mind that my educational roots lie in science, it's a paradoxical story. I will not be focusing on a particular work, not even on the theatre in its narrow sense, but on a flow of life that brought me to the arts. What I will examine is dramatic expression as a means of transformation. It is about overcoming, as Madeleine R. Grumet (1978, 50) succinctly puts it, the disjunction of feeling and form.

Scene 1: Showing Off

Had I been asked if theatre had any meaning for me in childhood I probably would have been ignorant and disparaging.

> The theatre . . . what . . . you mean the pictures (movies)? No! Oooh you mean where they do plays an' stuff. Well . . . I 'avn't bin there 'ave I. That's posh stuff what toffs goes to. Iss just people prancing about on a stage showin' off like. Can't understand 'alf of it anyway. Closest I'd get probably would be a busker outside along the queue.

My heavy Gloucestershire dialect, learned in a poor working class neighborhood, was a source of embarrassment when I went to a middle class elementary school. We, in turn, mocked and developed a prejudice against people who spoke as if they had pebbles in their mouths. I saw the theatre as part of this other culture; it felt oppressive to me, and elitist. Being a working class child pressed me to 'know my place'; even dialect, my own voice, was not seen as legitimate. It surely didn't encourage me to express much of anything except perhaps anger. Those who did 'express' themselves—such as actors—I saw as showing off, the opposite of being seen and not heard. I probably was envious of their opportunity to be authentic and to have voice.

Early schooling, however, did provide an important initial key which unlocked the box of alienation: I was able to go to nursery school from the age of three in a working class neighborhood. After, I attended a British infant school which practiced open education. Activities at both schools included expressive arts and play; concrete learning activities also enabled me to create my own meaning and knowledge.

Scene 2: Windows and Voice

This real, dramatic, and expressive pedagogy ended when I passed the eleven-plus exam and went to grammar school. One might expect that its harshness (somewhat like the school in *Dead Poets Society* but not as severe) would squelch the embryo of self nurtured by my elementary schooling. It appears, however, that I had enough of self to withstand, resist, and even benefit from the traditions of the grammar school.

My paucity of language skills did not permit much expression through that mode. Mostly, the way English was taught was like being hit across the head with a log. Shakespeare was taught in a didactic manner, a manner exactly the opposite of how I later learned he could live. As well, it was taught and acted with a stilted, refined accent—a double turnoff. Ironically, real Shakespearian speech would probably have been closer to my 'illiterate' Gloucestershire accent than to BBC English. I later saw the full beauty of Shakespeare in film—particularly *Romeo and Juliet*—where the reality of the times were married with a colloquial approach to the language. Understanding the nature of the Globe Theatre—Shakespeare for all—and populist drama in those times helped me to re-understand. The cultural aberrations and elitist abuse of theatre and drama were clearer.

In the meantime, what expressive windows existed for me in the grammar school? One theme, believe it or not, is science. The curriculum in science was based, for at least fifty per cent of the time, on scientific investigations. It was personal, practical, and relevant to my interests. I did better in the sciences and maths because cultural deprivation and my relatively poorer English skills did not affect my marks in these areas. Also, within the symbol system of maths and science, I started on an equal basis with my 'culturally richer' peers. Since we were able to specialize early, I took maths, physics, chemistry, and biology as the core of my curriculum. The symbol system of science and its practical and personal inquiries were an emancipatory route for me. It enabled me to experience and create my own meaning. A second window which kept me interested in school and allowed me to develop a more positive self-esteem related to sports—track and field, specifically pole vaulting, and rugby. Apart from the positive feedback I got from playing for school teams and winning regional championships, sports provided an outlet for deeply rooted aggression as it related to my class-conflicted ego.

I lived in other worlds in adolescence; a second, darker world, which contrasted quite sharply with school, was that of the street. I belonged to a working class gang. We were called Teddy Boys because we wore drain pipe trousers and velvet-lapelled long jackets reminiscent of the Edwardian era. Our life was characterized in the usual gang way—initiations, social sorties together, illegal activities, and fights. It was an expression, if destructive, of our alienation. I still bear the physical and emotional scars of that time. It almost claimed me forever, but other values won out. I recently saw *The George McKenna Story*, about a young black principal who tries to reach the kids in his ghetto school—Washington Preparatory High School, I think it was. He gradually reclaimed the school and the kids from violence, drugs, criminal activity, and hopelessness. One scene captured the contradictory dramas that I am trying to portray. As his staff and students participated for the first time in the school district's Shakespearean Festival inside the gym, the principal was outside, at the rear of the building, dealing with a very tense physical confrontation between two gangs. The juxtaposition of these two incidents was a vivid visual image for me.

I did, however, experience some significant glimmers of expression through poetry and drama. One moment gave me hope in English and a chance to use poetry to express my voice. "Ode to a City's Dawn" was written when I was eleven. In contrast to the bare passes in English which I usually achieved, I received ninety per cent for this poem. The first four lines I can remember:

> Oh dawn when the streets are still cold and wet,
> The early bustle hasten to work
> While in other regions of the town
> Blinds there are still drawn down

I could name class-consciousness.

In an all-boys school I took the part of a woman in a school play as I began my intermittent involvement in drama. Whereas playing a woman, for a working class lad, was somewhat traumatic, I had to learn to empathize with and portray what another person might experience. These two incidents signalled the potential for success in areas other than science and math and were the start of explorations which moved me elsewhere.

There was yet another world, another people, besides school people and street people, which had an electric impact in terms of bringing me closer to the expressive arts. It gave me a voice and sense of expression which has been unparalleled in my life. It was music—I played guitar, washboard, tea-chest, and double bass and sang(!), firstly in skiffle music (folk and bluegrass) at age thirteen. By fifteen and through twenty-two, I was a semiprofessional musician playing traditional, mainstream, big band, and modern jazz in local clubs and finally, as the Beatles emerged, I played in a successful rock group. The genres of blues, jazz, and rock as forms of protest music, particularly rock for the working class, gave me vital, dynamic, visceral, and emotional expression—as it did for our audiences who participated through dance. It not only gave me a vehicle for expression of my feelings, but, with the social commentary of the lyrics, enabled me to participate in a type of self-education and transformation. All of these experiences—informal education, science education, sports, the gang—were telling for me in a way that music clearly showed. They all were *dramatic forms of expression*.

Scene 3: Teachers' College

At college I moved further towards the humanities through a study of a broad range of education-related subjects. I especially remember relearning about children and adolescents through literature and autobiographical activities. At this point literature suited me—during my late teens I had discovered I could read and understand. It opened up other human worlds, many related to suffering, the human condition, and emancipation. I had read many British and North American authors and most of Sartre. What is most important about this era is that I discovered teaching, especially in the way I had been taught in elementary school, as a form of expression, as well as student politics, as I continued to work for myself and the underdog. My interest in drama was stimulated by the rich life at college. I saw many plays; one which I remember vividly for its impact was *No Exit* by Sartre. I played Marco, a dark, swarthy Italian (!), in Arthur Miller's *View from the Bridge*, understanding then the link between ethnicity and class in North America. The dramatic greening of Richard Butt was helped by increasingly realistic Shakespearean films and by the revolution in British drama (I recall *Look Back in Anger*, by John Osborne) which moved from a focus, in classical style, on aristocratic life to what we called "kitchen sink" drama: ordinary people and the *angst* of daily living, a significant step in the renaissance of drama as a form of populist expression.

Scene 4: Canadian Education

Teaching, mainly science, gave me the opportunity to use the child-centred methods that I had experienced as a child, but I moved from traditional science investigations into questions of personal interest to my pupils, and I used many simulations and games. It was but a short step to role playing—for example, portraying the behavior of molecules from which we could gather data to illustrate various gas laws, or role playing the biographies of famous scientists.

Now in Canada, I became more familiar with populist drama. Through an introductory course at university I learned to create dramatic meaning and express this in the form of playlets. I particularly remember directing a multimedia piece, including dance, of our integration of Bernard Shaw's *St. Joan* and the musical *Hair* as it related to the status of women. In relation to women and voice I found *Something Unspoken* the most intriguing of Tennessee Williams's plays. In this play, two older women live together in a conversation of utter gentility and politeness. "Would you care for some more tea dear"? "Oh! How thoughtful of you dear." In reality this superficiality hides their absolute hatred of each other. Williams paradoxically uses the powerful voice of drama in a contradictory way to show voicelessness. Ken Mitchell, Canadian playwright and friend, with whom I played rugby, wrote a play called *Cruel Tears* about sadness, powerlessness, and tragedy in the lives of Western Canadian truckdrivers. It was loosely based on *Othello*. Humphrey and the Dumptrucks, a well-known Canadian folk group, played the Shakespearean chorus. Ken would sit in the audience each night, listen anonymously to conversations, and incorporate his interpretations of their ideas into the script for the next day or week. There were quite a few populist drama groups across Canada which lived in small towns for a while in order to develop a play based on the community's joys and sorrows. After the performances the audience was invited to contribute, from their experiences, vignettes of their lives in mining or farming communities. Social animation, often community development, and sometimes protest were the result. At the time I was still involved in student politics—getting more participation for students in what went on in the Faculty of Education. One significant outcome of this critical stance related to the traditional pedagogy, particularly at the graduate level, in education courses. I got really sick and tired of students being required to read their boring fifty-page papers that skipped from one 'expert's' quote to another with nothing of themselves invested or risked. For my presentation, with three wood ticks still remaining in my head from a recent sojourn in the bush, I played guitar and sang, among other things, "What's It All about, Alfie?" and used cartoons to role play prehistoric people trying to problem solve how to move major boulders from one place to another. I thought that this was just as pertinent to the course, Philosophy of Educational Administration, as those boring papers, and perhaps more motivating.

Scene 5: Teacher Education

Just at this time I was given a teaching fellowship at university while completing my master's degree. Having been a critic of teacher education, as a student politician I felt I had to practice what I preached even more than those I had criticized. Fortunately, being in science education and having been unusually socialized through informal education into self-directed learning, I was able to provide concrete student-centred learning experiences which we used as a basis for personal and collective reflection. Science education, however, became less and less my focus as I moved into general pedagogy, curriculum, professional development, and school improvement courses.

My predisposition toward the pedagogy of personal expression melded well with *The Journal of Curriculum Theorizing (JCT)* community, which I had discovered early in my university career, particularly the work of Bill Pinar and Madeleine R. Grumet as it related to autobiography. It linked well with my own early experience in teacher education. It was from this base that Danielle

Raymond and I evolved collaborative autobiography as a means for understanding teachers' knowledge and development. The process provides a powerful means through which the teacher can express who she is and who she wishes to become. In our experience, it is very energizing and empowering for teachers. It enables significant renewal and professional development. This approach highlights *storytelling* as a dynamic and culturally appropriate form of pedagogy. We have used it, as well, to change our mode of conference presentation and in our scholarly publications.

Meanwhile, in undergraduate teacher education, I began to use autobiographical activities and storytelling to embed professional development in personal history. We also began to use more simulation, role playing, psychodrama, videotape productions to illustrate our stories, to enact practicum events, and to express how we wished to be as teachers. At this time, in pursuing another emancipatory interest of mine—multiculturalism—I reviewed the literature as to what teaching strategies reduce racism and prejudice. Among other activities that provided experiential learning, self-reflection, personally and socially relevant interactions, and self education (all quite Deweyan in flavour), the set of activities that seemed to have special impact was role playing, psychodrama vignettes, and creative projects in drama and the arts. This literature review reinforced my intuitive move towards the use of dramatic and expressive activities as an emancipatory pedagogy. In fact, in the conference version of the paper, I opened with the following playlet about my own life and ended the paper by looking back at it.

> The setting is a working class household. The father had made bigoted racial comments on many occasions. The son, sixteen years old, and the father had argued many times before about racial issues. The scene opens within the latter part of such an argument, when the ires of both antagonists have been well stoked with volatile fuels.
>
> SON: *(in heated exasperation)* "You don't like the wogs, the frogs, the ities, the chinks, the pakis. You don't like the toffs—they have all the money. You don't like what your kids want to do—especially me. Who the hell do you like?
>
> FATHER: *(exploding with rage . . . spluttering, red-faced)* Don't you goddam well come'ere with that posh school crap. You know nuthin. You bloody upstart . . . *(father continues*

general tirade about the thanks he gets for working his guts out to provide a roof over his son's head and food on the table . . . but gradually subsides with a hurt look and posture. He slumps back down in the chair).

SON: *(seeing an opening mounts a second assault with accusatory venom)* What about those two blokes you work with then? Eh! What about John and Bryce? Eh! . . . *(pause)* You *like* them don't you? Don't you? You 'ave fun with them. I've seen you. Go on . . . Admit it. You like 'em. They're black aren't they? *(Triumphantly)* They're black.

FATHER: *(winces, recoils angrily in Archie Bunker fashion, at first, then gradually deflates, looks more sensitive, human and speaks quietly.)* Thas different ent it. I know them. We work well together. They're good blokes.

The vignette between father and son with which we started this paper reflects the fact that working class individuals can be racists. It also, however, illuminates that windows through this racism can occur within the pedagogy of day-to-day interactive, personal, cooperative experience which provides for self-education and personal growth.

Within the graduate course where I used collaborative autobiography, I had always encouraged students to use various forms to express their stories; but I was more ready, now, to risk role playing and other forms of dramatic expression both for oral presentations in class and for written work. This led to a tremendous variety of creative expression in class, including playlets which required us to participate in recreating an event in someone's life. We could better understand by 'being there.' I particularly remember Irwin Warkenton putting himself, and his competence as a teacher, on trial with dialogues between judge, defendant, and jury. Greg Nixon wrote his play *Effulgence and Effluvium* as part of this course. We performed this play alongside a drama by Charles Hart at JCT (1987), with me playing Greg (the teacher), him playing the Great White Buffalo, and John Martini taking the part of the superintendent in his school on the Indian reserve where he teaches. What a rich way to have the professor understand the contradictions of a graduate student's situation! If we wished to communicate, represent, re-present, and express a life situation for pedagogical, developmental, or scholarly purposes, we felt that drama was a most effective medium. The audience appeared to agree.

With my colleagues, I have tried to explore how to use dramatic expression further. Judy Bopp, my colleague from the *Four Worlds' Project*, and I asked small groups to exchange stories of incidents they had experienced involving racism. Then they created a role play and performed it twice; the first time the audience observed. During a brief break they planned several interventions in which a member of *another* group would step in and transform the situation during the second performance. This proved to be a powerful way both to understand and to transform the reality of racism.

We have now taken collaborative autobiography into the field to work with school staffs on professional development. David Townsend and I use dramatic expression for a variety of purposes including acting out fears related to the commitment, work, risk, and courage required to engage in self-initiated, school-based staff development; representing the stress of daily work life; portraying one group member's story of a past event that influenced the way that person currently teaches; and acting out envisioned images of how they wish to be in the future.

Scene X: Beyond Words

I have tried to convey how I came to see personal dramatic expression as emancipatory pedagogy. This, of course, is not new to drama educators, but it was new to me. I have done this in the light of my own life experiences but, to bring a deeper meaning, I would like to cast it the light of a theory of how we can live. "Brighter Than a Thousand Suns: Facing Pedagogy in the Nuclear Shadow," an article by my friend and colleague David Smith (1988), is the source of this less individualistic and less egocentric window; he calls for a pedagogy whose form more appropriately expresses our feelings than nuclear war. He speaks of the limits of our languages such as scientism or the traditional cognate disciplines; he speaks of the ultimate resistance of things to be fully named and the pull of freedom.

> Given that the language which dominates (us) allows us to speak but also prevents us from saying what cannot be said in it (any discourse is at the same time a violence against discourse), how should we conduct ourselves in a manner which, while acknowledging this contradiction, ensures that we do not also give up on our own regeneration? (Smith 1988, 275)

The dramatic expression of story is a culturally universal way of understanding, re-understanding, portraying, communicating, and experiencing. While still contradictory, it offers a balance to the languages of other disciplines. What it can uniquely offer, beyond even its multidimensionality which swamps logic with its richness, is that it is malleable and ductile; it is about form, finding form, but it is formless. It does not tyrannize us with as much preformation of knowledge. The learner is able to freely explore and consider the forms that meaning and feelings can take. It enables the ambiguity of life to be lived which "calls for a response" (Smith 1988, 277)—interpretation. Thought and action are not separated but can live together in 'the play.' Dramatic expression is an interpretive pedagogy which "calls out to us from within the heart of what we do not understand and for which we may not at present have words. Pedagogy then becomes a vocation to live and act within the difference between what we know and what we do not know" (Smith 1988, 276). This pedagogy offers us an invitation to *act* in all senses of the words. It provides "grounds for our action rather than acquiescence" (Grumet 1978, 39). In interpreting and reconstructing our past, present, and futures, we move beyond what we *thought* before through action. In exploring these notions through acting them out we are able to rehearse the possibility of transformation.

26

NOREEN B. GARMAN

The Drama of the Classroom: Dramaturgy as Curriculum Inquiry

In my early years I took elocution lessons. I was the first generation of kids in my family to be introduced to the arts by 'taking lessons.' I also took violin and piano (which never really 'took'). My younger sisters took ballet. Once a week my mother would take me on the streetcar to Mrs. Brown, my elocution teacher, who was dedicated to improving my oral delivery as well as my poise in front of an audience. Each week I performed various dramatic readings for her and my mother. I turned out to be one of the stars in her many recitals and, later, a leading character in my high school productions. I was not a very good actor but I liked being in a play. It made me feel involved. For me, a drama was where ordinary events were given extraordinary meaning and I was a part of it. There was something special in the story of the drama which could be experienced. It made more sense than the passive, boring world of school ideas. It was alive!

While I was still in high school I was introduced to the theater. My first encounter with Broadway came when I went to a performance of G. B. Shaw's *Major Barbara*. The cast included Charles Laughton, Burgess Meredith, Cornelia Otis Skinner, Eli Wallace, and Anne Jackson. Years later I would still remember the dynamic energy of that incredible group. How extraordinary it was to be able to live in another world with them for a little while, in such total immersion of the psyche. I could feel the dramatic nuance of conflict and motive, of dissonance and emotion. I discovered the power in the vicarious experience of the theater.

In the late fifties I managed to take in the best of the musicals and plays that the 'legitimate theatre' had to offer. I made a pilgrimage to Broadway whenever possible and frequented the traveling company productions in Cleveland. It was in the local theater, however, that I discovered some of the most exciting playwrights. I was especially intrigued with the works of Anouilh,

Genet, Beckett, Pinter: authors who had come to be associated with the Theater of the Absurd. My favorite was Luigi Pirandello.

Pirandello introduced me to a recurring theme in the world of the theater: an exploration of relativity in one's perception of reality. In Pirandello's plays I discovered a coming together of art and life, of fixed form and moving vitality. Pirandello's particular vision reflected the dichotomy between art and life, between the fixed and the movable. What distinguished his plays for me was the way in which he moved beyond the use of the stage in its traditional presentation. He seemed to be probing the whole nature of convention of stage reality. It was reminiscent of the favored device of the Elizabethan and Jacobean theater, that of the play within a play. Pirandello challenged the conventional distinctions between appearance and reality by constantly switching levels. When I saw *Each in His Own Way* and *Tonight We Improvise*, I realized that the security of the audience was undermined to the extent that no one knew whether he/she was sitting next to an actor disguised as a member of the audience or a 'real' person. In this way my theatrical experience mirrored Pirandello's vision of life as an indefinable and unstoppable process where security of perception is mere illusion.

My passion for the theater remained through the years. As a high school English teacher (and director of plays) I was able to use the aesthetic as the subject matter of teaching. I think I have always had a sense of the potential 'drama of the classroom' but in those days it was intuitive, often muted. I was all too often influenced by the dominant tradition of schooling and implicit assumptions about the way classes are supposed to be. Early in my doctoral career, I was involved with English education but found more fascination in the Curriculum and Supervision Program. Clinical supervision became my primary field, with curriculum as a secondary study.

I wish I could say that my aesthetic sensibility continued to grow as a part of my doctoral study, but it didn't. It was compartmentalized. One part of me continued to go to the theater whenever possible, but the arts had little to contribute to the mechanistic world view I was studying in. My early introduction to curriculum was especially so. I dutifully learned the efficiency of behavioral objectives, scope/sequence, and task analysis, but there was nagging dissonance. I didn't realize it then, but I was bothered by the way in which the language in the curriculum field was being construed. Educators discussed curriculum as if they were talking about construction projects. (The concept of curriculum was analogous to a blueprint.) In the early 1970s 'learning theories' were touted as the basis for curriculum making. In the education literature, curriculum was separated from instruction just as learners were separated from teachers. It was such a struggle for me in those years to study in the field of curriculum because there seemed to be no language to help think about how teachers, pupils, and subject matter become involved in the significant events of the classroom.[1] Later, when I began to teach curriculum courses, I called this involvement an "educational encounter." To others the notion of 'learning' might be at the center of curriculum, but to me the educational encounter was the centerpiece.

There is real power in the concept of curriculum.[2] To me it suggests that there is an explicit nature within educational experiences capable of being articulated through word and action. In another sense, there is a sanction granted within the idea of curriculum from which we derive permission to create educational encounters. This special sanction allows us to imagine involvements where people come together to 'encounter' learning actively, where intellectual progress comes through personal and collective insights from the dramatic effects of classroom events and ideas. I think of educational encounters as being primarily for the generating of knowledge rather than for the transmission of reified knowledge. Yet there must be a scenario to guide the action and actors to participate willingly in the classroom events in order to create the learning encounter as it is lived out. Thus, we are continually faced with the dichotomy of the fixed nature of a written scenario (planned ahead of time) on one hand, and the fluid nature of the unfolding classroom experience on the other. This is the essence of the educational encounter. This is also the essence of curriculum inquiry. In true Pirandellian style it represents the tension that exists between the refining process of one and the limitless motion of the other. The dichotomy between fixed form and movable vitality is the dichotomy between art and life as Pirandello construes it.

The Drama of the Classroom

Classroom events, like dramatic presentations, are contrived. They are constructed by educators to create a representation with a heightened sense of reality (not a replication of ordinary, everyday activities), much like the playwright who recognizes that meaningful human action is theatrical in nature. Yet, because of the implied sanctions within the concept of curriculum, we are able to contrive situations and invite people to become involved in ways that no other institution can, not even the theater. We can fashion special scenarios which allow participants to get in touch with a unique level of understanding through their own involvement in a community of learners. The 'drama of the classroom' represents a mode of understanding different from the traditional cognitive versions of school learning. Learning happens when the events of the classroom unfold, when participants feel the nuance of conflict and motive, dissonance and emotion, as part of the intellectual process. In order for this to happen the participants must be 'actors,' that is, they must feel their own sense of belongingness, their own place in the drama. All who are involved must recognize that important knowledge is being generated as the events unfold. It is important to find ways to capture this knowledge, to 'textualize' it through continual disciplined inquiry. Thus, curriculum inquiry is part of the dramaturgy because it deals with the eventfulness of curriculum.

Several years ago I designed an educational encounter for my classes in clinical supervision. As I replayed this particular scenario for several classes of novice supervisors I was struck by recurring patterns as a result of our participation. I decided to 'study' the effects in a formal research project. A summary of the events of the educational encounter are as follows: Participants were asked to assume the role of supervisor and to view a film episode of a high school English class in session, observing the classroom situation, recording the events for subsequent analysis and conference practice. After viewing the film episode, the participants as supervisors were asked to respond in writing to the following questions: (1) What was the teacher's intent of the lesson? (2) To what extent did she achieve her intent? (3) How would you rate the overall performance of the teacher during the session? Using their observation notes and the answers to the questions, the supervisors discussed their views concerning the quality of the teacher's performance and the classroom as a social setting. A general exchange of opinion and judgement ensued. In many cases they formed triads to play out a conference between the teacher and supervisor with an observer to monitor the process. After the participants had the opportunity to hear the prevailing tone of the discussion and, in some cases, to experience the consequences of the conference, I invited them to become "clinical supervisors." (It is at this point that the events begin to mark the climax of the drama.) They were given copies of the lesson transcript as an example of clinical data. They were then asked the same questions. The results of this second response to the questions provided the basis for analysis of the transcript. It also illuminated the discrepancies between their first and second set of responses. They had the opportunity to experience and understand the difference between their opinions and often premature judgments based on random notes and presuppositions on one hand, and careful analysis of a written record (or text) of classroom events on the other. The dissonance that was often created by their actions was a powerful force in their learning. Participants became inquirers in that they examined the data as it unfolded from the class in order to gather insights about the practice of supervision which they were studying. Thus, the educational encounter had at its center the evolving knowledge about practice in clinical supervision. It provided a common experience base (a world of reality) from which to verify, explain, and interpret the events and meanings through curriculum inquiry.

I called my formal research project "The Mousetrap Study."[3] I realized that I was studying a world where supervisors had come together in a scenario designed to study clinical supervision—to put it another way, supervisors who were studying themselves in the practice of clinical supervision. In my own case, as a teacher of supervisors, I could shape the curriculum in order to participate in the world of learning about practice; as a supervisor, I could experience the consequences of certain supervisory actions and concepts; as a researcher, I could discover the sources and methodologies for inquiry regarding the teaching and supervision; and as a searcher, I could revisit the compelling abstractions in my own esoteric world. Borrowed from Shakespeare's Hamlet, the famous device of a play within a play provided a way to imagine the interaction between two (or more) worlds of reality. In Hamlet's 'real world' the circumstances of his life are at odds, in need of verification and explanation. Hamlet devises a play to replicate the critical events of his world involving his stepfather, the king, whom he believes to have killed his father. *The*

Mousetrap, as Hamlet's play is called, lies at the center of Shakespeare's play (Act III, scene 2). As Hamlet views *The Mousetrap*, he also observes the king's reaction to the play and thereby convinces himself of the king's guilt. The interaction of the two worlds leads to disclosure, and all that follows is a direct result of what has been revealed. And so it is in this study as curriculum inquiry. The significance lies in a dual representation. One view of the educational encounter reveals the 'real world' events of the clinical supervisors' actions. Another view reveals the world of teaching/research circumstances. This is, after all, a classroom occurrence which can be examined by all for meaningful features, the eventfulness of curriculum. It is the 'real world' of the classroom under consideration. And just as Hamlet's 'real world' and *The Mousetrap* are constructed by Shakespeare to create a representation with a heightened sense of reality, so too are educational encounters constructed by educators for similar purpose. Educational encounters are involvements where the events are charged with meaning, where action is given meaning by being part of larger action, where knowledge exists as it is being produced and recorded at once. This is the phenomenon under study in curriculum inquiry.

The drama of the classroom offers the curricularist an important frame of reference. It seems to me that if one can get in touch with 'the dramatic' of classroom events, one can sense the essence of school learning. Academic activities are often criticized, accused of being formal exercises that are empty, devoid of life-giving energy. How often we hear "But that's academic" as a contrast to "That's in the real world." By understanding the notion of 'the dramatic' in classroom events, we have the chance to create the classroom as a real world. We have the opportunity to experience reasoning-in-action in the company of a community of learners engaged in similar inquiry. We have a place where our natural energies (attention and wonder, excitement, fear, expectations, and the rest) are channeled. We are actors in the most fulfilling drama the education establishment can produce.

NOTES

1. Although the University of Pittsburgh, where I studied, had a doctoral program in Curriculum and Supervision, the curriculum in the department focused on the practical world of technical methods and procedures of practice. I discovered the writings of Pinar, Macdonald,

Greene and others quite by accident. My professors (later my colleagues) referred to scholars in the Reconceptualist school of curriculum as "fuzzy thinkers" and discouraged students from such esoteric ideas. They were generally condemned as having no practical application to the "real world of curriculum."

2. I have come to realize that curriculum studies are central to the study of education. Curriculum is perhaps the only field of study which the educational establishment can claim. Periodically we educators remind ourselves that we have been given the responsibility for a special kind of education, often identified as schooling—the academic universe in which classroom events are the fascinating and elusive realities. Furthermore, that which we call learning is not the exclusive domain of schooling any more than healing is the exclusive domain of medicine. We sometimes forget that all human sciences (psychology, sociology, anthropology, etc.) deal with human learning. Thus learning is not the exclusive domain of those in the discipline of education; however, curriculum is!

3. Results from "The Mousetrap Study" were first presented at the Association of Teacher Educators Annual Meeting, 1984, under the title "Stable Data and Clinical Supervision: Research on Supervisors' Observational Judgment." The study is widely reported in N. Garman, "Clinical Supervision: Quackery or Remedy for Professional Development." *Journal of Curriculum and Supervision* 1, 1: 148-157.

27

WILLIAM H. SCHUBERT

Curriculum Inspired by Scrooge or "A Curriculum Carol"

No art form has had greater impact on my outlook than theatre. Few works of theatre have influenced my vision of curriculum and teaching as much as *A Christmas Carol* by Charles Dickens. Originally written as a novelette, the play and film versions have affected me profoundly. I vividly recall those December evenings in the 1950s, sitting with my parents in our Indiana farmhouse, watching Alistair Sim as Ebenezer Scrooge become converted from disgruntled miser to joyful altruist. Each holiday season Scrooge's journey, his curriculum of spirits and remembrances, still brings a tearful eye of gladness in human possibility. In fact, the most moving scenes in all literature for me are those of conversion. Thus, conversion is the first of nine themes from Dickens's *A Christmas Carol* that influenced my teaching in elementary school, and it continues to affect my inquiry into curriculum and teaching.

Theme One: Conversion

For me, "conversion" is not only a term that pertains to religion of one doctrine or another, as meaningful as this may be to human lives. More broadly, conversion is the result of a leap in perspective that enables one to see the world and to *be* in it with greater perspective. Such perspective pushes beyond the taken-for-granted and everyday toward a deeper and richer image of practical ethics and justice. Curriculum, then, for me, is a design of events that brings about conversion.

I saw this clearly as the director of *A Christmas Carol* on some seven occasions with sixth grade classes over the course of the several years of my elementary school teaching career. In that experience I not only saw Dickens's characters on stage, but a kind of symbolic image of my students being converted. Their participation in Dickens's roles heightened my conviction that their own conversion was the essence of my efforts to design curriculum and teaching. Concomitantly, the journey of experiences leading to conversion was their curriculum. As a teacher, it was not my job simply to implement the predetermined curriculum of 'higher authorities', nor was it my job to design fully the conversion of my students. Rather, it was a joint venture in which my students and I, along with the spirit of possibility which we could become, would enter into growth. If this sounds mystical, then much of life needs to be acknowledged as mystical. The mystical character of the universe and therefore of education has been set aside too long in favor of the technical side which seeks to mold or program people.

Curriculum, I became convinced as a teacher, is not worth the journey if it does not convert those who participate in it (students and teachers) into something better. Such a process is vividly portrayed by Dickens in Scrooge's journey. Early in the play Scrooge denounces his altruistic nephew, Fred, for an invitation to Christmas dinner. Scrooge's office reverberates with his scolding of Fred:

> What's Christmas time to you but a time for paying bills without money; a time for finding yourself a year older and not an hour richer? If I had my way, every idiot who goes around with "Merry Christmas" on his lips should be boiled with his own pudding and buried with a stake of holly through his heart. You keep Christmas in your own way, and let me keep it in mine.

And to two gentlemen who asked Scrooge to contribute to charity, he barks that he will contribute nothing and adds:

> Let these deserving people of yours go to the establishments [prisons and workhouses] I have mentioned. [And to Fred's observation that many would rather die] Then let them do that and help decrease the surplus population. I'm busy. Good afternoon to you.

Confronted with prospects of his own death and the torturous punishment for an uncaring life received by the ghost of Jacob Marley (Scrooge's former business partner) and the ghosts of Christmas past, present, and future, Scrooge's curriculum culminates with the viewing of his own gravestone. He frantically responds:

> No, spirit. Oh, no, no! Hear me! I am not the man I was. I will not be the man I must have been but for this lesson. I will honor

> Christmas in my heart. I will try and keep it alive in the Past, the Present, and the Future. I will not shut out the lesson that all three spirits have taught me. Oh, tell me there is hope, that I may sponge away the writing on this stone.

Afterward – the next morning and throughout his remaining life – we are told that Scrooge

> did everything he promised and infinitely more. He became a persistent visitor to his nephew's home, and even took Fred into business with him. He raised Bob Cratchit's [his clerk] salary to a figure that left that bewildered gentleman gasping: and to Tiny Tim [Cratchit's lame son], who did not die, he was a second father. He provided doctors for the little lad, and very soon Tiny Tim will have his wish: he will be able to run and play like the other boys. As for the three spirits, Ebenezer Scrooge never saw them again. That was due to the unchallengable fact that Scrooge, for the rest of his days, helped keep alive the spirit of Christmas.

The words used in these quotations are taken from the radio rendition of the play that I found in an eighth grade basic reader on a shelf in my first sixth grade classroom. The words still ring clear to me as if I am hearing them through the voices of seven different groups of sixth graders. To this day, some fifteen to twenty years after teaching these students, when I watch, read, or listen to *A Christmas Carol*, I am imaginatively thrust back through my own personal history to my journey as an elementary school teacher, and to the conversions I experienced in my outlook on curriculum and teaching revealed in the themes discussed here.

Theme Two: Personal History

Each time I reinterpret the personal history of my teaching, I reflect on the centrality of curriculum inquiry to my work as a teacher. That the fundamental curriculum question (What knowledge and experience is most worthwhile?) is surely symbolized and was probably stimulated for me by Dickens's *A Christmas Carol* becomes increasingly clear on each of my encounters with the text. The pervasive conversion of Scrooge occurred because his teachers (the spirits) were able to tailor curriculum (influential experiences) to his autobiography. The artistry of Dickens portrayed for me the reconstruction of experience that runs through the educational philosophy of John Dewey. Moreover, seeing Scrooge's conversion through the medium of my students as actors was a living symbol that reconstruction of their experience was impossible without attention to each student's life history.

For quite some time I did not understand why Dickens announced early in the story (before Marley's entrance): "Marley was dead as a doornail . . . There was no doubt that Marley was dead. This must be understood, or nothing wonderful can come from the story I am going to relate." Through years of working with the play, however, I concluded that Marley represented the cancerous death from greediness and callousness that Scrooge (and any of us) can unwittingly allow to grow within. The curriculum of conversion emerges as a vivid vision both of what we are that we do not wish to be and of what we might become. Through the artistry of the spirits (curriculum developers) who heuristically posed these images, Scrooge became a full partner in the imaginative recreation of himself and of a sense of goodness unique to his autobiography. Only by genuinely involving Scrooge in the development of his curriculum, by tapping his connections with his past in new ways, could the full range of expertise be brought to bear on curriculum as reconstructive conversion.

Upon realizing this, I saw not only the need to individualize curriculum in light of student backgrounds, but I understood that students have a quality of expertise in their own experience that no one else could provide. Scrooge asked the Ghost of Christmas Past if he would travel to the "long past," to which the spirit responded, "No, your past." The work of curriculum and teaching was not merely to *make curriculum relevant*, to fit the prespecified to the student; rather, it was to enable the student to re-vision the personal past, present, and possible futures as a prelude to reconstruction. In Scrooge's case, his childhood sense of goodness and parental neglect were allowed to re-enter him. His visits to the poor and destitute, the ill and oppressed who existed because of the kind of miserliness he exemplified, and the gnawing personification of *want* and *ignorance* in the form of two gruesome children who charged at him from under the festive robe of celebration of the Spirit of Christmas Present, as well as the prospect of his own demise, together brought a new sense of meaning and direction for Scrooge.

Theme Three: Moral Direction

Merely a new sense of direction does not imply a better one. But who dares say what is better? Should those who educate simply reflect current social practice? If they do, how does education make society better? If, in contrast, educators decide to prespecify what is better (that which will 'improve' the individual and society), do they not overstep their role and indoctrinate? Is there an alternative to mere perpetuation of values on the one side and indoctrination on the other? This dilemma has plagued me over the years; however, I have come to believe increasingly (with Rousseau and Dewey) in a basic human goodness, embryonic though it may be, which is portrayed by Dickens as Fred responded to Scrooge's early disdain of Christmas:

> Christmastime . . . the only time I know of, in the long calendar of the year, when men and women seem by one consent to open their shut-up hearts freely, and to think of people below them as if they really were fellow passengers to the grave, and not another race of creatures bound on other journeys. And therefore, uncle, though it has never put a scrap of gold or silver in my pocket I believe that it *has* done me good, and will do me good. . . .

Theme Four: Unrelenting Confidence

Herein lies a belief that potentially outweighs the evil that many contend is fundamental in human character. Critic Joseph Gold sees Scrooge's conversion as "a plea for the society itself to undergo a change of heart, [to be] converted from closedness to openness, from frigidity to warmth, from isolation to brotherhood, from death to life" (Gold 1972, 147-148). I share this assessment and further see these conversions not so much as a change in humankind, but as a bringing out of that basic goodness that lies, often dormant, deep within.

The assumption of basic human goodness, intuitive and axiomatic though it may be, allows me to share authority with students as I actively respond to the basic curriculum question (What is worthwhile to experience?). My confidence, thus, is that if given genuine opportunity to ask this question about their own lives, learners will move toward a kind of growth that pursues such questions as; How does what I experience contribute to the quality of life I might lead? What kind of life do I want to live? How can I create it? How does this life influence others? How can I contribute to a better society and to the world? Although I am convinced that a great variety of responses to these and related questions will emerge from students, I am confident that the experience of pursuing them is itself a curriculum of most worth. Fred, too, had an unrelenting confidence that a basic goodness lay dormant in Scrooge and that one day the right influences would bring it to rebirth.

Theme Five: Integration

The curriculum questions illustrated above, when they infuse the experience of students, make the continuous reconstruction of life and outlook the central curriculum project. The spirits helped Scrooge address all of the disciplines of knowledge, but not as systematic bodies of knowledge set out in advance. Instead, the spirits led Scrooge through a Deweyan progressive organization of subject matter, starting with the *psychological* (interests) and moving to the *logical* (disciplines of knowledge). Scrooge began with momentary concerns and interests of his everyday life (making money, getting food and sleep). Marley's ghost caused him to reflect on his own past and challenged him to question the contributions of his life. A tour into memory of his childhood and youth guided by the Spirit of Christmas Past led Scrooge to see both a basic goodness within him and reasons for his transformation into miserhood. The Spirit of Christmas Present allowed Scrooge to see more clearly the expanded consequences of his preoccupation with making and retaining money—consequences for Fred's family, the Cratchit family, and the poor and destitute more generally. Together, the Spirits of Christmas Present and Future juxtaposed images of what Scrooge's life was at present with the possibility of it becoming more fulfilling to a larger community and, thus, to himself. The conversion of Scrooge joined education and life and it integrated curricular areas as they spoke to his emerging sense of meaning and direction.

Seeing this transformation in light of my students who acted it contributed to my increased quest to see student transformation as the ultimate goal of curriculum and teaching. This was not entirely a transformation toward what I wanted students to become. The project of curriculum was to decide together what was most worthwhile to become and to be. At its best such a project inextricably linked schooling and life and it naturally clarified how to use the disciplines of knowledge to move toward a continuously improved ideal of the worthwhile.

Theme Six: Drama and Story

As Marshall McLuhan (1967) warned, the message of the medium can massage us so thoroughly that we hardly notice its power. The medium I observed was, of course, that of my students as actors, as interpreters of a story. It took me some time to realize that their deep involvement in enacting the story symbolized neglected forms that curriculum and teaching could take. Story has long been the great teacher of humankind throughout history, as Kieran Egan (1986) ably argued. Concomitantly, acting is a formalization of story in play. Ironically, play, story, and acting have little place in most school activities. In fact, educators seem to want to overcome these great motivators in silly efforts to move children toward the dreary pseudoefficiency of adulthood.

Upon realizing the detrimental character of such a move, I began to ask: How can we make this (any required subject matter) into a meaningful story? How can we act out the story with the spontaneity of childhood play? I can recall no learning situations that were more effective and fulfilling than those built on these questions. What's more, were I to return to elementary or secondary school teaching I would strive more fully to enable learning to evolve from story, acting, and play.

Theme Seven: Common Knowledge

From the start I was amazed at how eagerly students responded to participation in *A Christmas Carol*. I gradually learned that the reason for this was more than the profound message of the story, more than a chance to enact a story in the form of play, and more than the compelling words of a master storyteller. It was all of these, but it was even more a sense of familiarity. Versions of Dickens's *A Christmas Carol* infuse our culture. The students knew the film versions with Reginald Owen (1938), Alistair Sim (1951), and recently George C. Scott (1984) as Scrooge. They even knew versions that involved Mickey Mouse, Bugs Bunny, and Mr. Magoo, among others. All of these versions seemed to blend into one giant acquaintance, one familiarity, a common experience.

Seeing the power of involvement brought by this common cultural experience led me to ask how I might tap other dimensions of the common experience, the common knowledge of my students, to build learning experiences. We began, then, to develop curriculum and teaching from popular mass media such as television, movies, and music. I only scratched the surface, but I continually asked myself how I could use the form of extant interests and preoccupations to reach new knowledge, skills, attitudes, ideas, and values. For example, I would ask how the design of a popular game show could be a vehicle for learning. I would ask how the substance of a popular situation comedy might be a starting point for understanding a perennial cultural or historical conflict. I would challenge students to criticize techniques of deception in commercials.

Theme Eight: Outside Curricula

Just as Scrooge's conversion was not limited to a separate academic exercise, I concluded that meaningful alteration of perspective in my students must take into account the broad context of educative sources in their lives. The spirits led Scrooge to reconsider the curricula of his family, home, vocation, avocation, friendships, school, nonschool organizations, and cultural values. Each of these influenced his sense of purpose, his image of possibility. The spirits, as curriculum makers, had to know Scrooge as a whole person in order to help him transform.

I often think of the curricular prescriptions made with little or no knowledge of those who are supposed to benefit from them. There is a desperate need for teachers to have time, expertise, and opportunity to know their students well. Without such knowledge it is impossible, or purely relegated to chance, to develop a curriculum that is meaningful.

Theme Nine: The Theory Within

I have come to think the great job of all persons is to continuously refine and reconstruct the 'theory' (or network of ideas) that guides their lives. With this assumption, I conclude that it is, in turn, the job of those who develop curriculum and those who teach to make the reconstruction of personal theory possible. Just as Scrooge was enabled to become his own curriculum director, we in the curriculum field (and all who teach) must give away our job in order to keep its spirit alive.

Conclusion

My experience with *A Christmas Carol* by Charles Dickens has directly influenced and/or symbolized many dimensions of my inquiry about curriculum and teaching. It helped me realize that the undergirding purpose of curriculum and teaching is to convert students (and teachers for that matter) to new perspectives. And it is a conversion that comes from students as much as from teachers' design. It must emerge collaboratively because meaning must be connected to life history and students are the authors of their autobiographies; thus, it is necessary to consult their expertise on matters of their own growth. For learning experience to be merely new, change *qua* change, is not enough to qualify as worthwhile and meaningful growth. It must be directed toward improvement of personal and social life, and thus be governed by moral direction. To choose to involve students in the design of their conversion through study of their personal histories is to exert a faith, an unrelenting confidence, in their moral character or basic goodness.

This cooperative curriculum development is a kind of integration that joins interest and effort, personal knowledge and the disciplines, and school and life as symbolized in the conversion of Scrooge. Such integration can be facilitated by an artistry of teaching that taps familiar experiences in the culture, engages students in playfulness of drama and story, and builds upon the curricula of nonschool experiences in student lives. Finally, the goal of curriculum as conversion is to enable students, as Scrooge was enabled, to continuously reconstruct perspectives that fashion lives experienced as ever more worthwhile.

28

MAX VAN MANEN

A Childhood Reading

"And that is how Ciske the Rat came to our school:

" 'Today we are going to get something that will give us much joy,' said Maatsuyker, the principal. as we were just finishing our morning cup of coffee before the start of school. 'A transfer. Boy oh boy, he has quite a reputation for criminal behaviour already. In and out of juvenile court. Fighting with a knife . . . And he will be in your class, Bruis!'

"The latter was meant for me.

"I regarded him somewhat coolly, because Maatsuyker was in the habit of acting rather pompously and overbearingly. Especially towards me, because I had been teaching for only a fortnight. He knew that he could not impress the other teachers, but with me he was still playing up his authority.

"Maatsuyker looked at me with a certain glee which annoyed me. He immediately passed me some pedagogical advice: 'If I may counsel you, then let him know straightaway who is boss. Put him up against the wall and use your hands if you got to. That kind of kid only has respect for physical authority, if you know what I mean. Give him a licking so that he will think twice trying anything with you.'

"'No way,' I replied curtly. 'Then the kid knows instantly that in truth you are afraid of him.'

"'A nice challenge for Bruis!' said Ms. Tedeman. 'Bruis still has ideals. Well you can practise your pedagogic skills, young man.'

"Ms. Tedeman is a likable spinster teacher in her fifties. She has lost some of her enthusiasm for teaching, but she still has her heart in the right place for the fifty-plus children in her class."[1]

How do children enter our adult lives? How do they acquire significance, concreteness, reality? As I reread these opening lines from Volume 1 of the trilogy *Ciske the Rat*, the story and atmosphere revisit me with a vague vividness that characterizes childhood memory. I am rereading a childhood reading. I am reading my childhood. During my visit to the Netherlands I have managed to locate an old yellowed copy of the novels by the Dutch author Piet Bakker. The books are out of print now. And this copy, which I recovered from an antiquariate bookstore, upon opening, pours out the same papery scent that my parents' books possessed. Thirty years ago these books were already antiquarian. The aging pages show brown spots like the skin of my mother's hands. I recall how turning the dry and fragile pages would release this not unpleasant musty odor. This slight smell of stale paper dust and dried glue somehow belongs to the story of the life of Ciske and his teacher. The story belongs to my childhood. But it also confronts me with my own aging, my mortality in the light of the youth of my own children. And as I now skim the pages of this book I skim off the memories of my early school years. Why did these books appeal to me? From my present point of view, the author Piet Bakker was led more by a sense of realism and humanity than by a motivated understanding of pedagogy. And yet what was so appealing in these stories was the difficult but growing caring relation between a less-than-perfect teacher and a troubled child. Did I, as a child, identify with Ciske? Or did I identify with his teacher?

"Jorisse nodded to Ms. Tedeman's words. He had a story.

"'When, last year, we made a field trip a police-van stopped at the station just about six yards from our group. And out of the car emerged a heavily shackled fellow. Of course the children were all eyes. And the chap scarcely saw me or he shouts: 'Hi teacher!' Indeed it was a former student of mine! And what does the schlemiel do? He starts singing: Twinkle, twinkle little star . . . ! And suddenly I see him in front of me! The third desk near the window. A nice boy with brown eyes and a grey sweater. A pleasant open face. So then it really bothered me when I saw him being led away by two cops. I mean, I did not get upset by my former student, but by those cops. No don't laugh so stupidly! I felt that those men should keep their hands off one of my kids. Crazy, of course. And then I looked at the children around me. They stood there so charmingly with their backpacks and their cheery clothes, and I thought: God knows who of you will end up in one of those police-vans. Yes, that was a lousy start of a day's outing with my class . . ."

The Ciske trilogy awakened first my desire to become a teacher, to want to make a difference in the lives of children. But I was ten years old then, still a child myself! Can a child have a pedagogic interest in the welfare of another child? I believe that as a child I developed a caring relation to Ciske. But the relation was a readerly experience. I was understanding something that I could not yet explain. The story of Ciske spoke to me but I could not tell why it had such appealing power. It simply "spoke" to me. Do I have words for the experience now? How can a teacher communicate what it means to develop a caring relation to children? What I realize now is that this book is structured like a composite of stories, anecdotes. Bruis is the authorial voice. And he tells anecdotes about Ciske—about his own life as a teacher with the child Ciske—as if he were entering in a diary everything that seemed worthwhile recounting as it happened during the day. What makes the anecdotes so effective is that they each seem to tell something important about teaching, about the failures, promises, disappointments, and possibilities of our pedagogic living with children. Yes, stories or anecdotes are so powerful, so effective, so consequential in that they can explain things that resist straightforward explanation or conceptualization. Anecdotes explain indirectly by evoking images of understanding of the significance of an experience.

"'There he is,' Maatsuyker suddenly announced.

"At the end of the hallway stood the Rat. Leaning against the wall. His head hardly reaching the coat pegs. A smallish boy. Maatsuyker right-a-way walked up to him, like a man who had an important mission to fulfil. There he stood: Big, enormous, and assuming in front of that little Rat. A blush of anger crept to my face when I saw how, without any ado, he dealt the boy a slap in the face. And I heard him shout in a high-pitched voice: 'Can't you properly take your hat off your head?! That is what we are used to here. Remember that! Hat off stinker!'

"The jerk! All children walk in the hallway with their hats on. The kid was utterly surprised by the unexpected attack. Maatsuyker wanted to reach out again but slyly and smoothly the Rat ducked away from his flailing arm, and before Maatsuyker knew the Rat skittishly ran away. And then I saw how he had obtained his nickname. That sly shifty escape had something animalistic, really like a rat who is chased by a yelping dog.

"But just as he wanted to run onto the street Vermeer walked through the door. He always arrives a bit later at school because he has to take his daughter to kindergarten. Vermeer caught the rat in his arms and carried the struggling and kicking boy to Maatsuyker.

"'Come on little deserter!' he smiled.

"At that point I quickly walked up in order to prevent any more incidents. I was furious! That stupid and awkward Maatsuyker had ruined my intention to greet the Rat normally, like I would have greeted any other newly transferred student to my class."

The Ciske trilogy is hardly an example of high literature. "Folk novel" this genre is called in Holland. And the three volumes were among the dozen or so books that my parental home possessed during my elementary school years. How these books entered our house I do not know. By the time I developed a hunger for words, they were simply there on a small shelf next to an ornamental ironwork statue that my father had welded for a hobby. My parents never seemed to pay much attention to the books (my father read only newspapers), and so I moved several of them to my tiny bedroom-corner under the eaves. Consequently, I had finished reading the Ciske novels (as well as an adult text on human sexuality and other less memorable works) before I had completed grade five. For several years the Ciske novels were amongst the most frequently reread texts in my modest but steadily growing library.

"'I'll take him to my class right now,' I said resolutely. And without waiting for a response from the dumbfounded Maatsuyker, I turned to the Rat: 'Let's go mate!' For a moment he looked at me. He had large grey eyes. Eyes with a wild glance. And yet incredibly beautiful. Those eyes in that pale face with lank colourless hair and thin lips. Those eyes were the only thing really striking in that shabby child's body.

"In that glance there was something like 'What do you, big guys, all want from me!' and I could not help but wink at him, in which he probably read: 'Just let them drop dead, Rat! Come on along!' Because he walked very tamely beside me through the corridor."

The Ciske novels were well suited to my circumstances. I attended an inner-city Dutch school where a street kid like Ciske would not have felt out of place. There were several Ciskes in my class. Often these kids evoked in me a mixed sense of pity and fear. Pity because I sensed that they were not loved by anyone, at home or at school. Fear because I sensed their growing hardness and immunity to the damaging effects of the poverty, abuse, and neglect around them. Ironically, as a child I did not fully realize that my elementary school had been an inner-city school of questionable quality; that realization came many years later when I became a teacher. Then I received my first teaching appointment at the same school. But not after I was warned about the rough-trade nature of this lower working-class school whose students simply were not destined for higher goals such as grammar school or academic high school preparing for university or professional career. Few finished high school at all. Most were largely children without a 'future.'

"To be honest, my meaningful wink was meant more as a protest against the meddlesome interference of Maatsuyker than as a sign of sympathy for the kid. Maybe also because I felt ashamed for the school. The school is for the children a piece of civilization. Our modes of conduct need to be decent. Even the littlest beggar has a right that his teacher is a considerate, gentle person. I am not at all opposed—and neither are the children—to the occasional rap. But Maatsuyker does it in such brutish, vulgar manner.

"So when we entered the classroom Johnny Verkerk screamed: 'Sir—that's the Rat!' And then I did really the same as Maatsuyker, because promptly Johnny received a rap on his knuckle hard skull.

"'Finish your math,' I growled. 'I did not ask you for any advice did I?'

"There shone a certain contentment in those big, grey eyes of the Rat . . ."

I am thirty-some years older now, and as I continue to reread pages from the Ciske novels I gain some insight into the charm of this text. This child, Ciske, is an enigma. He is the original stranger, the child who brings the adult to puzzlement because the adult does not understand the child and does not know what to do with the child. The child is as unfathomable, as bewildering as a wild animal. And yet in so many ways this child is the product of an adult world. The adult does not realize that he is already deeply involved in the child's problems.

"I harbor genuine envy to those real and experienced teachers as Vermeer and Jorisse. They seem to know almost immediately and naturally what tone to use with any particular student. I don't in the least. I still got to learn that from a few hundred children. And they unfortunately are my guinea-pigs, that is their bad luck.

"When the Rat stood at my desk the class was quietly working at the math problems that I always put on the board before school starts, to please the eager kids. But I could not help noticing how continuously some eyes wandered toward the Rat. The latter was standing there, as an accused who is determined to keep his mouth shut in front of the Bench's Magistrate.

"'Well, tell me what is your name, comrade!' I said as naturally as possible.

"But the Rat must have detected something unnatural, something artificial or phony in my voice, because he looked at me with those strange eyes and remained silent. 'You won't suck me in that easily!' that face said."

How does one find the right tone, the right words for each child? That is surely the question that is at the heart of our pedagogic lives. The teacher's task is not merely to find an opening, a way of reaching the child. As if it is not difficult enough to detect what language, what words, what gesture, what kind of tone can breach the barriers that separate any particular child's world from an adult's understanding and good intentions. The teacher must also do something with the language. The teacher's aim is not to battle, to penetrate, to violate the child's inner nature, rather the teacher's intent is pedagogic, to establish a pedagogical relation wherein it is possible to distinguish what is good and what is not good for the child.

"Damn, what incredible eyes that boy has in his head! Pearlgrey with dark, scintillating pupils. An ill-omened glow smoldering in those eyes. The eyes of an animal!

"'Well that is babyish,' I responded with an air of indifference. 'You don't even dare to say who you are?'

"Again he looked at me with a stony stare, and then I did something stupid.

"'Perhaps you would rather tell your name to the man from the hallway?' I said mockingly. What an ass I was to resort to Maatsuyker as some kind of bogey-man! I became annoyed, when

the Rat haughtily shrugged his shoulders. His face did not betray the least amount of fear.

"I said curtly: 'Go and sit in that front desk, boy-with-no name!'

"Henry Berg moved over as if someone with the plague was coming to sit next to him. I knew for sure that he would come to school tomorrow with a note from his mother, 'that she does not appreciate her son to have to associate with such riff-raff.'

"The Rat walked to his desk. Impassively.

"I had suffered my first defeat.

"'Take out your reading books,' I instructed to the class."

That is how Volume 1 of the trilogy *Ciske the Rat* begins. A journey into the lifeworld of a child without a 'future.' Or, at least, without any prospect that I, even as a child, understood as no future—delinquency and crime. And so the rest of the book reads like a pedagogical thriller. How can a teacher make a difference in the life of a child-without-a-life, a kid who desires no future because life has already no life at all. There are no rules, no principles of knowledge that can tell the teacher what to say, or how to say or do the right thing when the child is there. What is the difference that makes a difference between a life and no life? Does this sound sentimental? Does this appear naive to my present adult reading? I take the Ciske novels back 'home,' to Canada. Something has remained the same. And I am still attuned to stories, prompted by this reading of memories of childhood. But now I listen to stories or anecdotes that are more concretely (rather than fictionally) connected to life.

Indeed, the anecdote is probably the most common device by which people talk about their experiences. When teachers speak of their daily practice, then they tend to do so at the hand of anecdotes. I am tempted to believe that among teachers, and also among parents, anecdote is the natural way by which particular concerns of living with children are brought to awareness. Better yet, anecdotal narrative allows the person to reflect in a concrete way on experience and thus appropriate that experience. 'To anecdote' is to reflect, to think. Anecdotes form part of the grammar of everyday theorizing. In a reflective grasping, anecdotes recreate experiences, but now already in a transcended (focused, condensed, intensified, oriented, and narrative) form. And thus, the act of 'anecdoting' as concrete reflecting prepares the space for pedagogical reflection and for action-sensitive understanding.

As I talk and work with teachers I hear many anecdotes about teaching, school, and the children or adolescents they teach. Moreover, my wife, who is a teacher, also often comes home with stories. Sometimes the stories are inspiring, reflecting the joys of teaching and living with children. Sometimes the stories are disturbing; they may resemble the life of Ciske—except that there is a heightened reality to the stories I hear now, because, most often, I already know these children, not fictionally, but concretely, in flesh and blood.[2]

NOTES

1. The paragraphs in quotation marks are selections I have loosely translated from the first chapter of Volume 1 of the trilogy *Ciske the Rat* by Piet Bakker (Amsterdam/Brussels: Elsevier, 1944).

2. For more elaborations about the pedagogical and methodological significance of "anecdote" see my *Researching Lived Experience: Human Science for an Action-Sensitive Pedagogy* (London, Ont.: Althouse Press, 1989 and Albany, N.Y.: SUNY Press, 1990); and "By the Light of Anecdote" in *Phenomenology + Pedagogy*, Volume 7 (1989); see also *The Tone of Teaching* (Richmond Hill, Canada: Scholastic TAB Publications/Heinemann Educational Books, USA, 1986) as a text illustrating the use of anecdote in down-to-earth phenomenological writing.

29

JOEL TAXEL

Roll of Thunder, Hear My Cry: Reflections on the Aesthetics and Politics of Children's Literature

Mildred Taylor's *Roll of Thunder, Hear My Cry* (1976) is a novel about a young, African-American girl's gradual awakening to the brutal reality of racism in Mississippi in the 1930s. Perhaps more than any fictional work written for young people I've encountered since my days as a graduate student, *Roll of Thunder* has influenced my thinking about the possibilities afforded by literature to provide aesthetic pleasure and to raise issues of critical social and political importance. Consequently, the book has become a benchmark, a literary work against which others are measured and compared as well as one that has enabled me to join the concerns of my scholarship to those of my teaching.

For the past ten years I have been on the faculty of the Department of Language Education at the University of Georgia, where I teach courses in children's literature. Although my graduate education included extensive coursework in children's literature, my major area of concentration was in curriculum studies, specifically in the sociology of the curriculum. I was drawn particularly to research that critically scrutinized textbooks, to studies concerned with such aspects of schooling as the hidden curriculum, and to analyses that looked at television and literature as significant components of the curriculum and popular culture. These interests were reflected in a dissertation that examined a seventy-seven year sample of children's fiction about the American Revolution (see Taxel 1984) and blended my undergraduate background as a history major, and a growing passion for children's literature, with a view of schooling and the curriculum informed by the theoretical and methodological perspectives of the sociology of school knowledge.

The Sociology of School Knowledge

Critical curriculum scholarship of the past decade and a half has raised fundamental questions about the nature of schooling and especially about the knowledge that is created and transmitted by an institution increasingly seen as central to the reproduction of social inequality (Apple 1982, 1986; Giroux 1983). In contrast to the long-cherished view that schools are the 'great equalizers' serving as engines of democracy, sociologists of school knowledge see schools involved in the transmission of what Williams (1982) referred to as a "selective tradition." Williams argued that although educational systems claim to be transmitting knowledge or culture in "an absolute or universally derived sense," they actually transmit radically selective versions of both. He suggested further that there is an essential and necessary relation between this selective version of knowledge and culture and the existing dominant social relations (Williams 1982, 186). That is, schools confer preeminence on the language forms, world views, ideological, historical, and cultural perspectives of the dominant social groups, thus legitimating—as logical, natural, and/or the result of merit—the power, prestige, and status of these groups in society. At the same time, schools historically have slighted, ignored, and even denigrated the language, culture, literature, and history of subordinate groups.

In documenting the extent to which the world views and perspectives of women, people of color, and the working class either are excluded from textbooks and literature or subjected to misrepresentation or distortion, research in the sociology of school knowledge provided important validation of the existence of a selective tradition. This emphasis on the reproductive aspects of school knowledge and popular culture, however, led to the neglect of Williams's (1977) crucial reminder that selective traditions are the result of "a process," the product of resistance, struggle, and contestation. More recent research is, in fact, beginning to show that despite the historic dominance of the perspectives of, for example, white, Anglo males in our history texts and in our literature, there are and always have been voices of women and people of color that sought to counter and resist this dominance or hegemony. It is my view that Mildred Taylor is perhaps the leading contemporary African-American voice of resistance and opposition writing for young people (Taxel 1989a; Taxel, in press).

On the Relation Between Aesthetic and Sociopolitical Values

My interest in the politics of school knowledge and literature led me to join others challenging the view that when evaluating literature, aesthetic criteria are the only criteria worth considering and that such criteria are understood best when examined apart from the social, political, ideological, and historical forces that shape them. Although this viewpoint has been under assault for some time, the belief in the possibility of a set of purely literary criteria for the selection of the best books for children has proven to be remarkably persistent. This point was made painfully apparent to me as a graduate student soon after I completed a pilot study for my dissertation. It had become my practice to give copies of all the papers I wrote to the professor with whom I had done most of my course work in children's literature, this despite the fact that he no longer was serving as my major professor. Several weeks after giving him the paper, I went to his office to see if he was ready to discuss it. I found him standing in an area where there were a number of other students and members of the faculty. He responded to my query about the paper with a tirade about how my analysis of the novels constituted a fundamental violation of these literary works. My questions, he screamed before the now silent gathering, while perhaps appropriate to raise in relation to textbooks, were not the sort one asks of literature.

This outburst left me stunned, embarrassed, and angry. However, I soon came to understand that this very personal attack on me and my study reflected an approach to literature and literary analysis that undoubtedly was an essential component of this man's world view. I refer to the widely held belief that literature and art in general are objects to be contemplated and revered, that they exist for their own sake and occupy what might be termed an "ethereal realm" standing outside of politics, ideology, and even history.

Questions about the relation between sociopolitical and aesthetic values assumed even greater importance to me in Georgia because, for the first time, I was teaching courses in children's literature. My dissertation, by design, had focused almost entirely on sociopolitical, ideological, and historical questions, but I felt my courses needed a better balance between these concerns and the important aesthetic considerations involved in evaluating and selecting literature for children. However, despite immersing myself in the work of critics taking an exclusively aesthetic approach to the analysis of children's literature, I found myself even more certain of the soundness of the position of those, like Kelly (1984, 3), who argued that "so-called literary approaches are specific cultural allegiances wrapped in the mantle of art and labelled handle with reverence." I became convinced that the indissoluble connections between language, history, institutions, moral questions, and personal strategies make it impossible to separate questions of meaning from more explicitly aesthetic and stylistic considerations (McCann and Woodard 1972, 5). Consequently, I was increasingly comfortable with the view that in all writing—but especially in writing for children—consideration of questions of morality, politics, cultural preference, and affinity are unavoidable and need to be seen as an essential part of the responsibility of the critic.

Nevertheless, it was apparent to me that I was not giving sufficient attention to aesthetic considerations and that I was guilty of a sin of omission that essentially was the flip side of that which I had criticized. That is, many mainstream critics ignored the sociopolitical issues that were of concern to me, while I tended to slight the aesthetic values they believed were the *sine qua non* of children's book criticism. Clearly, the balance I sought had not yet been achieved.

As I struggled with these questions, research in the sociology of school knowledge was beginning to address the issues of resistance, contestation, and opposition. This interest was most readily apparent in investigations of student response and resistance to those aspects of the selective tradition taught in their schools (Anyon 1981; Willis 1977). Other research was discovering and recovering 'oppositional' works of literature and examining the dynamics of the responses of various groups of readers to literature. It is now clear that there are striking parallels between basic tenets of resistance and reader response theories. This is because both the reader of a literary work and the child in the classroom construct meaning on the basis of a complex set of factors such as age, experience, level of cognitive development, background, gender, race, etc. Consequently, those investigating literary response, as well as other classroom phenomena, cannot assume that all readers/students will derive the same meanings they do from a text/classroom (Taxel 1989b).

Teaching students at a southern university who are overwhelmingly white, conservative, and, to a remarkable degree, unreflective about race and racism makes the personal, idiosyncratic nature of response an especially crucial consideration when discussing books like *Roll of Thunder, Hear My Cry*. Indeed, the controversial, often painful qualities of this book make it as potentially divisive and alienating as it is liberating or emancipatory. The fact that I have used *Roll of Thunder* in every literature class I have taught for the past ten years indicates just how positive my classes' encounters with Cassie and the rest of the Logan family have been.

Undoubtedly, the most significant early experience with *Roll of Thunder* occurred during my third year at Georgia when I first taught the doctoral-level seminar that evolved into the course "Women and Minorities in Literature for Young People." My interest in the sociopolitical and ideological dimensions of literature for children was new and novel to the students in this class. On the other hand, many of them were more sophisticated than I was about such matters as character and thematic development, point of view, tone, the analysis of style and symbol, etc. In other words, our strengths complemented each other and this seminar proved to be decisive in my own development as a critic and teacher of children's literature.

My students and I concluded that it is the role and the responsibility of the critic to attend to both literary and sociopolitical concerns and that indeed the two were related in ways that we had not previously understood. We came to see that demands for realistic, nonstereotyped characters, and for historical accuracy and authenticity in writing about, for example, the black experience required that authors be skillful storytellers, have the ability to develop well-rounded, believable characters, and avoid the didacticism and pedanticism that have been so central to the history of children's literature. *Roll of Thunder* provided a concrete illustration that it *was* possible for a literary work to be satisfying on all levels.[1]

Roll of Thunder, Hear My Cry

In accepting the prestigious Newbery Medal for *Roll of Thunder* Mildred Taylor (1977) spoke of the enormous gap between what she had read and been taught about African-American history in school and what she knew about that history from her own experience and from the oral tradition of her family. In pointing to this "terrible contradiction," Taylor provided a sense of the painful distance between the lived experience of her people and the exclusion and distortion of that experience in the dominant culture. It was this contradiction that fostered her "driving compulsion to paint a truer picture of black people." Taylor's speech also provides a remarkably clear definition of the selective tradition.

> There were no black heroes or heroines in those books; no beautiful Black ladies, no handsome Black men; no people filled with pride, strength, or endurance. There was, of course, always mention of Booker T. Washington and George Washington Carver; Marion Anderson and occasionally even Dr. Ralph Bunche. But that hardly compensated for the lack-luster history of Black people painted by those books, a history of a docile, subservient people happy with their fate who did little or nothing to shatter the chains that bound them, both before and after slavery. (Taylor 1977, 404)

Over the years, it has become my practice to preface class discussion of *Roll of Thunder, Hear My Cry* by reading Taylor's speech. In so doing, it often occurs to me that while writing the book, Taylor surely must have envisioned as at least part of her audience, readers much like those who sit in my classes. My students generally are bright, decent, well meaning, and committed to becoming good people and good teachers. However, like virtually all who grow up in our society, their understanding of race and race relations has been shaped and often distorted by the insidious racial stereotypes that continue to dominate literature and the media. Mildred Taylor clearly understood this:

> I wanted to show the endurance of the black world, with strong fathers and concerned mothers; I wanted to show happy loved children about whom other children, both Black and white, could say: "'Hey, I really like them. I feel what they feel.'" I wanted to show a Black family united in love and pride, of which the reader would like to be a part. (Taylor 1976, 405)

I am certain that Taylor would be delighted by my students' responses to her book and would feel that she had succeeded in opening to them another perspective on black history. My students come to love and identify with Cassie and the rest of the Logan family. Many experience for the very first time a sense of disgust and outrage at a social system that determines a person's worth on the basis of something as superficial as race. Student journals and our class discussions often are punctuated with poignant confessions of the involvement of the much-loved family or friends in the kind of racist behavior they come to abhor as they perceive it through the eyes of Cassie and her family. Of course, I do not claim that this book transforms my students into activists committed to social justice. However, for many, *Roll of Thunder* provides a crucial first step toward the reassessment and rejection of a set of previously unquestioned assumptions about the world.

Roll of Thunder, Hear My Cry is the second book in a series that chronicles the hard-working, fiercely proud, independent, and community-minded Logan family's struggle to maintain dignity, self-respect, and their land in rural Mississippi in the 1930s.[2] Narrated by Cassie Logan, a bright and spirited nine-year-old, *Roll of Thunder* provides a vivid, strikingly realistic, account of Cassie's growing awareness of the vicious and unrelenting racism that confronted African-Americans in the South during the Great Depression.

The Logan children are protected from the full force of racism because, unlike their neighbors who are sharecroppers, they own a four-hundred acre tract of land and because their elders foster in them a sense of racial pride and the belief that they are inferior to no one. Significantly, the stories of family struggle and resistance that are presented throughout the novel are reinforced by consistent patterns of action that provide Cassie and her brothers with "models of social action" that they emulate when confronted by the painful realities of the "Jim Crow" caste system, an apartheid-like system that denied them the most elemental human rights and considerations.

The Logans are among the most vibrant, splendidly characterized families in all of children's literature. Big Ma is the matriarch of the clan who, with her late husband, had purchased the land the family tenaciously clings to. Her daughter-in-law Mary Logan is a tower of strength who teaches at the local elementary school and oversees the management of the family homestead even as she shoulders most of the burden of raising four children. David Logan, husband and father, is the cement of the family to whom all look for strength and guidance. This is the case in spite of the fact that he is frequently away from home working on the railroad to earn cash needed to pay the taxes on the land. Cassie's brothers include Stacey, the thoughtful first-born, whose occasional impetuousness often leads to trouble; the sensitive Christopher-John, and the prideful, manly "Little Man."

Crucial to the development of these and other characters is the skillful way that Taylor uses speech to reflect each character's race, social class, and level of education. Thus, David Logan, his mother, and the children speak an authentically rendered, non-standard, Black, Southern dialect. Mary Logan speaks a more standard form of English indicative of her college education, while Mr. Jameson, a prominent white lawyer who is representative of those whites who risked their safety and fortune by aiding African-Americans in their struggle against racism and injustice, talks in a manner reflective of his education and social class. By constructing believable, fully developed characters and by placing them in compelling, often gripping situations, Taylor succeeds in commanding the attention of her readers. As a result, her politics and perspective on the African-American experience never become self-conscious or more important than her story. Indeed, it is precisely because Taylor's historical and political perspective is a natural outgrowth of her masterful construction of character, setting, and story that *Roll of Thunder* is the subject of this chapter.

Easily the most significant event in Cassie Logan's painful initiation into the bitter realities of Mississippi's caste system occurs when she accompanies her grandmother to the nearby town of Strawberry. On this day, Cassie first is humiliated by Lillian Jean Simms and then thrown to the ground by the haughty white girl's father, Charlie. As Cassie notes at the conclusion of this traumatic episode, "No day in all my life had ever been as cruel as this one" (Taylor 1976, 87).

In the aftermath of the events at Strawberry, both Mary and David Logan discuss the incident with Cassie, and it is during these conversations that the values and principles (the model of social action) that Taylor claims were the foundation of her own childhood, and which she found so noticeably absent in the books she read as a child, are articulated. Mary Logan encourages Cassie to understand that in the world outside their house, "things are not as we would have them be" (P. 95). Despite all that has transpired, Cassie is unable to comprehend that her humiliation is a consequence of Charlie Simms' belief that Lillian Jean is better than she simply because she is white. Mary then explains that in order to justify slavery, "the people who needed slaves to work in the fields and the people who were making money bringing slaves from Africa preached that black people weren't really people like white people, so slavery was all right" (P. 96).

By providing historical understanding of the development of the ideology of white supremacy, Mary Logan helps Cassie to better understand her traumatic experience. The child's immediate reference to her Great-Grandpa Luke, a slave who repeatedly ran away, makes it clear that this is not the first conversation of this kind and that family and group history often are used to provide perspective and understanding of the struggles of the present.

Family gatherings that recur throughout the novel are critical moments of unity and bonding where a "storied tradition of resistance"[3] is passed on to the young. As the Logan elders place the family's history of struggle and resistance within the context of the history of African-Americans in the United States, a sense of connection between past and present emerges. This storied tradition of resistance also provides the foundation upon which the Logans cultivate their children's strength, will, and determination to survive.

David Logan's conversation with Cassie about Strawberry occurs in the midst of the remains of a stand of trees decimated years before by a white man named John Andersen, an incident detailed in *Song of the Trees*. Referring to the biblical injunction to "turn the other cheek," David tells Cassie:

> But the way I see it, the bible didn't mean for you to be no fool. Now one day, maybe I can forgive John Andersen for what he done to them tree, but I ain't gonna forget it. I figure forgiving is not letting something nag at you—rotting you out. Now if I hadn't done what I done [to save the trees], then I couldn't've forgiven myself, and that's the truth of it. (Taylor, 1976, 133)

David explains to Cassie that he resisted his desire to give Charlie Simms "a good thrashing" because of the need to consider the likely results of such an action. While urging Cassie to weigh carefully the consequences of her response to Lillian Jean, he does make one thing very clear:

> There are other things . . . that if I'd let be, they'd eat away and destroy me in the end. And it's the same with you, baby. There are things you can't back down on, things you gotta take a stand on. But it's up to you to decide what them things are. You have to demand respect in the world, ain't nobody just gonna hand it to you. How you carry yourself, what you stand for—That's how you gain respect, but . . . ain't nobody's respect worth more than your own. (PP. 133-134)

Cassie heeds her father well. While her self-respect demands that the encounter with Lillian Jean Simms in Strawberry be neither forgiven nor forgotten, Cassie's response is so carefully and skillfully conceived and executed that her 'payback' of Lillian Jean remains forever between the two of them.

Most of the hundreds of readers with whom I have discussed *Roll of Thunder* speak of the optimism they feel at the conclusion of the book about Cassie's prospects for the future. This optimism is born of their sense that Cassie's family has nurtured within her the strength, will, and determination to maintain her dignity and self-respect in an environment that denies her and her people the most basic human rights. This optimism is, however, tempered by readers' awareness that the irrational, deeply rooted bigotry that the Logans confront persists to this day and that its institutionalized forms (the "Jim Crow" laws) remained in place for decades.

In this chapter, I have discussed some aspects of the politics of children's literature and suggested that critics be as explicit in addressing such matters as they are in dealing with more strictly literary concerns. The notion of a politics of literature often is greeted with skepticism, trepidation, and even hostility.[4] Certainly, and in defense of such a response, there is no lack of precedent for the debasement and subversion of literature by those espousing both progressive and conservative political agendas. I have chosen to discuss *Roll of Thunder, Hear My Cry* precisely because it provides such a dramatic illustration of the fact that this need not be the case. Mildred Taylor has shown that it *is* possible to articulate a progressive politics and historical vision in a form that sacrifices neither historical accuracy nor aesthetic value. In so doing, Taylor—along with others who write for young people (such as poet Eve Merriam and social historian Milton Meltzer)[5]—has created literary works of art that teachers, writers, and readers of all ages would do well to consider.

ACKNOWLEDGMENT

My thanks to Susan Taylor Cox for her helpful comments and suggestions on an early draft of this chapter.

NOTES

1. My article "The Black Experience in Children's Fiction" (Taxel 1986) is a direct outgrowth of this and similar seminars.

2. The other published books include the novel *Let the Circle Be Unbroken* (1982) and three novellas, *The Song of the Trees* (1975), *The Friendship* (1987), and *The Road to Memphis* (1990).

3. I am indebted to Susan Taylor Cox for suggesting this term.

4. For an expression of this sort of concern voiced in a response to my article listed in note #1, see Aitken (1988). I respond in Taxel (1988).

5. See, for example Taylor Cox's (1989) interview with Merriam and Meltzer's (1989) discussion of the social responsibility of the writer.

30

NOEL GOUGH

An Accidental Astronaut: Learning with Science Fiction

Many of my favorite stories are known popularly as "science fiction" (sf),[1] and some of them have also become very significant in my work as a teacher educator and curriculum scholar. The value I place on certain sf stories, and my fondness for the genre as a whole, has resulted from a succession of fortunate accidents, each of which has predisposed me to take advantage of the next.

Childhood Dreams

One of the more plausible stories of modern biological science suggests that our inherited characteristics and the circumstances of our conception result from many chance occurrences. If that is so, then chance has it that I was born a boy in England in 1944 and that I have a brother six years older than me. A result of the latter accident is that my brother's reading preferences were an early influence on my own tastes. Thus, at the age of six I was not only following the adventures of Rupert Bear (and other favorites of my agemates) but also sampling books and comics preferred by older readers. Among these was the boys' weekly paper *Eagle* with its lead comic strip, "Dan Dare: Pilot of the Future." Dan Dare's colorful exploits were the stuff of many a boy's dreams in the drabness and depression of postwar Britain. He took the values of our heroic Royal Air Force into space and, more importantly, his adventures were set in a future from which science and technology had eliminated many of the most demoralising aspects of our existence. When I embarked with Dan Dare's Interplanetary Space Fleet to venture to Venus and beyond I escaped from the food shortages and rations, the cold and damp houses (coal was rationed too), and the runny noses and congested lungs that were endemic to England's soggy, smoggy atmosphere.

My brother and I were lucky to be acquainted with Dan Dare, because in 1951, only a year after his comic strip debut, our family emigrated to Australia, where *Eagle* was not widely distributed. This brief acquaintanceship was enough to whet my brother's appetite for sf, which grew steadily in the ensuing years. My own literary tastes were more diverse, but my brother's collection of sf formed a large proportion of our shared library and the Grand Masters of the genre—Isaac Asimov, Ray Bradbury, Arthur C. Clarke, and Robert Heinlein—soon became familiar names. However, my knowledge of their work and of sf in general remained superficial for many years. Indeed, between 1950 and 1967 I read nothing which appreciably altered the impressions of sf that I had formed on my flights of fantasy with Dan Dare. The only value I attributed to sf beyond that of escapist entertainment was its celebration of the virtues of science *per se*.

During my high school years I began to reject quite consciously the Christian theology of my parents and to put my faith in science. By the time I had completed my undergraduate degree in biology I was confident that the meaning of life resided in neo-Darwinian evolutionary theory. Had I been asked to do so, I could have defended assiduously the scientific optimism of my Dan Dare daydreams. But I had no reason to articulate such a defence, and I certainly did not recognise the complementarities between my faith in science and my childhood dreams.

Childhood's End

One day in 1967, when browsing in the Education library at the University of Melbourne, I came across a small collection of novels on educational themes—*The Prime of Miss Jean Brodie, Blackboard Jungle, To Sir With Love* and the like. Among them was *Childhood's End* by Arthur C. Clarke (1953). I had read and enjoyed several of Clarke's short stories in the anthologies of sf that I occasionally had borrowed from my brother, and I thus recognised the incongruity of his novel in this collection. *Childhood's End* is not about schooling, and I suspect that it came to be in the Education library by accident, perhaps on the strength of its title alone. Whatever the reason for its presence, my curiosity was aroused and I took a chance on reading *Childhood's End*. It is no exaggeration to say that doing so changed my life.

Childhood's End begins just as humans are about to take their first steps into space. The space race and the arms race are halted by the arrival of extraordinarily powerful alien beings who become known as the "Overlords". At first the Overlords are a mysterious presence, and they hide their physical form from humans for fifty years (it turns out that they resemble medieval conceptions of Satan). During that time they take benevolent control of the world and eliminate ignorance, poverty, disease, crime, and the fear of war. But the children of this new golden age are strange. They begin to dream of floating among distant suns and wandering on alien planets and, eventually, all they seem to do is dream. The Overlords reveal that their purpose on earth can be likened to "midwives attending a difficult birth," their duty being to supervise and protect the children through a metamorphosis which will "bring something new and wonderful into the world." Eventually the children are all that remain of humankind and, in the book's powerful metaphysical climax, they dematerialise—along with the earth itself—to become what their dreams prefigured: the children are at one with an omnipresent cosmic "Overmind." The Overlords observe this final stage of human evolution with a deeply ambiguous sense of loss: for all of their technological sophistication, they are incapable of joining the Overmind. As one of their number says: "Yes, we are the midwives. But we ourselves are barren" (Clarke 1953, 153).

I recall being fascinated and oddly exhilarated by my first reading of *Childhood's End.* I was surprised by the apparent paradox that a story about the end of the world could seem so hopeful, but I felt myself empathising with Clarke's aspirations for what humankind might become. I was also surprised that a story founded on the mystical concept of human transcendence could remain within the bounds of scientific plausibility and, moreover, be told using such stereotypical props of sf as extraterrestrial beings and spaceships and other wonderful machines.

I have revisited *Childhood's End* many times since that first reading, and its literary flaws have become more apparent. Human characterisation is minimal and the dialogue is often stilted, but I am still moved by the predicament of the Overlords and share Clarke's sense of wonder as he imaginatively documents the marvels of the universe and dramatises his beliefs in the possibility of human transcendence. Clarke is at his best when his mind's eye is on the big picture, as it is in his depiction of the last moments of the earth's existence (as seen by the departing Overlords):

> In a soundless concussion of light, Earth's core gave up its hoarded energies. For a little while the gravitational waves crossed and re-crossed the Solar System, disturbing ever so slightly the orbits of the planets. Then the Sun's remaining children pursued their ancient paths once more, as corks floating on a placid lake ride out the tiny ripples set in motion by a falling stone. (Clarke 1953, 188-189)

It is not just the metaphoric reference to water that reminds me of the climactic lines of Herman Melville's *Moby Dick* (". . . then all collapsed, and the great shroud of the sea rolled on as it rolled five thousand years ago"). Clarke's lines may lack Melville's fluidity and economy, but both writers know how to put humankind into perspective—against vistas of such magnitude and magnificence that events like the sinking of the *Pequod* and the dematerialisation of the earth appear as infinitesimal fluctuations in vast sweeps of time and space. However, through their respective central characters, each writer also demonstrates that such events are by no means trivial. Thus, the sombre tone of the concluding passages of *Childhood's End* does not invite us to mourn for the earth but reflects the tragic meaning of its destruction for the Overlord Karellen:

> There was nothing left of Earth. *They* had leeched away the last atoms of its substance. It had nourished them, through the fierce moments of their inconceivable metamorphosis, as the food stored in a grain of wheat feeds the infant plant while it climbs towards the Sun . . .
>
> Six thousand million kilometers beyond the orbit of Pluto, Karellen sat before a suddenly darkened screen. The record was complete, the mission ended; he was homeward bound for the world he had left so long ago. The weight of centuries was upon him, and a sadness that no logic could dispel . . .
>
> For all their achievements, thought Karellen, for all their mastery of the physical universe, his people were no better than a tribe that had passed its whole existence upon some flat and dusty plain. Far off were the mountains, where power and beauty dwelt, where the thunder sported above the glaciers and the air was clear and keen. There the sun still walked, transfiguring the peaks with glory, when all the land below was

> wrapped in darkness. And they could only watch and wonder; they could never scale those heights. (Clarke 1953, 189)

Childhood's End altered my conception of what science fiction could be and stimulated my curiosity about the place of scientific rationality in the human imagination. I began to read more widely in the literature of science—not only sf but other stories of scientific inquiry and the history and philosophy of science that lay claim to being "nonfiction". I also began to use sf in the courses I taught in teacher education, particularly studies in teaching biology and science. After *Childhood's End* my cosmological explorations were no longer accidental, though it took yet another chance occurrence to forge the links that now bind my affection for sf with my work in curriculum studies.

A Child in Time

In search of further revelatory experiences I returned to my brother's collection of classic and contemporary sf. At first I was disappointed by the scarcity of such revelations in the stories told by the most popular sf authors. Fortunately, some of Arthur C. Clarke's best work appeared in the years that immediately followed my first reading of *Childhood's End.* The 1968 movie *2001: A Space Odyssey* (for which Clarke coauthored the screenplay with director Stanley Kubrick), the short story "A Meeting with Medusa" (1971), the novel *Rendezvous with Rama* (1973) were every bit as awe-inspiring as *Childhood's End*, and each in some ways surpassed it. Thus sensitised, I could hardly fail to notice that one of Clarke's nonfiction books, *Profiles of the Future* (1973), was listed in 1975 as a suggested text for an elective course, "Educating for the Future", within the teacher education program I was then coordinating. The course was about to lapse because the staff member who was responsible for it had suddenly resigned. Shortly thereafter, I took the opportunity to teach and to further develop this course, now known as "Futures in Education", and it has remained an important focus for my work to this day.

Since *Childhood's End* I have encountered the works of several sf authors whose artistry with the written word totally eclipses Clarke's. Of these, Ursula Le Guin has done most to nurture the germ of personal consciousness that was planted by Clarke, the realisation that imaginative journeys into vast reaches of time and space can be much more than escapist fantasies. We can return from such journeys genuinely moved. Le Guin provides a useful analogy in her novel, *Always Coming Home* (1985, 10-11): a girl is on a journey from which she makes a short detour to visit her family in a nearby town. She recalls, "I had been to Madidinou many times, of course, but this time the town looked altogether different, since I was on a journey beyond it". The best sf has a similar effect: it makes the present—and particularly the moral choices and judgments that we perceive within it—look "altogether different." This applies as much to the stories we tell in curriculum study as to any other aspect of our lives.

Le Guin sets novels like *The Left Hand of Darkness* (1969) and *The Dispossessed* (1974) in the far future, in carefully constructed fictional universes. In each of these stories Le Guin creates unfamiliar yet magnificently realised environments which are integral to the interplays among her characters (who may or may not be human but who are always *characters* and not mere ciphers). The haunting clarity of Le Guin's prose allows simple visual images and motifs—a shadow on snow, the play of sunlight in a courtyard—to be woven almost imperceptibly into complex metaphors which resonate with the actions and existence of her subjects. The wholeness of Le Guin's vision of alien worlds invites us to accept them as familiar and subtly alters our perceptions of ourselves and our own times and places. I certainly believe that I returned from Gethen, the wintry setting of *The Left Hand of Darkness*, and from Le Guin's vividly personalised account of a solitary human envoy's interactions with its androgynous inhabitants, with a more sensitive and enlightened view of the politics of human sexuality and gender.

An added attraction of Le Guin's sf is that it has also been a source of questions for my own curriculum inquiries. For example, in *Always Coming Home*, she tells stories of the Kesh, a people who "might be going to have lived a long, long time from now in Northern California" and whose stories are written as translations of "their voices speaking for themselves." One brief story is told by the grandchild of a man called Fairweather. We are told that during Fairweather's adolescence "he learned arboriculture with his mother's brother, a scholar of the Planting Lodge . . . and with orchard trees of all kinds." Fairweather lived in a time and place when "none of the Valley pears was very good, all were subject to cankers, and most needed irrigation to bear well." He asked people in the north for help in obtaining different varieties and, by crossbreeding northern seedlings with a pear tree he found growing wild above the oak forests, "he came upon a strong, small, and drought-hardy tree with excellent fruit... This is the brown pear grown in most orchards and gardens, and people call it the Fairweather pear." There is much more to this deceptively simple story, which occupies less than two pages of a long novel, than can be examined here. But one of the story's chief delights is Le Guin's postscript to it:

> TRANSLATOR'S NOTE:
>
> *. . . he learned arboriculture with his mother's brother . . . and with orchard trees of all kinds.*
>
> We would be more likely to say that he learned *from* his uncle *about* orchard trees; but this would not be a fair translation of the repeated suffix *oud*, with, together with. To learn *with* an uncle and trees implies that learning is not a transfer of something by someone to someone, but is a relationship. Moreover, the relationship is considered to be reciprocal. Such a point of view seems at hopeless odds with the distinction of subject and object considered essential to science. Yet it appears that [Fairweather's] genetic experiments or manipulations were technically skillful, and that he was not ignorant of the theories involved, and it is certain that he achieved precisely what he set out to achieve. And the resulting strain of tree was given his name: a type case, in our vocabulary, of Man's control over Nature. This phrase, however, could not be translated into Kesh, which had no word meaning Nature except *she*, being; and anyhow the Kesh saw the Fairweather pear as the result of a collaboration between a man and some pear trees. The difference of attitude is interesting and the absence of capital letters perhaps not entirely trivial. (Le Guin 1985, 274-275)

The difference in attitude is indeed interesting; moreover, it is the *difference* between the Kesh view of learning and our own that gives the story a critical edge. Fairweather's story, and Le Guin's translation of it, questions the taken-for-grantedness of existing conceptions of curriculum and learning, and it matters little whether the Kesh exist "in fact" or that they are a speculative fiction of Le Guin's imagination. The facts of the story's existence and of our critical responses to it are more than enough to provide questions for curriculum inquiry. As Le Guin says in a preface to *Always Coming Home*:

> The difficulty of translation from a language that doesn't yet exist is considerable, but there's no need to exaggerate it. The past, after all, can be quite as obscure as the future. The ancient Chinese book called *Tao teh ching* has been translated into English dozens of times, and indeed the Chinese have to keep retranslating it into Chinese at every cycle of Cathay, but no translation can give us the book that Lao Tze (who may not have existed) wrote. All we have is the *Tao teh ching* that is here, now. And so with translations from a literature of the (or a) future. The fact that it hasn't yet been written, the mere absence of a text to translate, doesn't make all that much difference. What was and what may be lie, like children whose faces we cannot see, in the arms of silence. All we ever have is here, now. (Le Guin 1985, xi)

Le Guin thus reminds us that the value of a narrative excursion to other times has little to do with its status as historical or scientific 'fact' or speculative fiction. What matters is the wisdom and virtue that may grow in us as we respond critically and creatively to such stories here and now, in the present within which our pasts and futures are enfolded.

The essence of what I have learned from the stories of Arthur C. Clarke, Ursula Le Guin, and other writers of sf is that I am a child in time. They have helped me to understand that I am at the centre of my own history and have helped me to locate this history somewhere—and some*when*—radically indeterminate in any conception I might have of the evolving universe. The stories of science—astronomy, geology, ecology, and evolutionary biology—opened my mind to vast perspectives of space and time past, but in those stories I seemed to be situated at the edge of reality, or uncomfortably perched on the tip of time's arrow, with a narrow and restricted view. The stories of science fiction have helped me to realise the vast *imaginative* perspectives of space and time future. It is a humbling experience to sense oneself as a child in time—as a small, wondering, growing, and purposeful speck of consciousness—indeterminately and ambiguously located (but not lost) within an infinite timescape. And here, now, it feels like a good and useful metaphor for what I hope I am being and becoming as I tell my own stories of curriculum, teaching, and learning with my own children, colleagues, and colearners.

NOTE

1. Most connoisseurs, critics, and creators of science fiction prefer the abbreviation "sf", to "sci-fi." An advantage of "sf" is that it can also be taken to denote "speculative fiction" (an all-embracing term which includes any stories set in the future, regardless of whether or not they are furnished with the scientific or technological hardware of conventional science fiction) and/or "science fantasy" (stories which are ostensibly set in the future but which are characterised by magic and fantasy of the faery sort).

31

ALEX MOLNAR

The Significance of *One Flew over the Cuckoo's Nest* for Curriculum Workers

I read *One Flew over the Cuckoo's Nest* twenty years ago. It was then and it is now, to my mind, a useful metaphor for thinking about schools and the problems of schooling. To me, the characters are eerily accurate portrayals of people I have met in school, particularly Big Nurse and McMurphy. Big Nurse has the smiling face and relentless logic of a primary school teacher who admonishes the class to be "good boys and girls." She is someone who most often controls with a smile and through manipulation, not with the use of physical intimidation. She is one of the countless institutional "helpers" whose help often hurts the beneficiaries of their ministrations. As I read Kesey's description of Big Nurse, I thought about my second grade teacher and about a student named Rudy. Rudy was not a very pleasant kid, and with his angular face and painful smile he wasn't very easy to look at. Not the sort of fella either adults or children are drawn to. Rudy was always in trouble with our teacher for some infraction or other. The scenario was familiar to everyone in class. Rudy would do something that our teacher disapproved of (my second grade teacher disapproved of a lot—it seemed as though I spent a good part of second grade shut up in the utility closet), and she would grab him by the hair and pull him off into a back corner of the room to sit and reflect on his misbehavior. One day Rudy came to school with a crew cut. On that day when our teacher went for his hair, it was too short for her to get hold of, so, after several unsuccessful attempts, she made Rudy stand by his desk. Just stand there. And she started in exclaiming in a loud, irritated voice that she knew why his name was Rudy. It was because he was a rude little boy who would never do anything right. And Rudy just stood there with that painful smile on his face. Rudy was never a friend of mine and I never knew what became of him after second grade. But I wanted to cry for him that day.

And McMurphy. Growing up as I did, in a blue collar community, at a time when kids got kicked out of school for things like not wearing belts with their blue jeans and classes and corridors were always only an incident away from chaos, McMurphy was my kind of hero. Even at twenty-four, even after teaching for three years, I saw his acts of rebellion as encouraging and hopeful. I also realized that the schools I experienced as a child and as an adult contained the same struggles that locked McMurphy and Big Nurse together. I remembered all the phony hall passes, the disappearing ink thrown on a study hall teacher, running through the halls chanting, food fights in the cafeteria, and students who had their jackets pulled off, had chairs thrown at them, and had their heads bounced off of tables for who can remember what anymore. And I remember Ken, the kid with the kind of long, slicked-back, DA haircut that John Travolta would try to imitate years later, who dropped out of school rather than cut his hair. It wasn't a political statement and it wasn't really an expression of personal freedom; at least it was never thought of that way. He just wouldn't do it. And like McMurphy, he accepted the price to be paid.

The characters in *One Flew over the Cuckoo's Nest* were real to me. They evoked and helped give meaning to countless incidents I experienced over the course of my own schooling and as a teacher. Since reading *One Flew over the Cuckoo's Nest*, I have never been able to shake the sense that for those of us whose lives are taken up with schools (institutions sociologists like to compare to prisons and mental hospitals for good reason)—well, aren't none of us getting out alive. The story conveyed to me, in terms I could understand in the marrow of my bones, the relentless and remorseless quality of schooling in Western industrial cultures. It is, of course, inevitable that schools be so. They are one of the principal institutions by which our culture reproduces itself. And if we struggle, as I think we must, we will always be, as curriculum workers, struggling from inside the institution. We will also (like McMurphy) always appear to 'lose' in the end—if we don't understand what we are doing and why.

When I finished *One Flew over the Cuckoo's Nest*, I was left with the conviction that (if we Westerners are to find it at all in this vale of tears) transcendence lies down the road of resistance, criticism, revolt, even though the cause was lost before we were born. Perhaps that's why I have always been so impatient with curriculum thinking that seems little more than an apologia for the industrial order and its needs. Taking the acutes and chronics on the psychiatric ward of *Cuckoo's Nest* as a metaphor for curriculum workers has helped me to see that we can be toadies and sycophants like the acutes; we can withdraw into whatever passes for our internal mental dialogue like the chronics and speak to no one but ourselves; but we will never transcend the institution that defines our work unless we resist. Unless we remain, like McMurphy, outsiders on the inside, we are as absurd and impotent as Chief Bromden was at the beginning of the story. If I extend the metaphor, it is possible to see that the chance we have to influence each other and students positively by our example is related to the decision we make. Neither the chronics nor the acutes could set the stage for their own transcendence. They were captured by the institution, its assumptions, and its demands. They needed the example of McMurphy to transform their understanding of themselves and to recognize the possibility of reclaiming their humanity. The problem for curriculum workers is that it is not possible to emulate McMurphy and to act in ways that are 'practical' in terms of curriculum development. The two possibilities cancel each other out.

Yet another problem arises when we realize that the imperative to reproduce the industrial order is rooted in the very nature of contemporary curriculum. As Ulf Lundgren points out, the modern idea of curriculum cannot be separated from the historical development of industrial culture. The fact that modern school curriculum is a creature of the radical separation of social reproduction from social production means that thinking about and doing curriculum work is, by its nature, a schizophrenic activity. It also makes the various pleas for curricular relevance to productive activities outside the school that sweep through our profession from time to time absurd on their face. The social relations that called modern curriculum into being make it impossible for school curriculum to be in some way organically related to social production and thus 'relevant'. The nature of curriculum makes the gap between theory and practice and between school work and real work inevitable.

Denied any possibility of a real connection to the productive work of society, it is understandable that the principal rationale for the curriculum is 'preparation' for this, that, or the other thing. Learning by doing the thing itself is impossible because the thing cannot, by definition, be a part of school. What is possible in school is a surrogate for the real thing: the curriculum. This helps to explain why so much of what goes on in school has the same quality of 'adjusting' people to circumstances that therapy does. Just as mental institutions ostensibly adjust their patients for life in the real world by marching them through a series of more or less defensible therapeutic rituals, so too, schools attempt to adjust their students for life in the real (that is, productive) world by marching them through a series of more or less defensible activities which in the end are to leave the students prepared for the 'real' world.

Students, sensing the inherent irrelevance of the activities of schools and finding little pleasure in them in their own right, have long since perfected a variety of means of resisting either actively or passively. (Indeed, the schools are filled with McMurphys who could, if we paid attention, teach us a lot about how to transcend our circumstances.) Meanwhile educators' lives are made even more complicated because they are faced not with the task of simply preparing their charges for life. Educators are forced to struggle to adjust children to the curriculum, which is, in turn, to prepare them for life. This is the situation that the familiar old saw "learn this because you will need it next year" is intended to rationalize for students (who are faced not with one, but with two levels of abstraction from the everyday life they know lies outside the schoolhouse door).

Curriculum practice is for the most part concerned with making the best of these difficult circumstances. How can students be most effectively taught *x*, *y*, or *z* in a way that does not lead to open rebellion or withdrawal on a massive scale? On the other hand, students, particularly those from very advantaged or very disadvantaged groups, are forever wondering, What's the point of this dumb stuff? Unlike middle class kids, they find the curriculum cannot even be justified as a rather distasteful experience that is necessary to get through in order to be eligible to learn and do what they want in the productive world. It is easy to see why curriculum practitioners, principals, teachers, and curriculum coordinators beg for suggestions—while at the same time rejecting them as fast as they are offered. The advice sought by curriculum practitioners is the sort of advice Big Nurse might seek: how to go about the task of providing institutional help effectively and efficiently. The advice offered, if it is worth anything, would be like the advice offered by McMurphy: the problems are inherent in the enterprise; the best hope for salvation is to thumb your noses at the established order and its assumptions.

Since it is a function of the nature of curriculum itself, the tension between what school practitioners want and what curriculum theorists have to offer will never be resolved. The problem that keeps rearing up, despite the best efforts of our profession to paper it over, is that in order to be connected to the productive activities of life and thus inherently meaningful, the curriculum must (impossibly) cease to exist. Obviously, to bring this message to a struggling principal or teacher is to be dismissed as, at best, impractical.

It need not be disastrous that practitioners cannot do what theorists recommend and theorists cannot recommend what practitioners want to do. In some ways the tension in the relationship between theory and practice in curriculum can be seen as roughly the same as the tension in the relationship between Big Nurse and McMurphy in *Cuckoo's Nest*. The tension inherent in the situation creates the potential to help liberate students and ourselves, just as Chief Bromden was liberated by the struggle between McMurphy and Big Nurse. Thus, our task is not to bemoan the existence of the tension and look for ways to make it go away (which will never be successful). Our task is to learn how to use the tension to our advantage.

In drawing the distinction between curriculum theory and curriculum practice, I am not drawing a distinction between people who work in universities and those who work in schools. There are, on average, probably as many McMurphys in the schools as there are Big Nurses in universities. I am trying to make a distinction between apologists and outlaws. Curriculum theory is, in my view, a task for outlaws, wherever they work.

All of this sounds a little too romantic and naive to me. I'll try to explain a little more clearly. Cultures need outlaws to challenge, and push, and prod them into defining and redefining themselves, even as they reject the outlaws' message as impossible and destructive of the established order. So too, it is important for students that outlaws struggle against the conventional wisdom and trite pieties of school curriculum. It's not really even a question of good guys and bad guys (although my metaphor runs the risk of making it sound that way). For one thing, McMurphy would not have been such a hero without Big Nurse and the context within which their struggle took place. He would have been just another barroom brawler. His heroism was a function of both his person and his circumstance. He was an outlaw *in a mental hospital.*

Curriculum outlaws can be outlaws only within the context of institutional schooling. The institution and the outlaw call each other into being. Don't confuse so-called curriculum theorists who spend their time formulating obscure esoteric texts with outlaws. They are better compared to the chronics in *One Flew over the Cuckoo's Nest*. Nor should the tinkerers and apologists, with their endless technical fixes, be compared to outlaws. They are best compared to the acutes. In the one case we have hallucinatory babbling that cloaks self-absorption and utter ineffectuality, and in the other we have shadow boxing with the illusion of change. Neither provides a model of the kind of effort that can inspire transcendence. In fact, both are very relevant to the system. The chronics can be dismissed as a lost cause and left to play in their fantasy worlds. The acutes provide lots of opportunities to demonstrate that the system cares and is working hard to improve the lives of the people it 'serves'. McMurphy stands out from both the chronics and acutes because he is *in* the system but he refuses to be *of* the system. He neither went away, like the chronics, nor accepted the system's assumptions, like the acutes. He simply stood and said No. He refused to be digested whole.

When I think of the act of an outlaw that inspires and encourages, I think of McMurphy betting that he could lift the old water therapy control panel. He couldn't and he didn't, but he tried, and his effort was inspirational. In that sense the effort and struggles of outlaws are social acts. They help those who witness them know that they can survive failure and defeat and not be destroyed. These acts affirm that in most of life it is effort that cuts across the grain that generates new possibilities. They also affirm that often life is not well served by attaining every goal. I would reverse the old maxim "nothing succeeds like success". I would argue that nothing succeeds like failure. As it stands, schools not only encourage the attainment of cheap successes, they promote a fear of failure. Yet without the inspiration of failures like McMurphy's, many successes would probably never have seen the light of day.

What, then, is to be done? The institution of schooling will always be the outlaw's enemy. Schools don't much want outlaws; they want chronics, and acutes, and the cases of successful adjustment to the ways of the "Combine" they can point to in order to prove that they are doing their job. They surely don't intend to honor (much less hire) outlaws. So what, then, is a poor curriculum person to do? Here is where my metaphor breaks down. In *One Flew over the Cuckoo's Nest*, McMurphy, Big Nurse, Chief Bromden, and the others were distinct characters. In life it is rarely so clear cut. That is, McMurphy, and Big Nurse, and the Chief probably live inside of all of us. Sometimes one will be stronger, sometimes another. There are, for example, plenty of primary school teachers who are not Big Nurse. As we all do, they serve the system. However, from time to time they also have the capacity to conduct what Gandhi called "experiments in living," or to organize what Freire called "revolutionary projects," or to do what McMurphy may have called simply "raising hell." For school teachers, principals, and others who work in schools and universities to perceive that the "Combine" does not control every nook and cranny of their life and work, and to tumble to the idea that they might have a little of McMurphy in them, they need encouraging examples. They need to experience what it is like to think and act like an outlaw.

We can all at various times play McMurphy and help free others by our example, and we can also at times be freed when someone else plays McMurphy to our Chief Bromden. Since you can never tell when McMurphy might pop up in you or in someone near you, the possibility of transcendence is always at hand. In that sense we are all responsible for each other—which is as close to hope as any of us are likely to get.

32

GEORGE WILLIS

A Personal Inquiry into the Curriculum of Melville's *Moby Dick*

My favorite piece of literature is Herman Melville's *Moby Dick*. That novel has spoken to me more directly and more compellingly than has any other work of art. Certainly it has influenced me personally, and this influence in shaping my personal world view has no doubt also influenced how I think and act professionally. I think that curriculum inquiry is concerned fundamentally with how to tell good stories about what happens to people in educative situations. Really, that is the basic pedagogical problem which educators are always faced with. If the situations are truly educative, then people learn something: what happens to them has meaning and significance, and they change their lives for the better.

I think these suggestions provide a good way of understanding the novel, or at least the *Bildungsroman* (the novel of development, especially character development), which for me *is* the novel, since I find I am seldom interested in hearing stories about people who never learn anything. (Unfortunately, contemporary American media and popular culture constantly bombard us with stories attempting to dignify such people.) Hence, I am interested in autonomous, meaningful, significant, and moral actions and in telling good stories about them. I think this is the heart of curriculum inquiry. And even though I cannot separate these four characteristics—the autonomous, the meaningful, the significant, and the moral—of actions which interest me, I find I can often recognize them when they occur, and I always feel compelled to attempt to make sense of them for myself and others.

In this way of understanding the world any good novel is one which contains such actions and is therefore inherently educative, for such actions indicate someone is learning something worthwhile. The experience of the author or the characters in the novel is mediated by the world around them, but their experience becomes part of the world which mediates the experience of the reader. Thus, to me a good novel is one in which author and reader enter into an inherently educative relationship; their own experiences—whether in writing or in reading—are mediated through sympathetically identifying with the experience of a character who learns something worthwhile. In such a novel there is much for everyone to learn. These ideas also apply to other types of art, I think, even where there is no narrative, such as in painting, music, or dance. In good art of any kind there is always worthwhile experience, something for everyone to learn. So even where there is no spoken voice there is always a story.

In any case, my first experience with *Moby Dick* came when I was in the sixth grade. At the end of that year the teacher decided it was time to introduce her students to what she told us were "the classics." She had gone to the school library, dug out a number of what to most of us at first seemed to be terribly large and formidable books, and had them stacked on her desk at the front of the room. Whatever her reasons, she chose *Moby Dick* as the book I was assigned to read, and she handed it to me.

I remember at first being somewhat intimidated by the physical size of the volume itself. Just holding it in my hands told me it was a far longer and far weightier book than any I had previously read completely. But there was something about it which fascinated me. As I turned its pages it seemed to grow bigger in every way, and somehow I liked the way it looked, I liked the way it felt, I even liked the musty odor it exuded. It seemed to me to be significant in ways that I was only partly ready to comprehend. Something about it seemed to invite me to partake of mysteries which somehow promised to be bigger than any I had yet imagined. And when I read it through, I was not disappointed, even though I hardly penetrated into those mysteries very deeply. I read it almost entirely at the level of simple narrative, enjoying the story itself while at the same time being mildly perplexed and slightly annoyed about how the characters and action varied from the usual good-guy-hero-overcomes-bad-guy-villain story line I had come to expect from the adventure stories and the cowboy movies which up until that time had molded my perceptions of what a narrative must be. I felt a certain kinship with Ishmael, the narrator, but I did not understand his lack of involvement in determining the action of the story. I also remember being sometimes interested in and sometimes bored by the long-winded descriptions of different species of whales and the physical accoutrements of whaling, such as the fittings of the large ship and the small whaleboats; and I was completely baffled by Ishmael's—really Melville's—frequent and extended metaphysical musings. Long before I had finished reading the book, however, I knew it was something I wanted to return to, and I have many times.

Later I developed some strong personal identification with Melville himself, when I learned he had attended the same high school I attended in Albany, New York, and when I learned he had once been a rural school teacher, which I have also been. But most important in developing my personal identification with Melville has been developing my understanding of what *Moby Dick* says to me about how my life has been like Melville's and how inevitably it is like the life of any other person. Life confronts all of us with the same basic questions and the same basic tasks, he seems to say, even if we go about dealing with them in our individual ways. There is a lot to be learned in all this, of course, from our own efforts and the efforts of others. In many ways my own world view is consistent with Melville's.

One of the things I have learned is that my own compulsion for attempting to make sense of life's experience is the same compulsion Melville must have felt in writing *Moby Dick*. At the very least, it is the same feeling Ishmael claims compels him to narrate the story. Everyone remembers how *Moby Dick* begins, with the famous sentence "Call me Ishmael" (21),[1] the literary equivalent of the first four notes of Beethoven's Fifth Symphony. Most people recall that the book ends with the sinking of the ship, the *Pequod*. Few people, however, remember that the book actually ends with a short epilogue which itself begins with a quotation from the Book of Job: "And I only am escaped alone to tell thee" (p. 536). I contend that this epilogue, more so than any other part of the book, indicates clearly that Ishmael is deep down in his heart a teacher. He is the only survivor of the sinking, and he has a mission, to tell the tale, really *his* tale, for the tale is of much more than the actions and events which culminate in the sinking of the *Pequod*; it is of how he experienced those actions and events, of what he learned from them about himself, about other people, about the world itself, and about how to live wisely. It is a tale which is anything but trivial. He must, therefore, have learned something worth telling. His purpose, then, is fundamentally pedagogical. In fact, it may be that his pedagogical compulsion, which includes his ability to make the best even of life's worst situations by learning something worthwhile from them, is what has saved him in the end. He is the one member of the crew who neither remained indifferent to nor was torn apart by the physical and the metaphysical terrors of the voyage of the *Pequod*. Of course, we do not know for certain that Ishmael was at heart a teacher before he became a survivor, but we do know that throughout his voyage he was constantly a learner, for early on he tells us: "And as for me, if, by any possibility, there be any as yet undiscovered prime thing in me; if I shall ever deserve any real repute in that small but high hushed world which I might not be unreasonably ambitious of; if hereafter I shall do anything that, upon the whole, a man might rather have done than to have left undone; if, at my death, my executors, or more properly my creditors, find any precious MSS. in my desk, then here I prospectively ascribe all the honor and glory to whaling; for a whale-ship was my Yale College and my Harvard" (120).

In the first chapter of the book, speaking through Ishmael, Melville reveals his own fundamentally pedagogical purpose, I think, as he begins developing the extended and intertwined metaphors of the land, water, the ocean, and the voyage, the central metaphors he uses to embody his personal world view with its lessons about sympathetic identification among all people, about how all lives are fundamentally alike. Indeed, in the first paragraph itself Ishmael explains himself by saying: "Whenever I find myself growing grim about the mouth; whenever it is a damp, drizzly November in my soul; whenever I find myself involuntarily pausing before coffin warehouses, and bringing up the rear of every funeral I meet; and especially whenever my hypos get such an upper hand of me, that it requires a strong moral principle to prevent me from deliberately stepping into the street, and methodically knocking people's hats off—then, I account it high time to get to sea as soon as I can," and he quickly adds, more by way of explanation than apology, "There is nothing surprising in this. If they but knew it, almost all men in their degree, some time or other, cherish very nearly the same feelings toward the ocean with me" (21).

Whether or not we believe this explanation, Ishmael's highly personal introduction of himself to us is characteristic of the pedagogical method he employs throughout his story: he looks deeply into things, speaks his mind freely, and leaves us with far more questions than answers. What, for instance, is the metaphorical significance he ascribes to water, the source of the "damp, drizzly November" of the soul and at the same time the source of every soul's catharsis? What metaphorical power has the ocean to draw us along the paths of our own lives? About these and many other questions, Ishmael continues with this observation:

> Say, you are in the country; in some high land of lakes. Take almost any path you please, and ten to one it carries you down in a dale, and leaves you there by a pool in the stream. There is magic in it. Let the most absent-minded of men be plunged in his deepest reveries—stand that man on his legs, set his feet a-going, and he will infallibly lead you to water, if water there be in all that region. Should you ever be athirst in the great American desert, try this experiment, if your caravan happen to be supplied with a metaphysical professor. Yes, as everyone knows, meditation and water are wedded for ever. (P. 22)

And referring to the image of ourselves we see whenever we look into water, he suggests, "It is the image of the ungraspable phantom of life; and this is the key to it all" (23). And as had Ishmael, so I, too, having inevitably followed paths along the metaphorical streams and pools of my early life, have been led down from the mountain rills, where we all begin, to the gathering ocean, where the greatest part of our existence's journey awaits us.

In my case, the pathways I have travelled down have led to the literal ocean itself, since for nearly twenty years now my personal life and my professional career have been in Rhode Island, the Ocean State. It has been a place from which I have undertaken my own personal and professional ocean voyage in search of understanding. But, Melville seems to tell us, whether anyone is literally on the ocean, in the desert, in the mountains, or anywhere else, we are all fundamentally alike in sooner or later embarking on our own metaphorical voyages in search of the deeper meanings in life, and these meanings are found in the kind of personal meditation which Melville associates with water, meditation in which we immerse ourselves in the being of both the physical and the metaphysical world around us. This kind of voyage, he undeniably suggests, is significant.

Life's metaphorical voyage, however, is not without its potential terrors, even as a literal ocean voyage is not potentially without them. We never know what awaits us when we leave the safety and comfort of the land. But why else, indeed, do we need to make the voyage? Yet the land itself can be an even greater danger than the sea. As has Melville, I have discovered that we make our own voyages in ships largely of our own choosing, yet regardless of the specific vessels we have shipped on, our personal friends, professional colleagues, and even we ourselves can exhibit all the characteristics and foibles of the crew of Ishmael's *Pequod*. There are natural dangers enough before us, but we ourselves make more dangers of our own. There are no ready systems through which we can infallibly guide our personal or professional lives. We cannot make of life anything we want. Sometimes we can remain serene in our personal meditations, even in the face of professional chaos; sometimes we are drawn into that chaos, like the dangers of the sea, perhaps never to return alive. Is this statement too extreme? On this dilemma Ishmael early in the book expounds his views in memorializing the fearless sailor Bulkington, who scorned the safety of the land and was never to return. "[T]his six-inch chapter is the stoneless grave of Bulkington," he begins somberly.

> Let me only say that it fared with him as with the storm-tossed ship, that miserably drives along the leeward land. The port would fain give succor; the port is pitiful; in the port is safety, comfort, hearthstone, supper, warm blankets, friends, all that's kind to our mortalities. But in that gale, the port, the land, is that ship's direst jeopardy; she must fly all hospitality; one touch of land, though it but graze the keel, would make her shudder through and through. With all her might she crowds all sail off shore; in so doing, fights 'gainst the very winds that fain would blow her homeward; seeks all the lashed sea's landlessness again; for refuge's sake forlornly rushing into peril; her only friend her bitterest foe!
>
> Know ye, now, Bulkington? Glimpses do ye seem to see of that mortally intolerable truth; that all deep, earnest thinking is but the intrepid effort of the soul to keep the open independence of the sea; while the wildest winds of heaven and earth conspire to cast her on the treacherous, slavish shore?
>
> But as in landlessness alone resides the highest truth, shoreless, indefinite as God—so, better is it to perish in that howling infinite, than be ingloriously dashed upon the lee, even if that were safety! (PP. 115-116)

Not a happy prospect for a voyage each of us must eventually embark upon! Yet even in the face of such natural and human-made dangers to our inevitable voyages through life, Melville's world view suggests how within "that howling infinite" and within "all deep earnest thinking," the considerable consolation of contentment is bestowed on anyone who shares the fundamentally pedagogical purpose of Ishmael, the teacher at heart. Meditation and water remain, as Ishmael has told us, "wedded for ever." There are many personal and professional lessons to be derived from this. Anyone who deep down is a teacher has learned the voyage most worth making is never going to be all-serene, and there is no sense in refusing or hiding this truth. Accepting the terror-evoking truths about life's voyage is what makes Ishmael not only a survivor and a teacher, but a person content to accept what about life is as it must be. Pondering the voyage, he suggests, "Who ain't a slave? Tell me that. Well, then, however the old sea-captains may order me about—however they may thump and punch me about, I have the satisfaction of knowing that it is all right; that everybody else is one way or the other served in much the same way—either in a physical or a metaphysical point of view, that is; and so the universal thump is passed round, and all hands should rub each other's shoulderblades, and be content" (24). And as he observes about himself, "I am tormented with an everlasting itch for things remote. I love to sail forbidden seas and land on barbarous coasts. Not ignoring what is good, I am quick to perceive a horror, and could still be social with it—would they let me—since it is but well to be on friendly terms with all the inmates of the place one lodges in" (26).

Ishmael's acceptance of the terrors of the voyage is not unthinking, of course, nor something which always comes easily to him, despite his general willingness to rub shoulder blades or be on friendly terms with all around him; therefore, it does not lead to a complacent or totally untroubled contentment. Real terrors are real terrors. The most obvious terrors come from without but others come from within, and Ishmael in his meditations constantly examines his inner self, contemplating the darker side of the personal nature which he finds there, even though he shares it with the common nature of all humanity. In a meditation which begins on the simultaneous beauty of the ocean and the continuous cannibalism among the creatures that prey on each other within it, Ishmael ends by drawing some other contrasts, including a terrible one within himself: "Consider all this; and then turn to this green, gentle, and most docile earth; consider them both, the sea and the land; and do you not find a strange analogy to something in yourself? For as this appalling ocean surrounds the verdant land, so in the soul of man there lies one insular Tahiti, full of peace and joy, but encompassed by all the horrors of the half known life. God keep thee! Push not off from that isle, thou canst never return!" (270-271)

I have asserted that Melville's interest as expressed through Ishmael is, like mine, fundamentally pedagogical. A fair question, then, concerns the fundamentals of what Ishmael has learned: What is the essential curricular content of the story he tells? Given Ishmael's characteristic pedagogical method, that is no easy question to answer, for he himself never answers it succinctly or directly anywhere in the more than 500 pages that the typical edition of *Moby Dick* contains. He is typically ambiguous, as evidenced by his introductory assertion that an ocean voyage is the universal cure for the "damp, drizzly November" of the soul followed by his later admonition not to push off from the "insular Tahiti" which lies at the center of the universal human soul.

But, perhaps, no matter. Ambiguity is itself an answer, perhaps itself an autonomous, meaningful, significant, and moral action which invites a similar action in response. Each life may be a voyage, but each voyage ends in its own way, at its own landfall, with its own homecoming. And so on round. This much Ishmael seems to tell us. And near the end of his telling of the *Pequod*'s voyage, musing on his musings, he makes perhaps his clearest statement of what it is that he has learned:

> But the mingled, mingling threads of life are woven by warp and woof: calms crossed by storms, a storm for every calm. There is no steady unretracing progress in this life; we do not advance through fixed gradations, and at the last one pause:—through infancy's unconscious spell, boyhood's thoughtless faith, adolescence' doubt (the common doom), then scepticism, then disbelief, resting at last in manhood's pondering repose of If. But once gone through, we trace the round again; and are infants, boys, and men, and Ifs eternally. Where lies the final harbor, whence we unmoor no more? In what rapt ether sails the world, of which the weariest never weary? Where is the foundling's father hidden? Our souls are like those orphans whose unwedded mothers die in bearing them: the secret of our paternity lies in their grave, and we must there to learn it. (P. 464)

A hard lesson—no "perhaps"—to learn; we must die before we fully understand it. And so as Ishmael says at last, "Doubts of all things earthly, and intuitions of some things heavenly; this combination makes neither believer nor infidel, but makes a man who regards them both with equal eye" (359).

Do Melville's world view and Ishmael's example and advice speak to curriculum inquiry? I think they do. And what have I heard them say to me? Many things, many incomprehensible, mysterious, wondrous things; but, in short, nothing more ambiguous than only: "Be interested in autonomous, meaningful, significant, and moral actions, and try to tell good stories about them."

NOTE

1. All page references are to the 1961 New World Library Signet Classic edition.

33

THOMAS E. BARONE

Ambiguity and the Curriculum: Lessons from the Literary Nonfiction of Norman Mailer

All great literature, I think, lures he or she who experiences it away from the shores of literal truth and out into uncharted waters where meaning is more ambiguous. Some would-be readers are reluctant to board the boat. For on the solid ground are planted these confident, reassuring texts—from scientific treatises to journalistic reports—that offer apparently dependable, trustworthy, helpful accounts of how things really are. We call these texts "factual," "nonfictional," and the words they contain seem directly to correspond to actual phenomena, to real world objects that are guaranteed to be there when we reach for them.

So we may embark upon the reading of a literary text with some trepidation. What if, entranced by the formal beauty of the story, we lose sight of the shore? With all grounding gone, drifting aimlessly into a realm of fantasy where nothing is anchored down? Or maybe we will be swept down through a "gap" in the nonliteral text. This is the literary critic Wolfgang Iser's (1974) term for the deliberately positioned blanks in the narrative which the active reader must fill in with personal (and so indeterminate and ambiguous) meaning. I the reader must, Iser insists, imaginatively construct my own reality of what I read. But if, in squinting my eyes while trying to read between the lines of the text, my imagination fails me, won't I fall like Alice down into a nonsensical world where all is fluid belief and nothing is hard evidence?

Others among us may refuse to abandon the land because the open waters are simply no place to conduct daily commerce. Art, we believe, is for its own sake, while we need (to borrow a current phrase) "news we can use." So we may consent to leave port only at night. It is dark on shore then, reality having receded into a single shadow. With classes dismissed, why not venture, leisurely and harmlessly, out into the dreamy, romantic realm of the fictional text?

We work, therefore, on the land by day with what we think are the facts and tell playfully ambiguous stories as we drift on the dark waters of night. I confess that once, as a child of my culture, I felt reassurance in the tidiness of this conventional demarcation between fact and fiction. As a teacher I could not imagine learning anything substantial or useful from a text offering anything less than the literal truth. As a reader, I did not yet grasp how good literature really works; how it urges us to place the minutiae of daily life in an imaginary context, thereby estranging us from them; how it urges us out to a place just far enough offshore to turn and recognize these phenomena as features of what the aesthetician Susanne Langer (1957) calls a "virtual" world; how this imaginary world then stands against, and comments upon, the familiar qualities of life-at-hand, allowing us to see them in a new light.

Ultimately, I erased the boundary between the realm of the text which purports to give only the facts and that of the metaphor-laden story which dares to (as Sartre once put it) lie in order to tell the truth. But I did so haltingly, and not in a single confident stroke of understanding. Indeed, my insight came only gradually, after confronting a form of writing that aims to straddle the boundary between actual and virtual worlds, one foot firmly planted in each. These works are hybrids of textual species, essays/stories written in a literary style but shelved (curiously) in the nonfiction section of the library.

In 1963 Truman Capote claimed to have originated this new literary form. A "nonfiction novel" is what he called his chilling tale of two mass murderers, *In Cold Blood*. Capote later accused Norman Mailer of falsely claiming paternity of the genre. Mailer had subtitled his *Armies of the Night* (1968), an awarding-winning account of a protest march on the Pentagon, as follows: *The Novel as History; History as the Novel*. Works such as these which reported on public events in a personal, literary style soon came to be known as the "New Journalism," and they proliferated in the 1970s. Tom Wolfe (1979, *The Right Stuff*; 1969, *Radical Chic and Mau-Mauing the Flak Catchers*), Joan Didion (1969, *Slouching Towards Bethlehem*), and Michael Herr (1968, *Dispatches*) were among the most talented at critiquing important social events in a powerful manner that was at once artful *and* realistic. Of course a new art form is never created within a historical void, and the New Journalism, I learned, had its antecedents in earlier forms of literary nonfiction—in, for example, early nineteenth century British literary criticism, in eighteenth century travel literature, and in some forms of autobiography (Wolfe 1973).

But my awareness of the form first arose during that heated moment of history, the late 1960s. Then the frenzied flow of world events thrust upon journalism a new significance, while simultaneously causing consumers of the news to cast a suspicious eye upon traditional claims of objectivity. Weren't the media's claims to an unbiased presentation of raw information somewhat debased by their penchant for passing on, unchallenged, the establishment's version of the day's stories? The *new* journalism would, instead, intentionally suit up in an unabashedly personal style, presenting the facts, as proponent Dan Wakefield (1966) suggested, "imaginatively . . . in a full instead of a naked manner . . . in an artistic manner that does not diminish but gives greater depth and dimension to the facts" (87). A style, as it were, for land *and* sea.

And even though the new journalists never got around to fully exploring my own professional bailiwick, the high school classroom, it was *what* they had to say, the *substance* of their commentary, as much as their stylistic vitality that wrought changes in my personal and professional consciousness. In hindsight, it seems that two of these texts in particular helped me to navigate out there in those uncharted waters. Both books were written by that master of literary nonfiction, Norman Mailer. The first may now be recommended reading for (am I really this old?) an American history class. The focus of *Miami and the Siege of Chicago* (1969) was on the events surrounding the Republican and Democratic presidential conventions of 1968.

Recently rereading this book, I was reminded that the potential of a literary text will remain just that when the reader is unprepared to unleash it within a reading experience. In my initial (youthful) reading, I was not prepared to hear ambiguity in Mailer's voice. With many of my fellow Baby Boomers, my political self was, in Bob Dylan's memorable phrase, "busy being born"—and Mailer (along with non-storytelling philosophers such as Nietzsche, Niebuhr, and Marx) was serving as a kind of intellectual midwife. The sources of my outrage were those of the time;

civil wrongs and the stupid, immoral war. And soon my heroes were the dead ones, martyrs whose souls my fellow mourners and I were impelled to claim and share. In this most fertile soil the seeds of our frustrations had sprouted and yielded, as if overnight, the perfectly formed fruits of ideology, dogma, and moral certainty. We partook and were fortified for collective action, for righteous confrontation. It was the age of a new positivism, an outlook that offered the moral equivalent of the old scientific truth-mongering. We were a new breed of landlubbers, the kind that worked the soil for justice. How comfortable and secure were we in our knowledge that our actions were so ethically, well, *grounded*. Our complete contempt for the patently evil and ignorant establishment precluded the kind of doubts that arise upon cool, distanced contemplation out in a rowboat.

Certainly, as a novice high school social studies teacher my daytime mission seemed crystal clear. My curriculum platform, that nexus of personally held beliefs about what is educationally good, true, and beautiful, was as rigid as it was narrow. With George Counts and the other right-thinking progressivists whom curriculum scholars sometimes label "reconstructionists," I would dare, through my teaching, to build a new social order. Under my tutelage, the Roman Catholic teenagers of middle and upper class conservative parents in New Orleans, Louisiana, would be transformed into first-generation, ideologically correct McGovernites.

In retrospect the depth of my naiveté is (oh, you've already noticed?) stunning. We believed, I and my liberal-to-socialist peers (for we were legion, having infiltrated classrooms from coast to coast), that we could, by sheer dint of will, levitate above, and thus avoid becoming stuck in, the viscous contingencies pervading the institutionalized environment of the school. The righteousness of our cause would enable us to reshape the hearts and minds of the next generation in accordance with our own precious utopian vision. And if I, for one, could do *that*, how comparatively easy to will an interpretation on a text! For how else, save for blindness from the Light, can I explain my failure to treat Mailer's book as a work of art rather than as propaganda? What else could account for my missing, for example, the reserve in the authorial voice as it described my heroes, the leaders of the nonviolent New Left in somewhat less than flattering terms? ("They were," Mailer wrote, "ideological in their focus—which is to say a man's personality was less significant than his ideas" [Mailer 1969, 134].) And although my primary affections and allegiances always remained with the latest Kennedy to be slain, Mailer's subtle characterization of Eugene McCarthy would have been, back then, disturbing if fully absorbed. McCarthy was, in Mailer's eyes, both supremely intelligent and a romantic "who dared the incalculable wrath aroused in Lyndon Johnson" by his challenge to the President. But McCarthy was also gravely flawed, an aloof man, a hard man, and bitter in adversity: "too bitter even to express his bitterness, it leaked out of the edges of his wit, turned as punishment upon his own people...and leaking, seemed to get into the very yellow of his skin, his single most unattractive feature" (Mailer 1969, 121).

Today, the distance afforded by time allows for greater appreciation of the nuances in Mailer's text. A less passionate rereading offers the balance of cognition and emotion that characterizes a true aesthetic experience. This is not, of course, because the text has changed; rather, because I have evolved with the times. But only somewhat. For I remain deeply appreciative of the opportunity for coming of age in an irreverent, socially committed era like the 1960s, a time which fostered sensitivity to the imperfections of society, which opened our eyes to the plight of the less fortunate around us, to the groups of disenfranchised—including (since my eyes are still open) today's public school teachers whose professional autonomy and status have steadily eroded within our increasingly bureaucratized and depersonalized system of schooling.

So if today's rereading of *Miami* does not evoke in me the deep anti-establishment revulsion it once did, I am yet reminded that Mailer, more than any other literary craftsman I confronted in my youth, gave to me a permanent gift: Mailer gave me a direction in which to travel, if not, as I once thought, a final destination. His gift was a kind of moral compass to help me navigate responsibly across the ethically featureless ocean of the 1980s (and, I hope, beyond). Or perhaps these later years deserve a crueler metaphor. Maybe they are more like a sea of land, a parched and barren bed of sand devoid of moral signposts. The Great American Desert? This shift in metaphor seems apt because it is the very one that Mailer, in a triumphant work written in 1979, near the onset of the current moral drought, employs to characterize a significant part of the American landscape. (Recall that it was a Western president who brought the desert to so many of us. It was Palm Springs's Ronald Reagan whose simple and apparently sincere faith in mirages ["Over there! A Shining City on a Hill!"] was so seductive to many of my countrymen.)

The book is *The Executioner's Song* (1979) and the protagonist of Mailer's "true-life novel" (as he called it) was one Gary Gilmore. In 1977 this Utah native was executed for committing a set of heinous murders. In over a thousand pages Mailer painstakingly recreates the last nine months of Gilmore's life, from his murderous acts to his death in the electric chair. But like all great literature, Mailer's text, even while reciting the minutiae of a single life, transcends those seemingly isolated particulars. While meticulously introducing us to the actual conditions of Gilmore's world, Mailer suggests that we also view his life metaphorically. His story is, therefore, only ostensibly about one man's life and death. By filling in the "gaps" so artfully arranged by Mailer, the reader can recognize features of the soul of Gary Gilmore within the larger cultural landscape. Gilmore's crimes were literally senseless; free of purpose, devoid of meaning, they merely happened. Crimes of convenience. Observing the actions of Mailer's Gilmore, we gain a glimpse of what it means to engage in an extreme form of moral relativism, an *amorality*, that is, which represents the very antithesis of the dogmatic, tightly ideological posture affected by us 1960s types. We had envisioned reconstructing the world, the neighborhood of mankind, using very specific blueprints. But Gilmore, like many children of the 1980s, was merely an opportunist devoid of moral grounding and so incapable of withstanding the slightest breezes of circumstance. Of course Gilmore lashed outward, in violence. His whims were indulged within a bizarre theater of the cruel, while our present day self-indulgence is less obviously harmful. These days the sins of choice are those of omission, as, for example, the plight of society's less fortunate is ignored through a narrowing of the definition of who really are our neighbors.

But Mailer implies that vestiges of the westernness of Gary Gilmore remain within us. We are all, he suggests, sons of the pioneers, hyper-pragmatic and self-reliant (so the myth goes) frontiersmen, self-absorbed individuals undisturbed by the common condition. Joan Didion (herself a true master at disclosing the essence of life in the modern American West) articulated most eloquently Mailer's theme in her review of *The Executioners Song*:

> The authentic Western voice, the voice heard in *The Executioner's Song*, is one heard often in life but only rarely in literature, the reason being that to truly know the West is to lack all will to write it down. The very subject of *The Executioner's Song* is that vast emptiness at the center of the Western experience, a nihilism antithetical not only in literature but to most other forms of human endeavor, a dread so close to zero that human voices fade out, trail off, like skywriting . . .
>
> When I read this, I remembered that the tracks made by the wagon wheels are still visible from the air over Utah, like the footprints made on the moon. (In Manso 1985, 607)

We Americans are indeed inhabitants of a callow culture, a nation in its adolescence, one lacking the maturity that could provide a strong sense of who we are and where we want to go as a people. This partially explains, I believe, our infatuation with the tools which science gives us. With no clearly defined vision of our own we find it convenient to partake of the half-hidden values implicated in the use of technology. Well, why *not* use them? As the educational sociologist Margret Buchmann (1985) has noted, we believe that "our tools should not lie idle: where knowledge is valued for its instrumental qualities the charge to use it is almost implied." Of course this technological imperative (like our national malaise; indeed, like most of society's virtues and evils) has crept into our schools. There our shiniest tools, the ones that speak the loudest, the ones we teach *to*, are, of course, the standardized tests. Educators, we too are children of our culture, and have lacked the vision and the voice, the will to question where we are being led by our inventions.

Yes, the 1980s have been a chilling time for the 'non-western' teachers among us who still aspire to a restoring of the human voice to the next generation of Americans. But reading Mailer can help. Indeed, he points out to us two important signposts on the road to pedagogical (and maybe even national) maturity. The first says this: When we arrange the learning environment and select the activities in which we recommend that students engage, we are not performing a merely technical exercise. The humanities, the arts, the sciences, even 'computer science,' none of these areas of study are comprised of value-neutral content or 'thinking skills' to be acquired by students in a moral vacuum. Instead, our teaching and learning encounters are, as the title of yet another book of Mailer's suggests, "existential errands." We must take responsibility for the social and personal consequences which inevitably flow from our curriculum plans and their execution in the classroom. When we are vexed by external mandates that aim to deny us the autonomy we need to act as professionals, then we may move outside the classroom to confront the forces which presume to shape the nature of our work. But to do this responsibly we must first work toward articulating a personal vision of a more just, humane, and democratic society and begin to understand how the overt and the 'hidden' curriculum will inevitably promote or retard progress toward that vision.

But the message on the second signpost is more cautionary: Pay attention to history, it says. Remember how, in the 1960s, some of us had such a vision? Back then we lived within the narrow lines of moral certitude, just as in the 1950s it had been the facts themselves that blinded us to the values undergirding them. Now we know that the ennui, hopelessness, and drift of the 1950s (like the malaise of today) occupy one side of a coin. On the flip side are dogmatism, intolerance, polemicism. What Mailer does is urge us not to flip the coin, not to force a choice between fact and fiction, between knowledge and values, between final truth and possible meaning. In Mailer's work, as in nearly all good literary nonfiction, such choices are not made. Instead we are enticed to pull together and to accommodate two apparent opposites.

And so might it be in our curricular efforts. Just as Mailer has probed beneath the surface of actual events, crafting them into stories whose deeper, less apparent, meanings the reader is invited to explore, so we as curriculum designers must avoid awkward attempts at bluntly imposing on our students our facts and dogmas, our preformulated 'performance objectives,' our own personal visions, no matter how fully crystallized and dearly held. We should know by now to, instead, invite our students into that dangerous vessel which will float them away from the safety of literal truth and the twin seductions of ethical sloth and moral intolerance. We must do, that is, what the good storyteller does. We must design activities that entice them into paying careful attention to the social and empirical world around them. But we must leave "gaps" for students to fill in, holes which encourage them to actively intervene in the proceedings, to assume responsibility, to think critically about the significance of that which they have experienced, to wonder about how it fits into their own maturing outlooks on the world, to share their tentative thoughts with teachers and each other, to tear down and construct again any conclusions reached, and then to act.

Only then will our lessons for them be like Mailer's for us: Stay open, tuned in to the world and ready to change it. Use your judgment in considering how to make it better, even while avoiding any final pronouncements about its constantly evolving status. And so become accustomed to the doubts and anxieties inevitably involved in the exercise of that judgement. Learn not to submit to imperialism or tyranny in any guise—political, intellectual, technological, moral. Do not seek to escape from the responsibilities of freedom. Instead, why not get into the boat?

GEORGE WILLIS AND WILLIAM H. SCHUBERT

EPILOGUE

"The book comes to an end here, Bill, but it doesn't really conclude. Still, perhaps we should attempt a few final words on what we have found most evocative and memorable about the chapters we have read. There may be a few implications which still bear pointing out. If in our reflections in the prologue we helped readers to anticipate some of what they would find throughout the book, then the epilogue may at least bring the book full circle. Suppose you begin."

"Well, George, as I reflect on the impact of the book on me, I am struck by how clearly artists are risk-takers. Similarly, to perceive curriculum and teaching through the arts is to take a risk, to see new possibilities, new challenges. To see old forms in new ways pertains to this epilogue as well. Traditionally, an epilogue might represent closure, a summing up. For us, in a spirit of consistency with the author-artists of this book, 'epilogue' must be seen as an opening up, a fashioning of possibilities, new challenges, new risks to be taken. It is, in essence, the opposite of closure. So one more time we are in agreement.

"I have also been surprised by how full of surprises for me the authors have been. Most have been colleagues and friends over the years, individuals whose writings we have read often and with whom we have engaged in discussions at conferences and in other meetings. Given our familiarity with them and their work, I anticipated that their chapters would be predictable, but such has been far from the case. Their examples have provided evidence that educators' encounters with the arts seem to create a special kind and quality of understanding. I suppose I shouldn't have been surprised, for this had been our own personal experience, but we have indeed been gratified that some thirty-one colleagues have, in their own unique ways, shown us that they, too, are empowered through the arts."

"Yes, taking risks, not attempting closure, and living a certain kind and quality of experiencing are among the most striking things the authors' contributions have brought home to me, too. As we suggested before, the artistic examples in the book are forms of experiencing that are meant to be experienced constantly anew. That is understanding writ large, and there is something about that which is consistent with the etymological meaning of 'education' as a leading out. Yet how many school curricula are actually like that? And how many teaching practices? Far too few, I'm afraid. So I sometimes think modern society has lost its collective nerve. It wants everything to be safe. It wants to avoid all pain. It wants quick fixes. It wants everything to be systematized. So what does it get, in education, anyway? The quality of experience in schools inevitably suffers. Experience closes down instead of opening up. Instead of more possibilities for being most alive, there are fewer possibilities. And more and more people seem to expect and to accept their lives to be this way. Fortunately, the examples provided by the authors can help school people take heart, can help them trust their senses again. Not only is there risk in these examples, but there is a world of opportunity as well. Having now read all of the chapters many times, I keep seeing the world in new ways through them. My advice to others is to read them at least several times over and to keep in tune with the changes in yourself."

"Right. The inquiry and the conversation these chapters invite are, themselves, in no small danger of becoming extinct in today's high-tech world. We hope readers will continue on and refine educational conversation within the context of their experience with the arts."

"And that is what teaching is all about, is it not?"

"And that is what *both* teaching and 'curriculum-making' (as you called it earlier) are all about. Indeed, now that we are nearing the end of our own conversation, I see increasingly clearly that it is what turns ordinary conversation into the kind of dialogue we have been striving for all along. If the conversation is educative, then everyone participates and the quality of everyone's experience is enhanced.

"This kind of conversation does not happen automatically, however, just because someone spends some time with the arts.

What is artistic in what we have been describing must be linked with what is moral. To me, therefore, another striking feature of nearly all of the foregoing chapters is the integral connection of the aesthetic and the moral within their examples. Each day I am growing more fully to accept an observation that runs through the philosophic work of Alfred North Whitehead—that the moral is knowable in concrete situations only through an almost intuitive sense of pattern of self in context, an aesthetic awareness of the impact of one's life in the world. I once was impressed with Tolstoy's vision of art in *What is Art?*, and still am, but I now see it differently. He envisioned the best art as conveying a universal sense of interpersonhood and embodying traditional virtues of compassion for fellow human beings. This vision can hardly be faulted, but it must also be made concrete. Whitehead's aesthetic sense combined with Dewey's insistence on situational decision making reveals the unmistakable value of artistic reflection as a basis for understanding what is worth knowing, doing, and being—not generically, but in each of life's encounters anew."

"Bill, those comments—especially about compassion, the situational, and life—bring me to the other thing I find most significant about the chapters. The situational exists on two levels of living, I think. There is the individual person situated in relation to each other person alone. This is a one-to-one relationship. On this level the relationship is personal or there is no relationship. There is also the individual person situated in relation to the collective society. On this level the relationship is usually impersonal, but it need not be so if compassion enters in. Compassion means literally a suffering with. That is always personal. I am reminded of how Joseph Campbell in *The Power of Myth* suggests that suffering is inevitably part of experiencing, that through compassion one person can voluntarily share with others the experience of living. On one hand, life is always painful, but compassion is the healing principle which makes life possible in the first place and gives it the possibility of continuing; on the other hand, despite the suffering to which we submit ourselves, compassion enables us to experience 'the rapture of being alive,' as Campbell puts it. When we are willing to accept the experience of living for what it is, the suffering and rapture combine to give it its deepest meanings. I am with Campbell on this, and I think this is how the artistic combines the aesthetic and the moral. In this light, it seems to me that the chapters in this book exemplify compassion first on the personal, one-to-one level, but then raise it to the collective level, hence personalizing the relationship of authors and readers, of teachers and students, of—really—everyone and everyone else. The function of such artistic examples is not to eliminate the inevitable pain of living but to elevate everyone to the exhilarating experience of being truly alive. Surely we can consider curriculum and teaching in this same way. In fact, I think, the chapters collectively do.

"If I am correct about this, then these chapters work on both levels of situation, personalizing both individual and collective relationships. In so doing, they collectively express a powerful way of looking at and doing curriculum and teaching that is radically different from the ways that currently prevail in modern society but do not necessarily have to prevail in the future. In this sense they seem to me collectively to represent the development of what Campbell might describe as a new mythology about curriculum and teaching, a new and engaging way of metaphorically telling the truth about what is really important in education, about how to feel it, and think it, and live it. It seems to me this mythology represents something very real which has always been inside of compassionate educators waiting to get out. This mythology expresses something now powerfully subversive to how schools are usually expected to function in modern society, something which has always lurked just beneath the surface of the obscurity cast by the currently prevailing but dehumanizing myths. And now all this something is demanding to get out. That's big stuff. That's exciting stuff. We have before us what is really an old story about the human condition, but a story that people may be newly ready to respond to if only they can hear and feel its being told. If we can only open up all the possibilities that are there and help people live them—well, who knows what else can happen? We can all start living the organic connections between perceiving, thinking, and doing that are there in education in ways that reverberate in ourselves and others. Who knows, then, what kind of mysteries we encounter next?"

"You're right, George. The chapters in this book may indicate a collective turning point in how at least some educators have come to understand curriculum and teaching. That is big stuff. I'm sure we cannot suggest here any bigger implications. Let me, then, end this conversation by finally reiterating some points which we have raised before but which the chapters have made both evocative and memorable.

"To know situations, one's context in the world, is to be continuously engaged in the art of autobiography. To be so engaged, as the authors illustrate so well, is to allow the arts to help one become in greater touch with one's past stories, and to create the stories of one's present and future. These stories, when they tell the truth about human lives and when they are shared compassionately, are the essence of curriculum and teaching; they are what the authors tell us should be learned from the arts; and they are, in what they exemplify, reflections from the heart of educational inquiry. The only real epilogue for this book is in lives that share this understanding by continuing such reflective inquiry."

REFERENCES

REFERENCES FOR THE PROLOGUE

Apple, M. W. 1986. *Teachers and texts*. London: Routledge and Kegan Paul.

Bronowski, J. 1956. *Science and human values*. New York: Messner.

Coles, R. 1989. *The call of stories: Teaching and the moral imagination*. Boston: Houghton Mifflin.

Conrad, J. 1902. *Heart of darkness* (numerous editions).

Dewey, J. 1910. *How we think*. New York: D.C. Heath.

– – –. 1929. *The sources of a science of education*. New York: Liveright.

– – –. 1938a. *Experience and education*. New York: Macmillan.

– – –. 1938b. *Logic, the theory of inquiry*. New York: Henry Holt.

Egan, K. 1986. *Teaching as story telling*. London, Ontario: Althouse Press.

Egan, K. and D. Nadaner, eds. 1988. *Imagination and education*. New York: Teachers College Press.

Eisner, E. W. 1983. Can educational research inform educational practice? Vice Presidential Address at the Annual Meeting of the American Educational Research Association, Montreal, April 13, 1983. (Later published under the same title in *Kappan* 65 (7), March 1984, 447-452.).

– – –. 1985. *The educational imagination: On the design and evaluation of school programs*. New York: Macmillan.

Greene, M. 1973. *Teacher as stranger*. New York: Wadsworth.

– – –. 1978. *Landscapes of learning*. New York: Teachers College Press.

Guba, E. and Y. Lincoln 1981. *Effective evaluation*. San Francisco: Jossey-Bass.

Hamilton, D., B. Macdonald, C. King, D. Jenkins, and M. Parlett, eds. 1977. *Beyond the numbers game*. Berkeley, CA: McCutchan.

Highet, G. 1950. *The art of teaching*. New York: Knopf.

Jackson, P. W. 1968. *Life in classrooms*. New York: Holt, Reinhart, and Winston.

Lakoff, G. and M. Johnson 1980. *Metaphors we live by*. Chicago: University of Chicago Press.

Lincoln, Y. S. and E. G. Guba 1985. *Naturalistic inquiry*. Beverley Hills, CA: Sage.

Noddings, N. and P. J. Shore 1984. *Awakening the inner eye: Intuition in education*. New York: Teachers College Press.

Phenix, P. 1964. *Realms of meaning*. New York: McGraw Hill.

Pinar, W. F., ed. 1975. *Curriculum theorizing: The reconceptualists*. Berkeley, CA: McCutchan.

Pinar, W. F. and M. R. Grumet 1976. *Toward a poor curriculum*. Dubuque, IA: Kendall/Hunt.

Read, H. 1943. *Education through art*. New York: Pantheon.

Ross, M. 1984. *The aesthetic impulse*. Oxford: Pergamon.

Schubert, W. H. 1975. *Imaginative projection: A method of curriculum invention.* Unpublished Ph.D. diss. University of Illinois, Urbana-Champaign

Schubert, W. H. 1986. *Curriculum: Perspective, paradigm, and possibility. New York: Macmillan.*

Schwab, J. J. 1960. What do scientists do? *Behavioral Science* 5: 1-27.

———. 1969. The practical: A language for curriculum. *School Review* 78: 1-23.

———. 1970. *The practical: A language for curriculum*. Washington, D.C.: National Education Association (revision of 1969 version).

———. 1971. The practical: Arts of eclectic. *School Review* 79: 493-542.

———. 1973. The practical 3: Translation into curriculum. *School Review* 81: 501-522.

———. 1975. Curriculum theory: The practical and the educational. Presentation at the Annual Meeting of the American Educational Research Association, 1 April, Washington, D. C.

———. 1983. The practical 4: Something for curriculum professors to do. *Curriculum Inquiry* 13 (3): 239-265.

Short, E. C., G. Willis, and W. H. Schubert 1985. *Toward excellence in curriculum inquiry: The story of the AERA Special Interest Group on Creation and Utilization of Curriculum Knowledge*. State College, PA: Nittany Press.

Smith, L. M. and W. Geoffrey 1968. *Complexities of an urban classroom.* New York: Holt, Reinhart, and Winston.

Stake, R. E., ed. 1975. *Evaluating the arts in education: A responsive approach.* Columbus, OH: Charles E. Merrill.

van Manen, M. 1989. *Researching lived experience.* London, Ontario: Althouse Press.

Westbury, I. and N. J. Wilkof, eds. 1978. *Science, curriculum, and liberal education: Selected essays of Joseph J. Schwab*. Chicago: University of Chicago Press.

Willis, G., ed. 1978. *Qualitative evaluation: Cases and concepts in curriculum criticism.* Berkeley, CA: McCutchan.

REFERENCES FOR CHAPTER ONE

Arnheim, R. 1990. *Notes on art education.* Los Angeles: The J. Paul Getty Center for Education in the Arts.

Atkin, M. 1989. Can educational research keep pace with educational reform? *Kappan* 71 (3): 200-205.

Ayer, A. J. n.d. *Language, truth and logic.* New York: Dover.

Broudy, H. S. 1976. The search for a science of education. *Kappan* 58 (1): 104-111.

———.1979. The arts education: Necessary or just nice. *Kappan* 60 (5): 324-350.

Dewey, J. 1934. *Art as experience.* New York: Minton, Balch and Co.

Eisner, E. W. 1983. The art and craft of teaching. *Educational Leadership* 40 (4): 4-13.

———. 1985. *The educational imagination,* second edition. New York: Macmillan.

———. 1991. *The enlightened eye.* New York: Macmillan.

Gardner, H. 1983. *Frames of mind: The theory of multiple intelligence.* New York: Basic Books, Inc.

———. 1989. *To open minds.* New York: Basic Books.

Geertz, C. 1988. *Works and lives: The anthropologist as author.* Stanford: Stanford University Press.

Goodman, N. 1978. *Ways of worldmaking.* Indianapolis: Hackett Publishing Co.

Greeno, J. 1989. A perspective on thinking. *American Psychologist* 44 (2) 134-141.

Kagan, D. M. 1985. The heuristic value of regarding classroom instruction as an aesthetic medium. *Educational Researcher* 2 (6): 11-17.

Langer, S. 1942. *Philosophy in a new key.* Cambridge: Harvard University Press.

Phillips, D. C. 1987. Validity in qualitative research, or, why the worry about warrant will not wane. *Education and Urban Society* 20 (1): 9-24.

Polanyi, M. 1958. *Personal knowledge: Toward a post-critical philosophy.* Chicago: The University of Chicago Press.

———. 1967. *The tacit dimension.* London: Routledge and Kegan Paul.

Schwab, J. 1969. The practical: A language for curriculum. *School Review* 78 (1) 1-23.

Snow, R. E. 1986. Individual differences and the design of educational programs. *American Psychologist* 41 (10): 1029-1039.

Wittrock, M., ed. 1986. *Third handbook on research on teaching.* New York: Macmillan.

REFERENCES FOR CHAPTER FOUR

Blanchard, H. H. 1955. *Prose and poetry of the continental renaissance in translation.* New York: Longmans, Green and Co.

Chase, J. 1983. *During the reign of the queen of Persia.* New York: Ballantine Books.

Chodorow, N. 1978. *The reproduction of mothering.* Berkeley: University of California Press.

Dinnerstein, D. 1976. *The mermaid and the minotaur.* New York: Harper and Row.

Douglas, A. 1977. *The feminization of American culture.* New York: Avon Books.

Ehrenzweig, A. 1970. *The hidden order of art.* London: Paladin.

Frankenstein, C. 1966. *The roots of the ego.* Baltimore: Williams Wilkins.

Grumet, M. R. 1988. Pedagogy for patriarchy: The feminization of teaching. In *Bitter Milk: Women and Teaching.* Amherst, Massachusetts: University of Massachusetts Press.

Kakuzo, O. 1979. *The book of tea.* Rutland, Vermont: Charles Tuttle Company.

Kris, E. 1952. *Psychoanalytic explorations in art.* New York: International Press.

Langer, S. 1953. *Feeling and form.* New York: Charles Scribner's Sons.

Martin, B. and C. T. Mohanty 1986. Feminist politics: What's home got to do with it? In T. de Lauretis, ed. *Feminist studies: Critical studies.* Bloomington: Indiana University Press, 191-212.

Pratt, M. B. 1984. Identity: Skin blood heart. In E. Bulkin, M. B. Pratt, and B. Smith, eds. *Yours in struggle: Three feminist perspectives on anti-Semitism and racism.* Brooklyn, NY: Long Haul Press.

Robinson, M. 1980. *Housekeeping.* New York: Farrar, Straus and Giroux.

Sklar, K. K. 1973. *Catherine Beecher.* New Haven: Yale University Press.

Smith, D. 1987. *The everyday world as problematic.* Toronto: University of Toronto Press.

Stern, D. 1989. Crib monologues from a psychoanalytic perspective. In Katherine Nelson, ed. *Narratives from the Crib.* Cambridge: Harvard University Press.

REFERENCES FOR CHAPTER FIVE

Bruner, J. 1986. *Actual minds; possible worlds.* Cambridge: Harvard University Press.

Cremin, L. 1961. *The transformation of the school.* New York: Vintage Books.

Cronbach, L. 1975. Beyond the two disciplines of scientific psychology. *American psychologist* 30: 116-127.

Donmoyer, R. 1990. Generalizability and the single case study. In E. Eisner and A. Peshkin, eds. *Qualitative research in education.* New York: Teachers College Press.

_____. 1983. Pedagogical improvisation. *Educational Leadership* 40: 39-43.

Eisner, E. W. 1985. *The educational imagination.* New York: Macmillan.

———. 1967. Educational objectives: Help or hindrance? *School review* 75: 150-260.

———. 1969. Instructional and expressive educational objectives: Their formulation and use in curriculum. In J. Popham, ed. *Instructional objectives.* AERA monograph series on curriculum evaluation, no. 3. Chicago: Rand McNally: 1-18.

Gibson, W. 1957. *The miracle worker.* New York: Samuel French.

Gusfield, J. 1976. The literary rhetoric of science. *American Sociologist* 41: 11-33.

Langer, S. 1942. *Philosophy in a new key.* New York: Mentor.

Macdonald, J. 1966. Language, meaning, and motivation: An introduction. In J. Macdonald and R. Leeper, eds. *Language and meaning.* Washington, D.C.: Association for Supervision and Curriculum Development.

———. 1967. An example of disciplined curriculum thinking. *Theory into practice* 4: 166-171.

Macdonald, J., and B. Wolfson 1970. A case against behavior objectives. *Elementary School Journal* 71: 119-128.

Marcuse, H. 1964. *One dimensional man.* Boston: Beacon Press.

Noddings, N. 1987. Caring. *The Journal of Curriculum Theorizing* 3: 139-151.

Parlett, M., and D. Hamilton 1977. Evaluation as illumination: A new approach to the study of innovatory programs. In D. Hamilton, B. Macdonald, C. King, D. Jenkins, and M. Parlett, eds. *Beyond the numbers game.* Berkeley, CA: McCutchan.

Neiser, U. 1976. *Cognition and reality: Principles and implications of cognitive psychology.* San Francisco: W.H. Freeman.

Nisbet, R. 1976. *Sociology as an art form.* London: Oxford University Press.

Simon, R., and D. Dippo 1980. Dramatic analysis: Interpretive inquiry for the transformation of social settings. *The Journal of Curriculum Theorizing* 2: 109-132.

Spolin, V. 1963. *Improvisation for the theatre.* Evanston, IL: Northwestern University Press.

Waller, J. 1967. Identification of problem drinkers among drunken drivers. *Journal of the American Medical Association* 200: 124-300.

REFERENCES FOR CHAPTER SIX

Bakhtin, M. 1981. *The dialogical imagination.* Austin: University of Texas Press.

Berger, J. 1984. *Ways of seeing.* New York: Penguin Books.

Bishop, E. 1980. At the fishhouses. In *The Complete Poems: 1927-1979.* New York: Farrar, Straus, and Giroux.

Conrad, J. n.d. Heart of darkness. In *Three great tales.* New York: Random House Paperbacks.

———. n.d. Preface to The 'Nigger' of the Narcissus. In *Three great tales.* New York: Random House Paperbacks.

Danto, A. C. 1985. Philosophy as/and/of literature. In J. Rajchman and C. West, eds. *Post-analytic philosophy.* New York: Columbia University Press.

Dewey, J. 1934. *Art as experience.* New York: Minton, Balch & Co.

Ellison, R. 1952. *Invisible man.* New York: New American Library.

Faulkner, W. 1946. *The sound and the fury.* New York: Modern Library.

Foucault, M. 1972. *The archaeology of knowledge.* New York: Harper Colophon.

Gilmour, J. 1986. *Picturing the world.* Albany: State University of New York Press.

Goodman, N. 1976. *Languages of art.* Indianapolis: Hackett Publishing Co.

Hawthorne, N. 1969. *The scarlet letter.* New York: Penguin Books.

Iser, W. 1980. *The act of reading.* Baltimore: Johns Hopkins University Press.

Levi, P. 1988. *The drowned and the saved.* New York: The Summit Press.

Marcuse, H. 1978. *The aesthetic dimension.* Boston: Beacon Press.

Melville, H. 1981. *Moby Dick.* Berkeley: University of California Press.

Merleau-Ponty, M. 1967. *Phenomenology of perception.* New York: The Humanities Press.

Merleau-Ponty, M. 1964. *Sense and non-sense.* Evanston: Northwestern University Press.

New Yorker. 1989. Talk of the Town, 14 August, 1989.

Oakeshott, M. 1962. *Rationalism in politics and other essays.* London: Methuen.

Ozick, C. 1989. *Metaphor and memory.* New York: Alfred A. Knopf.

Percy, W. 1979. *The moviegoer.* New York: Alfred A. Knopf.

Sartre, J. P. 1956. *Being and nothingness.* New York: Philosophical Library.

———. 1965. *Literature and existentialism.* New York: Citadel Press.

Schutz, A. 1964. Making music together. In *Collected papers II. Studies in social theory.* Hague: Martinus Nijhoff.

———. 1967. Multiple Realities, In *Collected papers I. The problem of social reality.* The Hague: Martinus Nijhoff.

Stevens, W. 1964. The man with the blue guitar. In *Collected poems.* New York: Alfred A. Knopf.

Warnock, M. 1978. *Imagination.* Berkeley: University of California Press.

Woolf, V. 1962. *To the lighthouse.* London: Everyman's Library, J. Dent.

———. 1976. *Moments of being.* New York: Harcourt Brace Jovanovich.

REFERENCES FOR CHAPTER SEVEN

Bloom, B. H. 1986. Peak learning experiences. In B. H. Bloom, ed. *All the children learning.* New York: McGraw-Hill.

Broudy, H. S. 1987. *The role of imagery in learning.* Los Angeles: The Getty Center for Education in the Arts.

Epstein, J. ed. 1981. *Masters: Portraits of great teachers.* New York: Basic Books.

Foshay, A. W. 1987. The curriculum matrix. *Educational Forum* 51 (4): 341-353.

---. 1988. The curriculum matrix: Further thoughts. *Thresholds in Education* 14 (3): 8-10.

Foshay, A. W. and I. Morrissett, eds. 1978. *Beyond the scientific: A comprehensive view of consciousness.* Boulder, CO: The Social Science Education Consortium.

Hofstadter, D. R. 1980. *Gödel, Escher, Bach.* New York: Vintage Books.

Noddings, N. and P. J. Shore 1984. *Awakening the inner eye: Intuition in education.* New York: Teachers College Press.

REFERENCES FOR CHAPTER EIGHT

Bahti, T. 1982. *Southwestern Indian ceremonials.* Las Vegas: KC Publications.

Bakhtin, M. M. 1981. *The dialogic imagination: Four essays.* M. Holquist, ed. C. Emerson and M. Holquist, trans. Austin: University of Texas Press.

Bernstein, R. J. 1985. Introduction. In R. J. Bernstein, ed. *Habermas and modernity.* Cambridge: MIT Press, 1-32.

Black Elk, and J. G. Neihardt [Flaming Rainbow] 1961. *Black Elk speaks: Being the life story of a holy man of the Oglala Sioux as told through John G. Neihardt (Flaming Rainbow)* (Bison Book Edition). Lincoln: University of Nebraska Press.

Greene, M. 1988. *The dialectic of freedom.* New York: Teachers College Press.

Habermas, J. 1984. *The theory of communicative action.* Vol. 1. *Reason and the rationalization of society.* T. McCarthy, trans. Boston: Beacon Press.

Lame Deer, J. and R. Erdoes 1972. *Lame Deer seeker of visions.* New York: Pocket Books.

Noddings, N. 1984. *Caring: A feminine approach to ethics and moral education.* Berkeley: University of California Press.

Porter, E., ed. 1967. *From Henry David Thoreau: "In wilderness is the preservation of the world."* New York: Sierra Club-Ballantine Books.

REFERENCES FOR CHAPTER FIFTEEN

Bakan, D. 1966. *The duality of human existence: Isolation and communion in Western man.* Boston: Beacon Press.

Eisner, E. W. 1978. *The educational imagination.* New York: Macmillan.

Fromm, E. 1941. *Escape from freedom.* New York: Rinehart & Co.

Greene, M. 1978. *Landscapes of learning.* New York: Teachers College Press.

Grumet, M. R. 1988. *Bitter milk: Women and teaching.* Amherst: University of Massachusetts Press.

Koestler, A. 1978. *Janus: A summing up.* New York: Random House.

Macdonald, J. B. 1978. A transcendental developmental ideology of education. In J. R. Gress and D. E. Purpel, eds. *Curriculum: An introduction to the field.* Berkeley: McCutchan.

North, M. 1973. *Movement education: Child development through body motion.* London: J. M. Dent.

Polanyi, M. 1966. *The tacit dimension.* Garden City, NY: Doubleday.

Stinson, S. W. 1984. *Reflections and visions: A hermeneutic study of dangers and possibilities in dance education.* Doctoral diss., University of North Carolina at Greensboro.

———. 1985. Curriculum and the morality of aesthetics. *Journal of Curriculum Theorizing* 6 (April): 66-83.

———, D. Blumenfeld-Jones, and J. Van Dyke 1990. Voices of young women dance students. *Dance Research Journal* 22 (2): 13-22.

REFERENCES FOR CHAPTER NINETEEN

Freire, P. 1970. *Pedagogy of the oppressed.* New York: Herder and Herder.

Mitchell, L. S. 1928. Making young geographers instead of teaching geography. *Progressive Education.* 5 (3): 217-223.

Murray, J. W. 1978. The children build a city. In M. Speer, ed. *The City and Country School. Selected talks and articles.* New York: The City and Country School. (Reprinted from typscript prepared for presentation before a meeting of parents, c. 1945.)

Pratt. C. 1948. *I learn from children.* New York: Simon and Schuster.

REFERENCES FOR CHAPTER TWENTY-TWO

Beyer, L. 1988. Art and society: Toward new directions in aesthetic education. In W. F. Pinar, ed. *Contemporary curriculum discourses.* Scottsdale, AZ: Gorsuch, Scarisbrick.

Broudy, H. S. 1988. Aesthetics and curriculum. In W. F. Pinar, ed. *Contemporary curriculum discourses.* Scottsdale, AZ: Gorsuch, Scarisbrick.

Daignault, J. 1991. In W. F. Pinar and W. M. Reynolds, eds. *Understanding Curriculum as Phenomenological and Deconstructed Texts.* New York: Teachers College Press.

Eisner, E. W. 1985. *The educational imagination.* New York: Macmillan.

Frank, E. 1983. *Jackson Pollock.* New York: Abbeville Press.

Friedman, B. H. 1972. *Jackson Pollock.* New York: McGraw Hill.

Greene, M. 1978. *Landscapes of learning.* New York: Teachers College Press.

Grumet, M. R. 1976. Toward a poor curriculum. In W. F. Pinar and M. R. Grumet. *Toward a poor curriculum.* Dubuque, IA: Kendall/Hunt.

———. 1978. Songs and situations. In G. Willis, ed. *Qualitative evaluation: Concepts and cases in curriculum criticism.* Berkeley, CA: McCutchan.

Huebner, D. 1975. *Curricular language and classroom meanings.* In W. F. Pinar, ed. *Curriculum theorizing: The reconceptualists.* Berkeley, CA: McCutchan.

Kincheloe, J. and W. F. Pinar 1990. *Curriculum as social psychoanalysis: Essays on the significance of place.* Albany: State University of New York Press.

Musil, R. 1955. *Young Torless.* New York: Pantheon.

Namuth, H., and P. Falkenberg (producers). *Jackson Pollock.* New York: Film Images, Inc., 1951.

O'Connor, F. V. 1967. *Jackson Pollock.* New York: The Museum of Modern Art.

Padgham, R. E. 1988. Correspondences: Contemporary curriculum theory and twentieth-century art. In W. F. Pinar, ed. *Contemporary curriculum discourses.* Scottsdale, AZ: Gorsuch, Scarisbrick.

Pinar, W. F. 1972. Working from within. *Educational Leadership* 29 (4): 329-331.

———. 1988. "Whole, bright, deep with understanding": Issues in qualitative research and autobiographical method. In W. F. Pinar, ed. *Contemporary curriculum discourses.* Scottsdale, AZ: Gorsuch, Scarisbrick.

Pinar, W. F. and W. M. Reynolds, eds. 1991. *Understanding Curriculum as Phenomenological and Deconstructed Texts.* New York: Teachers College Press.

Potter, J. 1985. *To a violent grave: An oral biography of Jackson Pollock.* New York: G. P. Putnam's Sons.

Robertson, B. 1960. *Jackson Pollock.* New York: Harry N. Abrams, Inc.

Rohn, M. L. 1987. *Visual dynamics in Jackson Pollock's abstractions.* Ann Arbor: UMI Research Press.

Solmon, D. 1987. *Jackson Pollock: A biography.* New York: Simon and Schuster.

REFERENCES FOR CHAPTER TWENTY-THREE

Cassirer, E. 1946. *Language and Myth.* New York: Dover Publications, Inc.

Douglass, B. G. and C. Moustakas 1985. Heuristic inquiry: The internal search to know. *The Journal of Humanistic Psychology* 25 (3), 39-55.

Haggerson, N. 1971. *To Dance With Joy.* New York: Exposition Press.

———. 1986. Reconceptualizing professional literature: An aesthetic self-study. *The Journal of Curriculum Theorizing* 6 (4), 74-97.

———. 1988. Reconceptualizing inquiry in curriculum: Using multiple research paradigms to enhance the study of curriculum. *The Journal of Curriculum Theorizing* 8 (1): 81-102.

Palmer, R. E. 1969. *Hermeneutics*, Evanston: Northwestern University Press.

Pinar, W. F., ed. 1988. *Contemporary Curriculum Discourses.* Scottsdale: Gorsuch Scorisbrick.

Stake, R. and D. Trumbull 1982. Naturalistic generalizations. *Review Journal of Philosophy and Social Science* 7 (1 & 2): 2-10.

REFERENCES FOR CHAPTER TWENTY-FIVE

Grumet, M. R. 1978. Curriculum as theatre: Merely players. *Curriculum Inquiry* 8 (1): 37-64.

Smith, D. 1988. Brighter than a thousand suns: Facing pedagogy in the nuclear shadow. In T. Carson, ed. *Toward a renaissance of humanity: Rethinking and re-orienting curriculum and instruction.* Edmonton, Alberta: University of Alberta.

REFERENCES FOR CHAPTER TWENTY-SEVEN

Dewey, J. 1916. *Democracy and education*. New York: Macmillan.

Dickens, C. 1967. *A Christmas Carol.* New York: Simon and Schuster.

———. 1956. *A Christmas Carol.* In A. Jewett, M. Edman, and P. McKee. *Adventure bound*. Boston: Houghton Mifflin. (Adapted for radio by Walter Hackett).

Egan, K. 1986. *Teaching as story telling: An alternative approach to teaching and curriculum in the elementary school.* Chicago: University of Chicago Press.

Gold, J. 1972. *Charles Dickens: Radical moralist.* Minneapolis: University of Minnesota Press.

McLuhan, M. and Q. Fiore. 1967. *The medium is the message.* New York: Random House.

Schubert, W. H. 1980. *Curriculum: Perspective, paradigm, and possibility*. New York: Macmillan.

Schubert, W. H. and A. L. Lopez-Schubert 1981. Toward curricula that are of, by, and therefore for students. *The Journal of Curriculum Theorizing* 3 (1): 297-301.

REFERENCES FOR CHAPTER TWENTY-NINE

Aitken, J. L. 1988. Children's literature and the sociology of school knowledge: Can this marriage be saved? *Curriculum Inquiry* 18: 195-216.

Anyon, J. 1981. Social class and school knowledge. *Curriculum Inquiry* 11: 3-42.

Apple, M. W. 1982. *Education and power*. London: Routledge and Kegan Paul.

———. 1986. *Teachers and texts: A political economy of class and gender relations in education.* London: Routledge and Kegan Paul.

Cox, S. T. 1989. A word or two with Eve Merriam: Talking about poetry. *The New Advocate* 2: 139-149.

Giroux, H. 1983. *Theory and resistance in education: A pedagogy for the opposition.* South Hadley, MA: Bergin and Garvey.

Kelly, R. G. 1984. Literary and cultural values in the evaluation of books for children. Paper presented to the Annual Meeting of the American Educational Research Association.

MacCann, D. and G. Woodard. 1972. *The black American in books for children: Readings in racism.* Metuchen, NJ: Scarecrow Press.

Meltzer, M. 1989. The social responsibility of the writer. *The New Advocate* 2: 155-157.

Taxel, J. 1984. The American revolution in children's fiction: An analysis of historical meaning and narrative structure. *Curriculum Inquiry* 14: 7-55.

———. 1986. The black experience in children's fiction: Controversies surrounding award winning books. *Curriculum Inquiry* 16: 245-281.

———. 1988. Children's literature: Ideology and response. *Curriculum Inquiry* 18: 217-229.

———. 1989a. Children's literature as an ideological text. In H. Giroux and P. McLaren, eds. *Critical pedagogy, the state, and cultural struggle.* Buffalo: SUNY Press.

———. 1989b. Children's literature: A research proposal from the perspective of the sociology of school knowledge. In S. deCastell, A. Luke, and C. Luke, eds. *Language, authority, and criticism: Readings in the school textbook.* London/Philadelphia: Falmer Press.

———. in press. Reclaiming the voice of resistance: The fiction of Mildred Taylor. In L. Christian-Smith and M. Apple, eds. *The politics of the textbook.* London: Routledge and Kegan Paul.

Taylor, M. 1975. *Song of the trees*. New York: Dial.

———. 1976. *Roll of thunder, hear my cry*. New York: Bantam.

———. 1977. Newbery acceptance speech. *The Horn Book.* 53: 401-409.

———. 1982. *Let the circle be unbroken.* New York: Dial.

———. 1987. *The Friendship*. New York: Dial.

———. 1990. *The Road to Memphis.* New York: Dial.

Williams, R. 1977. *Marxism and literature*. London: Oxford University Press.

– – –. 1982. *The sociology of culture*. New York: Schocken Books.

Willis, P. 1977. *Learning to labor: How working class kids get working class jobs*. Lexington, MA: D. C. Heath.

REFERENCES FOR CHAPTER THIRTY

Clarke, A. C. 1953. *Childhood's end*. New York: Ballantine. (Page references are to the 1956 edition published by Pan Books, London.)

– – –. 1971. A Meeting with Medusa. In *The wind from the sun*. London: Victor Gollancz.

– – –. 1973. *Rendezvous with Rama*. London: Victor Gollancz.

– – –. 1973. *Profiles of the Future*, revised edition. London: Victor Gollancz.

Le Guin, Ursula 1969. *The Left Hand of Darkness*. New York: Ace.

– – –. 1974. *The Dispossessed*. New York: Harper and Row.

– – –. 1985. *Always Coming Home*. New York: Harper and Row. (Page references are to the 1986 edition published by Victor Gollancz, London.)

REFERENCES FOR CHAPTER THIRTY-THREE

Buchmann, M. 1985. What is irrational about knowledge utilization. *Curriculum inquiry* 15 (2): 153-168.

Capote, T. 1963. *In cold blood: A true account of a multiple murder, and its consequences*. New York: Random House.

Didion, J. 1969. *Slouching towards Bethlehem*. New York: Delta Books.

Herr, M. 1968. *Dispatches*. New York: Avon Books.

Iser, W. 1974. *The implied reader*. Baltimore: Johns Hopkins University Press.

Langer, S. 1957. *Problems of art*. New York: Charles Scribner's Sons.

Mailer, N. 1968. *Armies of the night: History as a novel, the novel as history*. New York: New American Library.

– – –. 1969. *Miami and the siege of Chicago: An informal history of the Republican and Democratic conventions of 1968*. New York: New American Library.

———. 1979. *The executioner's song.* New York: Warner Books.

Manso, P. 1985. *Mailer: His life and times.* New York: Simon and Schuster.

Wakefield, D. 1966. The personal voice and the impersonal eye. *Atlantic* 278 (6): 86-90.

Wolfe, T. 1969. *Radical chic and mau-mauing the flak-catchers.* New York: Bantam Books.

———. 1973. *The new journalism.* New York: Harper and Row.

———. 1979. *The right stuff.* New York: Farrar, Straus, Giroux.

CONTRIBUTORS

Ted T. Aoki is Professor Emeritus and former Chair of the Department of Secondary Education, University of Alberta, Canada, and continues his scholarly work as Adjunct Professor, University of Victoria, Canada. He has been acknowledged for his contributions to curriculum scholarship through his interests in critical social theory, phenomenological hermeneutics, and post-modernism.

Michael W. Apple is a Professor of Curriculum and Instruction and of Educational Policy Studies, University of Wisconsin-Madison and is a contributor to the understanding of relationships between ideology and education; his books include *Ideology and Curriculum*, *Education and Power*, *Cultural and Economic Reproduction in Education*, and *Teachers and Texts*. He has worked with governments, teachers, and activist groups in Europe, Latin America, and Asia to democratize education.

William Ayers is an Assistant Professor of Education at the University of Illinois-Chicago and Assistant Deputy Mayor of Education, Chicago. He is a writer, teacher, and consultant on school reform, teaching, and teacher education. His work can be found in *The Good Pre-school Teacher* and in numerous journal articles.

Thomas E. Barone is an Associate Professor of Education at Arizona State University and has written extensively about and within a literary tradition of educational inquiry. His writings have appeared as chapters of several books and in numerous journals, including *Daedalus*, *Curriculum Inquiry*, *Journal of Teacher Education*, *Phi Delta Kappan*, and *Educational Leadership*. Barone is currently writing a book which portrays one year in the life of an inner-city school.

Landon E. Beyer is the Chair of the Department of Education at Knox College and contributes to journals on social foundations, curriculum theory, and aesthetic theory. His work may be found in *Knowing and Acting*, *The Curriculum: Problems, Politics, and Possibilities*, and *Preparing Teachers as Professionals*.

Harry S. Broudy is Professor Emeritus, University of Illinois at Urbana-Champaign and has interests in the philosophy of education, aesthetic theory, curriculum theory, and art education. His publications include *Building a Philosophy of Education*, *Democracy and Excellence in American Secondary Education*, *Enlightened Cherishing*, and *The Uses of Schooling*.

Richard Butt is a Professor of Education, University of Lethbridge, Canada, and has interests which include curriculum praxis, professional development, classroom change, science education, and multiculturalism. The common theme across these different areas is an interest in emancipatory forms of education and research. Currently, he uses autobiographical inquiry as research into understanding the sources, evolution, and nature of teachers' knowledge. Parallel to this he works with teachers using autobiography for the purposes of professional development.

Robert Donmoyer is an Associate Professor of Education at Ohio State University. He also co-directs Ohio State's Educational Policy Center. Donmoyer's scholarly work has focused on research utilization. He has been particularly interested in developing alternative modes of inquiry in education. Some of these alternative modes of inquiry have been influenced by the arts. His articles have been published in various journals including *Curriculum Inquiry*, *Educational Researcher*, *Educational Leadership*, *Educational Administration Quarterly*, and *The Journal of Curriculum and Supervision*.

Elliot W. Eisner is a Professor of Education and Art at Stanford University. Professor Eisner's scholarly efforts have been devoted to clarifying the role of the arts in education. He has explored their use not only as a resource in fostering students' cognitive development, but as a powerful tool for understanding educational practice. His work in this area can be found in several of his books, including *Educating Artistic Vision*, *The Educational Imagination*, *The Art of Educational Evaluation*, and *Learning and Teaching the Ways of Knowing*. His forthcoming book *The Enlightened Eye* examines the role of artistic forms of inquiry for understanding schools, classrooms, and teaching.

Arthur W. Foshay is Professor Emeritus, Teachers College, Columbia University, and contributes to curriculum development and research and international educational assessment. He is a former President of The John Dewey Society and has received the Distinguished Contributions to Curriculum Award from the Curriculum Studies Division of the American Educational Research Association. Some of his work includes *Research for Curriculum and Improvement*, *Curriculum for the 70s*, and *Considered Action for Curriculum Improvement*.

Noreen B. Garman is a Professor of Education at the University of Pittsburgh. She contributes to such journals as *Journal of Curriculum and Supervision* and *The Journal of Curriculum Theorizing*. Her areas of expertise include supervision theory and practice, curriculum, and modes of educational inquiry. She is presently completing a book on interpretive supervision.

Noel Gough is a Senior Lecturer in the Department of Curriculum and Teaching at Victoria College, Australia. His teaching and research interests are in teacher education, curriculum study, environmental education, and futures study. He has pursued these interests through work in Australia, North America, and the United Kingdom and has contributed to books and journals internationally in these fields. He is the Australian editor of the *Journal of Curriculum Studies*.

Maxine Greene is Professor Emeritus, Teachers College, Columbia University. She contributes her expertise to the areas of the philosophy of education, aesthetic theory, arts education, curriculum theory, and teaching from existential, phenomenological, and pragmatic perspectives. Her publications include *The Public School and the Private Vision, Teacher as Stranger, Landscapes of Learning*, and *The Dialectic of Freedom*.

Madeleine R. Grumet is a Professor and Dean of the School of Education at Brooklyn College. She contributes to curriculum theory and feminist theory. Dr. Grumet is a series editor on feminist theory and education for SUNY Press, book review editor for *JCT: An Interdisciplinary Journal of Curriculum Studies*, the author of *Bitter Milk: Women and Teaching*, and co-author of *Toward a Poor Curriculum*.

Nelson L. Haggerson is a Professor of Education, Arizona State University. He is a poet and the author of numerous articles and chapters on curriculum theory, teaching, the nature of educational inquiry, and the mythopoetic nature of education. He serves on numerous editorial boards, is a past program chair for the World Council for Curriculum and Instruction, and past president of the Society for the Study of Curriculum History.

James Henderson is an Associate Professor of Education at Kent State University, specializing in teacher education and curriculum studies. He has published in a variety of journals such as the *Journal of Teacher Education* and the *Journal of Curriculum Theorizing*. He has just completed a general methods text which is based on a poststructuralist interpretation of teaching, *Becoming an Inquiring Teacher*.

Kenneth Kantor is a Professor of Education at National College of Education, where he is the Director of the Program in Instructional Leadership. His interests include English education and curriculum theory, and the blending of the two. He has published in *English Education, English Journal, Theory into Practice, Language Arts* and has contributed chapters in books.

Ann Lynn Lopez-Schubert is a home educator, an independent scholar, and an educational consultant from Chicago. Her interests include home education, progressive curriculum theory, feminist studies, hidden curriculum, inquiry paradigms, arts education, and peace and justice in education. She has published in such journals as *Teachers College Record*, *Educational Studies*, *Journal of Curriculum Theorizing*, *Journal of Thought*, and the *International Encyclopedia of Education*.

Wanda T. May is an Assistant Professor of Education at Michigan State University, specializing in curriculum studies, teaching and learning in the arts, and qualitative/critical inquiry. Her scholarship ranges from the conceptual analysis of curriculum materials to enacted curricula, professional development, and influences of popular culture and mass media on student understanding. Her publications have appeared in the *Journal of Teacher Education*, *Theory into Practice*, the *International Encyclopedia of Education*, and book chapters related to art education and curriculum development.

Gail McCutcheon is an Associate Professor of Education at Ohio State University. She specializes in qualitative research, curriculum studies, and collaborative action research. She has published numerous book chapters and articles in journals such as *Educational Researcher*, *Educational Leadership*, and *Theory into Practice*. She formerly taught elementary school for eight years.

Janet L. Miller is an Associate Professor of Education and Director of the Ph.D. program in Curriculum and Teaching at Hofstra University. She specializes in curriculum studies, gender issues, and teachers' knowledge and development. She serves as Managing Editor of *JCT: An Interdisciplinary Journal of Curriculum Studies* and has contributed to numerous journals on feminist studies, curriculum theory, and teachers' lives. She recently completed *Creating Spaces and Finding Voices: Teachers Collaborating for Empowerment*.

Alex Molnar is a Professor of Education at the University of Wisconsin-Milwaukee and a family therapist. Molnar is the author of numerous articles on educational and social policy and on structural and interpersonal responses to problem behavior in schools. He has edited *Curriculum Theory*, *Current Thought on Curriculum*, and *Social Issues and Education*. He is coauthor of *Changing Problem Behavior in Schools*. Molnar is consultant to *Educational Leadership* for its "Contemporary Issues" feature. He is currently at work on, *What Global Citizens Should Know*, a book of international perspectives on what the content of school curriculum should be.

William F. Pinar is a Professor of Education and Chair of the Department of Curriculum and Instruction at Louisiana State University. He is founding editor of *JCT: An Interdisciplinary Journal of Curriculum Studies*; he chairs the annual Bergamo Conference on Curriculum Theory and Classroom Practice. Recent books include *Contemporary Curriculum Discourses* (ed.), and *Curriculum as Social Psychoanalysis*, edited with Joe L. Kincheloe. Citing his central role in the recent reconceptualization of the curriculum field, the University of South Carolina Education Museum established the "William F. Pinar Collection." In 1989 Pinar was named by the Student Government Association as one of the fifteen finest teachers on the LSU campus.

José R. Rosario is an Associate Professor of Education and Director of the Urban Teacher Education Program at Indiana University Northwest. He has worked extensively in research and development projects in the U.S. and Latin America and has written on the history of childhood in the United States, aesthetic foundations of education, and school reform. He has held faculty and research positions at Inter-American University of Puerto Rico, the State University of New York at Geneseo, the High/Scope Educational Research Foundation, the Florida Institute of Education at the University North Florida, and the Chicago Teachers' Center of Northeastern Illinois University. He currently directs a multi-school district/university consortium for professional training and development consisting of three urban school districts, three teacher unions, and a university.

Louis Rubin is a Professor of Education at the University of Illinois at Urbana-Champaign. He specializes in curriculum studies, educational innovation, humanistic perspectives on educational theory and practice, educational policy, and the art of teaching. He consults and writes widely on these topics. His publications include *Process as Content, Life Skills in School and Society, Fact and Feeling in the Classroom, The Curriculum Handbook*, and *Artistry in Teaching*.

William H. Schubert is a Professor of Education at the University of Illinois-Chicago. He is a former President of the Society for the Study of Curriculum History and Factotum of Professors of Curriculum and is President-Elect of the John Dewey Society. He is Director of the Teacher Lore Project. He has published numerous articles on curriculum theory and history, inquiry paradigms, and curriculum development. His recent books are *Curriculum Books: The First Eighty Years* and *Curriculum: Perspective, Paradigm, and Possibility*. He is currently working on several books on teacher lore, teachers and learners as curriculum developers, and curriculum history.

Francine Shuchat Shaw is an Associate Professor of Educational Communication and Technology at New York University. Her interests are in curriculum theory and the integration of media arts, especially film and video production, across the curriculum. She has published numerous articles and chapters on these topics. Her current research is in progressive education. Her work at NYU includes both teaching in the areas of instructional design and television and producing educational programs.

Susan W. Stinson is an Associate Professor of Dance at the University of North Carolina at Greensboro, where she coordinates the dance education programs and also teaches in curriculum and foundations. Her research involves critical inquiry related to the place of arts in education, meanings of arts education to participants, and moral and aesthetic dimensions of curriculum. Her work has been published in *The Journal of Curriculum Theorizing*.

Joel Taxel is a Professor in the Department of Language Education at the University of Georgia. He is founding editor of *The New Advocate*, a journal concerned with issues related to the writing, publication, analysis, and teaching of children's literature. His book chapters and articles in journals such as *Curriculum Inquiry*, *Interchange*, and *Research in the Teaching of English* are concerned with linking the study of children's literature with critical perspectives on curriculum theory.

Elizabeth Vallance is Director of Education at The Saint Louis Art Museum and former administrator and faculty member at Kansas State University. Her interests in curriculum studies include the applications of art criticism to curriculum, and arts education. She has published in numerous curriculum journals including *Curriculum Inquiry* and *Theory Into Practice*, and was co-editor of *Conflicting Conceptions of Curriculum*. She is a photographer.

Max van Manen is a Professor of Education at the University of Alberta, Canada, and founding editor of *Phenomenology and Pedagogy*. He is interested in hermeneutics and phenomenology as a basis for the study of pedagogy. He has published numerous book chapters and articles in such journals as *Curriculum Inquiry*, *Theory into Practice*, *Interchange*, and *The Canadian Journal of Education*. His books include *The Tone of Teaching* and *Researching Lived Experience*.

Delese Wear is the coordinator of Human Values in Medicine at the Northeastern Ohio Universities College of Medicine, a program which integrates the arts and humanities into the study of medicine. Her interests include insights derived from literature for educational inquiry, and the nature of caring and other human values as a function of inquiry in professional studies.

George Willis is a Professor of Education at the University of Rhode Island. His interests include curriculum theory and history, evaluation, qualitative inquiry, aesthetics, and phenomenology. He has published numerous books and articles in such journals as *Curriculum Inquiry*, *Educational Leadership*, *Journal of Curriculum Studies*, and *Curriculum Perspectives*. His books include *Qualitative Evaluation: Cases and Concepts in Curriculum Criticism*, *Toward Excellence in Curriculum Inquiry*, and *Human Services in America*. He is currently working on *The American Curriculum: A Documentary History*.

NAME INDEX

WORKS OF ART INDEX